TOTAL REVOLUTION?

An Outsider History Of

Hardline

Phoenix X Eeyore

Warcry Communications

Total Revolution? An Outsider's History Of Hardline

This edition first published in 2022 by Warcry.

ISBN 978-1957452029

For information, submission guidelines, bulk requests, or general inquiries, please contact:

peter@peteryoung.me

Also published by Warcry:

Last Words, For War: Statements Of The Symbionese Liberation Army

The A.L.F. Strikes Again: Collected Writings Of The Animal Liberation Front In North America (Animal Liberation Front)

Animal Liberation Front: Complete US Diary Of Actions

Liberate: Stories & Lessons On Animal Liberation Above The Law (Peter Young)

Flaming Arrows: Collected Writings of Animal Liberation Front Activist Rod Coronado (Rod Coronado)

From Dusk 'til Dawn: An Insider's View of the Growth of the Animal Liberation Movement (Keith Mann)

Underground. The Animal Liberation Front in the 1990s (Various)

...This is The Book free of doubt and involution, a guidance for those who preserve themselves from evil and follow the straight path...

Quran 2: 2

Written/compiled by Phoenix X Eeyore.

First published 2021. Arc of Justice Angel Press.

This edition published by Warcry Communications, 2022. 2nd revision.

Note: The Quranic quote at the top appeared in the beginning of *Vanguard* #1.

Acknowledgment: Much gratitude to all who helped make this possible. Praise to them and God All F-ing Mighty. Credit goes to them, mistakes come from me.

Contents

1 Timeline overview

1984: *Maximum Rocknroll* (*MRR*) publishes first letter from Sean. Statement releases first cassette in the UK.

1985: The Apostles release *Smash The Spectacle* EP. *MRR* publishes interview with Beefeater and letter from Tomas Squip where he opposes abortion. Philly police bomb MOVE killing 11 people.

1986-1987: Sean runs Common Ground including distro of South African bands Screaming Foetus and Power Age. Sean puts out *No Master's Voice* zine.

1988: Sean runs No Master's Voice record label releasing LPs from The Apostles, Naturecore, and international compilation LP *The ALF is Watching and There's No Place to Hide...* (with songs from Beefeater, Toxic Waste, Power Age, Chumbawamba, Statement, and Oi Polloi). Also on that compilation, Vegan Reich released the track "Stop Talking—Start Revenging" about animal liberation. Youth of Today released the track "No More" opposing meat-eating. Straight edge band Hardball forms.

1989: *Minneapolis Alternative Scene* (*MAS*) publishes Vegan Reich interview. *MRR* publishes second letter from Sean. *MRR* publishes interview with punk band Rocks who had a logo of crossed M-16 rifles as in Hardline logo. Sean's ad in *MRR* requests a "straight edge, vegan bass player" for Vegan Reich. Sean founds Hardline Records and its first ad appears in *MRR*. Raid forms from ashes of Christian-oriented punk band One Way.

1990: Hardline Records releases EPs with Statement, Vegan Reich, and Raid.

1991: *Vegan Delegation* appears as early Hardline zine from Los Angeles. Early vegan straight edge zine *Ascention* comes out including an obscure Hardline manifesto. Additional Hardline zines appear such as *Justice* and *Praxis*. *Caring Edge* (Mike Karban) publishes interview with Sean/Vegan Reich. First Hardline "Survival of the Fittest" gathering in Memphis, TN. Hardball performs last show. Sean puts out first issue of *Vanguard* (c. 1991-1992).

1992: Ex-Hardball members Ryan Downey and John Johnson claim Hardline. Raid disbands and all members leave Hardline.

1993: Sean officially leaves Hardline. Ryan Downey puts out *Vanguard* issues 2-5 (nearly immediately retracting issue 3) and *Vanguard* 1+2 as double issue. "Memphis 3" (Hardliners) arrested for animal advocacy actions. Ryan leaves Hardline around the end of the year.

1994: Mike Karban puts out *Straight Edge Animal Liberation* (*SEAL*) zine. Jesse Keenan puts out *Cardinal Spirits*. Dave Agranoff puts out *Defense, Rescue, and Survival.* Micah Collins puts out *Destroy Babylon*.

1995: Michelle B. from Memphis puts out Hardline zines *Gaia Screams* and *Invictus*. Arrests of Hardliners in Utah and Tennessee for animal/Earth liberation actions. *Vanguard* 6 edited by Dave Agranoff comes out.

1996: *Vanguard* 7 (also by Dave) comes out and claims 16 Hardline chapters in 4 countries. Arrests of Hardliners in Utah for Earth and animal liberation actions. Arrests of Boston Hardliners for action against mink farms.

1997: Peter Young gets arrested on Mercer Island, Washington after an animal liberation spree but evades detention and goes underground for 8 years. Walter Bond gets arrested for burning down a meth lab in Iowa.

1998: Small group of Hardliners attempt and fail at organizing intentional community in Hawaii named New Eden Project. Sean re-enters Hardline, puts out *Vanguard* 8 and creates a Hardline Central Committee (HCC) in order to centralize authority in the group.

1999: Hardline website claims 19 chapters in 7 countries (a "chapter" may consist of as few as one or two individuals loosely tied to the group). The HCC turns out short-lived. Hardline dissolves and Sean organizes Ahl-i Allah (People of God) with Micah Collins. High profile campaign Stop Huntingdon Animal Cruelty (SHAC) begins in the UK against the Huntingdon Life Sciences (HLS), Europe's largest contract animal-testing laboratory.

2000: Ahl-i Allah claims 7 chapters in 5 countries.

2001: Ahl-i Allah dies out. The follow-up Taliyah al-Mahdi (Vanguard of the Messiah) website goes up. Walter Bond gets released.

2003: Via Taliyah, Micah celebrated the Space Shuttle Columbia explosion in 2003 (because the shuttle carried Israeli fighter pilot Ilan Ramon) and attracted notoriety via the Southern Poverty Law Center's critique.

2004: Ian Hamilton organizes Total Liberation Fest and Total Liberation Tour and places Taliyah and ex-Hardline people in line-up (such as Micah Collins, Dave Agranoff, Naj One, Amir Sulaiman, and Abdul Shahid Mustafa) alongside vegan straight edge and/or Hardline-affiliated bands such as Tears of Gaia, Purification, Gather, Cherem, Freya, and Purified in Blood.

2005: Police capture Peter Young and he serves two years for animal liberation actions. Taliyah al-Mahdi claims 7 chapters in 7 countries.

2006: Both Ahl-i Allah and Taliyah websites fade away.

2007: Peter Young gets released from prison.

2009: Earth Crisis releases the song "To Ashes" about Walter Bond.

2010s: Police arrest Walter Bond for Animal Liberation Front (ALF) actions in 2010. Walter attempts to restart Hardline with new group named Vegan Hardline. Walter converts to Islam and leaves Islam a few later, eventually rejecting Hardline as well. Nationalists in Russia and Eastern Europe adopt Hardline and organize gatherings. Sean posts Vegan Reich communiqué condemning fascism and racism. Tim Rule forms Bound By Modern Age record label and promotes neo-Hardline material including his own project Forward to Eden. Elgin James, vegan straight edger, and co-founder of FSU, begins work as advisor for the North American Animal Liberation Press Office.

2020: After serving 10 years, Walter Bond leaves prison and briefly forms Vegan Final Solution before former supporters accuse him of misanthropy and fascism. Micah Collins restarts Taliyah al-Mahdi's homepage.

2 Glossary

Ahl-i Allah (People of God): Shi'a-oriented Islamic follow-up group to Hardline with mix of Hardline and millenarian theological ideas (Daoism, Judaism, etc).

Ahmadiyya: Innovative Muslim sect that developed in Punjab, Pakistan (then British India) in the late 1800s with emphasis on reason and on the teachings of Hazrat Mirza Ghulam Ahmad as the most recent Prophetic revelation. Members of the Ahmadiyya constituted some of the earliest propagators of Islam in the United States after Muslim Africans initially brought the faith to Turtle Island shores in the 1600s.

American Indian Movement (AIM): Founded by Native Americans in 1968 to defend indigenous people against poverty, police, etc. They famously occupied Alcatraz (1969-1971), marched to DC the next year and, along with several hundred Oglala Lakota, had a showdown with the FBI at Wounded Knee in 1973 (ending with two Native Americans killed). In 1975 some members engaged in a shoot-out with the FBI at Pine Ridge reservation, leading to the nearly 50-year imprisonment of Leonard Peltier (Amnesty International maintains that he did not get a fair trial. He remains incarcerated). AIM activists also engaged in several cross-country walk covering thousands of miles calling to honor treaties, provide Native people with critical social services, restore stolen land, and end domination and control by U.S. govt./Bureau of Indian Affairs.

Anarcho-punk: Primarily originating with bands like Crass and Conflict in the UK, anarcho-punk overlapped with "peace punks" in opposing racism, capitalism, patriarchy, militarism, heteronorms, and eventually speciesism. Different bands had different angles, nuances, and emphasis but collectively they helped usher in a new generation of anarchists—people working for a stateless, egalitarian society.

Animal liberation: The principle that animals have value unto themselves and need human help to liberate them from cages that other humans have imposed on them.

Animal Liberation Front (ALF): A decentralized network founded in the UK in 1976 by Ronnie Lee and others (previously Band of Mercy) in which activists/cells attack fur farms/stores, slaughterhouses, hunts, laboratories that engage in vivisection, etc., and/or release captive animals (or protect ones in the wild from hunters). They aimed to commit no harm to humans in their defense of animals.

Crust/crustie: Originally a name drawn from the "crusty" appearance of certain punks, it evolved into its own aesthetic (black clothes, piercings, dreadlocks) and music (metal-oriented punk, death metal, etc.) and closely tied to anarcho-punk.

DIY: Short for "Do It Yourself" which emphasizes grassroots and independent productions such as low-budget recordings, labels, publications, and tour networks.

Earth First!: Founded in 1980 by Dave Foreman, Mike Roselle, Ron Kezar, Bart Koehler, and Howie Wolke, they had originally dubbed themselves "Rednecks for Wilderness" (which gives you an idea about the demographic that built the group). Without the Earth, we don't have anything else, so they believed in ridding ourselves of anthropocentrism (putting people first) and focusing on what we *need* to do (putting Earth first), often called ecocentrism or biocentrism. Dave Foreman, a lifelong Republican, eventually resigned around 1989 and a new generation of EF! activists took over. Spearheaded by more socialist-oriented people like Judi Bari, many others came largely from punk and hardcore scenes. They believed in direct action sabotage against industries harming nature. One of their slogans included "No Compromise in Defense of Mother Earth!"

Earth Liberation Front (ELF): A splinter group from Earth First!, the ELF did more radical actions (such as blowing up or setting fire to development projects rather than "just" putting spikes in trees to disable chainsaws or disable a bulldozer). While Earth First! could operate more openly in large groups, the ELF adopted the individual/small cell model of the ALF (also forbidding attacks against humans).

Five Percenters (also known as the Nation of Gods and Earths): Developed by Nation of Islam member Clarence 13X Smith in the 1960s (who would take the name "Allah"), they taught a decentralized version of NOI creeds and emphasized the Godhood of *each* Black man (they typically regard Black women as "Earths"). Although they tend to avoid pork, many smoke marijuana (known in Five Percenter language as "equality"). They use a system of numerology ("Supreme Mathematics") and esoteric, ad-hoc symbol and letter interpretation ("Supreme Alphabet"). For example, A = 1 = Allah = "the all in all" = Clarence 13X Smith (aka "Allah") = ALLAH = Arm Leg Leg Arm Head = the Black Man who has self-knowledge as God.

Hardline manifesto: Written by Sean of Vegan Reich, the single page manifesto formed the concise basis for the Hardline ideology, namely a call "for a movement that is both physically and morally strong enough to do battle against the forces of evil," thereby opposing capitalism, sexism, racism, speciesism, abortions, and homosexuality in accord with "the laws of nature" and belief in "one ethic—that all innocent life is sacred" (see Appendix 1 which also includes later variants of the manifesto by Ahl-i Allah and Taliyah al-Madhi).

Hardcore: Faster, harder, louder style of punk initially pioneered by bands such as Bad Brains and Middle Class in the late 1970s. Eventually merged with DIY punk, zine culture, and straight edge forming multiple and various hybrids of "hardcore punk" culture.

Kids: Hardcore term for anyone involved in the scene (often regardless of age).

Krishnacore: Bands like Shelter and 108 transitioned in late 80s-early 90s from straight edge to open advocates of ISKCON (International Society for Krishna Consciousness) often referred to as Hari Krishnas. As numerous hardcore bands and zines cropped up as devotees to Lord Krishna, the term "Krishnacore" began to apply to that particular scene. As Krishancore had nothing to do with Hardline (except that people from each scene debated with the people from the other one), I shall not give the scene any attention here. For more info on Krishnacore, turn to the experts (Dines 2014 and 2021; Stewart 2012).

MOVE: Not an acronym (it stands for "movement" because all life moves), the multi-ethnic/predominantly African American group started around 1972 In Philadelphia by John Africa (formerly Vincent Leaphart) and others who all adopted the last name "Africa" and who advocated a type of anarchism, primitivism, and abolitionism combined with sobriety, animal liberation, and Earth liberation. They rejected violations of "the system" and manmade categories and instead advocated defending all life based on "natural law," "Momma Nature," and the principle of Life as One. In 1985, when they had the majority of surviving members already in prison, Philadelphia police bombed their home killing 11 people. Some members remained imprisoned for 40 years. Only MOVE supporter and prominent journalist Mumia Abu-Jamal remains incarcerated.

Nation of Islam (NOI): Founded by W. D. Fard and Elijah Muhammad in the early 1930s, they gained most prominence through spokesperson Malcolm X. Regarding "the Black Man" as God (Fard in particular) in they developed a version of Islam that emphasized Black pride, Black liberation, Black businesses, self-discipline, and called for an independent Black separatist state.

Nihilism: Anarchist sectarian ideology developed especially in Russia in the 1800s with emphasis on abolishing morals, tradition, and destroying the state and society. Pioneers in assassination and sabotage.

Posi: Short for "positive" and refers to straight edgers who emphasized health, common ground, scene unity, and social justice as opposed to "negative" moralizing and self-righteous posturing.

Revolutionary Catechism aka *Catechism of the Revolutionist* (1869): Short booklet written by nihilist Sergey Nechayev, a friend of prominent anarchist Mikhail Bakunin (some say Bakunin co-authored it but evidence indicates otherwise). Sergey offered cold-hearted, fanatical, hateful, and deceitful tactics as a means to destroy tradition and the state. Hardline distributed it in the mid-1990s.

Scene: Local, regional, or global community of hardcore/punk kids.

Straight edge: Often shortened to sXe, started off as a 1981 song by DC hardcore band Minor Threat titled "Straight Edge."; often summed up as abstinence from intoxicants and promiscuity as in the lyrics of another Minor Threat song, "Out of Step" where songwriter/vocalist Ian MacKaye sang: "*I don't smoke, I don't drink, I don't fuck, at least I can fucking think.*" Typically symbolized by an X (often on the back of one's hand), straight edge developed into a movement through bands such as 7 Seconds, SSD, and later Youth of Today, Judge, Gorilla Biscuits, and a zillion others so diverse that some scholars have written: "Straight edge, then, is most usefully understood not as a movement defined by a monolithic set of beliefs and signifiers running consistently across social and geographic boundaries, but rather as a loose set of beliefs informing countless groups of youth and young adult cultural movements, who in turn express and communicate those beliefs in countless ways" [*Note: the authors also noted that "Despite media reports that have consistently described straight edge as a gang and the more recent scrutiny of FSU and other straight edge crews, the subculture is conspicuously absent from the National Gang Threat Assessment." They mused that police more likely described Juggalos* *[horrorcore rap group Insane Clown Posse fans] as a gang than they did straight edgers because they "contend that the police find a reflection of themselves in the traditional bourgeois and puritanical values of the straight edge movement and so to apply the gang label...would be a betrayal of self." While plausible, I'd add that ICP's emphasis on anti-racism and anti-cop rhetoric such as in "Piggy Pie" didn't help them win them over any badge-wearing fans; Linnemann and McClanahan 2019: 3, 10, 16*].

Symbionese Liberation Army (SLA): Syncretic socialist group that kidnapped Patty Hearst and forced the government to distribute food to working class neighborhoods. Police killed key founding members in a shoot-out in 1974.

Taliyah al-Mahdi (Vanguard of the Messiah): Also a follow-up to Hardline. Nearly identical to Ahl-i Allah except more revolutionary rhetoric and, with Sean's support, run primarily by Micah Collins. Existed roughly 2001-2006.

Ummah: The Muslim nation or global community of Muslims.

Vegan straight edge: Often shortened to xVx. Veganism + straight edge.

Vegan: Someone who does not consume animal products (meat, dairy, honey, gelatin, leather, etc.) either in their diet, clothing, glue, or other products.

Zines: Fanzines (fan-run magazines) constituted a huge part of the hardcore and punk scenes of the 1970s-90s. Sometimes produced with professional printers and circulation in the tens of thousands (such as major zines like *Maximum Rocknroll* and *Flipside*) but more often produced at home and through local print shops with circulation of 50-100 copies.

3 People list (and bands, zines, labels)

• **Sean Panno** (b. 1969) aka "Sean of Vegan Reich," aka Sean Muttaqi aka Shahid 'Ali Muttaqi: Main figure in the bands Vegan Reich, Captive Nation Rising, Pressure, the record labels No Master's Voice, Hardline Records, and Uprising Records/Uprising Communications, the zine *Vanguard*, and, by far, the most central figure in founding Hardline. Referred to here, for the most part, as simply "Sean" (because most people in the scene only knew him by his first name), he served as the initiator, most prominent figure, key founder, and normative voice for Hardline's ideology (even while other people prior to Sean and around him influenced him and helped organize the scene). He did not sign his name to many of his texts (including the manifesto, Vegan Reich lyrics, *Vanguard* 1, and *Vanguard* 8) yet no one disputed his authorship. Vegan Reich's *Hardline* 7" EP, released on Hardline Records in 1990, alongside two other EPs by Raid and Statement, marked the beginning of the Hardline scene.

• **Patrick "Rat" Poole** (b. 1966): One of Sean's oldest friends and earliest influences. As part of the British anarcho-punk scene, Rat had adopted a sober vegan lifestyle in the early 1980s. Although he certainly helped shape and influence Hardline, he never identified as such (nor as sXe). He attended the first Hardline gathering in 1991 but did not perform. Still based in the UK, he has participated in and produced an enormous amount of music over the last 37 years including bands and projects such as Statement, Unborn, The Apostles, Riot Clone, Arrogance, Muted Existence, Anorexia, and Cracked Cop Skulls.

• **Steve Lovett** (b. circa 1970): Vocalist and songwriter for Raid. In interviews, Steve has stated that he helped shape Hardline philosophy with Sean and turn the idea into an actual movement. He moved to California in 1992 from Memphis, Tennessee and left Hardline around the same time that Raid broke up. Because Steve began using intoxicants and rejected aspects of Hardline ideology, Hardline Records stopped selling the Raid records in 1993.

• **Ryan Downey** (b. 1975): MTV reporter in 1989, active in one of Indiana's first straight edge bands, Hardball in Indianapolis, Indiana. Officially joined Hardline around 1992 and left it at the end of 1993. Edited *Vanguard* 2-5 (all in 1993). After Hardline, Ryan returned to MTV and other mainstream news coverage interviewing celebrities such as Johnny Depp, John Travolta, and Miss Piggy. Vocalist in Burn It Down.

• **David Agranoff** (b. 1974): Originally from Bloomington, Indiana. Moved to Syracuse, NY in 1990s (now in Portland, OR). Put out 90s-zines such as *Voicebox*, *Defense, Rescue, and Survival*, *Unveil the Lies*, and edited *Vanguard* (1995-1996). Arrested several times for animal advocacy actions. In 2009, he collaborated with police against already incarcerated Earth liberation anarchist Marion/Marius Mason. Received subsequent pariah status among activists. Served 9 months in prison 2012. Wrote *The Vegan Revolution... With Zombies* (2012) and runs the *PK Dickhead* podcast devoted to all things Philip K. Dick.

• **Micah Collins** (b. circa 1977): Perhaps the Hardliner with the most number of names, going by 'Isa Adam Naziri, Mikhah David Naziri, Aboo Jamaal, and Micah Ben David/MBD (to name some of them). He put out Hardline zine *Destroy Babylon* in the mid 90s-early 2000s, helped facilitate the transfer from Hardline to Ahl-i Allah in 1999, and then ran the Taliyah al-Mahdi website 2001-2005 and later from 2020-present.

• **Naj One** (aka Foek aka Foekus aka Foeknawledge aka Harun Najwan al-Askari, b. Aaron Hunsaker): Perhaps, at the time, the most public and vocal proponent of Taliyah al-Mahdi outside of Micah Collins. White vegan straight edge rapper who joined the Total Liberation Tour of 2004. Eventually left the scene but gifted the world with the 2004 release *Foeknawledge* on New Eden Records.

• **Michelle Borok** (b. circa 1976): The most prominent female associated with Hardline, Michelle helped organize Hardline gatherings in Memphis, helped put out *Memphis Vegan*, networked with numerous pen pals around the world, and put out her own Hardline zines (*Gaia Screams* and *Invictus*).

• **Rod Coronado** (b. 1966): With Pascua Yaqui background and roots in punk and hardcore (Rod got into veganism and animal liberation via British anarcho-punk band Conflict), Rod began Earth and animal liberation activism in the 1980s, sinking two whaling ships in Iceland in 1986, working with Earth First! and then animal liberation actions in the 1990s, resulting in a 1995 arrest and subsequent imprisonment for the firebombing of a mink research center at Michigan State University animal testing lab and releasing mink from their farm. Although never affiliated with Hardline, as a widely celebrity figure in Earth and animal liberation circles, he attracted their support. Hardline zines regularly covered his case and Sean released benefit compilation *Ceremony of Fire* raising funds for his support committee.

• **Peter Daniel Young** (b. circa 1977): Perhaps the most well-known and widely celebrated animal liberation activist tied to Hardline. Although Peter never identified as Hardline, he saw their usefulness as bands like Raid, Vegan Reich, and Earth Crisis produced the soundtrack that inspired his actions that ultimately released thousands of minks and hundreds of foxes. He spent eight years as a fugitive and finally got arrested in 2005 and spent two years in prison. Has since written a book about his ideas and experiences on animal liberation and life on the run in *Liberate: Stories & Lessons on Animal Liberation Above the Law* (2019).

• **Walter Bond** (b. circa 1977, aka Abdul Haqq): Another more well-known Hardline-related activist. Known for burning down a meth lab (immortalized through the Earth Crisis song "To Ashes" in 2009) and then arson attacks on animal use industries such as a sheepskin factory in Utah. After his arrest in 2010, he served 10 years in prison, converted to Islam as Abdul Haqq then left Islam, had on-again-off-again relationships with anarchism and Hardline (which he attempted to revive under the name Vegan Hardline), ultimately rejected both by the time of his release from prison in June 2020, and then started the overtly misanthropic Vegan Final Solution website with fellow animal liberationist Camille Marino. For this, many former supporters and anarchists accused him of fascism, blacklisted him, and withdrew support.

• **Scott Beibin** (b. circa 1969): Formed a pen pal relationship with Sean around 1989. Put out early vegan straight edge zine *Ascention* in the winter of 1990-1991 which included an early Hardline manifesto. Joined Hardline in 1991 and, with his partner at the time, held most of the workshops at the first Hardline gathering. Left Hardline shortly after that. Started Bloodlink Records in 1992. Later went on to co-found Evil Twin Booking and Lost Film Fest. Now works with technology and ecology issues, hoping to use space travel as a means to save the planet.

• **Elgin James** (b. circa 1969): Together with others in Boston, Elgin co-founded FSU (Fuck Shit Up aka Friends Stand United) in the 1980s who fought off racists and robbed drug dealers. Elgin described this combination of straight edge with extreme violence as "hardline" but never identified as Hardline which developed later. In the 1990s and 2000s he played in bands such as Wrecking Crew, 454 Big Block, and Righteous Jams while FSU gangs spread across the country. Elgin left FSU in 2007 but got arrested in 2009 for a previous gang-related incident in 2005. He spent a year in prison right after the premiere of his first long film Little Birds in 2011. Moving out to Los Angeles and developing a career in the film industry, he most prominently co-wrote the popular Mayans MC television series. He also works as advisor for the North American Animal Liberation Press Office.

• **Shane Durgee** (b. circa 1973): Original singer for Framework (the band that turned into Earth Crisis after Karl Beuchner took over vocals). Also active in Gatekeeper and, briefly, in Hardline.

• **Tim Rule**: Founder of Bound By Modern Age Records in 2014 and behind the one-man band Forward to Eden in Hamburg, Germany, Tim remains of one of the few people still advocating some form of Hardline today—vegan straight edge plus millenarian militancy. In coordination with Micah, he released the latest Taliyah-version of the Hardline manifesto in the recent Forward to Eden release *Ready to Kill For the Cult* (2020).

• **Tim Yohannan** (1945-1998): Editor and founder of *Maximum Rocknroll* (*MRR*). Notorious for running a tight ship with authoritarian tendencies, socialist sympathies, and pouring his heart and soul into *MRR*. Loved and hated.

• **Mykel Board** (b. 1950): Well-known columnist for *MRR*. Notorious for trolling feminists, anarchists, socialists, vegetarians, and anything else deemed "politically correct" in the pages of *MRR*. Loved and hated.

• **Memphis Hardline**: Memphis had the most active and prolific Hardline scene and hosted most of the annual Hardline "Survival of the Fittest" gatherings (1991-1996), both during the period that Raid still performed as well as a few years after that. Scene figures included JP Goodwin (co-founder of Coalition Against the Fur Trade aka CAFT), Michelle Borok (*Gaia Screams*, *Invictus*) and vegan powerlifting champion Frank Winbigler.

• **Vegan Reich** (see below for variations of band members): Music project run by Sean as vocalist, guitarist, and songwriter. Vegan Reich rarely, if at all, played live in the 1980s. Most shows took place in the early 90s. They broke up after the release of their *Wrath of God* cassette in 1992. Vegan Reich re-formed with Sean plus new members in 1999 to record a new EP (*Jihad*) and perform one show in Indianapolis. They re-formed again (yet again with new members) in 2017 for a reunion show. Vegan Reich's entire repertoire from 1988 to 1999 consists of 11 original songs and one cover ("Sorry" by 4 Skins).

• **Raid**: The most popular Hardline band who started around 1989 and dissolved in 1992. Based in Memphis, Tennessee, Raid formed the center of the sudden surge of enthusiasm for Hardline in the early 90s.

• **Statement**: One-man band consisting of Patrick "Rat" Poole (b. 1968). Active 1984-present. Still vegan, still sober. Never identified as "straight edge" or Hardline. Close friends with Sean, Statement's approximately 13th release "Prepare for Battle" with the Hardline logo emblazoned on the front, came out on Hardline Records in 1990. Rat has, in more recent years, described himself as a misanthrope.

• **Captive Nation Rising**: Sean's post-Hardline reggae project put out one release on his own label in 1994 (apparently consisted of Sean plus studio musicians).

• **Pressure**: Sean's second post-Hardline band Pressure performed both reggae and hardcore. The band initially included Dominic Ehling and Jon Ewing (both of Vegan Reich) on bass and drums respectively, later Ray Rodriguez (Tension) on drums, and finally Chuck Treece (McRad, Bad Brains) on drums. They had three releases: *Destroy LA* (1996), *Hardcore Roots* (1998), and *Anthem* (2003).

• **Earth Crisis**: Inspired in part by Hardline and Vegan Reich, Earth Crisis soared to immense popularity and notoriety in punk and hardcore scenes. Known for spreading militant vegan straight edge metalcore far and wide. Although often lumped together with Hardline, they took a milder stance on abortion and never rejected homosexuality. Consisted mostly of members Karl Buechner (vocals), Scott Crouse (guitar), Ian Edwards (bass) and various others over the years.

• ***Vanguard*** (1992-1998): The major Hardline zine (although, as its first issue discussed only Hardline ideology and discussed no bands or music culture, one may well regard the first issue as a 10-page booklet rather than fanzine). Initially by Sean of Vegan Reich around 1992, it consisted of eight official issues, the first of which had canonical status and served as the ideological foundation for Hardline beliefs. Sean wrote the first issue in its entirety and contributed to some later issues. He directed the eighth and final issue in 1998. In between, MTV reporter Ryan Downey, of the bands Hardball and Burn It Down, edited issues two to five in 1993 and David

Agranoff, of Hardline zines *Defense, Rescue, and Survival* and *Unveil the Lies,* edited the sixth and seventh issues in 1995 and 1996 respectively.

• ***Destroy Babylon***: Perhaps the most prominent Hardline zine after *Vanguard*. Put out by Micah Collins from Cincinnati, OH it mostly ran from ca. 1995-1997. Issues 5-9 (coming out as late as 2005) seem obscure (can't even find reviews).

• ***Defense, Rescue, and Survival***: Another main Hardline zine, edited and published by Dave Agranoff who also put out *Unveil the Lies*, *Voicebox*, and went on to edit *Vanguard* 6 and 7.

• ***SEAL (Straight Edge Animal Liberation)***: Put out by Mike Karban (one of the "Memphis 3") in the mid-90s, SEAL continued the work Mike had started with his previous zine *Caring Edge* yet with more clear advocacy for Hardline.

• ***MAS***: Short for *Minneapolis Alternative Scene*. Forerunner zine to *Profane Existence*. Covered primarily the local Minneapolis scene. First notable zine to cover Vegan Reich. (No *MAS*, no Vegan Reich?).

• ***Profane Existence***: The most prominent North American anarcho-punk zine. Founded in Minneapolis, MN in 1989 by Dan "Troll" Susskind and others.

• ***Maximum Rocknroll (MRR)***: Initially founded in 1982 in San Francisco and run by Tim Yohannan (1945-1998), *MRR*, at its peak ran tens of thousands of copies per issue on a monthly basis and set a normative standard for many punk scenes. With the letters section, columns, scene reports, ads, and classified sections, *MRR* also provided a massive forum for internal punk debates and networking. *MRR* also helped spawn related projects such as the 924 Gilman Street club in Berkeley, Epicenter Records in SF, and the annual *Book Your Own Fuckin' Life* zine (1992 to 2011) which provided tons of info for punks to book their own tours and network with people, zines, and labels.

• ***HeartattaCk*** (spelled that way to emphasize HC for hardcore): Prominent hardcore zine (1994-2006) with a political and DIY edge (for example, refusing to review records that had a bar code on them). Run by vegan straight edger Kent McClard of Ebullition Records.

• **No Master's Voice** (1988-1989): Sean's first label, in between his work with Common Ground distro and Hardline Records. Released 3 records in 1988 (The Apostles, Naturecore, and the animal liberation compilation LP *The ALF is Watching and There's No Place to Hide…*).

• **Hardline Records** (1990-1992): Sean's label that kicked off the Hardline scene. It released three vinyl 7"s (Statement, Raid, and Vegan Reich) in 1990 and one Vegan Reich cassette, *The Wrath of God*, in 1992.

• **Uprising Records/Uprising Communications** (1994-present): Sean's post-Hardline, mostly hardcore/punk label which released Hardline-adjacent bands (e.g., Purification, Pressure, Burn It Down, Painstake, Tension, Racetraitor) as well as branched out into new territory such as reggae (e.g., Sean's own Captive Nation Rising), indie hardcore (e.g., Katsumoto, Dearlife), punk funk (e.g., Ricanstruction), experimental and progressive hardcore (e.g., I Am The Ocean, Dr. Acula), and hip hop (e.g., iCON the Mic King, The Crest and debut records by T. Mills and Taliyah-associate Amir Sulaiman). By far the most successful band Sean ever put out, Fall Out Boy had two releases on Uprising: the 2002 split 7" with Project Rocket and the 2003 full-length debut *Fall Out Boy's Evening Out With Your Girlfriend*. Since switching to a major label in 2005, Fall Out Boy has had worldwide hits and sales in the millions. Uprising does not seem to have released any music since Broadway's *Gentlemen's Brawl* in 2012. Sean published his father's novel *Animal Rites* on Primordial Press, a division of Uprising, in 2016.

• **Catalyst Records** (1992-present): Probably, along with New Eden Records, one of the most prominent vegan straight edge labels to support Hardline without actually advocating Hardline. Catalyst Records, for example, regularly ran ads in Hardline zines in the 1990s. Run by Kurt Schroeder of Birthright (who appeared on Sean's *Ceremony of Fire* benefit compilation for Rod Coronado).

• **Life Defense Communications**: One of the main producers of Hardline-affiliated music in Poland in the mid 90s. Run by Adam Malik (who now runs London-based hardcore record label The Essence).

• **Bloodlink Records**: Bloodlink put out a host of political hardcore with vegan and/or straight edge members such as Struggle, Chokehold, Atom and His Package, Groundwork, and Frail as well as more experimental-oriented work by bands like Pressgang, Girl Plunge, Denim And Diamonds, and Chromelodeon. Run by former Hardliner Scott Beibin, the label lasted from 1992-2004.

Vegan Reich band members in its various incarnations:

Vegan Reich circa 1987-1988 (song “Stop Talking – Start Revenging”):
Sean, vox and guitar
Brian, bass
Aaron Sperske (Doug & The Slugz, Armistice, Beachwood Sparks, Lilys, Pernice Brothers, Crystal Skulls, Ariel Pink’s Haunted Graffiti, etc.), drums

Vegan Reich circa 1989-1990 (*Hardline* EP):
Sean, vox and guitar
Sergio Hernandez (Amenity, House of Suffering), bass
Jon Ewing (Pressure), drums

Vegan Reich circa 1991-1992 (*The Wrath Of God* EP cassette):
Sean, vox and guitar
Dom Ehling (Pressure), bass
Ray Titus, drums

Vegan Reich 1999 (*Jihad* CD EP):
Sean, vox and guitar
?, bass
Andy Hurley (Racetraitor, KillTheSlaveMaster, Fall Out Boy), drums

Vegan Reich 2017 (live performance including live cover of “Sorry” by 4Skins):
Sean, vox
Eric Bartholomae (Racetraitor), bass
?, guitar, ?, drums

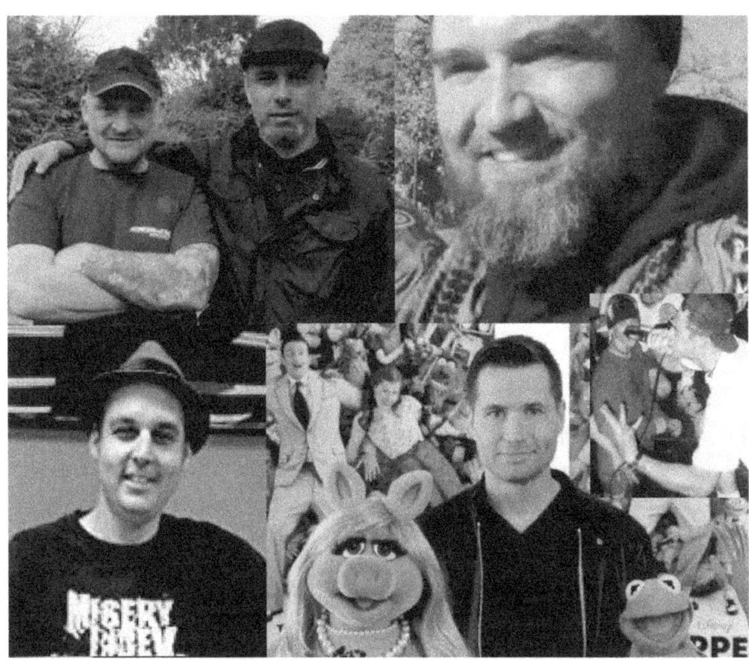

Some key Hardline figures: Top row, left to right: Rat, Sean, and Micah; Bottom row, left to right: Dave, Ryan (between Miss Piggy and the Hardline frog), Steve (singing for Raid in insert).

4 Introduction and overview: Why any of this matters

[Caveat up front: I write this for people who already at least know of Hardline. For those of you who have never heard of Hardline or possibly never heard of straight edge or even hardcore, you won't find a lot of description or background info here. Pardon the expression but you can "do your own research" on hc/punk]

Whether one calls it a "scene" or a "movement," Hardline started in the period between 1989 and 1991 with the former date marking the founding of Hardline Records by Sean in Laguna Beach, California and the latter marking the first Hardline "Survival of the Fittest" gathering in Memphis, Tennessee, headlined by the most popular band among Hardliners: Raid.

Hardline helped kick off vegan straight edge, inspire the band Framework and its more famous incarnation, Earth Crisis, engaged a number of activists in direct actions against animal-use businesses, and it stirred intense debate in the hardcore scene throughout the 1990s due to their extreme militancy regarding veganism and animal liberation (and, to some degree, Earth liberation), declarations of self-righteous purity and intolerance, open advocacy of vegan dictatorship, Darwinian survival-of-the-fittest macho attitudes combined with compassion-based and ultra-dogmatic concern for the welfare of animals and fetuses. Their loud opposition to abortion and homosexuality granted them a pariah status, stigma, and reputation that far overshadowed the actual number of people involved as well as their ostensible focus: creating effective means to achieve Earth and animal liberation.

Whatever one labels Hardline, Sean dissolved it by the end of the millennium. Aside from a variety of eerie apparitions (Walter Bond's Vegan Hardline/Vegan Final Solution, Eastern European nationalist appropriation of Hardline, and Shi'a-oriented post-Hardline groups like Taliyah al-Mahdi), Hardline essentially disappeared. On the surface, it may seem like a very small and scattered group of kids who very briefly got hyper-fanatical about living a pure, austere life for the sake of Earth/human/animal liberation only to backslide in their convictions a few weeks, months, or years later. If I believed that it amounted to no more than that, I wouldn't have compiled this oversized booklet.

Instead, I believe that, despite their obvious problems, small size, and seemingly irredeemable prejudice and arrogance, they point toward the power, potential, and need for small groups to organize along similar lines without those obvious problems. As Hardline seemed to employ the toxic and manipulative Revolutionary Catechism (see glossary) to some degree, activists can learn how to recognize and counter such approaches by seeing how it manifested in action. One can also gain insight regarding Hardline successes, failures, internal dynamics, public strategy, inherent contradictions, informal hierarchies, long-term vision, theology, innovation, duplicity, cognitive dissonance, and their attempts to resolve problems facing all life on Earth that have only increased since the 1990s. Whether or not the reader agrees… well, read on and judge for yourself.

Hardline has received relatively little attention by scholars presumably based on two assumptions: (1) as a highly marginal scene with very few members, it didn't matter enough to warrant more attention and/or (2) as a reactionary and militantly sectarian scene, it seemed to promote fascistic attitudes—especially in regard to homosexuals and women's reproductive rights.

This neglect seems to have led to a self-fulfilling confirmation regarding the first assumption. The less research attention devoted to Hardline, the more insignificant they seem. Yet, as even small scenes and groups can have a pivotal impact, we can ask: did Hardline? We may have trouble measuring impact but we can begin to at least survey the material here and get a better idea. Also, the above-mentioned neglect resulted in near-total lack of clear contemporary debate and analysis on the data and dynamics regarding Hardline stances (exaggerations and misinformation seem to have come from both pro- and anti-Hardline voices which, in turn, have muddied discussion of the topic).

Still, one might wonder: why does it matter?

If some people state that Hardline kicked off the vegan straight edge scene then we may want to know whether it did or not. It matters in terms of understanding how ideas and groups appear, develop, impact others, and disappear. It matters to know what happened and thereafter learn from successes, failures, and complex blends of the two. It matters in terms of better understanding social dynamics and how to recognize and avert Machiavellian power maneuvers (e.g., Revolutionary Catechism) and cognitive dissonance, replacing them with transparency, trust, vulnerability, gentleness, courage, and sensitivity. And hopefully, it can shed some light on sectarianism—not just in terms of advantages and disadvantages but also looking toward varieties of sects and "secular" prophets to better understand possibilities and types of social change—especially when addressing issues such as animal liberation in which activists must necessarily act on behalf of someone else: those who cannot vote, cannot speak, cannot organize against the system that routinely tortures, terrorizes, and slaughters them—typically beyond the sight of the masses who consume them and products made from their lives, their flesh, their pain.

Anarcho-punk had long advocated total liberation (Earth, human, and animal liberation) since the late 70s but if Hardline, even indirectly, helped consolidate the total liberation scene, then we might want to know about that too. After all, at least in its broad aims, Hardline propagated something that many activists could stand behind: the need to formulate a broad, action-based movement to address critical issues regarding the pollution and destruction of our Earth's habitats, the treatment of animals, and the oppression of Black and Indigenous populations across the world. However misguided or toxic one may regard the ultimate response by Hardliners, we still have to face both Machiavellian tactics and personalities in contemporary activist circles as well as the broad issues of eco-crises, animal suffering, and inequalities that remain with us today.

5 Thoughts on "Outsider History" and personal background

I write this as an outsider to Hardline scenes. I never paid much attention to them in the 1990s and I never met Sean, the founder of Hardline Records and co-founder of Hardline. I never met any Hardliner. By and large, most Hardline music (except for post-Hardline hip hop like Naj One and Amir Sulaiman) never appealed to me. The dogma seemed flat and rigid rather than creative and expansive. At the same time, I have understanding for Sean's interests (and can see some parallels between his interests and my own). In fact, I see much of his cause and vision as akin to my own. So when I offer critique (and I offer a lot), I do so in the spirit of both hoping he (or at least people like him) might hear it and providing a heads up to anyone working on the same or similar issues but has simply taken words at face value and could use a closer examination.

Sean and I both came of age in the 1980s US punk scene and rejected alcohol and drug use without identifying as straight edge or getting tattoos. We both got initially introduced to activism, at least in part, through the influence of our already politically active parents in general and specifically via nuclear disarmament protests in our teens in the 80s. We both maintained a particular fondness for Rudimentary Peni and the *Tao te Ching*. We both released political music compilations that included Chumbawamba. We both had close ties to antifascist anarchists, stopped eating meat in the 80s, remained on the fringes of anarchist scenes throughout the 90s, felt that civilization itself represented an enormous threat to the balance of life on Earth, and sought to integrate holistic "spirituality" with grassroots activism. We both opted for celibacy during a period in life when most guys want to have as much sex as they can. We both felt intrigued by monasteries. We both read theological literature while listening to hardcore punk. Both of us made music for a tiny audience (although his band eventually attracted far more attention and success than mine did). We both tended to avoid listing band members on our band's releases. We both ran small record labels and, around 1992, Tim Yohannan banned both of us from publishing ads in *Maximum Rocknroll* (Sean for his views, me because our music did not sound "punk" enough). We both read *The Autobiography of Malcolm X* and took a strong interest in the Nation of Islam, Black liberation, and primitivism. I got involved as a MOVE sympathizer in the 1990s and Sean would later claim MOVE as an influence on Hardline (for more info on MOVE see, for example, Boyette 1989, Wagner-Pacifici 1994, or Evans 2020). So we had our share of commonalities.

Yet, Sean's interests and choices also departed from my own. For example, I never felt that, as a male, my view on abortion (whether in favor or against) ought to matter to any woman. Choosing to abort or keep a fertilized egg or fetus seemed complicated enough for the woman who has to bear the consequences either way. She could certainly make that decision for herself without having to hear the opinions of myself or any other person—male or otherwise—who did not have to bear those consequences. I understand the apparent logic of wanting to defend the sanctity of "all innocent life," but, quite frankly, I see bugs as sacred and I still sometimes kill bugs. I also rescue bugs. I look at the circumstance. We can't avoid killing and violence in life to some degree. Seeking "purity" or "total consistency" seems like a dangerous pipedream. Life teems with contradictions (deal with it humbly rather than try to deny it). I see the violence of banning abortion and I see the violence of machine society providing abortions like a virtual habit. But I see the path to minimizing violence in both cases as the struggle to dismantle the state, build community, and choose degrowth and downscaling rather than more and more technology. Either way, I can't decide which instances a woman chooses to keep a child or get an abortion and it blows my mind that any man (vegan or not) would even have the audacity to attempt to tell a woman what to do with what grows in her womb.

In another example, Sean said he "hated" homosexuals. Maybe, in part due to growing up with a lesbian cousin whom I adored (and who schooled me on queer issues every time we met), I never understood that concept of hating people for their sexual preference. If anything, lesbians ought to rule the world (maybe a new band for Sean? Lesbian Reich! In fact, he needn't write a new manifesto because Valerie Solanas already did it for him in her 1967 *SCUM Manifesto*).

I also never went full-on vegan. If the abortion/homosexuality stances provided one bookend for Hardline's sectarianism, veganism provided the other. Fully aware of the moral superiority of veganism over vegetarianism, I consciously avoided internal and external pulls toward sectarianism and "purity." I would not eat animals that I didn't feel willing to kill with my own hands but will I eat food that uses animals or kills bugs in the process of harvesting grains? For now, yes. For better or worse, I simply picked a vegetarian lifestyle that I knew I could sustain my entire life without backtracking and, perhaps, gradual progression toward veganism (as society itself moved toward vegetarianism). While direct action certainly fills a function, in regard to education, I believe in people learning through example, practice, and insight that come from within rather than some sort of external moral authority dictating rules to them. As for structures (such as animal abuse industries), they change when people make them change.

Perhaps most significantly, like Sean, I read *The Revolutionary Catechism* aka *Catechism of the Revolutionist* in the late 80s/early 90s. Like Sean perhaps, I felt attracted by the implicit combination of "religion" and "anarchism." I really *wanted* to like it. And I *did* like the title... But the text itself... Absolutely horrific. It took the worst associations a person might have with "religion" and "anarchism" and combined it into one package by preaching absolute, unbridled fanaticism blended with callous Machiavellian manipulation and deceit. It framed "revolution" through categorical divisions of "us" and "them" and infused it with the crafting of tactically cold-blooded social relationships toward the singular goal of a massively destructive insurrection. Instead of talking about what type of society would replace the current one, it advocated the absurdly ass-backwards strategy that the more miserable you make a populace, the more likely they will engage in a mass uprising (you know who else adopted that strategy? The CIA in the covert war against the Soviets such as in Operation Splinter Factor). If such a strategy seemed psychopathic when Sergey Nechayev wrote it in the 1800s, it seemed even more insane when applied to today's technological police states, globalized power, and nuclear weapons. Yet, whereas the text made me wanna puke, Sean seemed to treat it like a blueprint for revolution.

So, we seem to have had both a number of commonalities and a number of differences. Obviously, that has shaped what and how I write about Hardline. Yet, I don't have an ax to grind, I would just like to see more honesty and clarity when people talk about the topic.

In regard to sects in general, I learned to separate issues where I disagree with issues where I agree. And then I try to listen, learn, and build on what matters. Sean, for the record, did not view Hardline as a sect. See, for example, the comment "No salvation in sectarianism" in his second version of the Hardline manifesto ("One God, One Aim, One Destiny," Appendix 1). Instead, because Sean/Hardline advocated theological pluralism, he seemed to think that that would suffice to disqualify a group as "sectarian." And, of course, it depends on how one defines "sect." I don't use the term pejoratively. I just mean something like a tight community that has clear ideas about the "in-group" and the "out-group" and exists in some degree of tension with mainstream society. A lot of sects, but not all, engage in a high degree of mutual "policing" in which members micro-manage one another's behavior, diet, consumption, and/or attire.

While I concluded that I had no personal interest in belonging to a sect, I felt that, from a more objective position, I had to admit that sects seemed to fill a purpose. In fact, I could see at least 4 functions: (1) *Counterculture*. Sects manage to create alternative cultures and enable more unified forces to present social, practical, and paradigmatic counterweights to dominant society. They can capture a holistic vision for the total transformation of society rather than focus on single-issue causes. (Individuals like me who remain all too tied to mainstream society could, even in a best-case scenario, transform that society only very slowly …and we do not seem to have much time); (2) *Consolidation*. While Greta Thunberg and Extinction Rebellion (verging on sectarianism) can shout "System Change Not Climate Change," actual sects can turn slogans into social visions by living them, demonstrating them, consolidating them, and voicing them through both words and actions more clearly than people integrated into and dependent upon the system they critique; (3) *Community*. Sects can provide an intense sort of community and can enable a type of egalitarianism and mutual aid that most people only otherwise read about; (4) *Efficiency*. Sects can channel and focus any particular activity—whether meditation, barn-building, art, gardening, therapy, commune construction, service-work, rehabilitation, and/or direct actions such as Earth and animal liberation—into effective living workshops and social factories which get more results—and often for a longer period—than other groups. By agreeing to agree on most issues and focusing on what members see as important, activity and resources can funnel through the group's collective vision rather than getting dispersed (as can happen in mainstream society when people all have their personal lives scattered about with jobs, schools, child care, families, entertainment, and often-separate social circles pulling people in different directions). Changing societal structures of injustice seemed to require a lot more concerted direct action than changing one's diet. Sects could provide that.

None of this meant that sectarianism did not also bring in a host of its own problems (dogmatism, elitism, violence, formal or informal hierarchies, collective delusion, etc.). Yet, as with any tool or medicine, in some cases, the benefits seem to outweigh the drawbacks at a societal level (each person involved has to determine whether it worked out that way for themselves at the micro-level or not). While people closest to a sect (such as ex-members or people who deal with them directly) tend to either glorify or revile them without much sense of nuance, an outsider perspective, uninfluenced by personal experience, can sometimes provide some nuance that other perspectives lack. In this case, we may look at Hardline as one attempt at forming a sect and, through a lens that acknowledges sectarian weaknesses and strengths, see how Hardline fared and what we might learn.

Hardline died in the late 1990s and its subsequent Muslim-oriented heirs (Ahl-i Allah and Taliyah al-Mahdi) did not last past 2006. So one might wonder why an outsider perspective on Hardline has any relevance today. My response:

1. As scholars tend to use the Hardline manifesto and interviews with Sean and/or other Hardliners as their primary sources, it can help to have a different perspective—especially one that brings in additional original sources and corrects some errors that have remained unchallenged. Summing up the material and resources in one location can also facilitate the research process for anyone interested in digging deeper.

2. As some nationalists in Europe have tried to claim Hardline, it can help to have a variety of voices clarify Hardline's largely anti-racist background.

3. Writing as an outsider, I may raise questions and concerns that insiders may have overlooked or disregard and which opponents to Hardline have consistently ignored. In particular, I find it worthwhile to think about the usefulness of sectarianism.

While most people tend to regard "sects" as something negative, Reinhold Niebuhr (the man who inspired the Serenity Prayer now used at 12-Step programs across the world) saw sects as a vital part of a thriving civil society in part because they segregated themselves from mainstream society and cultivated subcultures of resistance to domination. He critiqued "technological civilization" for making "stability impossible," for inhibiting reverence "of an ancestral order," for aggravating "the injustices from which [humans] have perennially suffered," for—via forced economic interdependence—cumulating "the evil consequences of these brutalities," and for imperiling "the whole human enterprise" (Niebuhr 1960: 276). In contrast, he said that the "absolutist and fanatic is no doubt dangerous; but ...also necessary" because they compose "the radical force in history" which can avoid sinking "into the sands of complete relativism" (Ibid: 222). Finally, with all the talk of sects, one might also distinguish between *types* of sects (Reinhold primarily had in mind non-violent groups like the Quakers or the Amish, never lived to see the Manson Family, Aum Shinri-Kyo, or Heaven's Gate, and did not seem to think of mainstream institutions such as West Point Military Academy as sects). We might also distinguish between *degrees* of sectarianism. On the very low end of sectarianism, I'd place things like straight edge, sports fans, police, activist groups like Extinction Rebellion, and party politics where people gather around certain activities and symbols, engage in occasional intense group actions, and share a sense of community without living together and easily integrate with non-members. At this low level of sectarianism, adherents certainly pay attention to who still participates and who doesn't but they don't punish people for leaving the group or scene. At the high end of sectarianism, I'd place things like most active military organizations, some police, Jehovah's Witnesses, ISIS, the Essenes, gangs, and the Bruderhof. And then we have any degree of sectarianism in between (e.g., groups such as football fan clubs, Thee Temple Ov Psychick Youth, public school systems, or Auroville). Again, I don't place a value judgment on "sect" or how high or low one rates on this scale. Personally, I'd rather join the Bruderhof than the police so the question of *type* of sect intersects with *degree* of sectarianism. I wouldn't take this typology very seriously (I just came up with it off the top of my head for the purposes of this book) but hopefully it gives a sense of roughly what I mean by "sect" (a group with a strong sense of social cohesion and/or tension with others and/or a system for socializing youth into a group norm).

Now, if we accept this proposition that sects can sometimes fill useful roles, then we may want to look closer at the dynamics that facilitate various aspects of sects such as their longevity, their effectiveness in sparking change, their ability to sustain committed activism, etc. I also have an interest in how genealogies of influences produce chain reactions of ideas and practices.

As with any outsider research, this process also brings limitations. I never attended a Hardline gathering or concert. I never met Hardline people in person. My data comes primarily from interviews and conversations with people who did all those things, zines that Hardliners published in the 1990s (or, to some extent, in the 2000s and 2010s in regard to post-Hardline scenes), the bands' own releases, and non-Hardline zines that covered Hardline, Vegan Reich, or related projects in the 1980s and 90s.

This means that I obviously didn't know much about Hardline when I started (and still remain largely ignorant now about "the real thing"). Yet, not letting ignorance stop me from doing stuff, I continued. I invariably skew the history toward my areas of interest, leaving out some things that may seem important to others while including minutia that seem completely trivial. That often boils down to a matter of taste (and time: I did not plan to work on this thing for ten years). I will likely get some details very wrong too (I also corrected some details along the way such as grammatical typos in quotes to make for easier reading—except when, for example, some Hardliners seem to intentionally use lowercase "i" as in "i am" presumably to signal less emphasis on the individual than a capital "I"). Although, in making tiny corrections one sacrifices a small bit of the original text's "authenticity," I feel more interested in communicating and discussing ideas and I think the text will flow more fluidly if readers don't get distracted by spelling or grammatical errors. Besides, ideas matter—not how well a person can spell.

I also let my own familiarity and bias steer to some degree (for example, I focus almost exclusively on the US even though I know a different study could do a better job at bringing in voices from Brazil, Poland, Belgium, Germany, the UK, and elsewhere). Yet it has gone more than 20 years now since Hardline died and none of the insiders have written a definitive work on the topic so this naturally results in a less-than-perfect outsider piece. If any reader suspects that I may have taken a quote out of context, they can look up the original source (which I provide when I can).

I have tried to keep true to the spirit of apparent intent of all authors without distorting their general message. Also, it may annoy some people that I included so much original data and quotes. Whatever. I think readers (and writers) deserve to see as much of an original text as possible. I put in as much as I did because see this project as a sort of consolidated data resource for others to do their own research on the topic. While I put in my two cents worth of views a little bit here and there and at the end, I mostly leave it to readers to draw their own conclusions about it. I could have put in even more from original sources but I leave that task to someone else (too much as it serves as little more than repeating the propaganda of the past without contextualizing it). One could easily fill several volumes with original Hardline material. I actually did *not* include a special section on veganism/animal liberation. First, the reader will quickly find no lack of references to animal liberation throughout the text. If Hardliners focused on anything, they focused on veganism and animal liberation. Second, I find it both obvious and the least controversial aspect of Hardline. Anyone who does not automatically support animal liberation, I cannot fathom why you would read this or how you can justify the massive imprisonment, torture, and slaughter of creatures, by and large, for human entertainment, taste, and a general unwillingness to take the time and energy to protect animals and resolve human needs by other means. Third, this planned booklet of 20 pages quickly, unexpectedly, and reluctantly turned into something resembling a circa 250-page book and I needed to save space.

I tried to organize the text in such a way that if you just want a hyper-short overview, you can look at the timeline. The Introduction will let you know if you want to read any more or not. This section on "Outsider History" provides a broader explanation about what I intended here, where I come from, and provides a list of caveats (if you have not already skipped past this section, non-academics might want to pass). The section "What have people said about Hardline?" gives a clearer idea of the reputation that has preceded Hardline in many punk and hardcore (especially vegan straight edge) scenes. It also provides a framework for thinking about Hardline social contexts (haters, bitter neighbors, lost potentials, allies/adjacents, true believers) as well as selected quotes from the last category to better explain how Hardliners thought and what attracted them to Hardline. The "Contrasting stories" section simply follows the format of people like Brian Peterson (2009) and Tony Rettman (2017). In their work on political/spiritual hardcore and straight edge respectively, they resolve the problem of "objective" writing by presenting a variety of first-hand accounts, views, and perspectives from various people via original interviews. Then they let readers decide what to think about it. By providing different people's views, one also builds up a more holistic sense of "reality" by hearing how a set of people in any given context viewed it. My own tweak to that format: almost all of the quotes come not from my own data but from existing resources out there in the world *and* I sometimes place quotes from the same person (often Sean) in contrast to something that person or someone else said. For a scene that emphasized consistency and uniformity of thought, it can lead to some perplexed head-scratching trying to figure out how they made sense of such apparent tensions and/or contradictions added up in their heads. Furthermore, I use this format as a means for people who want to argue the points to actually see in black and white what someone did or did not say.

I also used this "multiple view" format to highlight particular issues that have not received much attention such as Hardline's relationship to MOVE, characterizing Hardline as a "cult" or "religion," and the more esoteric or philosophical views about life, technology, and human nature. The next section "Timeline detailed" provides exactly that—a more detailed timeline for nerds who feel like really digging in-depth to stories and details about the progression of Hardline from Sean's earliest letter in *MRR* in 1984 to the resurrection of Taliyah by Tim Rule and Micah Collins in 2020. For anyone still awake and interested in my own thoughts, I offer "Afterthoughts and Looking Forward" where I try to capture points worth taking home from our visit with Hardline. Every decent booklet needs visuals which one finds in the Appendices along with entire texts such as the many variations of the Hardline manifesto (another nerd section). The glossary and people list provide the basics to people who would like some help in keeping up with all of the various people and groups involved. And, of course, I provide a list of references and links for anyone wanting to delve in further on their own. Although I originally planned a small booklet of approximately 20 pages, I realized that, as necessary as they seem sometimes, I hate such introductions. Because they invariably distort the material far more than something that lets people, as much as possible, speak for themselves. In the case of Hardline, mostly only Sean's voice has come forth even though he supposedly left

Hardline by 1993. Brian Peterson and Tony Rettman did a great job of including many more voices in regard to Hardline than anyone else had ever done. However, they did not quote much (or at all) from original Hardline sources, they did not dig up quotes from more obscure less-quoted Hardliners (no women for example), and they made no attempt to critically analyze Hardline which, I think, the material essentially demands. After all, allowing ex-Hardliners to simply offer their view today on it (no matter how much they diverge from one another) does not press the questions further and confront them with what they actually said at the time and their general lack of addressing that fact today (often glossing over details or blatantly revising the historical record such as former Polish Hardliner Adam Malik's recent attempt to claim in an online debate that most Hardliners did not adopt anti-homosexual stances in the 1990s).

Finally, while one cannot necessarily rely on any information here (or anywhere) as accurate, I try to substantiate claims when I can and I try to avoid stating any claims that I cannot substantiate. Yet, one can bear a couple things in mind here: First, no one has ever denied the absolutely canonical status that those four sources (Hardline Records, Vegan Reich, Hardline Manifesto, and, especially, *Vanguard* 1) have maintained within Hardline. Essentially Sean's words in any form held the highest and most normative status within Hardline. After that, a secondary tier developed with zines such as *Destroy Babylon*, *Defense, Rescue, and Survival*, and *Declaration* and books such as Jim Mason's *An Unnatural Order: The Roots of Our Destruction of Nature* (1993) and Screaming Wolf's *A Declaration of War: Killing People to Save Animals and the Environment* (1991) which all held relatively normative status. On the third tier, one finds a variety of texts from non-Hardline sources such as Earth Crisis lyrics, previously popular apostates such as Raid or Day of Suffering, and a host of literature such as *Earth First! Journal,* ALF-support zines, and a plethora of lesser-known Hardline zines (*Gaia Screams*, *Praxis*, *Contention Builder*, etc.). The quantitative proportion and corresponding authority looks very much like a pyramid when one lays it out.

Second, sourcing gets tricky at times as many Hardline texts do not cite an author and Hardliners—especially Micah and Sean—repeatedly wrote under pseudonyms online and offline. While a certain degree of anonymity seemed apparent due to the potential legal ramifications of essentially calling for or justifying the assassination of vivisectors and abortion doctors, the zine *Declaration* offered a frame for why zines like *Vanguard* and *Declaration* look like they do:

> …you find before you a magazine composed entirely of real subject matter. This magazine has no advertisements, interviews, reviews, or anything else along those lines. It is entirely writing that addresses the most important topics and forces that are changing and shaping the world we live in, forces that work sometimes in a positive light, usually in a very negative one. There are a few pictures in this also, they speak for themselves, they speak for the victims. They remind us that what is going on around us is not a joke, it is not alien to us, it is very tangible, and it is very painful. …I believe in mutual respect for all who take the time to educate themselves and get involved in any struggle be it the anti-drug war, earth/animal liberation movement, black and women's rights movements, or any other endeavor deserving of support and honor. That is who I am, and this is what I stand for (Declaration 1, c. 1995: 2).

While a certain anonymity, served clear functions at the time to avoid legal repercussions and keep focus on the issues rather than personalities (as illustrated above), it also had the effect of building a mystique of authority around Sean, diminishing transparency and corresponding accountability, and enabling a groupthink mindset that the "anonymous" author of *Vanguard* 1 insisted upon. No one has ever denied that Sean wrote *Vanguard* 1, Vegan Reich lyrics, Vegan Reich interview responses, or the Hardline manifesto. Subsequently, Sean's words take up a considerable amount of attention here because whatever Sean believed, Hardliners could reasonably expect one another to believe as well. As evidence, one will never find any Hardliner ever openly questioning or challenging *anything* Sean ever wrote. The closest this ever occurred (in the late 90s when Dave Agranoff began to—rather mildly—raise the question of changing some aspects of Hardline) ended very decisively with Sean stepping back in to oust Dave. Subsequently, whatever questions arise about sourcing for other texts remains almost a moot point. No one really cares. I did try to get it right but when I simply did not know—such as with *Declaration*, perhaps the most *Vanguard* #1-like zine in Hardline outside of *Vanguard* 1 itself, both in style, tone, and format (i.e., completely anonymous, no ads, often-prophetic or at least authoritative tone, etc.)—I just left it anonymous.

I tried to clear up confusion and lack of clarity when possible and substantiating any claims. Evidence and sources do not equal proof but at least they offer a stronger, clearer case than a debate of opinions. They also help fulfill the aim of turning this into a little resource database for anyone who wants to delve deeper.

But ultimately, if you feel like I did a really shitty job covering Hardline, I can only say this: please do a better one yourself. (Or, if you feel, like many people apparently do, that no one should cover Hardline at all or not nearly this much… oops. Too late.)

6 What have people said about Hardline?

Krishna is the straight-edge of the '90s and Hardline is the skinheads of the '90s.

- Steve Crudello (No Escape, *LongShot* #6 1991).

Within the hardcore punk scene from which it sprang, Hardline seemed nearly universally reviled. Indeed, some of the staunchest critics came from vegan straight edge scenes. Scholars, in turn, have (to some degree at least) built upon what others in hardcore punk scenes have said about Hardliners. Let's begin with a few comments from people in hardcore punk scenes and move on toward literature on the topic. We can divide commenters on Hardline into a few categories: *haters*—those who would dismiss Hardline simply by virtue of their involvement in punk rock, social justice, or their advocacy of veganism (I won't discuss this group because their reasons for dismissal have no relevance here); *bitter neighbors*—punks who shared some of Hardline's ideals but vehemently rejected Hardline as "fascistic," "right wing," "homophobic," etc.; *lost potentials*—people, largely in agreement with many Hardline stances, who might have felt temporarily swayed by Hardline until they found out about (or thoroughly thought about) all of their stances; *allies* or *adjacents*—those who either left Hardline or never identified as Hardline but remained close to it (distributing Hardline material or releasing bands with Hardline members); and *true believers*—those who actually joined and openly propagated Hardline at some stage.

We can see a fairly typical representation of *bitter neighbor* reception of Hardline in a *MRR* review of early Hardline zine *Vegan Delegation* in 1991: "Here's an easy way to spread your misguided message: conceal it among officious information and literature of genuinely caring organizations, make like you've got a clue, and march behind the banner of veganism. A self righteous suburbanite vents his sexual frustrations and tells us exactly why we should join the hardline cause. Count me in" (MW 1991). Or even more vehemently, in a review of *Praxis*, *MRR* wrote: "Get the fuck out of punk! All you fucked up vegan bashing, jock loving, rich white het male hardliners, go someplace that tolerates the mindless shit you pass off as a religion like a football field or [white power advocate Tom] Metzer's camp for tough boys. Fuck the propaganda in this shit rag. Stop tying in animal rights with fag bashing and telling women what they can't do. Let this zine die" (JX *MRR* 101, 1991). Previous issues of *MRR* gave better reviews. Sean distributed Screaming Foetus and got a positive review while his release of Naturecore and The Apostles elicited mediocre responses by Martin Sprouse. In December 1988, however, Martin gave Sean's first compilation release *The A.L.F. is Watching and There's No Place to Hide*... a glowing review in *MRR* stating that it set a "a good standard how compilations should be... powerful music with lyrical content centered around an important issue... I recommend this one!" so one might also count the straight edge Martin as a *lost potential* (Sprouse 1988). Most of the harshest opposition to Hardline came from this group. Anarcho-punk and straight edge bands such as Naked Angels (US), Crisis of Faith (Canada), Good Clean Fun (US), One X More (Netherlands), and Active Minds (UK) all wrote explicitly anti-Hardline songs. Prominent hardcore and punk zines such as *MRR* and *Profane Existence* boycotted and/or banned Hardline ads. Al Kowalewski of *Flipside* appreciated the vegan message but said that Hardline "reeks of fascism, right-wingism and just plain elitism" (Flipside 1992, 20). One of the harshest critiques came from the editor of *HeartattaCk*, vegan straight edger Kent McClard, who described Hardline as "gun-loving, homophobic, 'pro-life' ...hardcore-machismo ...[which] is as threatening to the American way of life as baseball, apple pie, and hot dogs. Like some flashy MTV orientated media trend, Hardline will burn itself out as all substanceless and disposable commodities do" (McClard 1991; see Appendix 2). Another harsh critique came as recent as 2016 from journalist Michael Little: "Muttaqi's megalomania and savage wrath are Biblical in proportion ... he obviously sees himself as a latter-day Jesus come to redeem us... All of Muttaqi's fanatical and homicidal threats seem to have been idle ones; as of yet we do not live under a vegan dictatorship, and I've heard of no murders of meat eaters. That said, Muttaqi is not just some hateful crank. People who support abortion and members of the LGBT community are at very real risk because of people like the assholes in Vegan Reich, who took and presumably still take a militant stance against legal abortions and gays" (Little 2016).

Paul Abrash, drummer for Crisis of Faith, wrote an article in the early 1990s entitled "No Tolerance For Hardline," where he described Hardline as "a dangerous hybrid of straight-edge fanaticism coupled with homophobia" and traced this type of conformity to straight edge itself such as when Ian MacKaye publically rejected meat-eating and, according to Paul, led to the "straight-edge mass embrace, more or less, of vegetariansm" (Abrash 1992: 16). To this, Ian responded in the pages of *Drastic Solutions*: "Even though I understand the unfortunate link between the Hardline people and the song 'Straight-edge' which I wrote when I was in Minor Threat, you have done me a great disservice by implicating me in their idiocy. Never have I been involved with that sort of intolerance, homophobia, and fundamentalism and your misleading mention insults the fuck out of me" (MacKaye 1992: 8). Vic DiCara of Inside Out (with Zack de la Rocha) and Krishnacore bands Shelter and 108 wrote of Hardline: "For the most part they were a bunch of asswipes even more 'holier than thou' than we were" (DiCara 2015). Other *bitter neighbors* appeared in Earth and animal liberation circles: *Live Wild or Die* called Vegan Reich and Hardliners "dickheads" and "scum" and Josh Harper of Talon Conspiracy called Hardline a "right wing sectarian…cult," adding "fuck Hardline and anyone who apologizes for it" (*LWOD* 7 1998; Harper 2014).

Lost potentials seem hard to track because they may simply lose interest rather than voice a public opinion but this example of a positive review of Vegan Reich's *Hardline* EP in *Factsheet Five* in 1991 indicates what the reception to Hardline *might* have looked like had they not emphasized opposition to abortion and homosexuality:

> Four songs of hardcore/speedmetal hybrid that take a definitive stances against all forms of animal exploitation (meat, cosmetics testing, dairy farming, leather, etc.). This band supports equal rights for all creatures, including human minorities. Their politics are similar to Consolidated's newest album. But their politics are nearly impossible to discern from the songs, and they've thoughtfully included a lyrics sheet and statement of purpose. There's also a discussion of the flaws in one-issue movements. As a supporter of veganism, I'm glad to see something this well-thought out and logical happen in the music world (Williams 1991).

Often it can seem difficult to distinguish between a *bitter neighbor* (punks supportive of veganism, activism, Earth liberation, and/or straight edge) and *lost potentials* such as in this excerpt of a review of *Vanguard* 7 by Scott McDonald in *Punk Planet* 19:

> …perhaps the greatest flaw of Hardline is that it pretends to have all the answers, forcing its adherents into the belief that the world is something that can be completely understood. Although the ideas offered in this zine are fucked up, I'm not too worried about them becoming massively popular—who can take seriously a zine in which the authors are too chickenshit to sign their names? (1997: 159).

Perhaps a clearer example of the loss of potential ally appeared in the *Earth First! Journal* who, without any follow-up commentary, published a letter from Memphis Hardline in 1992 yet, when a Hardliner named Jon Howell sent a letter in 1996 and clarified Hardline's anti-homosexual stance, the editor responded that Hardline "reeks of fascism" (Memphis Hardline 1992, Howell 1996). We can find other examples such as Vegan Earth Order whose ad in *MRR* clarified in regard to their Vegan Power shirts: "These are not hardline shirts. This is not a hardline group" and the first issue of *Militant Vegan* similarly clarified "IMPORTANT! The *Militant Vegan* is not a 'Hardline' zine, and we stand in total opposition to their patriarchal and heterosexist politics" (VEO 1993: 114; Militant Vegan 1993: 1).

Allies or *adjacents* seem like a fairly large and diverse group consisting mostly of vegan straight edgers who do not publically share some of Hardline's more controversial stances (such as in regard to homosexuality or abortion). We could understand them similarly to how *Vanguard #5* outlined its criteria for accepting ads in 1993: "*1) You are militantly vegan without slandering Hardline 2) You adhere to the Hardline philosophy or 3) You promote us in some way either through interviewing a Hardline activist or running our ads (without slandering us elsewhere in your product).*" In one prominent and influential example, Kurt Schroeder of the band Birthright and Catalyst Records said: "A lot of the people who got into hardline got into it for the same reasons they got into militant straight edge—it was this kind of elite, macho group. There were two sides to hardline—one was that side and the other was a more thoughtful side. A lot of the kids I knew were more intelligible about it" (Peterson 2009: 102). Later, Kurt spoke of "the huge influence that hardline and hardline bands had on the vegan straight edge movement in the beginning" and claimed: "Most of the vegan bands in the hardcore scene either had members who were hardline (or paid lip-service to the ideology), or were influenced by earlier hardline bands" (Kuhn 2010: 150). Within activist circles, we find, for example, Peter Young who has described how much Hardline bands (specifically bands such as Raid and Vegan Reich) influenced him: "I was skating the streets of Seattle, listening to Raid and something in me broke. …The fate that would have awaited myself and the animals had I continued as an inactive vegan stood to be far more horrific than prison" (Pike 2011: 38). Animal liberation activist Walter Bond wrote: "Throughout the 90s, Hardline bands like Vegan Reich, Raid and Green Rage got the youth focused like a laser beam on radical and fanatical Animal Liberation activism by blending the best elements of the struggles for Earth, Animals, anti-racism and anti-capitalism with the seriousness and purity ethic of the fundamentalist" (Bond 2011a). Elsewhere, Walter wrote:

> [Hardline's] central preamble and creed was called the "Hardline Manifesto." First disseminated by a little known punk rock band named "Vegan Reich". ...It could even be argued that Hardline was the progenitor of what latter would become known as "Vegan Straight Edge." ... Hardliners were much more than simply involved in a music scene. They were also instrumental in starting such hard hitting activist groups as [CAFT, (Coalition Against the Fur Trade)] and were instrumental in above-ground support of the Animal Liberation Front, Animal Rights Militia, Justice Department and others involved in the clandestine fight for Animal and Earth Liberation (Pieslak 2014b: 84).

Tim Rule of Bound By Modern Age Records in Germany said "I do not want to glorify or justify everything which the movement Hardline did or let happen/become of it later on, but still I feel like today's hardcore/metal music and the vegan straight edge movement as such wouldn't be the same if it wasn't for Hardline Records" (Ramirez 2018). Mack Evasion wrote in *HeartattaCk*: "The years from 1990 to 1997 saw vegan sxe kids—or a few of them—make hardcore a threat, maybe for the first time. Vegan Reich set it off in 1990; accurately capturing the urgency of the struggle for all life" (Evasion 2005: 30).

True believers often spoke of Hardline with the fervency of those enraptured with salvation. This has tended to turn off a lot of outsiders but, unfortunately, it means that, outside of quoting Raid lyrics or contemporary interviews with ex-Hardliners, few outsiders have quoted original sources without the purpose of either praising or deriding them. So here we have a few samples from Hardliners in their own words as they appeared in the 1990s and it may help explain both what attracted people to Hardline and how some of them thought when they identified as Hardline:

> **Jill (Cincinnati Hardline)**:
>
> I finally got around to asking Micah if I could read the infamous *Vanguard* #1. Soon I came to realize that Hardline's views were the same as my own. I could hardly believe that I agreed with what I read so strongly (*Destroy Babylon* 3, 1996: 57).

> **Anonymous/Attack on Eden Communications**:
>
> I hear the screams of a man in South America as he's beaten for collapsing under the hot sun during cocaine harvesting. I hear the piercing whine of jets and helicopters overhead. I hear the missiles being fired at civilian targets in Bosnia. I hear the cries of the animals tortured in labs, factory farms, and fur traps. I hear chainsaws clear cutting the rainforests, annihilating another 40,000

unknown species a year. I hear a woman whimper and shriek as she's beaten and raped. I hear a child cry to himself in Africa as he goes another week without food. I hear the crazed laughter of a power hungry dictator wielding nuclear arms. I hear the seas and skies choking and coughing as toxins fill their lungs. I hear it all, and it begins to meld until it all becomes a single sound, the sound of a drum. A drum that is pounding away the last years of an earth, an ecosystem, and a species' dwindling life. A drum that only be silenced with our apocalypse. And I fear that day is not distant (*Declaration* 1, c. 1995: 15).

Sean (Vegan Reich):

This society was built on violence against animals and people. Right now, in slaughterhouses and laboratories, animals are being tortured and killed. In every corner of the world jungles and forests are being uprooted or burned to the ground. Oceans are being pumped full of toxic waste, lakes are being drained and the skies being filled with pollution. All the while, whole species are being destroyed. To say that one cannot use violence to stop that is to in effect give support to those destroying this earth. For they know no morality, and they have not one ounce of restraint. They will do whatever it takes to ensure their profits and power. To deny violence as a means of resistance to their victims of rape and plunder, is to ensure that victims they will always be. This type of moralizing by people who accept the everyday comforts that this society offers (comforts gained by the brutal domination of the natural world by mankind) is nothing more than the words of sheltered idiots content with the status quo. For it can be nothing else—other than perhaps complete ignorance. For what else do they propose? That if everyone became vegetarians, the meat trade would vanish? Pleasant thought, but just totally unrealistic. Those dying don't have time to wait for that kind of evolutionary process. And this earth doesn't have time.

But let's pretend for just one moment we did have time to wait for the evolutionary process to end animal and environmental exploitation. What are these people gonna do in the meantime? What kind of lives are these people too pure to use violence gonna live? For their gas and oil is gained from violence to the environment. As is the plastic on their stereos and numerous other toys. Their cars violently pollute the sky just as their cities pollute the earth. If they're gonna live in this world, that their forefathers made, and accept the violence that it took and still takes to maintain the comfort that even they enjoy—yet condemn those who use, in comparison, relatively little violence, in an effort to end the continual physical abuse towards this earth and the life upon it, then it is obvious that it is not really violence for which they have a problem with, rather, only that violence which is not sanctioned by their master—the modern world. If they don't wanna live in a cave, removed completely free from this world, then they better make a choice of whose side they're on. Because as long as they live in this society, built upon and maintained by violence, they are a part of it. And either they are on the side of getting rid of the mess we live in, which will mean getting their hands dirty and fighting to clean this place up, or they are on the side of the status quo (which takes nothing except what they're already doing) (*Caring Edge* 1990: 22).

Tiffany (Indianapolis Hardline):

First of all, I want to make it clear that every single person on this earth should be Hardline! What I'm saying is that everyone has to change their complacent lifestyles or else the earth will die! Another matter I want to clear up is all the misunderstandings about Hardline being sexist. This is ludicrous. In no way whatsoever does Hardline advocate sexism. I have not yet encountered a sexist in Hardline. ...What I think is sexist is how a lot people assume I got into Hardline because of my boyfriend. Why can't they assume my boyfriend is Hardline because of me? If you want to know the truth we got into Hardline *together*, Amazing, huh? (*Vanguard* 2, 1993: 13).

Michelle Borok (Memphis Hardline, *Gaia Screams*, *Invictus*):

For Hardliners there is no choice, no compromise. Nothing is done "as we please". Pleasure is derived from a life liberated and the Hardline hand of justice dealt. If I am to live my life hoping to be free of guilt and be morally strong, I have no choice but to be Hardline.

The argument for personal choice is ludicrous. Personal choice, the vessel of truth to all politically correct liberals, has no meaning in the shadow of oppression. ...Hardline offers the truth and beauty of life. A fetus offers these same things. A baby in the womb symbolizes the power of life and creation, and the power of women. I find abortion an insult to my conscience and my femininity. This brings me to the issue of feminism and what women can offer to the Vegan Revolution. This is not a man's war, all about testosterone and machismo. Hardline fights oppression, injustice, prejudice, and discrimination. ...We as women have the power. We as Hardline, have the right and the might (*Vanguard* 6, 1995: 7).

Anonymous/Attack on Eden Communications:

There are so many problems to deal with in everyday life, for both you, I, and everyone around us. Financial dilemmas, maintaining a job, keeping our relationships going, just getting by from day to day can be quite stressful and draining. But we need to forget all of our personal petty little predicaments and take a look at the big picture. We have problems to solve that will determine if the Earth lives or dies, whether we will push species into extinction or salvage them, whether humans will stop their violation of one another and all around them or not, these are the real issues, these are the problems that need our attention now. It is up to every one of us to make conscious decisions ourselves and the world we live in. If you are not doing this you are being counter productive, in fact you are destroying what I and countless others are trying to rebuild, namely the ecological well being of our planet and a communal sense of respect that encircles *all* forms of life: human, animal, and plant. Take responsibility for your actions, then take into consideration the weight of your single life in the grand balance of things. You can make your voice heard, you can attack evil in this world on all sides and live in harmony with nature, or you can continue to demolish the Earth, massacre its animal inhabitants and enslave its human ones. It's up to you. Make a choice (*Declaration* 1, c. 1995: 29).

Mike (Messiah Communications):

My name is Mike, some people call me Talib. I am 29 years old. When I was around 14 years old, I started to think more critically. I started to question everything and became more aware of what happened and is happening around me. I changed my consciousness and became more active within different types of movements such as the anarchist or human/animal/earth liberation movements. Later came across the Hardline ideology, which made a lot of sense to me and lived by those principles over the years. Things have changed in my life since then though. Don't get me wrong. I still follow most of these ideas but I see them now more from a spiritual point of view. All Life and its creations are coming from the same source. If you try to submit to the Most High then I believe that standing up for the oppressed is also a part of worshipping Allah/Jah/God.

In this case nothing has really changed for me. I still try to live a compassionate life and to be responsible for my actions. I'm still raising my voice for the voiceless and the unheard. There are many things which make me smile. I have to admit that I smile especially when people succeed in fighting against tyranny and become independent and start governing their own lives. One of my biggest hopes is that one day, all people regardless of faith can peacefully coexist and that our planet will be saved and that justice will rule the world again.

I fear that time is running out though. Everyday people are being murdered, everyday the planet is being more and more depleted and sucked dry, everyday animals are being tortured and killed for human lust and greed. I fear that one day we all have to pay the price for this. I fear that we will all become more and more enslaved, controlled, manipulated and that there is no chance for us to resist this from happening. Spiritually, I fear that I cannot please the most highly spirit with my actions. Those are my biggest fears but my hopes defiantly overwhelm them (Bahr 2010).

Dave Agranoff (*Vanguard* editor 1995-1996):

Hardline is an ideology, is more than anything. No other movement, no other philosophy, no other ideology has made the connections that hardline has made. That being connections to racism, sexism, speciesism all kinds of things. Hardline is the only philosophy that acknowledges the fact that this is a result of mankind's alienation from nature. …It's so much easier when you can have a philosophy that encompasses all those in one simple belief-system (*Value Of Strength* 5, 1999: 52).

Michelle Borok (Memphis Hardline, *Gaia Screams*, *Invictus*):

It made me really sad when some people I really liked, and who I thought were liking me, stopped being friendly when I said I was Hardline. We were getting along very well in punk fashion until it came up and then all of a sudden I was an outcast. The first thing people will say of Hardliners is that they are judgmental, self righteous, all those things these people were to me. I wasn't angry, just hurt. I believe that the two friends are genuinely nice people. I just wish they'd give others a chance. You can't always judge a kid by his/her label (*Invictus* 1, 1995: 8).

Dave Agranoff (*Vanguard* editor 1995-1996):

During the last half of the 90s I was like a hardline robot totally dedicated like a machine to the ideology proposed in *Vanguard* #1 which was very much like a bible to me at the time. In 99 the hardline movement split, a minority who viewed hardline to [be] based on Muslim ideals copyrighted the name [and] declared many of us ideologically impure. …I still believe they were reading *Vanguard* incorrectly and at the time it was devastating to me. I had devoted everything to hardline for years (*Stuck in the Past*, 2010).

Brad (Buffalo Hardline):

For so long, being vegan straight edge was not sufficient enough for me. I need to be part of a movement not a 'youth crew.' My hatred towards institutions and individuals who denigrate the value of life and rape our world were (and still are) growing stronger everyday.

Even my views on militant intervention seemed unacceptable to most within the animal rights movement. It was incomprehensible to me that people who I thought shared the same beliefs as me thought violence was too extreme to liberate the innocent. Why were some of these kids who claim allegiance to the vegan straight edge ideals participating in other oppressive behaviors such as pornography? Why was it that so many who believe in animal liberation at the same time believe that killing an innocent baby is a woman's right? I didn't understand and I was confused. Where was the sincerity in others that I held so deeply? Where was the consistency?

...Hardline is the only logical extension of our quest to liberate the earth and all its inhabitants. The decision was already made for me. I now know there is no alternative. Society, and all of its selfish destructive behaviors has forced me to the extreme. I did not choose this life-style. In order to counterattack this species' war against nature, I must be Hardline. Michelle of Memphis Hardline wrote it best: '*For hardliners there is no choice, no compromise. Nothing is done as we please. Pleasure is derived from a life liberated, and strong. I have no choice but to be Hardline.*' A revolutionary force such as Hardline is needed if there is to be any hope for earth, animal and human liberation. We are the only movement that is not afraid of violence to liberate the billions of innocent lives who suffer as a result of humanity's sins.

I am far from perfect. I make mistakes. I am not afraid to admit that at times it's a difficult life-style. There is so much more I need to learn, but I now know that this is the only movement that lives by the highest ethic in accordance with the laws of nature. For animals in the slaughterhouses, for the women raped daily by society, for the indigenous peoples fighting for their culture, for the lives of the unborn, for my own liberation... This is why I must adhere to the Hardline ("No Alternative but Hardline," *Unveil The Lies* 1, 1996: 19).

Michelle Borok (Memphis Hardline, *Gaia Screams*, *Invictus*):

As Hardliners, our beliefs aren't limited to single issues, and our concerns shouldn't only be local. Our European chapters have proven that Hardline knows no geographical boundaries. Maybe someday we'll have the opportunity to hear of a Tokyo or Seoul Hardline chapter. Everything takes time, but we can try to speed up the clock. Do all that you are able from whatever location that you are from. Every action counts. At the very least write letters to foreign embassies, and express your discontent diplomatically, but with that undeniable Hardline flair. Our movement is so wonderfully unique in that we are devoted to total earth liberation, not scenes or single issues. There is only one issue: the war isn't over until all innocent life is liberated (physically and from emotional distress based on human civilization), and the Earth can exist without human bondage and torment ("Animal Liberation," *Vanguard* 6, 1995: 22).

Anonymous/Attack on Eden Communications:

> I hear the drum again, but this time it signifies not the dying of our home. This time it is a call for revolution. This time it pounds in time with my heart, and flows through my body. This time it pushes me against the flood of aberration humanity has become, in hopes of beginning anew, in hopes of changing this world before it perishes. Wake up to the suffering around you. Open your eyes to the death we are implementing into every aspect of our lives (*Declaration* 1, c. 1995: 16).

That sums up quotes from the different types. Yet, as with life in general, the facts often don't fit into neat and simple categories. Earth Crisis, for example, first hoped to get released on Hardline records and sounded positive about Hardline initially. *Persist* fanzine asked singer Karl Buechner "Do you believe in and/or support the hardline movement?" and he responded, "Yes. I along with every other Earth Crisis member are completely against outright promiscuity. It will always lead to lies and destruction. If two people love each other and want to hit the sack that's cool with me. If it's two men, two women, a man and a woman, I don't care. There's more important issues that need attention right now. Promiscuity is what needs to be dealt with." (Persist 1993: 24). Three years later, Karl sounded more unequivocal: "Earth Crisis are not a hardline band. Earth Crisis is a vegan straightedge band. That's what we've always been, are now, and forever shall be. We are not homophobic" (Svitil 1996). Guitarist Scott Crouse (also of SECT and Path of Resistance) later said: "Earth Crisis originally wanted to be on Hardline Records. Framework was very close to being on Hardline, and Earth Crisis seemed like an even better fit. We began to realize though that Hardline was a lot more than just veganism and straight edge. We disagreed strongly on a few of their viewpoints, basically it was too rigid in its overall agenda, and homophobia was a part of it. ...Don't get me wrong, we were fans of, and inspired by a few of the hardline bands, but ultimately we decided hardline didn't represent us and chose to carry on under the title vegan straight edge" (Ramirez 2018). Or, for example, take this interview with Shane Durgee, vocalist for Framework (which eventually turned into Earth Crisis without him), and member of "Hardline" band Gatekeeper:

> **xYosefx**: Since you brought up Hardline, what exactly was the relationship of the early Syracuse straight edge scene to Hardline? I know that, for a while at least, Hardline was pretty big in Upstate NY. In some early interviews (in Shadows and Tall Trees fanzine, for instance) Karl talks about Earth Crisis wanting to sign to Hardline Records and says that the members of the band

> agree with Hardline completely. Was this due to a misunderstanding of what Hardline espoused (particularly around the issues of homosexuality and abortion) or was there genuine agreement? Where did you stand on Hardline, especially around those two rather controversial issues? I know that in Gatekeeper you were the only non-Hardline member, yet you still put the Hardline logo on the demo layout. Where do you stand on these issues today?
>
> Shane: I'm actually surprised to see that Karl ever said that. My memory of the whole thing was that Ben and I were the only ones that actually proclaimed to be Hardline back then, and that was short lived. Other hardliners eventually moved to Syracuse, but I had thought Earth Crisis had shed the label pretty much in their infancy. That said, I only know that for me I didn't fully understand Hardline as a rigid set of laws. The homophobic thing really bugs me, although I had definitely ranted about it back then: "Sex is for procreation. Anything else goes against nature!" It honestly only took weeks for me to step back and listen to myself and realize I didn't even feel that way about any of it. I was just posturing (xYosefx 2009).

Similarly, Tom Lang of the *Our Struggle* zine in Austria seemed to promote Hardline in his zine but quickly added a caveat in *MRR* writing: "I do definitely not agree with what the Hardline said about homosexuals" and called Hardline views "plain and simple stupid" (Lang 1994). Rob R-Rock, vegetarian straight edger in Naked Angels (who released an anti-Hardline song) and perhaps the first xVx rapper, critiqued Hardline in a 1990 letter to *MRR* and sent a shout out to Hardball, two of whose members would soon go Hardline. Rob later released the Hardball 7" on New Start Records and, while the band complained that they never received copies, Rob later stated: "This record was obviously a joke, and was not a serious effort on our part" (R-Rock 1990 and 1993). Or, for example, take Dustin Hall from the band Gather who described Hardline as "fucking pathetic," "bullshit moral constructions," and added "I hate the few people I know of now who still regurgitate the old Hardline rhetoric on message boards" yet, when Vegan Reich had a reunion concert in 2017, he made sure to attend (Mittens XVX 2007; Vegan Reich 2017a). While this may seem odd, Sean's remarks seem to imply that, strange as it may sound, Vegan Reich never qualified as a Hardline band: "No Vegan Reich lyrics pertain to this issue [homosexuality/abortion]; the band has no collective view on abortion" (Muttaqi 2019). As Hardline required belief in all of its tenets without exception, disbelief in one aspect of it disqualified a person/band from claiming Hardline. Likewise, Patrick "Rat" Poole of Statement, responsible for one of only three records released on Hardline Records, also denied ever identifying as Hardline (correspondence with author 2021). In other words, as Hardline never had a formal organization, much less one with a transparent membership list, the questions of which person or band really "was" or "was not" Hardline quickly turns into a very murky and unconstructive enterprise (which I do not plan to resolve here even though I do hope to make it easier to grasp/bypass that endeavor). Some people whom one might not have guessed (such as Scott Beibin of Bloodlink Records) did identify as Hardline at one point in time (Scott even held the workshops at the first Hardline gathering). At the same time, other people, such as Statement or Earth Crisis, whom people often assume to have identified as Hardline, did not. Such confusions have made it more difficult for researchers who attempt to discuss Hardline in a cursory manner because no clear documentation or study exists.

Academic coverage of Hardline 1999-2004

Yet, now we turn to what academics have looked at and reported in regard to Hardline. Here, we can work our way chronologically from earliest works to most recent. Craig O'Hara, writing about the punk scene *The Philosophy of Punk* (1992/1999) from an insider-to-punk/outsider-to-Hardline perspective, seems like the first to discuss Hardline in a book. He had little positive to say:

> In the first edition of this book I was reluctant to mention the tiny "hardline" scene. Back then it was limited to a few groups with few releases and very small following. I did so only to point out the idiocy of their movement and intentions. Since then, it has grown exponentially with the shit metal band **Earth Crisis** at its axis. While I applaud the band for their animal rights and Earth First! style endorsement of political action, the overtly reactionary puritan bullshit they espouse is only good for a mocking laugh at best. This band and the many they have influenced were preceded by the SoCal band **Vegan Reich** (try not to laugh at the name). The band **Vegan Reich** with their record label No Master's Voice had become pretty popular within the scene while espousing very controversial views. Among those views were veganism, an end to animal experimentation, and eventually a peaceful anarchist society. Also present were views which were blatantly sexist, homophobic, and totalitarian (O'Hara 1999: 149).

Craig then went on to cite examples of this from Sean's letter to *Profane Existence* in 1990 (he also quoted from Sean's interview in *MAS* 1989 but did not cite the source). Regarding sexism, Craig noted that Sean considered "women to be completely equal to men, both in the struggle & in relationship" but he did "not think we are the same." Craig then critiqued Sean's advocacy of "pre-set natural roles" and "the family structure" as "blatantly sexist and could easily justify domination" seemingly conflating the concepts of "sameness" and "equality" which Sean attempted to distinguish (Ibid: 150). Craig seemingly missed Sean's lack of clarification of what he meant by "pre-set natural roles" and "family structure." Except for the issue of abortion, Sean did not (and has not ever as far as I have seen) express any views arguing for inequality of the sexes. Therefore, it seems more likely that Sean meant "heterosexual" in reference to pre-set natural roles and family structure. He *may* have meant that women ought to tend to children more than men but he never said or even implied that. Then Craig critiqued Sean's statement that "homosexuality can be seen as nothing but a deviation from nature [and therefore] must be spoken out against and combatted." Then, turning to the Vegan Reich interview in *MAS*, Craig noted that Sean advocated "a dictatorship by Vegans who would help speed up the natural evolution process by re-educating those who can be, and weeding out those beyond help. After this has occurred and the human race is drastically reduced in population…" (but clipped off the end of Sean's sentence which continued: "…the dictatorship can be dissolved and true anarchism can flourish"). Craig then summed up his view of Hardline: "Dictatorship, mass murder, and fascism are not very Punk or tolerated by most Straight Edgers" (Ibid). Most later scholars tended to avoid such a partisan tone against Hardline yet none of them followed Craig's example of citing early primary sources beyond the Hardline manifesto or Vegan Reich lyrics.

Police investigators Michelle Arciaga and Al Valdez seemed to fire shots off with one of their hands half-covering their eyes. Al wrote that, after Vegan Reich started Hardline in the early 1990s, "Surprisingly, almost overnight the Straight Edge vegan (Hardline) movement gained nationwide popularity" and "Many of the young kids who get involved in Straight Edge move on to Hardline, ALF or racist skinhead membership and affiliation. Be safe!" (Valdez 2000). Of course, Al did not cite any evidence for Hardline's nationwide popularity (instead conflating it with vegan straight edge) or specify how many straight edgers turned into racist skinheads. Nor did he add "police" to that list but he could have (I have seen a police message board where several cops bonded over their shared past as kids from the scene and former edger Jeremy Nelson of the Ogden police has even showed off his tattoos, see Sangosti 2021). More accurate, but still without citing sources or number of groups, Al wrote "Hardline Straight Edgers began creating their own local ALF groups, made up of three to 10 members, to act independently 'on behalf of animals.' These individual cells, with no central leadership or structure, began to commit 'direct action' terrorist acts against businesses that sold animal products" (Valdez 2000). Michelle Arciaga wrote of Hardline's origins: "In the summer of 1987, five young men from Memphis, Tennessee, formed a hardcore band. Since all five came from Straight Edge backgrounds, they shared common beliefs. However, front man Sean 'Hardline' Penn had a radically different view of the basic Straight Edge opposition to drugs, alcohol, and tobacco. The group named their band Vegan Reich because all the members were avid animal-liberation activists" (Arciaga 2005). Not only did she conflate Raid (from Memphis) with Sean of Vegan Reich (from Laguna Beach), she also got Sean's last name wrong (a mistake repeated by Abraham 2008, Abraham and Stewart 2017, and others). This leads one to believe that the "inside source," whom she corresponded with, consciously misled her to make her sound stupid. If so, it worked.

More scholarly work did not, however, necessarily entail accuracy. Erin Foster, who focused on the scene in Salt Lake City and described Hardline as a "self- proclaimed subdivision of straight-edge" that advocated "releasing captive animals, slashing tires of bar patrons (whom they believe will later drive drunk), and physically injuring any other individuals whom they see challenging their 'rights' for purity" (Foster 2001: 100-101). While most of this may have applied to some members of the SLC scene (even though Sean very much downplayed any connections to straight edge), the idea of "physically injuring any other individuals whom they see challenging their 'rights' for purity" sounds purely speculative, ambiguous, and/or a gross misrepresentation of the ethical basis for animal liberation. For example, Hardliner Jon Justice claimed in *Praxis* 1991 that he suckerpunched Ron Guardipee from Brotherhood/Overkill Records because he opposed animal rights and had talked shit about Hardline—the only instance I've seen of Hardliners bragging about gratuitous violence—but even that instance had nothing to do with attacking someone who challenged "rights for purity" (Praxis 1991: 12-13). Furthermore, the ethics of militant animal liberation simply recognize unnecessary harm to animals as unacceptable and apologists for such harm as ideological accomplices. Again, any violence perpetrated against apologists (right or wrong) does not seem to arise from a concern about purity but striving for justice and defense of animals. When scholars depict it in such a frame, they make it seem like a foreign concept. But if most people witnessed another person physically attacking a horse for no reason or torturing a dog in the street then, if they could physically intervene, they would. Militant vegans, including Hardliners, simply extended the logic of this physical response to the attacks and torture that take place toward other animals behind walls rather than in public streets.

In 2003, James Patrick Williams wrote a dissertation entitled *The Straightedge Subculture on the Internet: A Case Study*, but conflated Hardline with straight edge, using the term "hardline straight edge." Although James read a post that described the actual Hardline scene, he dismissed it for lack of evidence:

> One forum participant offered a definition of "hardline." He said, "HARDLINE is not STRAIGHT EDGE there are massive differences. Hardline is vegan, pro life and no drugs, booze or sex. It involves violence. And militant Animal Rights action. Hardliners do not call themselves straight edge. They are their own unique subculture." While this definition may be true for this particular participant in his own local area (somewhere in New Zealand), I found little supporting evidence from other forum participants. This and other subcultural terms were oftentimes interpreted differently by members of the forum. It is therefore necessary to highlight divergent interpretations within straightedge groups in order to avoid fixing terms that are fluid (Williams 2003: 114).

Yet, if James had actually read Craig O'Hara's book which he cited elsewhere, he would have found precisely such "supporting evidence" regarding the New Zealander's definition of Hardline (even if he did not like what he saw). As with other scholars interested in straight edge, James leaned heavily on Beth Lahickey's interview-based *All Ages* (1997) which gave no attention to vegan straight edge or Hardline.

Academic coverage of Hardline 2005-2007

In 2005, Peter Staudenmaier wrote that Hardline "grew out of the Straight Edge movement" and situated it among "rightwing" tendencies in animal rights currents. In "Ambiguities of Animal Rights," he wrote:

> ...animal rights sentiment has frequently served as an entry point for rightwing positions into left movements. Because much of the left has generally been reluctant to think clearly and critically about nature, about biological politics, and about ethical complexity, this unsettling affinity between animal rights and rightwing politics—an affinity which has a lengthy historical pedigree—remains a serious concern. While hardly typical of the current as a whole, it is not unusual to find the most militant proponents of animal liberation also espousing staunch opposition to abortion, homosexuality, and other purportedly 'unnatural' phenomena. The 'Hardline' tendency, which in the

> 1990s spread from North America to Central Europe, is perhaps the most striking example (Staudenmaier 2005: 6-7).

Peter's work—unrelated to punk studies—marks one of the few, if only, mentions of Hardline in strictly political science/social ecology studies. Peter later published this same commentary on Hardline in his recent book *Ecology Contested: Environmental Politics between Left and Right* (2021) with a mention of Walter Bond and Camille Marino's Vegan Final Solution.

In 2006, two other scholars whom James Williams had cited, Robert Wood and Ross Haenfler, put out perhaps the most influential work on the topic of straight edge. Yet, both of them tended to portray Hardline as a marginal subset of straight edge and generally devoted very little attention to it. Robert Wood wrote in his book *Straightedge Youth* of a "new variation... commonly known as *hardline straightedge*, or simply *hardline*" that initially "referred to the level of militancy of one's 'claim' or identity as straightedge" (Wood 2006: 45). Robert continued:

> Hardline appears to be a sort of orthodox reconstruction of straightedge culture. In addition to the historical focus on drugs, this manifesto places hardline squarely amidst more recent issues such as animal rights, abortion, and environmental awareness. Since the early 1990s, mainstream media have been quick to characterize hardline as representative of straight edge culture in its entirety. In reality, however, hardline comprises only a minority of the straightedge subculture (Wood 2006: 47).

Robert quoted Raid lyrics and a significant portion of a statement from Bloomington Hardline but seemed unaware of its origins and many of its views.

For example, Robert mentioned briefly that Hardline addressed abortion but ignored the question of Hardline's stance on homosexuality as well as belief in a "Lifeforce" or the extent of its veganism (including minimizing car usage—see *"Religion" and "Cults"* section in this volume). Robert did not get it all wrong, however, as indeed, Project X and Elgin James of FSU have used "hardline" in this sense as he said. Robert cited John Porcell (Shelter, Judge, Youth of Today) who claimed that his band Project X in 1988 put out "a real hardline straightedge record...[an] I-am-gonna-kick-your-ass-if-you're-not-straight-edge type thing" (Wood 2006: 45). And true enough, Elgin James of FSU stated that this type of hardline originated with Al Barile of SSD: "DC invented straight edge, Al invented hardline. ...If some punk rock relic is drinking a beer at an all-ages show, Ian MacKaye... he might shoot him a dirty glance... Al and his crew would knock you out"

(2004). Yet, Robert seemed to conflate this type of "hardline straight edge" with Hardline and thereby led later researchers down a misleading detour. (As far as I know, the two scenes, FSU and Hardline, never had anything to do with one another in the 90s—but what do I know? Ask Alex of Boston Hardline. Or Pete Wentz who has supposedly hired FSU for security).

Perhaps the most prominent book on the topic of straight edge, entitled *Straight Edge* by Ross Haenfler, barely mentioned Hardline. He wrote that a "minority of sXers, labeled 'militant' or 'hardline' by other sXers, are very outspoken, donning X's and sXe messages at nearly all times and confronting their peers who use drugs" and "a vegan sXe offshoot called 'Hardline' was very outspoken and confrontational" (Haenfler 2006: 49, 78). Without mentioning Hardline by name, Ross wrote of "militant" straight edge as more "hypermasculine" and more "likely to be homophobic. Essentially in some ways they resemble the agro skinheads present in the early punk scene" (Ibid: 88). This type of glossing over of Hardline seems to have contributed, in part, to both the academic marginalization of Hardline and the depiction of it as a subset of straight edge/vegan straight edge when a more accurate description would mark Hardline as that which sparked vegan straight edge but differed from it notably. It also promoted some stereotypes about Hardline without actually citing Hardliners themselves or naming names (Ross mostly used Earth Crisis as a representative of this type of militancy even though they have, as far as I know, never critiqued homosexuality—only promiscuity regardless of sexual preference).

In a 2005 doctoral dissertation entitled *The Authentic Punk* and which cited Beth Lahickey, Alastair Gordon wrote of Hardline as a "militant straightedge doctrine" with a "zero-tolerance approach to substance abuse and intoxication," incorrectly identified "the New York band, Vegan Reich," and blurred distinctions between anti-abortion straight edge bands and Hardline (Gordon 2005: 131).

With another focus, Donald Liddick wrote in *Eco-Terrorism: Radical Environmental and Animal Liberation Movements* about "Peter Young, convicted for releasing thousands of minks from fur farms in Iowa, South Dakota, and Wisconsin" who upon getting arrested in 2005, "was prosecuted under the Animal Enterprise Protection Act of 1992" and "was sentenced to two years in prison and $254,000 in restitution." He then quoted from a letter he received from Peter:

> In the mid-90s, the straight-edge scene saw an emerging consciousness on the subject of our treatment of nonhuman animals, and many of the bands I was getting into at the time (most notably Earth Crisis and the intentionally provocative Vegan Reich) pushed the Vegan ethic through their lyrics. ...At first it was the message of nonconformity that attracted me, as well as the

> rejection of the party scene, which I saw as rather degenerate. As I began to give more thought to lyrical content, I began to find myself more appalled by what I was learning about what humans did to nonhumans for greed. My supplemental reading solidified my feelings that this was an injustice of the greatest scale, urgency, and magnitude. ...In remaining motivated for over a decade now, I would credit in no small way my rejection of the many numbing agents society throws at us which lead to apathy such as drugs, alcohol, television, and frivolous internet use. ...The only justification I need for illegal activity on behalf of sentient beings is that it works (Liddick 2006: 84-86).

Also in 2006 (referencing Beth Lahickey and early work by William Tsitsos and Robert Wood), we find an interesting academic article that remarkably passed peer review. Written by Steven Hamelman, who identified as straight edge because, as "a rock'n'roll junkie" and vegetarian *prior* to straight edge he abstained from intoxicants and promiscuity: "...I was, ironically, already a confirmed Straight Edger when the rockers and fans who would grow up to form the official straight edge movement were still in nappies" and yet, he added, "I am, of course, not straight edge after all, largely because I'm 'older'...Furthermore, I don't hang with a straight edge crowd, don't slam or mosh... and don't particularly like the music of any of the official straight edge bands" (Hamelman 2006: 189-190). In his article, he aimed to show how straight edge completely failed as a protest movement. He never mentioned Hardline but he did cite the 1999 *TIME* article on Salt Lake City violence. He mentioned Hardliners Josh Anderson (for his firebombing), Ryan Downey (in passing in a completely different context), spelled Steve Lovett's name wrong, and quoted Raid lyrics without identifying any of these people as Hardline. Steven declared: "In sXe circles, to be an animal-loving teetotaler with a taste for hardcore is not inconsistent with aggression, hostility, militancy, or even murder" (Ibid: 192). As a movement, straight edge failed, he insisted, because it supposedly protested against protest making it a tiny insignificant minority: "nothing straight edge says or does can be taken seriously by anyone who loves rock'n'roll. Nor would it be an exaggeration to suggest that for these same reasons, straight edge must also fall flat as protest music. ...A mutiny on board the pirate ship of rock'n'roll could only be termed an aberration, an anomaly, a futile endeavor" (Ibid). Citing early work by William Tsitsos, Steven seemed to allude to Hardline and/or militant straight edge when he referred to a new "generation of Straight Edgers ...rebelling with the ultimate goal of becoming agents of control with the power to impose rules on others" (Ibid: 194). As the article goes on, so does Steven's confidence of his conclusions: "We're familiar with what it, Straight Edge, dislikes, and we know the lengths to which Straight Edgers will go to hold their ground in defiance of what they emphatically aren't" (Ibid: 196).

At this point, I can't resist inserting a quote from *MRR*. In responding to the rumor that "*MRR* is anti-straight edge," Tim Yohannan wrote: "most of the staffers at *MRR* are indeed straight edge, meaning that they don't drink or do drugs, are vegetarian or vegan, and are clear thinkers. They have been this way for a long time, too. Brian Edge, Martin Sprouse, Katja, etc. are longtime adherents of this outlook. I smoke tobacco, but that's it. Walter, Chuck, Joel Wing, Chris Dodge, and John Yates are about as clean cut as you can get. Mike LaVella is a longtime friend to the whole DC approach" (*MRR* 73, 1989).

In other words, many straight edgers "hide" so well among people who do not agree 100% with them that researchers don't even notice them. No researcher that I know of has turned to *MRR* staff looking for straight edgers. They go to Ian MacKaye, SSD, and *TIME* magazine coverage of Salt Lake City and they find what they want.

Weirdly, Steven suggested straight edgers "are as far removed from reality as" Christian fundamentalists Dave Noebel (who critiqued the Beatles for their immorality) and Bob Larson (who blamed rock music for every problem under the sun). Even though Steven identified himself as straight edge (in a very broad sense), he switched to a narrow definition of sXe in his article as he critiqued people in the scene asking, "are Straight Edgers capable of having good record collections?" Quoting ex-straight edger David Schulz, Steven wrote that, "after a couple-few years," straight edge "began to suck so badly," and added in his own words: "Harnessing rock music to voice their protest against [the] senselessness [of drugs, alcohol, and promiscuity], Straight Edgers paradoxically make crooked (curved) life look (and sound) a lot better than it actually is (Hamelman 2006: 204).

Academic coverage of Hardline 2008-2010

Referencing Craig O'Hara in an article entitled "Punk Pulpit: Religion, Punk Rock, and Counter (Sub)Cultures" (2008), Ibrahim Abraham began discussion of Hardline within the context of religious studies and wrote: "Hardline became notorious for its militant, but deeply reactionary politics. Vegan Reich called for a dictatorship of the vegans and the rallying cry, 'in defence of all life,' came to encapsulate violently pro-life, misogynist and homophobic attitudes" (Abraham 2008: 4). The next year, 2009, Brian Peterson gave the most attention to Hardline that anyone had ever done up until then in his interview-based book *Burning Fight: The Nineties Hardcore Revolution in Ethics, Politics, Spirit, and Sound*. Here, he provided multiple interview excerpts from Sean Muttaqi and others associated with Hardline.

Rather than the section on "Straight Edge," he more discussed Hardline in the sections on "Animal Rights" and "Spirituality," where, in the former section, he wrote: "The hardline movement played an important, albeit controversial, role in nineties hardcore due to their stance on animal rights, sexuality, abortion, and other issues" (Peterson 2009: 85).

In another interview-based book, *Sober Living for the Revolution*, Gabriel Kuhn termed the "hardline movement" the "most ardent wing" of the "vegan straight edge movement," which Gabriel characterized as the "new school," third wave of straight edge (Kuhn 2010: 13). Although focused on straight edge and radical politics and including interviews with a wide range of straight edgers, Gabriel chose to restrict the selection to those who "maintain a clear distance to politically ambiguous ideologies" (Ibid: 14). This led to the exclusion of any potential Hardliner interviewees from the book although the topic came up a bit such as in the interviews with Kurt Schroeder of Birthright/Catalyst Records and Ian MacKaye. The only real technical information on Hardline appeared in the straight edge timeline where Earth Crisis and "Vegan Straight Edge" appeared in 1991 and, with a line connecting the two topics, he wrote in the section under 1993: "Hardline movement forms, centered around California band Vegan Reich and its frontman Sean Muttaqi; the band releases a 'Hardline Manifesto' with a 7" by the same name in 1990; in 1994 Muttaqi founds Uprising Records; some from the scene, Muttaqi included, turn towards Islam" (Ibid: 10). So he got the years right but the placement of Earth Crisis earlier in the timeline than Vegan Reich sparked the online ire of DaveMoral (probably Dave Agranoff) who responded:

> I think it's clear from browsing this book, how far off the timeline is about the emergence of the Hardline Movement and Vegan Straight Edge generally, and quite frankly the obvious and blatant ignoring of the Hardline Movement's (and Vegan Reich's) contribution to politics in the Straight Edge and hardcore scene and the very formation of the entire Vegan Straight Edge scene, that the author knows next to nothing about the Hardline Movement and its origins. He would be well served with reading the interview with Sean Muttaqi in *Burning Fight* just as a starter. ...Hardline, in fact, was the only group within the hardcore punk scene that specifically stated its abstinence from drugs and alcohol were tied to its politics. ...One could, and probably should, consider Hardline to be something distinct from vegan straight edge and not merely the "more militant" version of vegan straight edge simply because Hardline had a very specific platform and was not a mere sentiment as is vegan straight edge and was indeed an organization with chapters and memberships (Stephanie K. 2010).

To this, Gabriel responded:

> You don't need to worry: I've read Sean Muttaqi's statements in *Burning Fight*. They include lines like the following: "In regards to what some people perceived as 'homophobia' was the stand hardline took that if you were hardline, you could not be gay, that homosexuality was not part of a healthy, natural lifestyle from its perspective. People took that and wanted to jump to conclusions and would say hardliners were homophobic [...] It was a case of a sort of reverse P.C. fascism where they were saying, 'If you don't believe what we believe then we're going to make demagogues out of you.' [...] In general, I think the P.C. liberal crowd is just as eager as the 'Christian Right' to make other people believe in what they believe and to enforce their views." To be honest, this reflects a pattern that I see illustrated by your comment as well: whenever hardline is critiqued, the critic is called ignorant, ill-intentioned, or both. I never get the sense that self-identified hardliners at least somehow understand how offensive and frightening hardline was to a lot of people—and, no, not evil capitalists, but many women, queers, their allies, and generally everyone who feels uncomfortable when folks claim to be judge and jury based on supposed "righteousness" and "purity." If there was any indication for self-reflection, I might see hardline differently—although I admit that being anti-abortion and homophobic (I'm sorry, but Sean's explanation does not convince me of the opposite) is enough for me to question people as companions in "actively pursuing a fundamental social change in order to create free and egalitarian communities," which is how radical politics are defined in the introduction to *Sober Living*. So these are the reasons why hardline is "obviously and blatantly ignored," not because I know nothing about it—as far as I am concerned, I know too much about it, as I could have done with a few less frustrating discussions back in the day (Stephanie K. 2010).

Instead of conceding to any actual problems with Hardline stances (such as Sean saying he "hated" homosexuals or Hardline celebration of assassination of abortion doctors), Dave pretended to understand Gabriel's arguments and said "I agree, Hardline could have stood to better articulate their positions vis-a-vis abortion and homosexuality in so far as how they would relate to those effected by their views." Dave's argument then asserted that (1) Hardliners "never used militant language toward homosexuals or threatened violence to homosexuals as a group," (2) yes, they "did use militant rhetoric regarding abortion, [but] that was aimed exclusively toward providers when it was employed" and "was almost always pretty much tangential to the main thrust of their militant rhetoric," (3) Hardline "stance on abortion was/is consistent with early women's movement figures like Elizabeth Cady Stanton and Susan B Anthony," (4) aaah, *kids*! ("A softer approach was probably warranted. Then again, what can one expect from mostly teenagers?"), and (5) no one "in the early 90s ...would legitimately fit your definition of 'working to form egalitarian communities'" (successfully showing that he did no more than "browse" *Sober Living*). Readers can view the rest of his arguments in light of this book in general and draw their/your own conclusions.

Also in 2010, Petra Stěhulová published a bachelor's thesis containing perhaps the most extensive study so far on neo-Nazi straight edge: "NS Straight Edge took all the essential elements of the Straight Edge subculture in its original form, but each element also serves to promote the ideology of National Socialism (so Neo-Nazism)" (Stěhulová 2010: 54). She built in part on Ross Haenfler's book and looked at Hardline as an outgrowth of straight edge. Yet, Petra did her own research on Hardline as well and quotes from the Hardline manifesto. Except for the quote above, Petra wrote the entire paper in Czech. But, with some approximate online translations, you can get an idea of what she covered. For example, she looked at how neo-Nazis' approached Hardline. Essentially, she noted how the neo-Nazi straight edgers know that most straight edgers—including Ian MacKaye—have antiauthoritarian views but they didn't care. They knew Hardline and Vegan Reich had anti-racist views but they didn't care. Some of them got interested in Vegan Reich and Hardline precisely because others had accused them of "militancy" and "alleged intolerance". When they looked closer, they felt attracted by Hardline's quest for "purity" and "justice" which sounded very much like what they thought. In Petra's words (roughly translated):

> According to Hardline, life is sacred for all humans and animals. Equality of rights is also important for them. NS Straight Edge, on the other hand, argues that it is important for them to stop the white man's genocide, and therefore they can defend themselves against the sources of this genocide, which they consider, among other things, capitalism and liberalism. Immigrants are considered to be instruments of white human genocide. However, NS Straight Edge states that they are not interested in the genocide of immigrants, but in their return to their own countries (Ibid: 39).

Then Petra quotes the neo-Nazis themselves:

> But let's say something about [Hardline's] demand for the protection of everyone's lives—even blacks and yellows. For us Europeans, the goal is to stop the genocide of white people—in this sense we have the sovereign right in self-defense to get rid of both the sources of genocide (capitalism, liberalism ...) and the tools of this genocide, i.e. immigrants. However, we are talking about the survival and development of the Aryan man, not about the Holocaust

> of people of color (which does not fit into the media image of the NS)—from which we derive our activities. So let the blacks, etc., rule in their homelands [as] they want... (Ibid: 40).

Back to Petra's words: "Hardline further declares that people who interfere with the rights of others lose their own rights and one may therefore take action against them. NS Straight Edge interprets this as justification for war and revolution. Through war and struggle, NS Straight Edge wants to protect against those who want to disrupt the quality of life of the white race and its identity" (Ibid). And if all that sounds a bit creepy… well, from the sections I tried to translate, I got that feeling too. It felt difficult to tell if Petra wanted to do an academic description of neo-Nazis, an advertisement for them, or both. It seems like an inherent problem with much of academia. [*Note: it also reminds me of a warning from Willona Sloan many years ago: "Remember: there is a fine line between providing information about an issue and providing free advertisement. So, keep that in mind if you decide to write about white power" (Sloan 1998: 15)*].

Building on Robert Wood's book, Jason Torkelson (2010) wrote: "Hardline is a term used to describe straightedge adherents who are intolerant of persons who are not straightedge, violent, and/or militant about their beliefs more generally. … A majority of interviewees stated in their narratives that their conception of hardline straightedge led them to question the authenticity of straightedge, their tie to straightedge, and/or the space they once believed straightedge gave them from mainstream culture" (Torkelson 2010: 266). Jason did field research too: "Even former hardliners themselves seemed to question their own ties to straightedge as a result of their own actions. For instance, Randy, the Minneapolis waiter who also self-identified as a former militant, told me that introspection into his own militant behavior eventually led him to believe that straightedge was not real" (Ibid). Jason briefly discussed veganism in the straight edge scene but neither used the term "vegan straight edge" nor mentioned British anarcho-punk animal liberationists, Krishnacore, Earth Crisis, or anything related to Hardline.

Academic coverage of Hardline 2011-2015

In 2011, Gabriel Smith attributed the strong presence of straight edge and Hardline in Salt Lake City to local Mormonism (which also imposes a social ethic of abstinence from drugs, alcohol, and sexual promiscuity): "Given the evolution of SxE philosophy from its inception, through its second wave in the NYC hardcore scene, and into Hardline, it is clear that a deeply religious community would serve as the breeding ground for the enacted violence of the mutated ideology" (Smith 2011: 644). Gabriel S. did not always clarify distinctions between violent straight edgers and Hardline yet did offer one particular insight not provided by others. Gabriel S. noted that the Hardline manifesto

> utilized vague metaphors to represent its mission: 'The true hardliner must strive to liberate the rest of the world from its chains—saving life in some cases, and in others, dealing out justice to those guilty of destroying it.' The ethereal 'justice' here has proven an interpretive problematic for the SxE movement of the new millennium. Semiotic ambiguity in SxE culture enabled the fundamental ideological shifts through the various stages of the movement (Ibid: 635).

This point seems noteworthy because linguistic ambiguity can fill extremely useful social functions and it seems accurate to observe that Sean specifically, and Hardline in general, employed ambiguous terms for both legal purposes (to avoid potential incrimination) and to allow interpretational flexibility for both speakers and audience.

Seemingly unaware of Ibrahim's work, Sarah Pike also discussed Vegan Reich in a religious studies context in 2011 in the article "Religion and Youth in American Culture," writing "a popular underground hard-core punk band of the early 1990s called Vegan Reich and fronted by Muslim singer/songwriter Sean Muttaqi, a vegan and animal rights advocate, also urged teenage followers to adopt pro-life views" (Pike 2011: 41). Her examples of Islam in punk mostly focused on taqwacore and the Kominas with no mention of Hardline or its heirs. In 2013, she looked at similarities between Christian rites and conversion experiences and those who "committed to radical activism" and "express their conversion through ritual actions of protest" (Pike 2013: 36). Here, Sarah quoted Peter Young on the influence of Raid but she described them as "vegan straight edge," not Hardline, and she referred to Vegan Reich as a "straight edge band" (Ibid: 38, 40). In this article, she mentioned punk connections to Islam with no examples and she discussed Sean Muttaqi without mentioning Islam. Continuing to connect Hardline to religious studies, Anthony Fiscella discussed Hardline in the context of interactions between punk scenes and Islam (including taqwacore) in "From Muslim Punks to Taqwacore: An Incomplete History of Punk Islam" (2012a). Basing in part on Brian Peterson's work and a now unavailable outtake interview with Sean from the Edge documentary, Anthony briefly discussed the development of Hardline into Ahl-i Allah and Taliyah al-Mahdi, perhaps in more depth than any other scholar but, with only a few paragraphs written, that does not say much. Also, Anthony seemed ignorant of the fact that Sean released *The A.L.F. is Watching* compilation on his own label and neglected to note that Sean Muttaqi and taqwacore carry the same Arabic root *taq* (piety/fear). Furthermore, Anthony's zine *Varieties of Islamic Anarchism* mentioned Hardline briefly and described Taliyah as "perhaps the first modern group of Muslim anarchists" (2012b: 12). That sounds either grossly oversimplified at best and delusional or terribly misinformed at worst [*Note: Yes, Taliyah grew from a largely anarchist punk context and may sometimes sound anarchist or cite anarchists but "they," essentially Micah, have given no indication through their own structure (e.g., Micah's, and to some degree Sean's, absolute centrality to Taliyah) or beliefs (e.g., their apparent lack of advocacy of statelessness in either praxis or statements) to suggest any type of commitment to anarchism*]. Anthony's later dissertation work (2015) only mentioned Hardline briefly but noted how Michael Muhammad Knight described in one of his books (actually *Blue-Eyed Devil: A Road Odyssey through Islamic America*) Mike's personal interaction with Naj One of Taliyah around 2005 (cited in full in the section below entitled *Post-Hardline 1: 2000-2006*).

Joe Mageary's (2012) doctoral dissertation on hardcore mentioned Hardline but leaned on Ross Hanefler (2006) and Robert Wood (2006), defined Hardline as the "militant branch of Straight Edge," and incorrectly associated Hardline with "anti- immigration beliefs" (Mageary 2012: 27).

In 2013, building in part on Gabriel Kuhn's work, William Tsitsos expanded the attention given to Hardline by contrasting US and European types of political straight edge. Entitled "An International Comparison of the Politics of Straight Edge," the article characterizes the US-based vegan straight edge scene (e.g., Earth Crisis, Vegan Reich, and Hardline) as focused on personal morals and the European political straight edge scene (e.g., ManLiftingBanner, Refused, and Lärm) as one that emphasized socialistic challenges to social structures such as capitalism. Quoting from Brian Peterson's work, Bill wrote:

> Hardline clearly had a broader, more political focus than early straight edge. However, this political focus still interpreted problems as rooted in individual, moral failings. ...the radical and revolutionary politics of hardline seemed mainly to focus on attacking the most visibly corrupt actors, rather than the structural causes behind them. In fact, Sean Muttaqi explained the demise of hardline as a consequence of its excessive emphasis on individual morality, stating that "*Hardline lost any aspect of militancy and was all-consumed with minute details or inward shit. It was like how inwardly introspective can you get about where something was grown and whether a chocolate bar had an*

> *ounce of caffeine in it? It got absurd to the point where they weren't getting anything done (Peterson 2009: 489).*" Although Muttaqi described these "inwardly introspective" debates as contrary to the radical goals of hardline, they were, in fact, consistent with hardline's fixation on individual morality as the root of larger problems. In this sense, hardline was a quintessential product of the neoliberal United States, a society that it did not hesitate to criticize (Tsitsos 2013: 206-207).

Francis Stewart and Ibrahim Abraham co-authored the article "Desacralizing Salvation in Straight Edge Christianity and Holistic Spirituality" (2014) wherein they discussed Hardline briefly: "The adoption of militant environmentalism by a small group of Straight Edgers created the 'Hardline' subcultural schism, which included the band Vegan Reich, fronted by Muslim convert Shahid Ali (Sean) Muttaqi, which epitomized the violent and often patriarchal attitudes of the almost exclusively male Hardline tendency" (Abraham and Stewart 2014: 85). The same dynamic duo followed up in 2017 with a similar theme of religious studies applied to punk and hardcore in general.

Also in 2014, Sarah Amber Preston's master's thesis entitled "Rebelling Against Rebellion: Resistance and Tensions in Straight Edge Subculture" (2014) addressed "hardline" briefly. She wrote, for example, "By way of simplification, there are three noteworthy evolutions in principles which complicate the original [straight edge] movement: 'cruelty-free,' Krishna-core, and 'hardline'" (Preston (2014: 14). Yet, as Sarah based her definition of Hardline on Jason Torkelson's definition who, in turn, took his definition from Robert Wood, she only referenced militant straight edge groups like SSD and made no mention whatsoever of any Hardline group or scene.

Another master's thesis in 2014 appeared in Australia by J. E. Donovan entitled "'Hardcore Makes Me Sick': Truth, Youth and Unity in Australian Hardcore Punk Subculture." J.E. wrote:

> Inspired by the Minor Threat song, Al Barile, from Boston band SSD, appropriated sXe as a life philosophy. In this tough environment of the Boston scene, sXers embraced a pack mentality, and were renowned for beating up non-straightedgers at shows. sXe, as an extreme view became known as 'hardline', from Vegan Reich's EP of the same name, (Vegan Reich 1990), though it is also called militant sXe. Under the influence of proponents such as Sean Muttaqi from Vegan Reich—it became an even more aggressive and puritanical enactment of the sXe ideals and veganism. Lyrics such as "If you're not on my side, you're a target in my eyes" (Vegan Reich 1990), indicate the extreme radical intolerance of drug-takers, meat-eaters and in particular, edge-breakers (Donovan 2014: 109-110).

J.E. built on previous work by Ross Haenfler, Craig O'Hara, Robert Wood, Beth Lahickey, and William Tsitsos and also did independent interviews with local straight edgers: "some of my informants were more adamant in their rejection of hardline than others. For [TP], Straightedge is a very positive phenomena for those for whom it is a private affair: 'but, if your one of these new hardcore, hardline sXe fuckwits, fuck off I don't care. You're as relevant to me as a Nazi skinhead. I don't give a fuck" (Ibid: 116). To this J.E. surmised: "In one sense, those who criticise hardline sXe, sXe conformity, preachy sXe and sXe posers and fakes, are, themselves, being divisive. ...On the other hand, however, my informants understood such criticism being limited to those whose own actions worked to undermine the harmony hardcore, or a particular hardcore scene" (Ibid: 120). J.E. cited Elgin James attributing the origin of "hardline" to Al Barile of SSD but did not elaborate on Hardline beyond what appears above (Ibid: 127).

The same year, Alan Parkes discussed Hardline in "This Small World: The Legacy and Impact of New York City Hardcore Punk and Straight Edge in the 1980s"(2014) where he identified Earth Crisis with Hardline: "The ideas expressed by bands such as Earth Crisis would ultimately form a distinct social circle in hardcore known for militancy: hardline. Hardline and its strict vegan message developed a national following in the mid-1990s" (Parkes 2014: 65) After quoting lyrics to "Firestorm" by Earth Crisis, Alan continued to imply Earth Crisis led to Hardline (rather than vice versa), writing:

> Beyond merely straight edge, some militants strongly advocated extreme ecological ideologies, vegan- ism, heterosexuality, and an anti-abortion philosophy. Hardline, as this became known, was its own sub-group within straight edge and hardcore. Moreover, straight edge militancy grew out of the selectivity of membership. ...Of course not all militant members adhered to hardline principles, and many were even critical of them, such as Boston straight edge band Slapshot (Ibid: 74-75).

Again, Robert Wood's work, which Alan relied on, had derailed another academic's understanding of Hardline. Alan clearly knew about Vegan Reich and the issues of veganism, abortion, and homosexuality as well as "militant ecological views" that most obviously distinguished Hardline from militant straight edge. He just seemed unaware of actual Hardline history and bands (aside from Vegan Reich). In the end, Alan wrote:

> Hardline, as distinct from just militant straight edge, with its inclusion of militant ecological views, was largely overlooked by the media but disrupted the scene as much as the straight edge militancy that Reesor was identified by [reference to 17-year old straight edger Colin Reesor who fatally stabbed 15-year old Bernardo Repreza]. The lyrics of hardliners represented the severity of their convictions. Southern California's Vegan Reich addressed their contempt for abortion, meat eating, and the use of drugs in their song "I, The Jury." With a sense of moral superiority they declared, "*I won't hesitate... To infringe on your rights, to take them away, to be judge and jury, and make you fucking pay, for the crimes you commit day after day, 'cause only with you stopped will our lives be truly free!*" This encouraged more factionalism and exclusivity. While hardline never formed any significant following in New York City, like it had in surrounding scenes and on the West Coast, it grew out of the reestablishment of straight edge and militancy in New York City's scene (Ibid: 76).

When a scholar begins with straight edge as their vantage point, it increases the likelihood that they will view and describe Hardline from that lens, overlooking other relevant aspects and angles. Perhaps, most significantly, it tends to downplay the extent to which Hardliners gradually drifted away from emphasis on hardcore music culture and more toward activism and animal liberation actions.

Building in part on Donald Liddick and Ross Haenfler's work, U.S. Defense Department-financed researcher Jonathan Pieslak addressed this perspective to some extent when he put out two articles in the same journal in 2014 entitled "The Music Cultures of Radical Environmental and Animal-Rights Activism (REARA)" (Pieslak 2014a) and "A Collection of Interview Correspondences with Incarcerated ALF and Vegan Straight Edge/Hardline Activist Walter Bond" (Pieslak 2014b). Both of these articles discussed Hardline which Jonathan characterized as an "ultra-conservative, right-wing form of militancy" (Pieslak 2014a: 47). Jonathan continued: "The militant and self-identified 'hardline' side of sXe animal rights and veganism emerged... [when in] 1990, the California band Vegan Reich released the EP, Hardline, a collection of four songs that would codify the ideology of the "hardline" movement, define its violent position, and infuse a more metal sound into sXe music" (Ibid: 48). Jonathan clarified that "not every militant xVx-er [vegan straight edger] is 'hardline,'" implying that the entire distinction turned on whether an activist identified as "pro-life" or "pro-choice" (Ibid: 47). Jonathan also wrote:

> Vegan Reich was perhaps the most important band in establishing the 'hardline' movement and was followed soon thereafter by other "hardline"

> groups like Raid and Abnegation. The rise of xVx militancy, in which the single issue of violent eco-animal rights defense defined the sub-genre, was catalyzed to a large extent by the band, Earth Crisis. Although groups like Chokehold and Conflict were also influential in pioneering militant ideology in xVx, Earth Crisis was more important in popularizing—if we can use this term for describing such a small group—the movement's worldview (Ibid: 49).

According to Jonathan's analysis, the Vegan Reich track "This Is It" demonstrated "the perspective shift from 'just looking out for myself' ('posi') to 'hardline' on the issue of animal rights and veganism" (Ibid: 48). In this sense, Jonathan somewhat contrasts with William Tsitsos' analysis by framing 'positive' straight edge as personal and private on the one hand, and, on the other, Hardline as a collective social enterprise in relation to animals and veganism. [*Note: Or, put another way, we might frame them as a range of both degrees and types of activism ranging from moral concerns to structural concerns on one vector and low-degree (personal) concerns to high-degree (group) concerns on the other. So a person might, for example, display high moral concerns about sobriety or veganism on a personal level but manifest low structural concerns (William Tsitsos' critique of Hardline). Alternatively, one might contrast narrow personal concerns with group concerns (as in Jonathan Pieslak's assessment of Hardline). See chart below for a visual representation of how one might conceive of the alternative framings (with Jonathan emphasizing how the group-oriented Hardline contrasts with personal posi-core below and William emphasizing how the moral-oriented Hardline contrasts with structural concerns or European vegan straight edgers such as Lärm and Refused).*]

Potential social expressions of vegan straight edge

	MORAL CONCERNS	STRUCTURAL CONCERNS
G R O U P	Hardline (e.g., group-focused ethics, eating meat/drug use as "sinful," concern for animal welfare, mutual monitoring of sexuality/consumption habits, organizing a morally-based xVx scene, etc.)	Large-scale activism (e.g., changing scene structures, mass-mobilizing, jobsite organizing, eco-socialism, organizing co-ops, communes, national/global campaigns for structural reforms, organizing protests, alternative economies, boycott of profit-driven animal industries, organizing xVx festivals, building local DIY scenes, anti-militarism, etc.)
P E R S O N A L	Posi-core (e.g., focus on personal health, leading a xVx lifestyle, "positivity," listening to xVx music, tattoos, etc.)	Small-scale activism (e.g., direct action, attending protests, attending xVx shows, union membership, passing out flyers about veganism, graffiti, putting out a zine, minimizing personal consumption, etc.)

One might describe a key difference between moral outlooks and structural outlooks as follows: Moral questions ask people what decisions they will make whereas structural questions ask what decisions they **can** make and how to shift the organization, selection, or parameters for potential decisions. A moral outlook might ask, "why does a person choose to eat meat, why does a woman get an abortion, or why does a scientist choose to perform vivisection?" A structural outlook might ask, "why does society industrialize animal products, how do women get unwanted pregnancies, and what socio-economic forces encourage scientists to choose animals for testing?" A moral outlook might draw conclusions about individual scruples (e.g., "evil," "weak," or "greedy" people make "corrupt" decisions). A structural outlook might frame answers more along lines of market or societal forces (e.g., profit-based economics, colonialism, patriarchal institutions, or opportunities for jobsite union organizing). If a moral outlook wants to make "better people," a structural outlook fights for "better opportunities."

Although laid out as boxes, one might conceive of both vectors as a spectrum and even blended where the ranges can vary in accordance to any given person's (or group's) response to a particular issue.

Vegan Reich, "This Is It"

This is the final solution to mankind's endless transgression, for earth's liberation
a vegan revolution.

Beyond the confines and false divisions of alignment with color, age, or fashion
no alliance given to any nation to earth alone is our devotion.

Guided by the purest convictions to harm no innocent life for our existence self reliant
and free of the addictions that lead the weak on a path of destruction.

We've attained perfection in ideology there's no others of comparison.
The highest stage in mankind's evolution without question is Veganism.
And with this higher wisdom we offer you salvation but be warned,
if you refuse it you'll face extermination.

Cos it's no personal decision nor a matter of opinion when the choice you make
destroys all life in the ecosystem.

Your victims have been voiceless so we've spoken for them.
Now tired of wasting our breath, there will be no more talking.
This is it, no second chances, take heed it's your last warning.

You'd better lock yourself inside because the storm is fucking comin'
(Cited in Pieslak 2014: 48-49).

Perhaps most notably, Jonathan seems first among scholars in reproducing the Hardline manifesto in its entirety as well as the first to bring animal liberationist Walter Bond into the conversation about Hardline (even publishing Walter's call to start a revival of Hardline named "Vegan Hardline" and Walter's detailed interpretation of the Hardline manifesto). Here, Walter explained his appreciation for, history with, and understanding of Hardline and its eventual demise:

> I was always attracted to how the XVX (Vegan Straightedge) message preached abstinence and compassion from an aggressive and absolutist point of view. …I have always admired [Dave] Foreman's Earth First! in part because it was so politically syncretic. Much like Vegan Hardline and early XVX some views were very conservative and others very liberal. …When we speak of 'Hardline' we are not speaking about absolutist Veganism or sXe, per se. 'Hardline' was a fairly holistic and codified worldview and lifestyle. …When I was a kid I was in a crew called VFL (Vegan For Life). We leaned towards hardline, and were at times very myopic in our worldview. We got into fights

with drunks and druggies more than we factually helped Animals or promoted Veganism. But we all grew out of that mentality as we aged. … Hardline really does not exist as it once was. In 2009 before my arrest, I was attempting a revival but to no avail. … As the leadership of the Hardline Movement turned more and more towards orthodox religions, Hardlines' relevance within activist circles began to wane. Simultaneously Hardline drifted further and further away from the music scene it had helped spawn. …What is certain is that religion changed the scope and focus of Hardline and it became a different animal from there on out (Pieslak 2014b: 51, 73-74, 79, 84).

Walter continued then to describe his vision for a new Vegan Hardline movement:

Vegan Hardline is in effect the rebirth of the Hardline Movement. We use the title "Vegan Hardline" to differentiate from the generic word "hardline" (which simply means "rigid in a belief"). After this any changes are of degree and not of kind. We are not going to innovate or stray from ANY of the tenets of the Hardline Manifesto. It is still our preamble and centerpiece of the ideology, unchanged and unspoiled. However, outside of the manifesto we shall build things anew. We will not be bound by the Hardline literature of yesteryear, the cults of personality that were rife within the movement, or any dissention into religiosity. "Under the principles of the Hardline Ideology all shall be permitted to do as they please as long as their actions do not harm in anyway the rights of others". As pertains to religion, spirituality or beliefs in the afterlife, this means a Vegan Hardliner may hold any belief (or none at all) as they see fit. But Vegan Hardline, in and of itself, is not a religious dogma and will forever remain secular.

…In the Hardline movement there was much debate over what constituted "deviant sexual acts". In Vegan Hardline we are not going to concern ourselves with issues such as masturbation or celibacy. Biologically speaking sex has a purpose, that purpose being procreation (all nature proclaims this). With procreation comes a lifetime of responsibility. Which is why we do not practice promiscuity and we faithfully uphold the sanctity of traditional family values. Sex is meant for a man and woman that are deeply committed to one another and ready to deal with the results, namely childbirth and rearing. Originally Hardline was a leadership/membership organization with official chapters all reporting to a central committee, not so in Vegan Hardline. Time and experience have taught that membership organizations are easily infiltrated and often attract people that have more of an emotional need to climb a social ladder within a group setting than becoming effective revolutionaries.

…Vegan Hardline is a revolutionary movement and not a reformist one. We do not mean revolutionary in the way that advertisers use it. Nor, do we mean it as just another social justice buzzword. A revolutionary idea is one that

> cannot co-exist with the present society, because the two are fundamentally incompatible. When we speak of a truly Vegan world, as opposed to just a Vegan diet, we are talking about a human world that does not encroach on any other species' life (insofar as is possible). A human society that does not expand or build its technology into other beings' living spaces. A human world that favors a river's right to life over the need for electricity to power its machines. It's literally impossible for that human society to be formed out of this one. ... Of course we think that the practice of Veganism is not only necessary but must become mandatory if we are ever to live in a safe and sane world.
>
> ...Human beings are in the higher order (strictly in the Darwinian sense) of primates, as such raw Veganism is our natural diet. Also, being Animal Rights activists in the extreme we view the eating of Animals dead bodies, the drinking of Animal secretions and the consumption of calcified bird menstruations as being as disgusting and sinister as cannibalism!
>
> ...In Vegan Hardline we reject the 'victim stance'. Our species is often victimized by its own, true enough. Racism, sexism, classism and war are all prime examples. But in comparison with what the human race is doing to Mother Earth and her Animal Nations, what we are doing to ourselves is trivial.
>
> ...Whether you are a rich white person from an affluent community or a poor Puerto Rican from prison (like yours truly) is largely irrelevant. If you're concerned, if you care, then the burden is on you to set things right. ...In Vegan Hardline we are not defeatists, we believe that the tide will turn once we are willing to pay the price that such a change demands. How pathetic is it that your average drug dealer or gangster is so willing to risk life and limb (or take another's away) over a few stinking dollars but those that feign such deep concern for the compassion and rights of others blanch in fear at the idea of Militant Intervention and personal risk or injury in defense of the innocent. It's time we began heeding the alarm instead of endlessly ringing it (Pieslak 2014b: 84-85, 87, 89-91).

The extensive interaction between Jonathan and Walter also raised a question about the degree to which researchers might impact their interviewees. At one point in their exchange, Jonathan wrote "There is an irony here: by trying to broaden the scope of inclusion to embrace a variety of causes (left-wing causes like worker's rights, racial equality, social injustice, gender/queer rights, etc.), these movements actually narrowed the scope of their appeal because everyone had to agree on more issues." To this Walter replied, "I agree with you 100% on this" (Pieslak 2014: 68). According to Jonathan's homepage, "Jonathan is presently working on a team project exploring the mobilizing influence of media in Jihadi-Salafi movements, funded by a Minerva Grant from the U.S. Department of Defense" (Pieslak 2021). So we can see where Jonathan's ideological allegiances seem to lie and we can bear that in mind when we read his analysis:

> One might compare the ideological shift in xVx towards what Bond describes as a general radical anarchist agenda to the re-orientation of EF! ideology. My speculation regarding the xVx scene today is that it has been assimilated into the larger framework of 'politically correct' sXe or general Marxist/anarchist/anti-industrial capitalist values (Pieslak 2014: 68).

Academic coverage of Hardline 2016-2019

Tony Rettman, in 2017, put out another interview-based book. Entitled *Straight Edge: A Clear-Headed Hardcore Punk History*, Tony's book marked a milestone for Hardline as the first one to devote an entire chapter exclusively to Hardline (pages 265-277). Tony provided no commentary or introduction to the chapter but let the interviewees speak for themselves. He selected a variety of voices (although no females from Hardline), including key Hardline figures such as Sean Muttaqi, Steve Lovett (Raid), Rat (Statement), and Ryan Downey (Hardball/*Vanguard*) who composed at least 80% of the chapter as well as a few voices opposed to Hardline such as Ron Guardipee (Brotherhood), Vique Martin (*Simba* zine/Revelation Records), and Dan O'Mahony (Carry Nation and others). Sarah Pike, citing Sean again, finally mentioned Hardline by name in her book *For the Wild: Ritual and Commitment in Radical Eco-Activism* (2017) framing it as a divisive subset of straight edge where most straight edgers "were more accepting of reproductive choices and sexual orientation" (Pike 2017: 160).

Only one work that discusses punk rock and sectarianism seems to mention Hardline, and then, only briefly: Mitch Douglas Daschuk's PhD dissertation, *"What Was Once Rebellion is Now Clearly Just a Social Sect": Identity, Ideological Conflict And The Field Of Punk Rock Artistic Production* (2016). Here, Mitch wrote only a short passage on Hardline but it seems interesting in how it exemplifies how academic focus on one area can get things so wrong in another area:

> While [Ian] MacKaye expresses discomfort recounting how he and Minor Threat "accidentally" instigated a particularly violent sub-faction of hardcore subcultural participants, it is nevertheless crucial to recall that the "hardline" straight-edge movement employed violence and intimidation in a symbolic economy that already accredited violence as a particularly desirable form of currency (Daschuk 2016: 213; Bracket in Kuhn quote by Daschuk).

The only mention, in fact, in the entire dissertation of veganism or animal liberation (aside from a fleeting mention of Propagandhi as a self-described "Animal Friendly Anti-Fascist Gay Positive Pro-Feminist" group and mentioning their song title "Animals Are Not Biological Machines") comes through a discussion of NOFX's lyrics in their 1988 LP *Liberal Animation* which included their reactionary mocking of animal liberation.

In *Punk Rock is My Religion: Straight Edge Punk and 'Religious' Identity* (2017), Francis Stewart continued discussion of Hardline in religious studies, writing:

> Hardline Straight Edge is the term used by Straight Edge adherents to describe those who joined believing, or rather utilising, it as a funnel for their tendency or desire for superiority, militancy and violence. The band Earth Crisis is commonly blamed as a reason for the attraction of such people due to their public advocacy of waging war with those who abused animals and dressing in a military manner—camouflage trousers, bandanas. However, it could be argued that their lyrics or certainly their intentions were misrepresented by some of their followers and that their "attack" was actually one of education, protest and compassion rather than physical violence. Haenfler recounts his experiences of observing violence by hardliners when attended the annual hardcore music festival Hellfest in 2001 (Stewart 2017: 40).

Francis continued:

> In the US, Muslim punk bands emerged within early formations of Straight Edge, specifically in relation to the vegan hardline scene. Some key Straight Edge figures such as Sean Muttaqi from the band Vegan Reich converted to Islam (although was also influenced by Rastafarianism, anarchism, the Black Power Movement and Liberation Theology) and created groups such as Ahl-i Allah (army of Allah) and Taliyah al-Mahdi (Vanguard of the Messiah). Songs by Vegan Reich covered topics dealing with veganism, ecology, jihad and their own identity within the scene (Rage of a Prophet). Later material espoused anti-abortion and anti-LBTQ views, which run counter to typical punk attitudes (if we can even assume such a thing exists). There is a common theme [in Muslim punk contexts] of struggling with multifaceted identity that is composed of layers that have limited access to dominant discourses and power for change (Ibid: 57-58).

In the (so far) only scholarly article to focus exclusively on Hardline, entitled "Reich Vs. Reich: Sex Economy and the Hardline Subculture" (2018), Brian Hughes examined Hardline through the lens of Wilhelm Reich's theories.

This included Reich's conception of fascism as a "bio-psychic formation …originating in the bio-energetic forces that animate libido, shaped socially and expressed politically," "sexual repression," "reactionary sexual ideology," and "homoeroticism" (Hughes 2018: 83-84, 90). Brian wrote of "Hardline's idiosyncratic fascism, particularly as pertaining to its mysticism and homophobia" while speculating that Wilhelm Reich's own "pathologization of homosexuality" stemmed from a dualism between "the real object rationally produced on the one hand [i.e. sexual work democracy] and irrational, fantasizing production [i.e. pathologized homoeroticism] on the other" (Ibid: 96-97).

> Hardline, despite its explicit anti-fascist political stance, is best understood as a fascist formation in the Reichian sense: a mystical modality of sexual biopathy, characterized by homoerotic social rituals and a delinquent romanticization of 'purity' and the 'natural order' (Hughes 2018: 77).

Brian seems first among scholars in looking beyond Sean Muttaqi, the Hardline Manifesto, and contemporary interviews to examine other sources such as *Vanguard* #8 (a segment at least), Micah Collins' *Destroy Babylon*, and Dave Agranoff's *Defense Rescue, and Survival*. After quoting one piece from an issue of *Vanguard* that described leading German Nazis (such as William Shirer) as homosexuals, Brian quipped: "Obviously, such a statement, and the rhetorical and ideological context in which it occurs, is logically inconsistent, rhetorically fallacious, and factually wrong. William Shirer, for example, was neither gay, nor a Nazi, nor even German. He was an American author, broadcaster, and historian, who wrote the wildly successful popular history *Rise and Fall of the Third Reich*" (Ibid: 86).

In 2019, Gabriel Kuhn followed up *Sober Living* with a more internationally-oriented *X: Straight Edge and Radical Sobriety* that addressed specific themes related to straight edge such as: collectives, religion, scene reports, debate, and recovery. Although Gabriel did not interview any Hardliners, he did include a debate about Hardline (from Joey Leyva's *Out From The Shadows* zine in 2006) and he included Hardline in the glossary. He defined Hardline as:

> a radical political movement espousing vegan straight edge and, according to its manifesto, advocating 'an ideology that is pure and righteous, without contradictions or inconsistencies.' Hardline was influential in straight edge culture throughout the 1990s and is strongly associated with the band Vegan Reich (2019: 10).

Finally, the most recent mention of Hardline in academic texts appears in a conference presentation by Chrisa Christoforidou in 2020 titled "Deconstructing Straight Edge Lyrics and Music: The Straight Edge Total Liberation Ethics." Building, in part, on work by Gabriel Kuhn, Jonathan Pieslak/Walter Bond, and Robert Wood, she wrote:

> Such issues of animal rights and radical ecology were often advocated by a variation of the straight edge subculture that emerged during the late 1980s and early 1990s and distanced itself from the mainstream straight edge. This variation, which is commonly known as hardline, brought much controversy into the scene, due to the militancy and extremity of the lyrics and hardline practices. However, a Syracuse band which is often acknowledged as a musical vanguard of hardline straight edge (Wood 2006: 51), Earth Crisis, is by many considered to be one of the most influential hardcore bands (Christoforidou 2020).

As this last example of identifying Earth Crisis as Hardline shows, one occasionally runs across minor scholarly errors. We can review a selection of such "faux paws" here. We see an early example in Ross Haenfler's claim (repeated by Jonathan Pieslak) that "Youth of Today, for instance, is largely credited with first promoting veganism and animal rights in their song, 'No More' (1988)" (Haenfler 2006: 13; Pieslak 2014: 48). Youth of Today advocated vegetarianism—not veganism—and Ray Cappo's insistence on defending dairy consumption provoked strong critique from Hardliners. Later, Gabriel Smith confused the Hardline timeline by more than a decade in writing, "Nearly fifteen years after Youth of Today bound animal ethics to the movement, a militant bastardization of SxE began to appear on the hardcore scene. A new splinter called 'Hardline' spawned from the roots of vegan-SxE hardcore" (2011: 634). This type of characterization also reverses the relationship between the two: if anything, Hardline spawned vegan straight edge—not the other way around. In both of these cases the more famous and more socially acceptable Youth of Today gets more credit while Hardline gets less. Some minor errors like Sean's name also inadvertently distort the timeline. For example, Sarah Pike wrote "In 1990, Vegan Reich, led by singer Sean Muttaqi who had converted to Islam…" (Pike 2017: 160; also similar in Pike 2011: 41). Sean did not use a last name publically in 1990 and did not convert to Islam or adopt the name Muttaqi until 1995 or later (see also Stewart 2017 who similarly placed the name "Muttaqi" on Sean retroactively. To clarify: Sean never publically identified as both Hardline and Muslim simultaneously even if he covertly did so when he "re-entered" Hardline in 1998 and wrote in *Vanguard* 8 under the pseudonym "Ishraq Furqan"). Also, when Sarah wrote, "Vegan Reich was accused of being antigay," she opened for an unnecessary ambiguity that Sean's "I hate homosexuals" remark had quickly dispelled (Pike 2017: 160; Sean/Vegan Reich 1989b). Anthony Fiscella identified Vegan Reich as from Los Angeles (actually Laguna Beach lies outside of LA) and, citing Anarchopedia, repeated the "Sean Penn" misnomer (Fiscella 2012: 268). Anthony's dissertation (2015) incorrectly identified Racetraitor as a Hardline band and incorrectly translated Ahl-i Allah as "Army of God," a mistake repeated by Francis Stewart (Fiscella 2015: 365; Stewart 2017: 57).

Along with technical errors, we can note errors of omission. While one could name a long list of books and articles that *could* have mentioned Hardline but did not (or only mentioned Hardline in passing in contexts that seemed to warrant closer attention), we can note the following: Ross Haenfler's work, Richard Kahn's encyclopedic entry "Environmental Activism in Music" (2013), and Dave Ensminger's *The Politics of Punk: Protest and Revolt in the Streets* (2016).

First, in *Straight Edge* (2006), Ross Haenfler quoted Vegan Reich's lyrics to "I, the Jury" in association with intolerance in the straight edge scene—not in association with Hardline. Also, the song does not vilify people for "breaking edge" and I cannot even see that Hardliners ever used the term "breaking edge" when someone had a drink or a smoke. Elsewhere Ross noted that veganism "had become such a significant part of sXe by the late 1990s that many sXers gave it equal importance to living drug and alcohol free" but either did not know or did not want to credit Vegan Reich and Hardline with sparking that scene (Haenfler 2004: 432). Second, Richard Kahn mentioned Earth Crisis, Dave Rovics, Earth Liberation Front, and vegan straight edge but not Hardline or Vegan Reich even while mentioning other bands. Richard wrote: "Other punk and hardcore bands also notable for espousing environmental and animal rights politics include Goldfinger, Propagandhi, Rise Against, and Oi Polloi" (Kahn 2013: 416). Third, Dave Ensminger not only ignored Hardline completely, he ignored animal advocacy, veganism, vegan straight edge, and gave more attention to Throbbing Gristle, Antonin Artaud, and medieval monk Francois Rabelais than Earth Crisis, ManLiftingBanner, and the Total Liberation Tour of 2004. Straight edge in general barely got mentioned (mostly in passing by Alec MacKaye or Mark Andersen), the term did not appear in the book's index, and, even the extensive discussion about Positive Force in DC did not clarify Positive Force's own strong straight edge influence and leanings (encouraging temperance rather than requiring absolute sobriety). Ironically, Dave quoted Ian MacKaye: "The printed word, when it's typed up and looking nice, people think it's the truth, but most of the time it's incredibly slanted—it's just misinformed writers, or it's not telling the whole story" (Ensminger 2016: 17).

Obviously, I type up my own version of history right now as I repeat the quote. Yet, while none of us—including MacKaye—can tell the "whole story," we can find degrees of inclusion and accuracy alongside degrees of acknowledging one's own impartiality. Dave's book included an academic caveat: "This book is not an attempt to collectivize the entire conscience of punk in a definitive form, for instance, it does not shed light on the WTO protests, cascading contemporary queer politics, or recount the recent Occupy movement, all of which have punk antecedents…" (Ibid: xiv). Yet, even in the caveat, Dave made no mention of animal advocacy, veganism, straight edge, Hardline, primitivism, Earth First!/Earth Liberation Front, CrimethInc., MOVE, or Total Liberation. That said, we do not always know why scholars choose the focus that they do. One researcher wrote to me: "I intentionally deplatformed [Hardliners] because of what they were saying about women in the interviews, and the demands they were making about how I could write the article." I don't present any of these errors to determine the "truth" but a community creates consensus when all its voices can come to the table. I can't bring all those voices in but I tried here to bring a much larger variety of voices than we have so far heard in regard to Hardline.

Finally, for a selection of non-English works that mention or discuss Hardline but which I did not discuss here see Bulatova 2016 [Russian], Fernandes 2015 [Portuguese], Hrafnsson 2021 [Icelandic], Lesko 2012 [German], Meden 2011 [Slovenian], Mulder 2010 and 2011 [German], and Vaďura 2018 [Czech].

7 Contrasting stories

This sections aims to display some of the more obvious contrasting accounts within Hardline (and a couple voices from outside of Hardline), whether by different people or, in several cases, the same person presenting different stories. Some stories contrast only slightly, some seem incompatible. Also, people change throughout life and the contrasts in the stories sometimes reflect that. Although I add a few minor comments here and there with additional info, I leave it to readers to determine which story, if any, they find most plausible. At least, all readers can see the same documented text here in order to better assess the plausibility of some instances (such as matters of historical record).

Caveat: readers may take notice that Sean's writings in 1988-1989 prior to Hardline do not necessarily apply to Hardline doctrine and the same goes for post-Hardline writings by Sean and Micah in Ahl-i Allah and Taliyah from 1999-onward. I include a broad time range, however, because it seems important to see both what preceded and followed Hardline. Readers can discern for themselves how much, if any, of those positions, statements, or actions seem to reflect a continuum or not and, if so, to what degree. Besides, until key former Hardliners adequately address the historical records (rather then deny them), it seems relevant to keep them on the table for discussion. [Animal liberation and veganism—interspersed throughout the sections rather than their own section].

This section addresses Hardline in relation to the following topics:
Abortion
Homosexuality
Patriarchy and pornography
Authoritarianism and leftism
Violence
Straight edge and vegan straight edge
Apostasy/Leaving Hardline
Origins
"Religion" and "cults"
MOVE
Nature and Human nature
Ethnicity and anti-racism
Size
Miscellaneous

Abortion

The question of abortion played a key role in distinguishing Hardline and setting it apart from anarchist animal liberationists and most vegan straight edgers because it provided perhaps the clearest "missing piece of the puzzle," so to speak, in the formulation of Hardline's "single ethic" that "that all innocent life is equal and sacred." The striving for both consistency and purity seemed to find resolution in the defense of fetuses alongside animals. Much like how straight edge took a mainstream conservative stance in relation to sobriety, Hardline's adoption of a stance common among evangelical Christians and conservatives created a similar effect of counter-countercultural twist to a mainstream moral theme during the 1990s. Although the position gained a degree of traction in non-Hardline vegan straight edge circles, it remained a minority position that ultimately lost the majority terrain to women's reproductive rights which, by far, took a dominant position in anarcho-punk and vegan straight edge scenes.

As in other instances, some former Hardliners have attempted to downplay Hardline stances regarding abortion. Yet, the abortion question played a big role in Hardline and Sean did advocate making abortion illegal.

Vanguard 6 (Spring 1995), edited by Dave Agranoff, featured a dead fetus on the cover. Inside, mentions of abortion appeared on at least six of the 26 pages including in the Hardline manifesto and in a two-page article that celebrated the assassination of abortion doctor John Britton. The article compared abortions to the Nazi holocaust, called the assassination "justifiable," and concluded: "We need to stand up for what we believe regardless of the cost to us. …The unborn babies and other victims of this ruthless age are too precious to ignore. It's our world—let's take it back!" Number of articles on capitalism in *Vanguard* 6: one. Number of articles on racism in *Vanguard* 6: zero. *Vanguard* 7 (Summer 1996), also edited by Dave, featured a dead fetus pictured on page 5. Inside, again, abortion appeared mentioned on at least six of the 26 pages. An anti-abortion article by Upstate Hardline celebrated the firebombing of an abortion clinic with the subtitle: "One clinic down, many more to go…" Number of articles on capitalism in *Vanguard* 7: zero. Number of articles on racism in *Vanguard* 7: zero. It can help to bears such facts in mind when reading their accounts and their priorities.

DaveMoral [probably Dave Agranoff]: "[Hardliners] did use militant rhetoric regarding abortion, and that was aimed exclusively towards providers when it was employed. Which was almost always pretty much *tangential* to the main thrust of their militant rhetoric, which was animal exploiters, *racists* and the capitalist system in general" (Stephanie K. 2010, emphasis added).

DaveMoral: "…[anti-abortion] Legislation would be a hard issue for Hardline to address, being generally against the system" (Stephanie K. 2010).

Sean: "Abortion is not a 'right', just as murder is not a 'right'. …Abortion must be made illegal!" (*Vanguard* 1+2 double issue, 1993: 17-18; re-printed in the 1995 interview collection).

Sean: "It [Hardline] also means being consistent and having one ethic regarding life across the board—be it animal rights or foetus rights" (Boston Hardline 1995: 1).

Jesse Keenan: (Memphis Hardline, *Cardinal Spirits*, Vegans For Life): "On Saturday, December 10th [1994], Vegans For Life held a silent vigil at an abortion clinic in Little Rock for the millions of children murdered every year by abortion. About 20 pro-life vegans showed up to give support to the idea that all sentient beings, regardless of age, sex, color, or species deserve a chance to live. We received many approving honks and waves of support. Vegans For Life is a Memphis-based group whose goal is to bridge the gap between the animal rights and pro-life movements. Quite often those involved in the animal rights community are assumed to follow the typical 'PC' doctrine of pro-'choice'. Vegans For Life has set out to clear up this myth and take a stand for all life" (Keenan, "Animal Rights, Human Rights, One Struggle, One Fight!" *Memphis Vegan* 5, 1995: 7).

Tiffany (Indianapolis Hardline): "Since you 'feminists' will not listen to anything a man has to say about certain issues (abortion), I will convey it to you (since I am a woman). Abortion—murder! The two go hand in hand. There is no difference" ("Hardline Women" *Vanguard* 1+2 1993: 13).

Scott Beibin (Bloodlink Records, Lost Film Fest, Evil Twin Booking): "I kind of agreed with hardline's abortion stance in that I viewed abortion at this time as being the same thing as killing animals, the killing of innocent life. It didn't make sense to be vegan and for abortion, if your reasons for being vegan were against the killing of innocent life. Over time my viewpoint on that changed drastically. My reasons for being vegan became very political and environmental and not just the ethics of killing. When you're vegan you are sometimes killing creatures because when your grain is harvested there are animals killed in the process. When your food is transported from one side of the country for the other, the emission from the trucks is partially causing cancer and killing people and animals along the way" (Peterson 2009: 97).

Kim Nolan (*Chicks Up Front*, *Bark and Grass*): "Although I embraced veganism and influenced a lot of hardcore kids to go vegan through the *Bark and Grass* cookbooks, I wasn't into hardline for one specific reason: they were pro-life" (Peterson 2009: 97).

Praxis: "If a pregnant woman can kill her unborn child then I should be able to beat my child. That's consistency. …If you're reading this you are probably vegetarian or vegan already. You are also probably anti-authoritarian. So how can you give one group rights yet deny another group of their rights? Your pro-choice, anti-life stance invalidates anything you have to say about other forms of oppression such as meat-eating, racism, sexism, etc. …There is no justification for denying a fetus its right to life. As an anti-authoritarian you should oppose all forms of oppression, not just a select few injustices that might be more convenient to you. …As many as 1 out of 3 abortions harm the mother. Besides when a woman dies from an illegal abortion it's nature's way of dealing out justice! …It's time to stand against all forms of oppression, torture, and murder! STOP THE SLAUGHTER—BAN ABORTION!" (*Praxis*, "The Political Side of Abortion," 1991: 54).

Michelle Borok (*Gaia Screams*, *Invictus*): "There is no room for compromise. Too many people have let their lives slip away with useless negotiation and pacifism. Let's look at the example of an admirable anti-abortionist named Paul Hill. He is an inspiration to a true militant activist. In his taking of a murderer's life, a man who made his living by killing babies, he saved hundreds of lives. …Not only did his glorious actions have a direct impact on the Florida clinic, but imagine the long term effects. The conviction of militant pro-lifers to bring about justice by any means necessary, has surely made young doctors think twice before giving their talents to local abortion clinics" (*Vanguard* 6, 1995: 4).

Dave Agranoff (*Defense, Rescue and Survival*, *Vanguard*): "There is no such thing as a 'safe' and legal abortion. …convenience is not more important than innocent life. The fetus is not a parasite or a tumor, it is a human life from the moment its DNA is formed [and] deserves a chance to be born" (Agranoff, *Forward to Eden: A Guide to Hardline Viewpoints*, c. 1995: 4).

Michelle (*Gaia Screams, Invictus*): "Aborting a fetus is not like removing a tumor. …Oh please, us women of color [*Note: Michelle has a Korean mother and Jewish-American father*] don't need your pity, or your advice. As a woman (of color), as a proud feminist, as a vegan, as a potential abortion, I oppose them vehemently. PC patriarchy today tells me to abort. …Abortion is an escape route encouraged by men. Oh well. As I said before, I'm not trying to make any converts, but when it comes to Animal Rights, keep your pro-death preaching to yourself. Don't condemn groups like Vegans For Life who bring the AR agenda to the mainstream pro-lifers" (*Invictus* 1, 1995: 21).

Sean: "The original ethic of veganism which informed hardline's view on this subject was that life was intrinsically sacred, whether human and animal. In that regard, we always viewed having a pro-life view as being directly connected to our veganism. Other key animal rights activists like Ronnie Lee, co-founder of the A.L.F., Animal Liberation Front, felt the same. Likewise, we saw the connection between eugenicists and the white power system that sought to limit population growth amongst brown and black people as a way of maintaining their dominance. We also understood the complexity of the situation, and were never so naive as to not see that abortion could sometimes be the lesser of two evils in certain scenarios" (Rettman 2017: 272).

Rat (Statement): "At that time I was opposed to abortion, I did see it as the taking of a life but my views on that have changed drastically over the years. I'm a misanthropist and think the best thing for this world is the end of humanity, so I don't want more humans, so every abortion is a better thing for the planet and all life up on it, so, abortions and homosexuality and definitely a step in the right direction for the end of humanity!" (Old Man's Mettle 2021).

Sean: "My point is not to say that each person in the group believes this or that—I mean, for instance, for me, abortion is not good, but it is permitted in Islam up to a certain time period. Again, even in Islam, it is not considered a 'happy' thing, but life is difficult, and not everything is meant to be perfect. On the other side of it, I think that too often in the west, it is used as birth control—or worse, population control by racists (planned parenthood in America, was created by a racist KKK woman to get black and Latino women to abort their babies)—so a lot of scary stuff there. On the other end, I do not want to be linked with right wing Christian groups on the other side either. I have my opinions on it, but it will just not be a focus. So no, we [Vegan Reich] won't come out trying to back peddle and change everything. Rather—we will focus on the issues most people can agree on, and on the others, I think, if we talk about it rationally and clear, not trying to force other views—then many people will respect that" (Keynes 2010).

Sean: "No Vegan Reich lyrics pertain to this issue [homosexuality and abortion]; the band has no collective view on abortion" (Sean Muttaqi 2021).

Sean: "One either believes in Hardline as a whole or they do not. Those who do not are not Hardline" (*Vanguard* 1, "What is Hardline," c. 1992: 5).

Homosexuality

The question of homosexuality perhaps most clearly demarcated Hardline's socially conservative position within punk and vegan straight edge scenes. If the question of abortion placed Hardliners in the company of fundamentalists and evangelicals, the vehement and vocal opposition to homosexuality placed Hardliners in the company of those same fundamentalists and Nazis (the Liberation Theologists whom Sean cited as an ally in opposition to homosexuality have never expressed hatred of homosexuals as he did. Even conservative elements of the Catholic Church tend to distinguish between Christian love for homosexuals and banning homosexual behavior—a distinction Sean clearly rejected in his 1989 letter). Hardliners attempted to justify their apparent outlier status in hardcore scenes by relativizing their stance as something in line with the majority of the world's population. Yet the "100 million Elvis fans can't be wrong" argument obviously had no legs to stand on, especially considering Hardline's eagerness to go against the grain in other issues. Considering their starting point from anarcho-punk, they literally had to go out of their way ideologically in order to hate on homosexuals (while some, such as Michelle and others maintained a quiet no-homosexuals-allowed-in-Hardline policy others such as Matt Praxis, Micah, and Ryan very much did not do that). When, years later, Sean would continue to attempt to justify Hardline's opposition to homosexuality, he cited "indigenous groups" in Chiapas as "VERY conservative" and presumably opposed to homosexuality (this seemed to indicate the Zapatistas). Yet, as anyone who paid attention to the Zapatistas knew, Subcomandante Marcos supported homosexuals from the very beginning and the EZLN—unlike Hardline—never banned homosexuals from serving. (Also, as far as I know, many indigenous cultures had far more accepting policies regarding homosexuality and transpeople than industrial societies and the local indigenous Mayan population of Chiapas have long had a term for trans-people in Tzotzil—*antz-vinik*, literally woman-man).

Anyway, even many people who could follow the line of reasoning of "a single ethic" in regard to abortion got lost in Sean's attempt to turn opposition to homosexuality into an activist platform. Although Sean would later claim that he merely attempted to restrict Hardline membership to heterosexuals, as the record shows in 1989 (in *MRR*) and 1990 (in *Profane Existence*), Sean's letters revealed such a strong antipathy toward homosexuals and homosexual behavior that he both blamed them for society's depravity and openly advocated combatting them. Although he began to tone the venomous attitude down by the time he wrote the Hardline manifesto and *Vanguard* #1, he very much integrated opposition to homosexuality into the core of Hardline (see, for example, his interview in *UNAxVOCE* 1990).

The idea that homosexuality represented decadent hedonism rang hollow in light of many heterosexuals engaging in the same type of pleasure for pleasure's sake (not to mention the enormous hetero-porn industry which Sean opposed but not as often or intensely as he opposed homosexuality). The idea that homosexuality did not serve nature's original purpose of sexual procreation seemed illogical in light of Hardliners simultaneously arguing for diminishing population growth for ecological reasons. The idea that homosexuality contradicted the yin-yang principle of a union of opposites did not seem to sit well with the idea that yin and yang embodies the very idea of "exception to the rule" and co-existing contradiction (a notable degree of influence Hardline, especially regarding sexuality and yin/yang but also ideas of Tao/Hardline as the "universal and enduring Way of Nature" and possibly even Sean's backseat leadership style came from Daniel Reid's personal interpretation of Taoist principles in his book *The Tao of Health, Sex and Longevity,* 1989: xi).

Part of Hardline's rhetorical defence focused on attacking the admittedly faulty terminology of "homophobia" which may have earned them a couple "debate points" or a moment's distraction but hardly helped bolster their arguments. Nor did their misleading equating of homosexuals with Nazis win any intellectual territory (e.g., *Vanguard* 5 and *Destroy Babylon* 2). Further, while attempting to prove that homosexuality went against "natural law," Hardliners also wanted to make claims about animal behavior for which they offered zero empirical support. Micah's offer to commit sodomy with anyone who could prove homosexuality compatible with natural law may have just shown how low a Hardliner could go in lieu of actual arguments. As Hardline waned, only Sean and Micah remained to sustain (explicitly or implicitly) the anti-homosexual stance via Ahl-i Allah and Taliyah. That said, to claim that anti-homosexuality did *not* constitute a major part of Hardline ideology in which all Hardliners implicitly or explicitly agreed would amount to an inaccurate re-writing of history as this section demonstrates.

Sean: "People can not be separated from their actions. …And that is why I hate homosexuals" (Sean/Vegan Reich 1989b).

Sean: "…homosexuality and drug use …are prime examples of the root evil that not only creates the possibility for such things as capitalism, but also help it thrive. And that root evil is weakness" (Sean/Vegan Reich 1989b).

Sean: "Homosexuality can be seen as nothing but a deviation from nature. And like all other deviations from nature, which have brought our world to the dreadful state it is in today, it must be spoken out against and combatted" (Sean/Vegan Reich 1990: 7).

Sean: "In regards to what some people perceive as 'homophobia' was the stand hardline too that said if you were hardline, you could not be gay, that homosexuality was not part of a healthy, natural lifestyle from its perspective. People took that and wanted to jump to conclusions and would say hardliners were homophobic and were out beating gay people up and had an anti-gay agenda. But those things never happened in hardline. …and with Vegan Reich, it was never an issue we sang about anyway. We'd do shows and gay people would come out just like anyone else. Violence never erupted between us and anyone over their sexuality. It was quite the opposite as individuals and as a band. …I always thought it was funny that Hardliners would get flak for simply deciding that homosexuality was a lifestyle they didn't want to engage in or stating they believed it was wrong. …So even though I can see how hardline's views on homosexuality were controversial and at odds with many people in the hardcore scene, I don't think it's legitimate to make the leap of considering hardline homophobic or that it was trying to oppress people" (Peterson 2009: 96-97).

Sean: "Active homosexuality was clearly verboten within the ranks. However, it would not be what I would class as 'homophobia.' There was never any goal to repress/forbid/harass or deny homosexuals their rights, as it were" (Muttaqi 2021).

J.P. Goodwin (CAFT, Memphis Hardline): "…we will welcome people as allies to win the most important battles (animal lib., environmental lib., etc.) even if they don't live up to the standards we live by. I'd sab a hunt with a homosexual or a drug user even though I oppose both. I wouldn't hide the fact that I opposed such behavior by any means. It's just that I have my priorities. Anyway, Joel from *Profane Existence* made it quite obvious that he wouldn't work with a Hardliner because we are anti-gay. Now, he may have political differences with Leonard Peltier or another political prisoner but still work with them. He even put out an Earth First! benefit comp at the time when Dave Foreman was their big figurehead. Mr. Foreman is quite right wing and very nationalist but Joel still worked with his group. But Oh No, he can't work with a Hardliner. Not even when the issue involved is animal rights, and nothing else" (Goodwin, *MRR* #115, 1992: 15).

Sean: "In order to clear up …misconceptions, the official Hardline view on sexuality is here laid forth. Intercourse exists for procreation. That is to say it came into being for that purpose alone. …Sexual attraction to other species of animals, prepubescent children and the same sex are obvious deviations from the natural order of things. …Hardline is about life. Our struggle [is] against the enemies of life" (*Vanguard* 1, "The Balance of Things" article accompanied by a yin-yang symbol, 1992: 9-10).

Adam Stępień Malik (Healing, Pain Runs Deep, Life Defense Communications, The Essence Records): "…even back in [the] 90s most individuals involved [in Hardline] would distance themselves from that statement [referring to the quote above from *Vanguard* 1]" (Muttaqi 2021).

Bound By Modern Age (Kevin of Cologne): "P.S. your NS [National Socialist] Hardline tattoo has nothing to do with real Hardline except that homophobic bullshit only a few hardliners were believing in" (*Bound By Modern Age* 3, 2015b: 6).

Praxis: "Many people are trying to say that Hardline is 'homophobic' meaning that we disagree with homosexuality because we are scared that we are gay ourselves. This is the most ridiculous thing that I have ever heard. Does this mean that since I think eating meat is unnatural, I'm really scared that I want to eat meat, or for that matter, since you think that so called 'homophobia' is wrong, does that mean that you are really homophobicphobic? Are you secretly scared that you think homosexuality is wrong? This makes as much sense as saying we're homophobic. …In nature, very little homosexuality occurs and when it does, that animal is often pushed out of the herd. Another problem with homosexuality is that in many places 'gay liberationists' are trying to have it taught in schools that homosexuality is fine and acceptable. What's next? Will we have people saying that we should teach that it's O.K. to do whatever they please in the name of pleasure? These special interest groups think only of themselves and not how their actions affect the society as a whole thereby infringing on the rights of everyone. …Although we do believe that homosexuality is wrong, the Hardline ideology, however, in no way advocates 'fagbashing', even though it does not fit into the natural cycle of animal existence, it does not directly affect the lives of others. I personally couldn't care less if two men or women want to stay in their house and say they 'love' each other but, when it starts to infringe on my rights, action will be taken" (Note: The author provided no source for the claim about animals—or anything else; *Praxis*, "Homosexuality and Fagbashing" 1991: 48).

Sean: "Yes, it would be easier if we toned things down and changed our agenda. Perhaps if we accepted homosexuality more people would accept Hardline. Perhaps if we permitted drug use from our members it would make their life in the struggle easier. Perhaps if we weren't so firm in our stance against abortion we could get more people into veganism. Maybe if we didn't stress veganism so much, we could get more people into environmentalism. And perhaps if we didn't stress any issue, we could gain more friends and in time they'd learn. And perhaps suicide is the only answer for those who can't live on their feet and stand by what they believe" (*Vanguard* 1, "The Hard Life," 1992: 8).

Declaration: "Sex drives exist for a single purpose, to ensure procreation of our species. But our sex drives are being used to sell products, to market everything from cologne to cars, to trap us in a huge marketing scam. Sex should be based on love and the desire to manifest that love in a physical form, while bearing in mind that sexuality exists to bring children in the world. To base sex on lust, desire, convenience, profitability or any other ignoble purpose is to deprecate a feeling and bond that is one of our most healthy and natural instincts. Do not let this defamation of our sexuality continue, take hold of your true sexual being and use that awareness to empower the natural state of sexuality that exists within us all" (*Declaration* 1, c. 1995: 20).

Ryan Downey (Hardball, Burn it Down, *Vanguard*): "…personally, the nature/nurture thing, I feel that either way it's [homosexuality is] still a disorder, whether it's caused environmentally …because there's a lot of people who are born alcoholic, people who are born obsessive compulsives, schizophrenics… They're still not viewed as acceptable things because they are deviations despite however 'natural' they may feel to the person. …I think what occurs between a man and a woman is natural and totally cool but we can't forget that sex is intended for reproduction. Because when you start forgetting that's when you have things like abortion and this and that. But to go to the extreme of like going out and doing it with people of the same sex or doing it with a tree or little kids or a dog or like anything that strays that far away to me I view as unnatural. ...homosexuals ask for a lot more than acceptance, They're asking for radical change in order to accommodate them. People that want to proliferate this 'Heather Has Two Mommies' and all these little pamphlets, they want to give them to first graders. You can't teach a first grader what a homosexual is when you have not even taught 'em about heterosexuals" (*Vanguard* 5, 1993: 7-8).

Rat (Statement): "i think too many people possibly saw hardline and thought 'that's what i want to be' when, myself, sean and others, were already that way. There were a few things with hardline that i didn't agree with, the homosexuality stance (being the main one), the family unit thing. i think as my ideas have 'progressed' i think i'm now quite far away from the hardline philosophy" (Bahr 2010).

Ryan (Hardball, Burn it Down, *Vanguard*): "I personally had no problem with gay people, ever, but I found myself arguing about hardline's stance on homosexuality with straight edge kids who otherwise agreed with us more often than I was doing much about animal rights. I am still drug-free, I don't eat meat, I don't believe abortion is correct, and it's been 18 years since then" (Peterson 2009: 95).

Ryan (Hardball, Burn it Down, *Vanguard*): "Ten years ago, even liberals thought that the topic of homosexuality was unsuitable for discussion with children. Nowadays, curriculum, teaching about the gay 'lifestyle' has been designed for first graders. ...Religious dogma aside, marriage serves the purpose of uniting two people, often times (but of course not always) with the intention of raising a family. This can only be done between a male and a female. ...For information concerning the Hardline view on homosexuality, pederasty, bisexuality, bestiality and sex with or without reproduction, write to your nearest Hardline chapter, we are all happy to talk" (Downey, "Homosexuality: Gay Rights, the Decline of Civilization and More," *Vanguard* 5, 1993: 21-25).

Monkeywrench: "Homosexuality ...is wrong. Our own bodies have proven this to us. We in no way advocate 'fag bashing'. I see that there is a difference between homosexuality and something like eating meat where another's life is at stake, however" (Praxis 1991: 31).

Dave Agranoff (Defense, Rescue and Survival, Vanguard): "'Intercourse exists for procreation. That is to say it came into being for that purpose alone. The pleasurable component of sex, the natural attraction between man and woman and the instinctual drive to engage in sexual activity, are to ensure the continuing cycle of life.'-Vanguard #1. As vegans we have seen the destructive effects of making important decisions governed by pleasure alone. ...The purpose of sex is also not pleasure, but procreation. ...When we stray too far from the purpose behind our actions is when we see the consequences" (Forward to Eden: A Guide to Hardline Viewpoints, c. 1995: 5).

Dave Agranoff: "[Q: probably at that time [early 90s] HL's stance on homosexuality wasn't that big yet?] A: Oh no, it was. From the beginning." (xCatalystx board 2009).

Dave Agranoff: "...unlike popular conceptions of Hardline, we have no stance against homosexuality. We however believe that sex came into existence for the purpose of reproduction and the balance of yin and yang energies" (*Vanguard* 6, 1995: 3).

Daniel Reid: "For men, masturbation represents an irretrievable loss of Yang semen-essence. ...ejaculations through masturbation or homosexual relations are regarded as being especially harmful to the Yang-essence and energy" (From his book *The Tao of Health, Sex and Longevity,* which Hardliners such as Micah have referenced, 1989: 221, 257).

Sean: "Drug use and homosexuality are related in that each is unnatural behavior which both are the cause and by-product of a disintegration of morality and fall from nature. These issues are not one of personal choice as they do infringe on the good of the whole, offsetting the balance of nature, and destroying what little we have left of that balance in our society. ...To understand the threat which homosexuality poses to the greater order of things, we must look at the true root and purpose of sexuality, how it is part of a natural balance and plan, and how modern concepts of sexuality seek to destroy that balance—upsetting the harmony that should be. ...We must take a stand against ALL that is not in harmony with the natural order of things. We've got to keep the forces of darkness from gaining any more ground if it's the last thing we do. For our children's sake, we've got to preserve what little we have left" (Boston Hardline 1995: 11-13).

Sean: "The epitome of sex being used as nothing more than for pleasure is homosexuality. ...In issue no. 77 of *MRR*, the question is asked (in the letter section) as to what is the difference between hating someone because of their skin color and hating someone because of their sexual preference. I will answer that. Even though someone may be born genetically fucked up, and be attracted to the same sex, they, at one point, have to make a conscious decision to follow through on those urges and thus they choose their sexual behavior. No one can choose their skin color, and beyond that, the color of one's skin does not reflect what type of person one may be, whereas being gay (which is a behavior) does i.e. A pathetic slave to desire" (Sean/Vegan Reich 1989b).

Sean: "Pleasurable activity which is natural and healthy—we embrace" (*Vanguard* 1, "The Balance of Things," 1992: 10).

Sean: "Influenced by vegetarian Anarcho-punk bands such as Conflict, Crass, and Flux—as well as Crucifix, @ state of mind and MDC, Vegan Reich carried on where these bands left off—taking the message of animal liberation and green revolution to an extreme not seen since" (Vegan Reich, back cover text on "Vanguard/The Wrath of God," 10" EP, Uprising Records, 1995). [*Note: The text cited Crucial Truth as the voice/source—a seemingly non-existent or super-tiny—zine, but it seems likely written—and certainly approved—by Sean himself. This particular quote provided a rare example of Sean giving credit to the pro-vegan, pro-queer, anarcho-punk band MDC as an influence on Vegan Reich. Sean has often cited The Apostles as an influence and even released a record with them in 1988 but I have never seen him mention that The Apostles had one or two openly queer members.*]

Scott Beibin (*Ascention*, Bloodlink Records): "I came down to the 'Hardline Gathering' and gave workshops on herbalism—I was very interested in alternative medicine since I was a teenager. When I went down there the way the ideas were being filtered into that scene was so incredibly comical. They were saying the Inca society was vegan or homosexuality doesn't exist in nature. The one thing I never connected with in hardline was the homophobia" (Peterson 2009: 95-96).

Brad (Buffalo Hardline): Through the hardcore music scene, I became aware of a movement. Deep inside, I knew Hardline was the next logical step in the war against oppression of all forms. I avoided the truth. For so long I hesitated partially because I was misinformed, and partially I lacked the strength to live all aspects of the Hardline ideology. Like many of our peers, I had preconceived notions about hardliners mainly concerning homosexuality.

I have never been the type of person who blindly follows what others say without question. So I decided to find out for myself what the Hardline movement was all about. What I found through talking to other hardliners was the ideals of Hardline were in fact the same that I had already accepted. My spirituality, my political beliefs, my loves and angers fell into place. The misconceptions that so many had, including myself were not based on truth but ignorance. The truth was revealed. There was no discrimination against homosexuals or anyone for that matter, only love for nature" ("No Alternative but Hardline," *Unveil The Lies* 1, 1996: 19).

Sean: "So too deviated, is the obsessive, addictive and domination oriented qualities of much heterosexual sex, where the incessant drive to engage in intercourse is not rooted in the instinctual urge to reproduce and the internal drive pushing one to achieve union and oneness (completing the balance of energy) with their natural counterpart, but rather, is based upon self-centered desire where each partner sees the other as merely a tool for their own gratification—having no real connection to each other and no place in the grand scale of things" (*Vanguard* 1, 1992: 8).

Micah: "…as far as gay 'rights' goes, I wholeheartedly agree! I have homosexual friends and I think that they should have the same 'rights' as everyone else. But just as you are not trying to make what promiscuous people do behind closed doors your business, we are not trying to make what homosexuals do behind closed doors our business. We simply are striving for much more balanced and natural sexual activity. Whatever people do, so long as it's not hurting anyone else, I couldn't care less because they are only hurting themselves" (Micah, speaking to Karl of Earth Crisis during an interview, *Destroy Babylon* 2, 1995: 21-22).

Micah: "Sodomy Contest: We at Cincinnati Hardline have received vast amounts of mail and verbal admonishments having to do with Hardline sexuality stance as stated in *Vanguard* issue #1. We have been called names like 'homophobic' (despite the fact that the very nature of our sexuality stance calls for confidence and security in one's own sexuality) and 'oppressive.' These slanderous claims are based on gossip and pure stupidity. …If you can prove that homosexuality is in tune with Nature, is healthy and balanced then I, Micah of Cincinnati Hardline and *Destroy Babylon*, will allow the homosexual of your choice to sodomize me or be sodomized by me! This is your big chance!" (Collins, "Sodomy Contest," *Destroy Babylon* 4 1996: 13).

Micah: "I am so fucking sick of Hardline always having to be on the defensive, all because a bunch of media propaganda-buying kids are too diluted by the sexual discordia of the Western mindset to understand the roles of human sexuality in the natural order. Hardline is <u>not</u> 'homophobic'! Get it through your fucking skulls! I'm not afraid of homosexuals, nor do I hate them. I simple disagree with the lifestyle which they have chosen to live …I am more than secure in my sexuality and I do not 'oppress' anyone! ….Nor can you bamboozle me into believing the sexual relationship (Yang and Yang) or two women (Yin and Yin) is balanced, healthy and in harmony with Mother Nature" (*Destroy Babylon* 2, 1995: 50).

Rat: "Well, firstly I never called myself hardline, I didn't feel the need to label myself that way. I had many discussions with Sean before I did the hardline record, as I didn't agree with the homosexuality stance, even tho it was a very minor point in hardline, and as many wrongly thought, it had nothing to do with homophobia, it was to do with how some thought humanity should go forward, the family unit, something far from my way of thinking" (Old Man's Mettle 2021).

xYosefx: "I'm not Hardline and never was (I've always been very queer positive & I'm pro-choice) but I'm vegan sXe & have a lot of friends who were involved in HL at one point. It's weird how it took that turn into ultra-fundamentalism (mostly pushed by Sean and Micah, of course). It WAS an anti-gay ideology however; in fact, in a 1990 interview for the Australian sXe zine *UnaXVoce* Sean said:

'The basic principles of hardline;

1. Being vegan.
2. No alcohol or any other drugs.
3. Anti-abortion, anti-gay.
4. Radical environmentalism—a rejection of modern civilization and all of its governments, countries and corporations who try to control/dominate and thus destroy nature.'

I've always found it sad that Hardline combined such great & radical ideas with the dead weight of homophobia & such" (*Crucial Times* 2006; also see *UNAx VOCE* 1990).

Sean: "The thing is, and I know this isn't a popular belief here—but people should be allowed to hold views that run counter to what popular cultural views are (or popular counter-culture for that matter): To deny that, is in itself, Authoritarian. …Furthermore, it seems that within the realm of say, the vegan straight edge scene, or modern anarchist movement etc., tend to be very selective about when and where they hold these overly highly exclusionary standards (i.e., will listen to their favorite rapper who doesn't think it's ok to be gay, will listen to their favorite metal band who are against animal rights, will visit their grandmother who might be against abortion and so on…). If people are willing to make those exemptions for the sake of their music collection or family ties, you'd think there should be some willingness to stand together on the barricades, in the common cause of the planet, and against real authoritarianism (i.e., the kind implemented by those actually in power).

…I'm not calling for unity with self-declared Nazis. What I'm saying is that within the masses of the world's population there are diverse groups of people who see themselves standing against authoritarianism, against oppression, etc. but may have different views than you regarding personal morality issues (based on their particular cultural, spiritual, religious background). Let's look at a few examples: Latin American Liberation Theologists. They have fought side by side with other revolutionaries who may not share their belief in God or certain moral viewpoints held by them since they are Catholic. Various indigenous groups—let's take the struggle in Chiapas as an example since this has long been generally supported by the 'PC' oriented aspect of the left—even though large sectors of that community are VERY conservative and would be at odds with a lot of their supporters in certain issues" (xCatalystx board 2009).

Catalyst Records: "Without vegetarianism, without veganism, without actively fighting the evils of sexism, racism and homophobia, straight edge becomes nothing more than a group of individuals whose common bond is the abstinence from drugs, instead of reaching the potential it has" (Originally from *Catalyst* zine 3, clipped by Dave Agranoff into his zine; Catalyst Records, "Straight Edge," *Defense, Rescue and Survival* 1, 1995: 12).

Sean: "I have lost touch with the Apostles over the years, but was friends with them, and never had some moral issues about it [i.e., their homosexuality]. Me, Andy and Dave had discussions back then about some of our differences (as well as agreement on some things), as I have done throughout the years with many people in my life, whether friends, family or work associates etc. who have different views and/or lifestyles than me" (xCatalystx board 2009).

Micah: "Now, white elitist PC kids want to cry that there is someone speaking at the Total Liberation Fest who doesn't agree with homosexuality (besides Ramona Africa). It isn't that such a person (me, that is) advocates violence against homosexuals, nor any sort of action whatsoever. Rather, his (my), religious beliefs —like the religious beliefs of almost the entire world—are opposed to it. As well, this is based on 8,000 years of Chinese Medical tradition, and Yin and Yang theories of coupling. It isn't a 'God hates fags' philosophy, it is an ancient way of life that seeks to harmonize the Yin with the Yang. Men are Yang, women are Yin. There is simply no harmony in two Yangs nor in two Yins. Thus, we oppose such unbalanced coupling (as does most of the world)" (Naziri, "Calling All Anti-Homophobes!, Protest MTV," *Indybay* 14 July 2004).

Micah aka Adam Naziri: "Go into ANY Masjid [mosque] and ask people if you or I are leading people astray by me opposing homosexuality. ... Most Muslims HATE homosexuality. ... Is all change good? Like if I broke your nose would that be a good change or a bad one? The Qur'an says homosexuality is haraam. You are a wanna-be Muslim and ANY one of over a BILLION Muslims would agree with that assessment" (from his post entitled "Fags Delete Messages When Proven Wrong," by Adam Naziri, *Indybay* 21 July 2004).

Micah aka Adam Naziri: "A *Mu'min* [Muslim] CANNOT be a homosexual. So what you are saying is inapplicable. I will not repent for calling a *kafir* a *kafir* [infidel]. If the individual wants to leave behind his homosexual lifestyle and enter the fold of Islam, then *al-hamdulillah* [praise God], I would proscribe him the Traditional Chinese Medicine that I have proscribed elsewhere (which has helped a brother leave behind the Sodomite urges of the hormonal imbalance that he was born with). ... We have never said we would bother to kill homosexuals. It is simply not worth it to us. ...I believe that homosexuals should be left to themselves as the Qur'an says. We should literally leave them to themselves and let them have their own secular society APART from an Islamic State. ...Generally when Islamic sources referred to homosexuals, it was speaking of homosexual pedophiles and YES, I do believe they should ALL be killed ideally" (from his post entitled "Fags Delete Messages When Proven Wrong," by Adam Naziri 22 July 2004).

Patriarchy and pornography

With Hardliners' obvious macho-posturing, weapons fetishism, refusal to acknowledge women's reproductive rights, and hysterical outrage over homosexuals, one can perhaps forgive many outsiders for lambasting Hardliners for sexism as well. However, evidence on this front seems lacking. Although Sean and a few early Hardliners (like Jon Justice) rejected "feminists" and Sean's first interview "jokingly" referred to "yeastie-infected-unshaven…[feminist] cunts," I could find no evidence of Hardliners (including Sean) speaking disparagingly of women and, in contrast, explicitly rejected sexism and advocated the equality of the sexes. They rejected pornography and, although only rarely mentioned, they rejected patriarchy too. While Dave Agranoff, perhaps one of the most clearly anti-sexist Hardliners, asserted the male role as central in dismantling patriarchy (an interesting position that placed men again in the center of activity and women as relatively passive bystanders), the emphasis on women's self-defense, workshops on women's health, and the section devoted to women activists in *Vanguard* showed that those who critiqued Hardline as sexist and patriarchal would have to make clearer arguments—especially if debating someone like Michelle of Memphis Hardline.

Furthermore, Hardline, like anything else, deserves contextualization. Its majority male membership and testosterone-laden machismo hardly differed much from the very same hardcore and straight edge scenes that critiqued Hardline the most. What evidence exists for sexism in Hardline that did not also apply to straight edge? Compared to the accusations of sexual predatory behavior by non-Hardline "pro-feminist" bands like Seven Generations (see Khanum 2021), I see very little evidence, if any. One may assume, however, that behind the accusation of "sexism" many people may submit that Hardliners opposed abortion and they classify this position as "sexist". So yes, if one defines "sexism" in that manner then one *de facto* defines Hardline as "sexist" alongside other anti-abortionists such as Mary Wollstonecraft, Susan B. Anthony, and Dorothy Day. If, however, one's criteria for "sexism" means behaving or believing as if females deserve less power than males, then I fail to see much evidence for that in Hardline. One finds much more evidence in their texts *opposing* sexism.

Dave Agranoff (*Defense, Rescue and Survival*, *Vanguard*): "Patriarchy is a system of male domination over women. Being a movement made up of all human beings fighting for the equality of all life in nature, we unite in the struggle against sexism. Besides the clear injustice of sexism, it deprives our movement of half the ability and knowledge we have potential for. When, in reality, we need all the potential we can get our hands on" (*Forward to Eden: A Guide to Hardline Viewpoints*, c. 1995: 3).

Sean: "As a movement made up of both men and women, we are unified in a struggle for equality between the sexes—working to end the reign of those who exploit existing differences to an unfair advantage, so as to gain domination over another" ("What is Hardline," *Vanguard* 1, 1992: 5).

Dave Agranoff (*Defense, Rescue and Survival*, *Vanguard*): "By accepting the idea that animals need rights given to them by human beings we continue to foster the patriarchal and speciesist ideas that animal liberation should be defeating" (*Defense, Rescue and Survival* 3, 1995: 5).

Dave Agranoff: "Smash the sexist bastard within… I'm not sure exactly what I wanna say…men are sick. We leer at women, in our minds we judge by what we see. The body is noticed and the soul is forgotten, a person is reduced to a set of tits and ass. Centuries of women struggling to know their freedom… Women proud and strong for themselves are reduced everyday by men. Most men are guilty of this crime every day.

In a time where every strong soul is needed to battle the evils of our world gone insane, it is more than just an obvious injustice to deprive women of equality. The most important warrior against the humiliation and injustice that is sexism is men. Too many times i think sexism is made to be an issue women need to fight.

In the end I think it is us men who hold the key to a world free of the sexist disease. We need to reassign the ideals that society places on a strong man. A strong man to me respects all. In the words of Jim Mason from *An Unnatural Order*: '*Instead of macho displays, the modern man can show genuine human bravery and strength. He can be brave enough to tackle the thorny strands of tradition that warp human society and threaten the living world. Men can have the strength to accept equal roles in the house, at work, in bed, and society as a whole. ...to build a culture that values empathy, altruism, and kinship with all others—regardless of sex, race, size, or species*'" (*Defense, Rescue And Survival* 2, 1995: 4).

Sean: "List of favorite things: Girls, Punk, Sex Pistols, Dead Nazi skins, Vitasoy, Trader Joes, Payless Shoes (home of non-leather steel toe), Paulina, Jessica Lange, Michelle Pfeifer, Jane Seymore, The two Miami Vice girls, Anarchy (the chaotic kind), Mykel Board, All Laguna Beach girls, the Germs, Bondage (with non-leather straps), Italian food, Italian Girls, (non-New York hybrids), Tofu, Jamaican women (natty queens), Mexican food,

All girls on above list, deals (not the drug kind), salad (not the green kind), The Apostles, Miami Vice, Saturday Night Live, David Letterman, Blonde girls, raging Scottish punk, Jimmy Cliff, Peter Tosh, Matabaruku [Matabaruka], The Epileptics (pre-Flux), Tom Likas, furniture" (Vegan Reich 1989a).

Michelle Borok (*Gaia Screams*, *Invictus*): "I'm so fucking sick of arguing pornography. There is nothing okay or acceptable about it as far as I'm concerned. …Breasts are glands. They are flesh. Breasts can be beautiful and erotic. Breasts can give life and pleasure. Breasts can be sucked, fucked, and eaten. Breasts can be served on the same plate as two thighs and a side of mashed potatoes. Breasts can be boiled, fried, or even baked. Ah, the sexual politics of meat…" [she goes on to quote from Carol Addams' book *The Sexual Politics of Meat*]" (*Gaia Screams* 1 1995: 6).

Micah: "According to the center for Mental Health Services, 42% of all women who are murdered in the United States are killed by their husbands. Every 15 seconds a woman in this country is beaten and every 6 minutes a woman is raped. … But what causes it? Are rapists born or made? Just as with racism and speciesism there cannot be one simple answer as to what causes such injustices. However there are in fact many things that contribute to them. In the case of sexism, pornography is a big contributor. Pornography turns people into abusers of others for personal pleasure and profit. Men become addicted to lustful images and then act them out in violent and sickening ways.

…Pornography is anti-Nature! Following natural and healthy instincts is a beautiful thing. It helps to keep our bodies and minds in tune and in balance with the Lifeforce of Nature. However, when any aspect of life is taken to a warped extreme and is out of balance, then drastic consequences follow. …Pornography exploits and dehumanizes women as discardable tools for the satisfaction of male lust, and children are abused mentally, emotionally, physically and spiritually to satisfy the hedonistic urges of pedophiles. …Real people are not seen as individuals, rather as a tool for a selfish means.

…Pornography is an industry, just like African slavery and just like animal agriculture, its industry is slavery! …Greedy capitalist tycoons see the demand for sex in this society, so in turn they supply this demand by taking advantage of innocent women who might need to support a family or pay her way through school. Pornography and greed feed upon each other. They go hand in hand.

…Pornography is anti-sex. Pornography promotes physical satisfaction without caring love, sex without responsibility, union without the obligation of consequences, and exercise of the mating privilege without reward to the immediate partner. Pornography is out of balance plain and simple! In terms of Yin and Yang sexual energies and fluids, there is no Yin sexual counterpart. The counterpart is an illusion. Thus making pornography (and the masturbatory fantasies that were meant to accompany it) not really sex at all! Rather a cheap substitute for sex, or rather an 'illusion' of sex. In this case pornography actually destroys the physical health of the male participant, as his 'Yang Chi' sexual essence is drained to complement and balance it (thus depleting his body of zinc and a myriad of other minerals that help to compose the body's cerebral fluid).

...The question isn't 'What's wrong with pornography,' the real question is 'What isn't wrong with pornography'! ...If the oppressed of this industry cannot muster the strength to fight this oppression, then we will fight it for them. All oppressive industries must fall, be it by resignation or by force. Now is the time to rise up" (Collins, "What's the Matter with Pornography?" *Destroy Babylon* 3, 1996: 65-67).

Indianapolis Hardline: "Pornography is a legal form of patriarchy" (*Vanguard* 7, "What Really Goes on Behind the Scenes," 1996: 13).

Dave Agranoff (*Defense, Rescue and Survival*, *Vanguard*): "Sexist...it makes me angry to think of someone giving the impression to people that i or anyone hardline is sexist" (*Defense, Rescue and Survival* 2, 1995: 10).

Sean: "List of fucked things: Girls, smell-skanky-rotten to the core-yeastie-infected-unshaven-intrenched and intwined with lard-bitchy-separatist-antiMykel Board feme cunts! ...South O.C. cops, Bush (the George kind), Quayle (the Dan kind), virgins, San Francisco/Berkeley, Deadheads/hippie scum..." (Sean/Vegan Reich 1989a).

Sean: "As to the sexist allegation—I take that in regards to the list of 'favorite things' where we listed some actresses, models & various other women, etc. I thought it would be painfully obvious that we were joking (when the first choice of both the 'favorite' and 'unfavorite' lists was girls and then talking about non-leather bondage & hating virgins, etc. I mean who could take this seriously?) and in fact, I don't see how we could have expected to seriously with such a ridiculous, irrelevant question as 'what are your favorite things?'" (Sean/Vegan Reich 1990: 7). [*Note: Sean described above the (seemingly self-made) interview he sent in to* MAS *(pre-*Profane Existence *zine) in 1989 which seems like the first zine to ever publish an interview with Vegan Reich.*].

Declaration: "When a man holds a woman down, and forces himself upon her, he has at that instant partaken in such a vicious act of hate that he no longer deserves to live. He has forsaken his right to life, because only sane human beings deserve to live, not corrupted vulgar scum that have no respect for themselves or any one around them. …I don't care why they did it, the fact remains that they did do it and they deserve what they've got coming. Because they were traumatized as a child, because they had a mental lapse, or because they were getting revenge is of no concern to me. They made a conscious decision to ravage another's body and mind, they have stained themselves with their own blood, and they should not escape retribution.

…Rape is an offense that will not go unanswered, desist or be killed. It's as simple as that" (*Declaration* c. 1995: 17, 20).

Authoritarianism and leftism

The question of Hardline's "right wing" politics perhaps remains the most confusing aspect of its legacy. Sean's co-opting of Nazi references such as "Reich" and "Vanguard" (the name of the British National Front's magazine in the 80s) backfired when nationalists in Europe took up Hardline's mantle and compelled Sean to publically reject any attempt to link Hardline with xenophobia, nationalism, racism, or fascism. Yet, if a number of neo-Nazis found straight edge a suitable tool to further the cause of white power, Hardline added a testosterone kick that, quite naturally, many neo-Nazis would find hard to resist: Self-discipline! Anti-porn! Answers to everything! Anti-gay! Purity, justice, and righteousness! What self-respecting vegan nationalist would not want to embrace Hardline? After all, if racist nationalists could embrace things like hip hop and a global faith founded by a Palestinian Jew, why would it matter to them if Sean and some of his band mates identified as people of color and rejected racism? Consistency has never ranked high on the list of nationalist logic but Hardline's claim of consistency would certainly appeal to some of them.

Furthermore, Hardline rejected both communism and capitalism which would also appeal to Third Positionist nationalists or national socialists who see Nazism as a third path alternative to communism and capitalism and green fascists might agree the idea of a vegan dictatorship. This section can at least clarify the facts. Sean has implied that he never advocated an actual dictatorship. These texts suggest otherwise. Although Sean never referenced Robert Anton Wilson's concept of a "serious joke," he might as well have.

The "semiotic ambiguity" of "Vegan Reich" as an intentionally provocative yet genuinely ideological name and attitude left more than one head scratching. The fact that the "left-right" binary brings its own problems to the table and Hardline consciously engaged in ideological cross-dressing led to never-ending and impossible-to-resolve debates about how to "really" classify Hardline. Yet, regardless of the terminology, the structure of Hardline never provided anything other than that of a purely informal authoritarian sect. Sean wrote a general script and maintained veto rights over interpretation of that script. He retained the sole authority to excommunicate people. No other person held the authority that he held. That said, yes, Sean did come out of the anarcho-punk scene and he did give occasional lip service to anarchist ideas and groups. Similarly, Benito Mussolini once took inspiration from syndicalism and had a love affair with anarchist Leda Rafanelli. Yet, whereas Benito completely disavowed anarchism in favor of fascism, dictatorship, and nationalism, Sean attempted to sustain an anarchist veneer around Hardline as an antiauthoritarian, antifascist, and technically leaderless movement while functioning as its de facto leader working toward a literal vegan dictatorship that would, as outlined in *Vanguard* 8, operate via guerilla cells taking over cities block by block, creating by force the justice that he and other Hardliners deemed necessary for Earth, animal, and human liberation. (For the record, Swedish activist and academic Andreas Malm recently advanced this type of idea terming it "ecological Leninism" and "war communism"—saving the planet through vanguard decrees imposed by force; see Kuhn 2021). But we need not attempt to place Hardline on a left-right scale to simple note what they said and what they seemed to do. Hardline sectarianism in itself need not imply fascism and Hardline advocacy of the *Revolutionary Catechism* need not imply anarchism.

DaveMoral: "[The] Hardline Movement …was a decidedly anti-fascist organization and everyone I have met that still holds an affinity with Hardline is strongly anti-fascist" (Stephanie K. 2010).

Sean: "The first step would have to be a dictatorship by vegans who would help speed up the natural evolution process by re-educating those who can be, and weeding out those beyond help. After this has occurred and the human race is dramatically reduced in numbers, the dictatorship can be dissolved and true anarchism can flourish" (Sean/Vegan Reich 1989a).

Sean: "The name Vegan Reich came about as a shock tactic, similar to Dead Kennedys, etc. If you think we ever believed in the real possibility of creating and maintaining a vegan dictatorship across the world, what can I say…" (xCatalystx board 2009).

Sean: "We do believe that a governing force, if you want to call it such, would be necessary after a revolution or insurrection etc. and do not buy the anarchist line that people left to their own accord would just act responsible and morally. However, at the same time—we neither believe in right nor left wing politics, with power being in the hands of an individual or group of individuals—as power most definitely corrupts. Thus, we are opposed to the concept of a dictator. Rather, the body of power that we envision would be somewhere between authoritarian rule and anarchism—as there would be a governing structure, with complete power and total control (which most would consider 'authoritarian')—yet the inner workings of such a structure would be set up along a decentralized line, with no individual holding any power whatsoever. That, along side an economic system similar to anarcho-syndicalism, would provide freedom for all—with the 'governing structure' ensuring the rights of defenseless people, animals, and nature against amoral people, and the non-exploitative economic system doing the same" (Edge 1990: 24).

Sean: "All shock value aside, we have never believed in achieving animal or human liberation by implementing an authoritarian system of governance. Our political stance has always been anti-fascist, and anti authoritarian" (Vegan Reich 2017b).

Sean: "There was a set of rules [in hardline], but we got the accusation of being fascist for having too many rules. There were anarchist roots to a lot of things in hardline, so there was always this internal friction between rules and not creating a hierarchy" (Peterson 2009: 485).

Irish-Moor Hardline: "As Hardliners, part of our struggle is to preserve the order of the natural world around us, and nature itself. Nature, beautiful in its diversity, is nevertheless distinctively simplistic—ordered in a concise fascism that suggests a larger hand in its creation—the hand of God. It is precisely for this reason that adherents to Hardline must avoid the dangerous trap of succumbing to the worship of nature itself. …Hardline should guide humanity back to its true root; the ONE, the only, THE CREATOR—The single source of all Life, and not the pagan ways fallen of the past. …If we as Hardliners succumb to the ideology of nature worship, we will find ourselves in bed with inherently racist groups like Earth First! and its openly white power and animal killing founder Dave Foreman and other, more frightening and outwardly fascist organisations. We must remember that the

Force that animates all of us has a universal Source, and is not merely the earth itself. This planet, this universe, are not God—merely attributes. In our search for spiritual practices that are congruent with our belief system, Hardline must be quick to discard the superstitious practices of pagan ancestry. Body piercing, for example—a fad popularized by this age's fascination with all things perverse—has its origins in backward sex acts ...Such demonic practices will always lead astray those who seek to tune themselves in with what is righteous and harmonious. Wandering in the deserts of desire by engaging in such practices... [the] truth seeker will find him/herself being led away from monotheism and progressive revelation, into the darkness and despair of polytheism, atheism, and Satanic fancy. ...Neo-fascism and racism are logical steps from adherence to 'ancient' traditions as they suggest a return to a nationalist identity. A full return to the past in its more spiritual sense would eventually lean towards an 'America for American[s]' and of course, a 'Europe for the Europeans'—as in ancient times—before the advent of multi-culturalism. Fascism, Satanism, paganism and 'Gaia worship' share a lot of similarities, with their emphasis on personal power, spiritual and physical pride, survival of the fittest, elitism and the like. 'Natural living' like that espoused by Earth First!—free from all technological innovation, good or bad—is surprisingly similar to 'Aryan living', as presented by the neo-Nazi 'camping' and 'out-door living' workshops in Europe. The answer for the Hardline individual on the straight path is to reject not only the mistakes of the modern man (with its technology and unsacred science), but also of so called 'primitive peoples' who have equally fallen from their Primordial state... For as much as the answer does not lie in modernism, neither does it exist within false notions of primitivism. ...Submission to the One, the guiding force for all Creation, is our only chance at redemption" (*Vanguard* 8, 1998: 9-10).

Sean: "It was a case of a sort of reverse P.C. fascism where they were saying, 'If you don't believe what we believe then we're going to make demagogues out of you.'...In general, I think the P.C. liberal crowd is just as eager as the 'Christian Right' to make other people believe in what they believe to enforce their views. As much as people wanted to criticize hardline for having its belief system, those same people wanted to enforce their beliefs in reverse. I personally think it's valid to hold an ideology or a religious view without having to fear being labeled 'fascist,' where going in you know that certain things aren't allowed and to expect others who hold that line of thinking to abide by the same rules. For instance, don't become a Buddhist monk and then complain that you're supposed to be celibate. Don't be straight edge and sneak a drink once in a while. Likewise, if you're born into a tradition where your lifestyle choices conflict with the rules of your church, or temple, mosque and so on then just leave it behind. Don't call people fascist because they have a different moral code than you adhere to" (Peterson 2009: 96-97).

Sean: "How about actual large scale confrontations between neo-nazis and their opposition that could include say everyone from anarchists and communists, Christians and atheists, gay and lesbian activists to Jewish groups? Should the atheist refuse to find common cause with the Christian against the nazis? Should someone who's gay not fight side by side (and vice versa) against the nazis with the religious Jew even though the latter may not approve of someone being homosexual? ....I just don't get it. Even though I'm against drug use, I never had a problem standing side by side at a protest or riot with crust punks I knew who were heroin addicts or drunks. Do I think their lifestyle is a healthy one? No. Do I want to fight them for it, or refuse to work together with them because of that? Of course not. Even though I am vegan, and believe violence is a legitimate option to stop vivisectors, etc.—I've never confused that with wanting to attack some guy on the street eating a hamburger.

...I'm not saying one should allow someone into an organization if they hold opposing beliefs to the tenets of that group. In fact, quite the opposite. I think we should all be allowed to define ourselves as we will, and even have self-imposed rules on what membership to said group requires, whether in belief or action. However, in the broader realm, I don't think it's good for societal or global harmony to cease interaction with those who do not belong to said group, or share your beliefs in their entirety.

Again, this is not to argue there is common ground with every person on the planet simply due to them being human. I don't want to be friends with someone who wants to kill me because of my race or religion, let's say. But I have no problem being friends with and interacting with those who respect who I am—yet have entirely different view points than me on everything from politics, to diet to religion, etc." (xCatalystx board 2009).

Sean: "I for one will no longer sit back and let these people destroy what little good is left in our society. You can call me a fascist or a homophobic or whatever. I don't give a fuck. This ain't some fucking game. ...What I'm saying is end the shit like, 'He eats meat but he's still pretty cool' and 'I don't care if he likes little boys, he's still against apartheid' and all that other common ground, mutual cause bullshit" (Sean/Vegan Reich 1989b).

Sean: "First of all, I'm the last person to cry victim, or hide from an argument. I've never tried to hide from things I've said, or beliefs I've had" (xCatalystx board 2009).

xChristopherx: "The resentment focused at you for your ideals is simply what happens in matters of public discourse, not 'PC fascism.' That phrase is utterly ridiculous and it attempts to liken objections and dissension to oppression. Perhaps normally you don't play victim or whimper, but your post that I quoted was almost strictly self-pity masked as a rebuttal. ...Doing a band of sufficient iconoclasm will bring you criticism, I'm sure you are aware of this, but one should accept this fact and defend one's position based on the intellectual merit of the critique, not by calling people bullies and throwing around foxnews pundits' slogans" (xCatalystx board 2009).

Sean: "My use of the term 'PC fascism' was not an attempt to resort to sloganeering. ...I don't have TV in my house and wouldn't watch fox if you paid me. That said, I have always found the overall use of the term 'fascist' to be a bit off base, since most people use it to describe all sorts of right wing groups or philosophies that bear no connection or resemblance to the actual fascist party and a belief in actual 'fascism'. With that in mind, if we can all agree that the term in either direction tends to be an oversimplification, then, by all means, I'm in support of dialogue that goes beyond ism, scism, over simplification or any preconceived notions. In terms of expanding beyond the initial post and my response to yours, I think you'll find the discussions have gone a bit deeper since then. And dare I say it on this board :), insha'allah, will continue to do so" (xCatalystx board 2009).

Sean: "Hardline condemns both Capitalism and communism which both see nature to be nothing more than a mass of resources for human consumption and exploitation. We denounce this modern society which was built on genocide, slavery and eco-terrorism and perpetuates racism, sexism, and speciesism" (*Vanguard* 1, "What is Hardline," 1992: 5).

Sean: "...many that justifiably hated capitalism, and in their efforts the fight against it, mistakenly took up its counterpart—communism—thinking it was the only option of resistance. Look at how many third world peoples ended up in misery, because of this mistake. They failed to see that communism was formulated on the same materialist misconceptions of existence that capitalism was. Based upon the same European ideal of civilization and 'progress' etc. Sure those two ideologies outwardly took different stances, but ultimately they were just different roads to the same (un)desired conclusion (of a materialistic state).

Likewise, with Satanism. Both modern Christianity and Satanism feed off each other. They both further the lie of mankind being born into sin, of evil having some power in and of itself. And that is just not the truth" (Muttaqi c. 2001).

Jon Street Justice (*Justice*): "JUSTICE ZINE: The one and only HARDLINE fanzine. If you can't stand all the whiny leftists from Berkeley, this is the zine for you. When we say 'no tolerance for ignorance' we mean it, and are willing to do something about it" (*Praxis* 1991: 14).

Sean: "Do you wanna know what's wrong with the Anarchist/ Commie/ Left wing/ Punk movement? Its adherents talk a lot about spreading their message to the working class and building a movement capable of bringing down the decadent capitalistic system—yet not only do they seem to have a complete disdain for traditional working class values, thus alienating those they speak of helping, they also champion such things as homosexuality and drug use that are prime examples of the root evil that not only creates the possibility for such things as capitalism, but also help it thrive. And that root evil is weakness. War, poverty, and capitalism etc. are not the real enemy—the underlying flaw in human character that makes it possible for such things to exist IS! It is the lack of inner strength and self-discipline that leads to the belief that one needs outside stimuli for happiness (be it money, power, sex or drugs), and that whatever one must do to get such things is justified by the end result of pleasure. Thus, wars are fought by men whose own body and mind were not enough of a sacred possession and had to have more material possessions and power to fill their void. Likewise, rape is committed by those who can't live without their fix of sex, and so turn to violence to get it, just as people starve so that the wealthy elite can overeat and amass wealth so that they can satisfy their thirst for pleasure. The hippy ideal of 'Free Love' which is running rampant within the alternative 'scene,' as well as homosexuality are just further examples of that weakness, where life is lived purely for pleasure" (Sean/Vegan Reich, *MRR* 79 1989).

Matt, JP, and Ryan (Memphis and Indianapolis Hardline): "We oppose this current governmental system, as well as communism and all other human centered governments because of all the oppression they have wrought. We fight for the protection of this planet and all of its downtrodden inhabitants regardless of their race, sex, age or species, and oppose all acts which go against nature's laws, including deviant sexual acts such as same sex attraction or attraction to young children or animals" (*Vanguard* 1+2 double issue 1993: 7).

Sean: "Immediately, we have to deal with saving lives today—through direct action. In conjunction with that we have to launch a massive educational campaign, be it through music, art or literature, to further enlighten people and gain numbers in our movement. With that said—we must not fool ourselves into thinking that the majority of the population (which fails to even see as equal, members of its own species, be it women, minorities, or members of different religions) will ever be enlightened as to the righteousness of animal liberation and the necessity of animal rights. ...in the here and now, it means creating a climate where one fears retribution for any acts of wrongdoing. Let our numbers increase and govern the streets with fear—so that no man or woman shall transgress on what is good and pure" (Boston Hardline 1995: 16).

Sean: "...our goal is not as you perceive. You keep looking at things in terms of western politics and culture—from one end of the spectrum (of anarchism) to the other (of fascism), thinking that we have to fit some sort of definition which you are familiar with—that our beliefs have to be rooted in European history, and attitudes—assuming that no other viewpoints and approaches have ever come to exist which were not based on your culture's outlook—and that is just a narrow minded, naive understanding of the world (which is the same way European colonialists looked at things as they condemned natives as being 'savage' and 'uncivilized'). We don't want a militaristic fascist state. We don't want crowded jails and courts. We don't want constant bloodshed. This is what we have now. We seek to go back to a time when man lived in harmony with the earth. A time before an egotistical individualism took over his soul. A time when the laws of nature ruled supreme and instinct still guided our way. If there is ever to be peace on earth, then order must be retained. Not according to our wishes, but to the balance of nature. ...As to your continued suggestion that we're totalitarian; would you also suggest that Native American cultures were totalitarian because everyone in the tribe had their place, and their assigned role? Was their strong tradition which ensured a continuance (for thousands of years) of a way of life that lived in balance with nature, be considered by you to be fascist? If so, then I suppose we would choose that 'fascist' existence, where the earth flourished, over your liberal 'democracy' where all life is on the brink of destruction" (Boston Hardline 1995: 21).

Jon Street Justice (*Justice*): "I don't believe in anarchy if that's what you mean. I do believe that many anarchist ideals can be applied in a 'perfect' government. Using the word 'perfect' doesn't work with govt. Man is not perfect. His creations are not perfect. We can get a lot closer to a perfect govt. by burning this one to the ground and starting from scratch, but there will always be room for improvement" (*Praxis* 1991: 13).

Sean: "First and foremost, Vegan Reich started out as an anarcho-punk band. Our members have always been committed anti-fascists, and the band has historically primarily been made up of people of color throughout its existence" (Vegan Reich communiqué 2017).

Sean: "Anyone who's followed Vegan Reich should know that we've always supported the Black Liberation Struggle and have always fought fascism in all of its forms" (Sean Muttaqi 2020).

Sean: "I will never let Vegan Reich be a mouthpiece to make people Muslim. It did not start as that, and it is not what it is for. If people see I'm Muslim but don't try to force it on them, it makes them respect Islam and me better. No one likes being forced to do anything" (Keynes 2010).

Sean: "From my current perspective as a Muslim, I have even less concern with what non-Muslims choose to do nor not do, as long as it's not oppressing others. The West as a whole has not chosen to embrace Islam as its guiding principle, nor Christianity for that matter, and the *Quran* is clear that there's no compulsion in religion, so really, what people want to do in a secular society, they're free to do. They might not make the same choices I make, or believe the same things I do, but I'm not about trying to force my religion down people's throats or be some type of morality police. I live the example I want to give and that's the extent of it" (Peterson 2009: 97).

Sean: "I for instance simultaneously believe in Islamic government for Muslims —I am Shia by the way:)—whilst at the same time also holding strong Anarchist beliefs. It may seem a contradiction, but it is not on a deeper level, see—I believe in the principle of non-authoritarianism, and the movement towards ALWAYS fighting government oppression—but I also see the human need to have order, and rules of law. So to me, it is very much the Tao. We need order, and the counter balance to order, is struggle and Anarchy—resisting too much control. There is no perfect static utopia, always movement. Change.

Likewise, I do consider myself a conservative on many moral issues, whilst perhaps also being a libertine on many matters. i.e. I am not an uptight Christian moralist who thinks sex is evil. So there are many differences within my own brain, Insha'Allah, that makes the point clear" (Keynes 2010).

Violence

Another confusing aspect of Hardline remains the question of violence. First, how does one define violence? Again, it deserves context. Most punks would not consider it "violent" to smash into one another in a mosh pit. Few punks, if any, would cringe at the lyrics of Misfits or Dead Kennedys simply because they sound "violent." Many would not consider it particularly violent to break into a fur farm, liberate mink, or destroy fences or cameras along the way. What about verbal threats? Celebration of assassinations? Lyrics that include death threats or description of rape? Would punks who listen to Judge consider Hardliners violent? Second, how does one know of or measure the purported violence of Hardline in relation to other people in the scene? Considering that so few Hardliners existed and those that did carried no official Hardline ID, one could, at best, say that the scene attracted some people who engaged in violent acts. In lieu of actual coverage of instances of key and undisputed Hardline figures engaging in unprovoked acts of violence against others in the scene, I cannot say that Hardliners stood particularly high on the scale of violence when placed in the context of either militant veganism, Earth liberation activism, insurrectionary anarchists, or macho-straight edge scenes.

Hardline has had a notorious reputation for violence which many of them, including Sean, seemed eager to perpetuate. In reality, however, most Hardliners only acted violently (if at all) against violent institutions (such as animal use industries). I have not heard of much (or any?) violence regarding Hardliners toward people for "breaking edge" or drinking alcohol. Below, one can read, for example, how Dave Agranoff described an incident in which supposed Hardliners joined a group of straight edgers in assaulting a kid wearing a potleaf t-shirt at a straight edge concert. Yet, Dave clearly demarcated that as something that went against Hardline beliefs saying they only "*think* they are hardline" (emphasis added) because "for those who are truly hardline, violence is only in defense." As sobriety merely served as a means to better organize revolution rather than an end unto itself, Hardliners seemed generally less concerned about sobriety than straight edgers and more concerned about justice. Their willingness to deal out "justice" (violence) seemed inextricably tied to their emphasis on compassion and respect for innocent life. The binding of these contrasts reminded me of what Amy McDowell has described as "aggressive and loving" attitudes among hardcore Christian punks and what Elizabeth Price described as "weaponized compassion" in vegan straight edge scenes (McDowell 2017; Price 2017). It feels almost as if many males have to compensate their "feminine" compassion and sensitivity to animal suffering with declarations of vengeance, justice, and violence to display a hypermasculinity that leaves no doubt as to their gender identity (or sexual preference). Of course, punk and hardcore feed into this dynamic. The preference for extremes and the attention span of punks will reward a band named Vegan Reich more than a band named Vegan Life. That said, one also needs to keep this in perspective and recall that many crews in hardcore such as DMS, FSU, Courage Crew, and others probably had both greater local numbers and a greater proclivity toward violence than Hardliners but did not gain nearly as much national or international notoriety (see Binelli 2007, Linnemann and McClanahan 2019, and Purchla 2011). Whereas non-Hardline gang-like hardcore crews could amass large numbers of locals (thereby increasing their power and potential threat of local violence), Hardline started out as an ideology with disparate adherents spread throughout the country and later the world. Predominantly one city at one time (Memphis during Raid's existence) provided the chance for Hardline to produce a similar effect. The later gang-like violence in, for example, Salt Lake City's scene seems more attributable to certain straight edge crews—not Hardliners. In fact, the most extreme example of intra-scene violence that I could find associated with Hardline appeared in a letter containing death threats supposedly received by Mike Bullshit (Go!) and sent by Jason of Blindside/Scooby Doo Records who purportedly wrote a vicious anti-homosexual rant (Abrash 1992). I could not get confirmation from Mike regarding the letter and if Jason did send it. And if Jason did have any connection to Hardline, it seems marginal (I could find no Hardline zine ever writing about Blindside or Scooby Doo Records for example).

Sean: "[*Q: I've heard rumors of knocking burgers out of peoples hands, beating up hippies etc. What do you think of this?*] A: We won't comment on any rumors. You will know when you are confronted by the REICH. You are either standing with the REICH, or you will be crushed under its wheels of progress. [*Q: Do you think everybody should stop eating meat?*] A: We don't care if they 'should' THEY WILL! [*Q: What are your views on drugs?*] A: We don't have 'views'—liberals have views. Views are opinions—we only deal with what <u>is</u>, and there is only one truth! You either face reality or are smashed in the face by it! As to the drugs—they will not be tolerated, nor will hippies, even if they quit doing drugs!" (Vegan Reich 1989a).

Sean: "Abuse of any substance is lame, and will be dealt with accordingly" (Vegan Reich 1989a).

Raid/Sean: "You believe in violence, well I do too. Yours is against animals, mine's against you" (Raid, *Words of War* 7" vinyl etching).

Sean: "Someone who is truly hardline, is a warrior for the liberation of this earth. They use the heightened awareness, and strength against the forces of evil destroying this world. And in that struggle we shall use what ever means necessary, be it weapons, martial arts, or explosives. Our numbers may never be in the majority—but our strength will be greater than all, and we shall gain world liberation" (Boston Hardline 1995: 2).

Sean: "See, all the Vegan Reich lyrics were militant against people we all agree are messed up—vivisectors and so on. Never sung about killing someone for eating meat. Even our one song against drugs was against people drinking and driving. i.e. we were never a militant straight edge band—most of our fans were drunk anarchists!!!" (Keynes 2006/2010).

Sean: "Anyone who's known me personally, like Rat, knows that I'm not out trying to be morality police with regards to what people do in their personal lives. That is not to say that I haven't been highly vocal in the past about what I think the optimum way to live is (especially during my Hardline years)—but even then, I was the last person trying to be Big Brother about what happens in someone's bedroom" (xCatalystx board 2009).

Declaration: "Militancy is not about indiscriminately killing all who eat meat and then putting a bullet in the heads of those who disagree with us.

….Militancy is about taking a revolutionary stance against the greatest threat to animals, humans, and the earth: the industry and its leaders. Militancy is a mindset. A mindset that emancipates our conscience and compassion from conventional protest tactics and elevates our cause beyond laws while focusing our anger and will into a more effective, coherent attack: an attack that is formed around two main components, direct action and ensuring that personal accountability for the industry leaders will be met. To let this system constructed upon animal suffering continue is intolerable.

…A call to arms is here, there can be no compromise in the defense of Mother Earth and all life upon her. Sympathy and concessions have failed, negotiations will not halt the maniacal generator of destruction mankind has become. We take a stand now in warfare or fall amongst the smoldering ashes of all the polluted beauty left in these demons' path" (Anonymous, "The Tide Will Turn," *Declaration* 1, c. 1995: 3).

Sean: "If you don't stand firm on the side of right, you're nothing but a waste of life. So you'd better choose a fucking side and not be sitting in the middle when the bullets start to fly. If you don't make a choice, it could mean your life. For if you're not on my side, you're a target in my eyes" (Lyrics to Vegan Reich's "No One Is Innocent," *Hardline* EP, 1990).

Sean: "My problem is not the concept of prison. For I think both prison and capital punishment are necessary realities in the world which we live. My problem is the use of these institutions and practices, to oppress minority groups or the populace in general, for holding certain beliefs, rather than for punishment of a crime. But as far as punishment goes, I do believe it is absolutely necessary for their to be consequences to negative actions in society" (Muttaqi c. 2001).

Sean: "Meat and dairy production is torturing, is killing, for no purpose, for your ego for the taste. Their blood you're spilling. …So expect no fucking mercy, if you're guilty you will pay. No chances to discuss it, you're gonna fucking hang. …What did you think, this was a college debate? This is WAR" (Lyrics to Vegan Reich's "The Way It Is," *Hardline* EP, 1990).

Sean: "Smoking a cash crop, I don't care if you die. But the animals tested, should they pay that price? …As you eat the flesh from another that you denied life, freedom is not just a one way street… So don't even say that it harms only you and 'It's your choice to make' Cos a weak link in the chain will break the whole thing. And that I cannot tolerate. …If you wish to remain then stay in your place, cos you fuck up again and I won't hesitate.… To infringe on your rights, to take them away, to be judge and jury for the crimes you commit, day after day. Cos only with you stopped will our lives be truly free!" (Lyrics to Vegan Reich's "I, The Jury," *Hardline* EP, 1990).

Declaration: "We are subconsciously persuaded to embrace the most acquiescent solution to our problems, that reap short term benefits but only exacerbate the dilemmas in the long run by compounding them with new ones. This results in a pathetic inability of our generation to cope with its hardships and obstacles. And, it should come as no shock or surprise that drug usage, be it alcohol, cigarette, or illegal drug, is the primary element in cultivating this revolting dependency.

…How will our children learn respect for others' bodies and their own when their peers are encouraging them to pollute their bodies, haze their minds and ignore the consequences? This is our future?

We must break every link in this chain of oppression. Communities must be educated and persuaded to abstain from any and all drug usage. Synonymously, drug lords must be taken down, executed if need be to bring them to justice. And their minions must be forced to cease as well, for as long as one dealer is left free to spread contamination, thousands of lives are in jeopardy" (*Declaration* 1, c. 1995: 23-24).

Sean: "The whole concept of what justice is, refers to what one rightly deserves. This separates into two intertwined elements: One, that this planet and all the downtrodden and oppressed life upon it cease to be exploited in any way, and hereafter gets treated equally and equitably. Secondly, that those who have wrought unmeasurable sorrow and pain, as well as those who continue to inflict wrongdoing upon the innocent, be made to pay for their evil deeds. That is Justice" (Boston Hardline 1995: 20).

Sean: "As far as whether we believed in using weapons or violence, yes. We absolutely did" (Rettman 2017: 269).

Sean: "Some of our influence was good and some of it was bad. I mean, Salt Lake City got so out of control that I don't know anyone who was too happy with that legacy. There were kids getting stabbed for drinking and shit like that, which was never part of our ideology at all" (Peterson 2009: 489).

Sean: "Meat eating and sacrifice are not pillars of Islam. Nor are they obligatory. Again, if one looks at it contextually, it is easily determinable that it is not inherently part of the faith itself. Every *Surah* of the Qur'an came to Muhammad (*sal*) in response to certain events that were taking place over a period of many years. In the case of halal dietary laws, before their implementation, many people were slaughtering countless animals, in very inhumane ways—wasting much of the food, and treating animals abhorrently. Living in a desert environment, vegetarianism wasn't a possibility and thus not a practical answer to this situation and problem. So what Muhammad (*sal*) said, and what the Qur'an says, is that one must treat animals fairly, and if one must kill to survive, they must do it in the most humane manner possible (and also, since only Allah can create life, the animals' life must be taken in the name of Allah, as only Allah has the right to end such a life). Never is indiscriminate murder encouraged or even condoned. Far from that, what was encouraged was that less killing be done—and that when it must be (for survival) that one must share the meat with the poorer members of society, and to be less gluttonous in one's eating habits, so that less life must be taken" (Muttaqi c. 2001).

Brendan Desmet (Groundwork, Absinthe): "Hardline was important for hardcore. It might sound shocking, but it was a logical extension of taking something to the extreme, which is important for people to do in order to understand the negative side of extremism" (Peterson 2009: 96).

Declaration: "Hunt the hunter. Invade his territory. Scare off the wildlife he wishes to murder. Track him down. Take aim and watch a monster die. Then look around at all the life you have saved, and be glad that there is one less assassin left in the forest.

...Vivisect the vivisector. Break into her lab, liberate the tortured animals and burn her science down. Amidst the inferno, strap her to a table, crush her skull, pour acid in her eyes, make her swallow gasoline, burn her skin, test cocaine on her and see how it deforms her baby, just as the vivisector did to the animals.

...Factory farm the industry leader. Steal them from their mother at birth. Confine them to a tiny stall after letting the animals go free. Never let them see the light of day. Feed them antibiotics, inject them with drugs, beat them, yell at them. Deny them social interaction, deny them life. ...They have a desire to acquire wealth at the expense of the animal kingdom and the well being of the Earth. This warrants their annihilation.

These crimes should not and will not go unpunished along with the scores of others committed on a daily basis in this 'free' world of ours. If you undertake an action willingly, be prepared to answer for its consequences. There is a universal mandate of justice to be answered to, and repentance is the only salvation if one wishes to be saved from the wrath of the natural order" (Anonymous, "Hunt the Hunter," *Declaration* 1, c. 1995: 4-5).

Sean: "We were not really expecting how much controversy our ad in *Maximum Rocknroll* would cause among straight edge kids. In the punk realm of Southern California, which had always had a huge gang influence, guns were never out of the ordinary. Even many of the anarcho-punks had guns. Circle One used guns in their band logo, as did the Apostles in England, among others. But our logo definitely freaked the fuck out of many people in the hardcore scene, especially the more posi-type kids. We had contemplated using AK-47s in our logo, as that was the sort of more traditional revolutionary gun imagery. But starting up in America, we decided to use guns with ammo that would be more readily available in the States should stuff pop off, so to speak. Placing the rifles on the X both referenced a link to Malcolm X, as well as us purposely trying to co-opt straight edge imagery to get kids into the revolutionary struggle" (Rettman 2017: 269).

Sean: "I am appalled at the treatment of child workers, not only by [major corporate brand], but by the majority of Multinational companies, as well as the national companies within most third world nations. Children and women should be the world's most protected treasures. They are the key to the future, and the key to the world's well being. How anyone can exploit those kids and then go home to their own children as if they have done nothing wrong is beyond me. And certainly, for any so-called Muslim country to allow this behavior, is deplorable, when the Qur'an specifically outlines the rights of children.

It is areas such as this that definitely make me believe in the need for jihad" (Muttaqi c. 2001).

Sean: "We got a lot more flak from around the country than we did back home. I grew up in the early eighties with a lot of gang stuff going on in Southern California. From the long standing Black and Mexican gangs, to the punk gangs that sprang from many of the same neighborhoods and general gang culture—from the Suicidal Tendencies stuff, and Circle One, to punk rock gangs like L.A. Death Squad (The LADS), and The League. Our scene was really violent. People were getting stabbed and shot. Even as I got older and involved in the anarchist movement, we were always about guns, and fighting with Nazi skinheads. So, to me, being violent was sort of second nature, so it just came out in our lyrics. …We were also very influenced by radical political groups such as the Black Panthers, which often used guns and those types of symbols on their literature" (Peterson 2009: 484).

Ryan (Hardball, Burn It Down, Time in Malta, *Vanguard*): "We were around a lot of gang culture [in Indianapolis, late 80s, early 90s]. We hung out with and some of us were in local gangs" (No F'n Regrets 2021).

Dave Agranoff (*Defense, Rescue and Survival*, *Vanguard*): "I could write a book about how stupid the sXe scene is in western Ohio. …this is not an anti-Straight edge article, this essay is about the scene in Eaton and Dayton, Ohio where i lived for the last year before i moved to Syracuse. I admit i never wrote this before because i was afraid of them… and that is the worst part. Being afraid of people in the hardcore scene. I hope i never see them again; if i do they will beat the shit out of me but i don't care because they will prove me correct. …[Snapcase show] This kid in the leather jacket was not dancing any harder than any of the sXe kids but one of the Ohio kids began to beat the hell out of him. The Ohio sXe person in question (J.C.) claimed the leather jacket guy had kicked him, but J.C. didn't seem to notice the 20 or so people that left because of how violently he and his friends were dancing. …I watched j.c. pick Brian (Militant Records) up off the floor and throw him on to the stage.

…1995 started out the same, even worse. …[Birthright and Everlast show] During birthright, my friend John was dancing and he was at the very front. From behind J.C. jumpkicked him in the back. …[Outcast and Sevin show] Half way through [Sevin's] set two heavy metal kids started dancing. One was wearing a pot leaf shirt, i regret not warning him, but since no one was dancing, i didn't.

Well, his presence was enough… J.C. jumpkicked the potleaf kid in the face and almost instantly the whole crowd of sXe kids swarmed on this poor kid. They dragged him outside and set his shirt on fire. …That kid was enjoying Sevin. Maybe if he had been allowed to dance he would have bought a tape. Who knows, a couple shows and a few records later, he might have become sXe. I assure you, he never will be now! …Fuck that—I have enough respect for the time in my life when i was sXe to think it should not have anything to do with hatred and intimidation.

Those kids are jocks, fucking tough guys that got a Youth of Today record and picked and chose what they wanted to believe from it. A couple of them think they are hardline. For those who are truly hardline, violence is only in defense. Attacking innocent kids at hardcore shows or to justify it is not an act of an enlightened person" (*Defense, Rescue and Survival* 2, 1995: 8).

Sean: "[Q: Don't you think working with ads like the one in MRR with all the facts and details about eating meat and drinking milk etc. will make people think more about their nutrition than confronting them with automatic guns?]

A: Presenting knowledge, and informing people about the realities of the world is a large part of what we're about. And it is an effective and essential element of the struggle. But so too is the gun, or any weapon. For words alone will not gain the liberation of our planet. The state will not sit back and let its power slip away. As soon as we (and this goes for peaceful movements as well) become a threat to them, they will not hesitate to use force to destroy what we have built. The guns are a symbol of our willingness to fight this war by any means necessary. They are a symbol of solidarity with all the exploited people in the world who take up arms to fight imperialist/colonialist/ and capitalist oppression. In a society built and run on violence—the gun, a creation of their violent existence, has become our last resort—the final option. The only means for their destruction" (Boston Hardline 1995: 22).

Sean: "We [Vegan Reich] had a very aggressive attitude towards anyone who wasn't vegan straight edge or whatever" (*Destroy Babylon* 2, 1995: 42).

Sean: "I don't want to force anything down anyone's throat. In fact, I think in general Islam is like that. Really a calm, peaceful middle path. You rarely will see Islamic 'missionaries' in the same way that you will see Christian ones.

Since I believe in the Unity of God, and I accept that the world religions all come from God in their essence, I don't feel that those who aren't Muslim are somehow doomed. In fact, I don't even feel that about people who aren't 'religious' in any way. We all come from Allah whether we know it or not, and ultimately to Allah, we all must return. So I am not on a Crusade. That said, I do believe in doing '*Dawa*,' and that is spreading the message of Islam to those who are interested in hearing it. But again, I'm not pushing it down people's throats" (Muttaqi c. 2001).

Sean: "Our belief is not one that is against violence. Rather, it is one against injustice. If a wild animal were to attack someone and that person defended themselves, that violence would be legitimate. On the other hand, when violence is used by oppressors to dominate, and enslave innocent life (that being life which has done nothing to harm them)—it ceases to have justification, and there is a crime. …Concerning absolute morals. If one was to base that on always telling the truth, rather than always doing what was right—look what happens in this situation: a family is hiding some Jewish people from the Nazis. The Gestapo shows up at their house and asks, 'are you hiding any Jews?' Since this family bases their absolute morals on truth, they cannot lie, and so tell the Nazis about the people whom they have hidden. The Nazis then capture the Jews and send them to death camps. Do you think that family really did the moral thing? Obviously not! …We won't let this happen. We will buy guns to protect ourselves and our loved ones against attacks, and we will use whatever means necessary to stop similar attacks that are committed against this earth and all of her inhabitants. That is not a contradiction to what we believe in. Our violence is not done for personal gain—be it wealth, or power—nor is our violence done for the purposes of enslaving or oppressing. What we do is done in defense of this earth, and in defense of all that is righteous and good, against those who seek to destroy what little we have left, so they can live lives in excess, and in transgression of the natural order" (Boston Hardline 1995: 3).

Sean: "I am in complete support of all animal liberation activity, whether violent or not. This is not to say that I believe in indiscriminate acts of violence, aimed at the common person on the street. No one is arguing for that. But against the institutions built on exploitation and the individual merchants of death, most certainly my views have NOT changed on how they should be dealt with" (Muttaqi c. 2001).

Sean: "I believe that it is the duty of the spiritually attuned person to serve Allah first, and that such service requires that justice is fought for, and equality of all life strived for. The Qur'an teaches us not to fear adversity in the battle, nor weigh the moral imperative against the odds of losing. If something is wrong we must fight against it. I am not talking about forcing people into belief. For certainly there is to be no compulsion in faith. But we cannot sit by and let injustice prevail" (Muttaqi c. 2001).

Hardline Inner Circle: "Our next objective must be to increase the number of those within our ranks, by spreading our message of salvation through the written word; in magazines and leaflets, music, public speaking and inspiration by deed (direct action). What we have to remember in this matter, is that different approaches have to be taken depending on who one is trying to reach. It is imperative that everything we do be well thought out, and done in the manner which will best convince the individual or group we are addressing. ...In each city, in every country, where the Hardline supporter resides, it is imperative that they start a local Hardline chapter to further spread the message which will ensure the growth of this movement. ...This means centralizing ourselves at one location (or more if necessary, but in close proximity) in each city, county, state, or country where we are active—combining our efforts in order to achieve a greater productivity, as well as benefit from a sense of community. A collective house would be the first logical step when a group's numbers are relatively small. ...In addition to all of this, buying food in bulk, as well as having a year or roof top garden, will save a lot of money on food, which is just one more reason for such an endeavor. ...The revolution is one whose end we may not live to see. It is one whose final victory may come too late to help those who are suffering today—in the here and now. Therefore, we must ...also concentrate our energies on the present day... to alleviate the suffering we can; liberating those who can't wait for a far off victory, and dealing out justice to those who deserve it today. The autonomous direct action cells that we start today for the purpose of isolated cases of action (be it monkey wrenching/environmental direct action, animal liberation, abortion clinic bombings, or political terrorism, etc.) will be the same cells who may be involved in serious guerilla warfare and revolutionary struggle for years to come, so it is essential that the organization of such cells be done correctly and with caution. Agencies of the state are already monitoring this movement, and have phone taps in place. They may very well have plants (spies) pretending to be activists. Therefore, it is essential that anyone starting a direct action cell (group) thoroughly check out all potential members. They might not be a spy, but if they're caught, you'll want to know if you can count on them to remain loyal and not turn you in. ...When you determine the relative safety of bringing in a new member, it is best to put them through a test (an action to prove their loyalty and also one that you can hold over their heads should they ever turn on you)" (*Vanguard* 8, 1998: 13-15).

Hardline Inner Circle: "[Phase 2: Internal organization] The cell that operates the safe house and the one that operates the sanctuary should not participate in the action , so that if the safe house is busted they'll have no knowledge of the direct action itself and vice versa (if the direct action cell is caught, they won't know the details of the sanctuary).

...[Phase 3: Going underground] Once a core infrastructure has been established in the movement, and a number of years has passed where the ideology has become fairly widespread and smaller actions have occurred, it will become necessary to dissolve the outward structure of Hardline before we will be able to move on to the final revolutionary goals of the movement. ...Once one's level of actions becomes too great, they may have to fake a public break with the movement (pretending to sell out, or give up etc.). Sometimes this may even have to be believed by the rest of the movement. For in the end, the main priority must be to the revolution and not to our own personal feelings of popularity and acceptance.

Eventually however, it will become necessary for the whole movement to go underground and appear to have dissolved.

...As individuals we will merge into other groups that we have a personal affinity for (be they political or religious, human rights based or animal/earth liberation etc.) and influence them subtly. New members at this point will be drawn in from the ranks of the new groups we are associated with.

...Along with this we must start establishing our own businesses from which to gain the money necessary to fund our actions and build communities away from society that can offer us the freedom to further develop our skills, and ultimately create a self-sustaining environment that will offer us and our families a safe haven for when society's inevitable collapse begins and the final stage of our revolutionary struggle is put into effect.

[Phase 4: The revolution] The first step in this process will be two fold. On one level, we must merge with whatever dominant force in our respective societies poses a challenge to the status quo (in so long as it isn't a group that we are morally opposed to) and join that mass in unified opposition to the state. In conjunction with this, our own attacks must be aimed at weakening the system, causing civil discord, unrest, financial collapse etc. Anything that can further speed up the inevitable collapse of society.

Next, as their control begins to weaken and society erupts into chaos, with martial law imposed, and power decentralized from the national government to more regional levels of military and civil authority, we must start moving inch by inch, block by block, one city, one country at a time, until we take back this earth.

...In the cities, the war will be against ALL aspects of oppression—their outlets, center of organization and defense mechanisms. One block at a time we will shoot, bomb and burn all manifestations of their wickedness.

Their butcher shops, liquor stores, pornography shops, abortion clinics, banks and police stations will all be destroyed. Property will be expropriated and given to the poor and the rich ruling elite will be drug from their homes and shot. In each city block we will clear away their trash and disease and leave notice that any business which deals in, or exists by, exploitation will be destroyed.

Grocery stores, restaurants, shopping malls etc. will be continually attacked until they cease to serve or carry any products that contain animal products or alcohol, or are produced through animal, human, or environmental exploitation.

One block at a time we shall create 'Free Zones' where all merchants of death and oppression have been cleared out, either being replaced by responsible businesses (which are collective or family run) or bulldozed, making way for nature.

In areas which have not been liberated, consumers of death will become targets. Meat and dairy will be poisoned or said to have been contaminated, to dissuade the public from purchasing them. Roads will be destroyed. Police and government officials attacked. Chaos will run rampant in the streets until the wicked SUBMIT.

From the country we shall cut off their cities from each other, attacking their transportation vehicles, downing telephone and power lines and barricading roads. Meat and dairy farms will be destroyed. Dams will be blown up and barbed wire fences torn down. Nature will reclaim what is rightfully hers.

...In every country the indigenous populations will be given back complete access to land usage. Religious and ethnic minorities will be ensured protection, and given autonomous zones for self empowerment if they so choose. The poor will reclaim what for so long has been stolen from them—and humanity will slowly begin to heal the wounds wrought by the wicked devils that run our planet.

...This reclamation will continue until we are victorious worldwide. Viva La Revolucion!" (*Vanguard* 8, 1998: 15-19).

Total Revolution?

Straight edge and vegan straight edge

The question of straight edge might qualify as the most confusing aspect of Hardline but it also seems like one of the most irrelevant questions. Because of the confusion and the typical association of Hardline with straight edge by outsiders accompanied by Sean's repeated denials of having much to do with straight edge himself, it seems worth clarifying the record but I cannot say it matters whether or not Sean ever called himself straight edge or not. People toss around labels hither and thither and Sean has seemed eager to attribute the coining of the term "vegan straight edge" to Rat of Statement but, for the record, we can see that the first public use of "straight edge vegan" seemed to come from Sean—not Rat—even if Sean currently would prefer to distance himself from his previous use of the terms and his claim that he and his crew would identify as "vegan straight edge" (as he said in *Destroy Babylon* 2, 1995). To the extent the question seems relevant at all, I'd say Sean did try to articulate a vision of Hardline in which activists strove for sobriety not as an end unto itself but to organize more effectively for revolution. Due to that distinction, he attempted to establish a scene in which people, ironically enough, policed one another *less* than militant straight edgers did in terms of sobriety. Hardline had bigger soy-based "fish" to fry and nit-picking over whether an activist drank alcohol or not mattered less than whether or not they would help liberate animals.

CombatMarshmallow on Hardline's "Wikipedia-Talk" page: "This page needs to be merged with Straight Edge. Probably will be. It's the same thing. With a few different 'rules'" (Wikipedia, 17 July 2015).

Robert Wood (scholar on straight edge): "Hardline appears to be a sort of orthodox reconstruction of straightedge culture. In addition to the historical focus on drugs, this manifesto places hardline squarely amidst more recent issues such as animal rights, abortion, and environmental awareness. Since the early 1990s, mainstream media have been quick to characterize hardline as representative of straight edge culture in its entirety. In reality, however, hardline comprises only a minority of the straightedge subculture" (Wood 2006: 47).

Wikipedia: "Hardline grew out of straight edge. The original logo of the movement was an outline of a large 'X' (a sign associated with straightedge) with two crossed M16 rifles inside it. Muttaqi has said that he was first exposed to the idea of fusing veganism and abstinence from drugs by an English punk named Rat. Rat had allegedly coined the term 'vegan straight edge' by the mid-1980s. However, Rat was doing little to spread his ideology while Muttaqi was transforming and propagating it" (Wikipedia 2020).

Earliest instance of "vegan straight edge" phrase in Archive.org zine collection as of June 2021: 1992, page 31, in *Book Your Own Fuckin' Life* #1, submitted by George Tabbs regarding band Iron Prostate writing "Geriatric, imbecilic, metamucil, vegan, straight edge drunk punk."

Sean: "For clarification, I've never personally been 'straight edge'—at least in terms of defining myself as such" (Dorff 2018).

Sean: "The establishment of Hardline …had almost nothing to do with straight edge. That association was later and had more to do with the genesis from an ideology into movement" (Rettman 2019).

Sean: "Influenced in large part by the resurgent Straight Edge movement, they [Vegan Reich] released their infamous 'HARDLINE' EP in 1990, which detailed this new ideology and declared war against animal exploiters, earth rapers and apathetic drug users against a powerful backdrop of rage filled hardcore (that combined the speed of the Bad Brains, with the fury of Judge and Integrity and the melodic overtones of Bad Religion)" ([*Note: text purportedly citing* Crucial Truth*—a seemingly non-existent or super-tiny—zine, it seems likely written—and certainly approved—by Sean*]; Vegan Reich, back cover text on "Vanguard/The Wrath of God," 10" EP, Uprising Records, 1995).

Sean: "We have never considered ourselves a straight edge band" (Vegan Reich 2017b).

Sean: "Vegan Reich needs a straight edge, vegan bass player" (Sean/Vegan Reich, *Maximum Rocknroll* August 1989c).

Phil (Vegan Delegation): "We've said this and we're going to repeat it: that Hardline has nothing to do with the Straight Edge dogma, militant or not. We honestly don't care for it, nor do we want to be a part of it. Our ideology requires the advocates to be completely drug-free, yes, but never 'Straight Edge.' How ridiculous. The band Raid 'was' self labeled 'Straight Edge', though long before their *Words of War* EP came out on Hardline Records. They no longer label themselves SE and if anyone asks questions about the crossed M-16s with the 'X', then please take note that that was the original design. Sean (of HL Records and Vegan Reich), always hated the whole Straight Edge scene, and he's the designer (or founder) of our M-16's logo. So why would he want it to affiliate with the typified 'X' as a SE emblem? He didn't nor will he ever?" ("The Hardline," *Flipside* 77 1992: 18-20).

Sean: "Tired of songs about friendship and unity? We are! And that's why we're putting out 4 E.P.'s by these militant Straight Edge/Vegan bands that your parents won't even come close to liking… VEGAN REICH, WILL OF IRON, PRESSURE, CLASS WAR Out in early 1990! This is the new breed!" (First Hardline Records ad, *Maximum Rocknroll* December 1989).

Sean: "Out Now! From the Originators of Vegan Straight Edge: Vegan Reich" (Uprising Records ad in *Destroy Babylon* 1, 2, and 4 1995-1996; *Defense, Rescue and Survival* 1, 1995: 16, as well as in *SEAL* 3, 1996: 13).

Sean: "…we were all kind of associated with the straight edge scene but even then, they thought that we were all nuts. We were kind of just showing up being like loc'ed up bangers and shit. I mean it was like straight edge but we would come with like bandannas on and tripping people out. …Someone would be like 'well what are you' and we'd say 'vegan straight edge.' I know that people now want to think of it as something new but it's not, we all used to call ourselves that. You can ask Rat from Statement. I've got letters from him from like 1985 with vegan straight edge written with x's all over his letter. You know? Some of these kids weren't even born then" (*Destroy Babylon* 2, 1995: 49).

Rat (Statement): "Ha, well, if you read about Hardline on Wikipedia, it states that I came up with the term Vegan Straight Edge. I've recently spoken to Sean Muttaqi (Vegan Reich) about this, and he confirms that it was me! Despite being drug/alcohol free for well over 30 years, my memory is terrible. …the first vegan straightedge band? Well, possibly Vegan Reich, but, for myself, and I think Sean, I've never called myself Straight Edge. I was drink/drug free before I'd even heard the term Straight Edge so I didn't see the point labelling myself as such" (Mittens XVX 2017).

Monkeywrench: "MONKEYWRENCH as a band despises Ron Brotherhood. His oppressive actions against HARDLINE were justly dealt with by Jon STREET JUSTICE. …If he is such an authority on what straight edge is, then he should know that by eating meat he is showing absolutely no respect for his body or the rest of the planet. Isn't staying pure what straight edge is about anyway?" (Praxis 1991: 31).

Rat (Statememt): "[Q: According to the "Legend" you seem to have been involved in the genesis of the VeganStraightEdge(VSE) thing, can you share that story with us?...] A: i wouldn't say i was involved in that, as i've never really claimed to be sxe as i was drink and drug free before i even knew what sxe was. So why should i label myself something that was 'invented' after i was that way? i think vegan reich kind of gave vsxe the kick start and pushed it to what it is today, so that doesn't directly have anything to do with me, altho, when i first met and hung out with sean for a month, he wasnt drink and drug free himself.

i don't feel any responsibility at all, because like i've said, i dont think it had anything to do with me. i guess i'm only disappointed that many people flaked out on being vsxe, and more importantly gave up veganism. that really pisses me off and i hope these people get what they deserve, turning their backs on the reality of meat and dairy" (Bahr 2010).

Vic DiCara (Inside Out, 108, Shelter): "So there we were, master conductors orchestrating our spiritual revolution through music—'taking straightedge to the next level of purity'—when, suddenly, something unexpected happened. One day we were busy preaching vegetarianism to the straightedge kids. Then the next day we were busy defending against the straightedge kids preaching veganism to us. It seems straightedge leapfrogged over our heads in a militant stride to an even higher level of purity. Enter the 'Hardline Vegans.' Our reaction to it frustrated me. If we actually cared about animal rights, why would we get defensive when someone comes along even more into animal rights than us? We weren't so much into animal rights, it turns out, as we were into being the holiest dudes this side of CBGBs. So when some holier dudes came along who were even more 'cruelty free' than us... instead of applauding or supporting them, we tried to shoot them down. Of course, it wasn't entirely our fault. For the most part they were a bunch of asswipes even more 'holier than thou' than we were" (DiCara 2015).

Jon Street Justice (*Justice*): "...drug use isn't a problem in its own right but a symptom of deeper underlying issues. ...The war shouldn't be on illegal drugs—but the desire people have to use them—as well as the legal ones. The thing is, our society cultivates the said desire. To effectively win the 'drug war' we must restructure society and let people know that the only meaning one's life has isn't an unending quest for pleasure" (*Praxis* 1991: 13).

Declaration: "Therefore, a drug free, vegan lifestyle is an essential foundation with which the individual can develop and walk along the proper, natural path that leads to sobriety, respect for plant and animal lives and union with the earth" (*Declaration* c. 1995: 12).

Rat (Statement): "Even if they never actually listened to anarcho-punk music, many straight edge vegans today don't realize that anarcho-punk played a big part in them going vegan" (Rettman 2017: 265).

Jon Street Justice (*Justice*): "HARDLINE is most definitely a completely different philosophy, lifestyle, and movement from straight edge. Straight edge is just a youth subculture. HARDLINE is a movement—musically, politically, and otherwise" (Praxis 1991: 13).

Sean: "I don't think hardcore or any musical based 'scene' has ever had the power in and of itself to change the world. However, being a youth based movement, and an expression of the wants and desires of certain elements within the younger generation, I think it has potential to play a part in creating change, when the tone of the movement is set by those interested in social activism (as was the case in the early days of hardcore and punk)" (Muttaqi c. 2001).

Tim Rule (BBMA, Forward to Eden): "In short: without Hardline there would be no vegan straight edge metalcore" (Rule 2021).

Pennsylvania Hardline: "Education, as in the case of most other problems, is the answer to the elimination of controlled substance use. Direct action is always justified against the evil suppliers of drugs whether it be the local pusher, liquor store, or even [major beer brand]. Remember that EDUCATION is the answer for the person considering drugs, TREATMENT is the answer for the user, and ACTION is the answer for the supplier. Any of these three steps feeds our struggle to overcome this evil" (*Vanguard* 7, "Why Oppose Drug Use?" 1996: 21).

Sean: "One of the problems that I see with vegan straight edge is that it is such a narrow issue. It is one of the things that HardLine is trying to go beyond. And maybe that's where HardLine failed because it seems that with some people all that HardLine is is vegan straight edge with a tougher image. I see a problem when you go to a show and you see these kids and it seems that that is the extent of their world view. They can make all of these radical statements about killing drug dealers or whatever, and that's all valid, I've said the same things in my life. But it's easy to talk like that in a little sheltered scene where no one can challenge you. ...that image of going around like you are the hardest person in the scene, but it's not reality. If you go into the heart of the ghetto and start talking like that, no one is even going to know what you are talking about. And if you just think that you are so hard then you're just going to get shot. It's funny 'cause most of the old scene here is like cholos and if you went around trying to fuck with someone for drinking a beer then you're just going to get stabbed. So I think it's a positive step for someone to be vegan and straight edge, but I would just like to see them have a deeper political understanding, and more of a realistic approach to the things that surround them. Those things are revolutionary but those things in themselves aren't going to make you a revolutionary" (*Destroy Babylon* 2, 1995: 42).

Fabio (Absence, Destroy Babylon): "Free love is a concept I am fascinated by and I won't tolerate any stupid conservative blinded white trash judgement on this. Straight edge was also conceived in my eyes within a conservative kind of life vision which overlooked the boundaries that Mother Culture has built around us. I think spirituality must help you realize who you are and what you stand for and should help you clear your head, fill your heart, clench your fists and fight. Everything leads to the realization that we are nothing and everything at the same time so we must pay respect to mother nature and all so called creation and feel as One with it, and this is one of the main reasons why I think it so important for us in western countries to embrace a vegan cruelty free lifestyle for example. As I said earlier, sometimes some people just focus on their own well-being and chant their whole life away and that is somehow kind of selfish in my eyes. I know I would never just focus on myself as I witness corruption and evil all around me every day and I don't want to escape reality. I can't escape reality. I want to look within myself yes, but I want to find the strength to stand up and fight against those who step on our brain every day. And this is why I call myself straight edge. This is the true reason" (Sparks of Dissent 2010c).

Steve Lovett (Raid): "We consider ourselves straight edge in the strictest sense, however we label ourselves hardline" (Edge 1990: 4).

Sean: "One can be a Muslim and still be a part of various *tariqas* or 'paths' as long as they don't conflict with the basic understanding that Allah is One. I mean, even though the message of Islam is universalism, if one is living in an occupied country, it would be in line with Islam's principles of Justice to be a part of a 'nationalist' movement to throw the oppressors out. Likewise, one could be a part of a martial arts society, and similarly, 'Straight Edge' is a path that one can be a part of while being a Muslim. ...One should not elevate western notions of morality above their religious background. By this, I mean, the notion of abstinence and purity runs through every culture and religion. However, within many of these same spiritual paths, are also certain beliefs that may on the external level seem to conflict with the western notion of purity or morality. For instance, many Native American Indians, who are absolutely against drug use, do use peyote in their spiritual ceremonies. Some Muslim holy men smoke a pipe. What one shouldn't do, is make the mistake of thinking that the 'Straight Edge' perception of reality and of right and wrong, is automatically superior to the ancient spiritual traditions' perception of such things" (Muttaqi c. 2001)

Sean: "Too much emphasis is placed on being straight edge for straight edge's sake. Having a clear mind, free of intoxication etc. only has value, and serves a purpose if one uses that heightened awareness and strength in a quest for something greater—be it animal liberation, class struggle or environmental action" (Boston Hardline 1995: 11).

Ryan: "[Hardball] was a reaction to the outright hatred, derision and bullying we received from punks and metalheads over our positive straight edge message. I had read about bands like Confront and Die Hard in *MRR* and then when I heard Judge, I was quick to adopt a more militant attitude of self-defense and outspoken pride. The metal, goth rock and darker punk I had been into before hardcore sort of came back to the fore for me when Dwid Hellion sent me the first Integrity demo. I realized there was a way to have my cake and eat it too with all of that. I saw the first ad for Hardline Records in *MRR* and struck up a friendship via snail mail and long distance phone calls with Sean Muttaqi, aka Sean Vegan Reich. Dwid and Sean remain two of my oldest friends and each had a significant influence on me in different ways" (Dorff 2016).

Steve Lovett (Raid): "Basically, Sean of Vegan Reich and I created the philosophy of the movement. As far as I'm concerned, the movement did not exist before the first three Hardline Records releases by Vegan Reich, Statement, and Raid. ...Hardline was essentially militant straight edge with an emphasis on radical veganism and environmentalism. Direct action was our chosen path to accomplish our goals. Hardline to me was built on the building block of straight edge" (Rettman 2017: 268).

Sean: "Unfortunately, other streams of thought came to dominate the general culture of straight edge—namely a rigid mind-set, and a sort of general conservatism. ...I'm still torn about hardline's association with straight edge" (Rettman 2017: 276).

Sean: "I am in support of [marijuana's] legalization. However, it must be said that very often it is in fact legal and many are just trying to use this issue as an area to push forward other agendas concerning marijuana. …And as far as marijuana goes, it is so hard to say how the modern west should deal with it. Many third and second world countries have a very healthy relationship so to speak with marijuana, very often using it for food, medicine, (even to relax with) etc. But I don't know if people in the west can handle that, as they don't have the cultural background of using it outside the realm of 'partying' etc. that seems to be the standard in the west. It is rather strange to make a plant in and of itself illegal" (Muttaqi c. 2001).

Hardline Inner Circle: "…also beware of the subtle addictions of junk food, video games and all unnatural things that pollute the body and distract us from our true purpose" (*Vanguard* 8, 1998: 11).

Steve Lovett (Raid): "I think we were the first vegan straight edge band" (xYosefx 2010).

Apostasy/Leaving Hardline

For all the talk here about sectarianism, Hardline organized as a general concept with a correspondingly sloppy organization. It couldn't organize in a genuine anarchist fashion because individual Hardliners or chapters (except perhaps an editor of *Vanguard*) had no "right" or position of autonomous power to make any innovations to its rather comprehensive doctrine. Yet, nor could Hardline organize in the fashion of a conventional sect because Sean attempted to steer the vehicle from the backseat and, once it really got on the road, he jumped out and let others take over the responsibility (without corresponding authority). Even during his brief period of claiming Hardline, Sean's *de facto* leadership could only do but so much. It couldn't make Hardliners at the first gathering in 1991 care any more about activism than music than they actually did. It couldn't police every single person who claimed Hardline in every city. It couldn't rein in the arbitrary violence by some people in Salt Lake City or even necessarily know which ones did or did not really identify as Hardline. It couldn't even edit every issue of *Vanguard*. By the time Sean attempted to impose a centralized order upon Hardline in 1998, it had already largely waned so its death knell at his behest a year later probably put it out of its tortured misery. Subsequently, with all the confusion regarding Hardline identity, it did not take much to join Hardline nor to leave it. Aside from putting out Hardline literature or a band, the most a person could do publically seems like wearing a t-shirt, telling people you identify as Hardline, or, at best, getting a Hardline tattoo. Indeed, that ink on some people's skin may prove the most long-lasting aspect of Hardline. Yet, privately, the very nature of clandestine direct actions meant that, unless someone got arrested, only a very small inner circle might ever know about which Hardliners engaged in animal/Earth liberation and which ones did not. Combine that with a scene that espoused (in *Vanguard* 8) a form of *taqiyya* in which members merely pretend to have left the community, and it makes for a very murky territory regarding who knows who "really" identifies as Hardline and who doesn't. Finally, in a scene in which the founder explicitly bailed (accompanied by other key figures in the same time period), how can those who remain (especially those who don't have key insider information) muster the justification to stay?

Sean: "...when living an ideology of action poses the risk of imprisonment, even the safety of that individual's life; when society is constantly tempting that individual with promises of acceptance, comfort and stability—it is easy to see, how easy it would for some to give up on their beliefs, give in and submit—choosing happiness (false though it may be) over a life of struggle. But no one ever said walking the Hard Line would be easy. No one should have thought it would be. Hardline is a hard way of life. It has to be. These times necessitate it. Never before has brutality reached such a level, on such as mass scale—and never before has the fate of ALL life been in such peril" (*Vanguard* 1, 1992: 7).

Sean: "I feel I owe you all an explanation as to why ...my active involvement within the Hardline movement is over for the time being. Ten years ago I began my journey along the road of resistance, not as a spokesman for a movement, nor as a singer in a band, but as a nameless face—be it in a crowd of demonstrators or alone doing action that can't be mentioned. That is where I was most content. The unknown revolutionary. ...But even with the success and the great fortune [of Hardline] there are still failures in those years. Relationships I let slide. Goals I did not pursue. Loved ones taken for granted—always too busy with 'the struggle.' Right or wrong, these things always tear at me—and it has come time for me to deal with them. My personal life has been on hold for ten years and until I deal with myself I will no longer be able to effectively deal with others. In retrospect, if I had been more balanced, it would not have gotten to this point where I have to choose one or the other, but then again, if I wasn't so focused and all consumed I would have never accomplished as much for the struggle in those years. So there are no regrets. Only an understanding that I've reached a point in my life where my involvement in the revolution needs to go back to that of being just a nameless face …to pursue my music and martial arts studies and the personal peace and spiritual harmony that I'm going to need if I plan on being around for another ten years of resistance" (*Vanguard* #1+2, 1993: 9).

Sean: "The biggest reason for leaving was that I felt conflicted because during hardline and with the problems we used to face I felt there was a big cultural disconnect between what a lot of the white, suburban hardcore kids were interested in and my own background. …Also, hardline in its very early days had people from different ethnic backgrounds who were influenced by different things, but as it went on, it clearly became more of what people were criticizing it for—a white, male group of kids who were into veganism, with a couple of extra things thrown in there almost for political points. For me, personally, I just couldn't take it anymore. So, Vegan Reich broke up, I left hardline, and I just started playing reggae and removed myself from hardcore for a while" (Peterson 2009: 489).

Sean "…in regards to the specifics of Hardline's emergence as a sub-scene within Straight Edge, I feel a little bitter-sweet about it. On the one hand, there's no denying that Straight Edge was the scene where Hardline really took off. On the other hand, I think it was precisely it residing in that milieu than caused it to be misunderstood, and part of the reason for my disbanding Vegan Reich in 1992 and leaving Hardline as well" (Rettman 2019).

Sean: "I myself left the movement precisely because I wanted to live a far less rigid lifestyle (and although I remained vegan and drug free, I wanted to casually date, travel, and enjoy life). It was never meant to be a path for everyone, nor even a permanent one for those involved. Just a militant revolutionary group fanatically focused entirely on the struggle" (Muttaqi 2021).

Sean: "For those within our ranks, the ones who knew yet turned away, betraying truth for fantasy, and the easy life that brings… You can't hide from reality and pretend that life's but a game. But while you're looking elsewhere, it will hit you like a train. …Apostasy, there's no greater crime. You're first on JAH list. This is your judgment day" (Lyrics to Vegan Reich's "Letter to Judas," *The Wrath of God* EP, 1992).

Dave Agranoff: "Sell-outs are not worthy of life" ("40 Pieces of Silver," *Defense, Rescue and Survival* 3, 1995: 13).

Sean: "Vegan Reich continued on for maybe a year after our final tour, which had numerous dates canceled due to phoned-in threats or complaints to the promoters and clubs. We were finding it harder and harder to get booked at hardcore or punk shows due to our notoriety. ...We finally made the decision to put the band identity to rest" (Rettman 2017: 274-275).

Sean: "There was a lot of F.B.I. surveillance and harassment and it got to the point where it became nearly impossible to keep the band going" (Peterson 2009: 489).

Brian Peterson: "Muttaqi found himself nearly powerless to participate in any type of direct action due to F.B.I. surveillance" (Peterson 2009: 482).

Sean: "Under constant surveillance by the FBI, direct action had become almost impossible for Vegan Reich to participate in, and as a band their militant message had gotten them blacklisted from clubs, their tours canceled and their ads banned from numerous magazines. Frustrated by their inability to carry on as either effective activists or as a functioning band, Vegan Reich called it a day after their 1992 release "THE WRATH OF GOD" ([*Note: text purportedly citing* Crucial Truth*—a seemingly non-existent or super-tiny—zine; it seems likely written—and certainly approved—by Sean*]; Vegan Reich, back cover text on "Vanguard/The Wrath of God," 10" EP, Uprising Records, 1995).

Micah: "The problem appears to me to be the fact that Raid and Vegan Reich (Former HardLine spokesbands) lyrics were taken too literally. People started planning for the 'storm' to come and sweep all the unrighteous away. They saw the Vegan Revolution as a specific date that all HardLiners should have marked on their calendars, when we should take up arms and stand on one side while the vivisectors, abortionists, factory and fur farmers and huntsmen stood on the other. Thus they planned for things on that dreamlike of a scale, attempting to recruit as many 'soldiers' as possible despite their level of commitment. However, that is not the way things will be played, they were never intended to be. Old HardLiners simply got delusions of grandeur as they saw so many join in such a short amount of time.

...When those who were in it, for selfish and material reasons, left then many of those envisioning a huge HardLine army became overwhelmed with hopelessness and burnt-out" (Collins, "Hardline Update," *Destroy Babylon* 1, 1995: 4).

Steve Lovett (Raid) in interview by Ryan about why he left: "A lot of it had to do with how I saw what the Hardline structure was, how, you know, some of my beliefs started to stray away from the original Hardline … I guess you could say 'doctrine.' For myself, because Hardline was a set thing, I couldn't try to change it just because my beliefs differed, you know? I wasn't gonna be, still trying to be on the bandwagon with different beliefs. So now I feel a lot more comfortable in the fact that I don't have to put a title on myself. People know I'm vegan. …I mean, Hardline, was something that existed before me and Sean sat down and talked about it. *Ryan: Exactly.* Steve: I'm not necessarily saying that Hardline is some mystical thing that's always existed. *Ryan: Oh. I thought you were (laughs).* Steve: No, I'm saying that pretty much I had all my beliefs and opinions before we even came up with this name 'Hardline.' …But Hardline sort of had a bad image and …some of my beliefs started to change. I just didn't feel the need to stick on to a name that wasn't me. Now, I don't have any problem talking about Hardline, it's not something that I've got any shame of because of the bad stigma that Hardline does have. I'm not saying that would have any reason to do with the reason why I initially stopped being Hardline. I remember one of the dudes in my band before I stopped saying I was Hardline or whatever, said that he wasn't really, I mean he all has the same beliefs—he said he's not going to be calling himself Hardline anymore and I had such a hard time accepting that 'cause I'm like, you know, 'why?' He said those exact same reasons that people turn it off too quick. I mean like *Maximum Rocknroll* …I mean (laughs). …*Ryan: Just out of curiosity, how do you feel about the Hardline stances on homosexuality and abortion?* Steve: Homosexuality, the way I look at it is—I don't necessarily want it around me. But I mean, I work with lesbians and homosexuals. …I had a lot of preconceived notions about gays originally too. …Abortion, I think idealistically I am against it. I believe that is, a fetus is a living thing. Being vegan naturally…*Ryan: You have to be consistent.* Steve: Right. However, you know also I know a lot of women a lot of girls whatever, I understand a lot of reasons why people would want to have abortions and as much as I think they're bullshit, you know, what can I do?" (*Vanguard* 5, 1993: 5-6, 9).

Sean: "…my involvement with hardline— I didn't regret having started it or having done it, but I found myself not happy with where it was going. We started hearing reports of actual right-wing people in Europe who were interested in us. It had started out as a fairly diverse group of people, but it became more and more a very white, middle-class, right-leaning type of thing. The same thing had happened to straightedge" (Sanneh 2013).

Sean: "I should clarify that I ceased identifying as Hardline, and left the movement in 1993 (after a three year involvement)" (Muttaqi 2021).

Sean: "The last official Hardline publication was *Vanguard* 8—the *Vanguard* which officially ended the 'movement' in the late 90s (in terms of an organizational structure etc)" (Muttaqi 2021).

Sean: "First things first. It's time for consolidation and centralization. In the early stages of Hardline this was not necessary, as all parties involved were in close contact and the various chapters were growing at the same time—forming in a unified manner.

...In addition most of the early Hardline literature was written by a select inner circle, assuring quality control and further uniformity of message. As more chapters have taken on the task of producing literature themselves, so too has the risk increased of poorly written, and/or inaccurate material being released.

If we do not act now to ensure the uniformity of thought and action, the majority we have will begin to erode, and our movement will be overrun with infiltrators, cowards, and reformists—our message being reduced to a pale imitation, if not an outright contradiction to its original glory.

Therefore, we are implementing an organizational structure that will ensure the survival and continuity of the Hardline—both in thought and in deed. This shall henceforth be referred to as the Hardline Central Committee (HCC).

All chapters must immediately report to the HCC in order to register their current status (operational or non-operational) as well as clarify their positions. Any group we do not hear from, or those who contact us but do not fall within Hardline's guidelines of belief and action will be terminated.

Once every six months we will publish an active list of Hardline chapters. Only those groups appearing on this list are to be considered valid and legitimate chapters. ...This issue of *Vanguard* represents a re-emerging of the Real" (*Vanguard* 8 aka "the last official Hardline publication," 1998).

Wikipedia: "In mid-1998 the subculture experienced a massive internal upheaval as Indianapolis Hardline member David Agranoff's attempts to weaken Hardline were sidelined by Boston Hardline. *Vanguard* number eight announced the reorganization of the movement under the authority of the newly created Hardline Central Committee (HCC) and castigated Agranoff and his comrades for softening the network's ideology through their refinement and development of it. This proved a wise decision as Agranoff later became a police informer. Chapters were instructed to report to the Committee for evaluation and were told in no uncertain terms that they would not be recognized as cells until they submitted to this review. Also in the issue was a document about the stages through which the Hardline revolution would progress which was presented as being from 1990, but had never before been seen and was suspiciously contemporary feeling" (Wikipedia 2020).

Steve Lovett (Raid): "I was tired of all the Hardline dogma and rules. Some kids had this holier than thou attitude, like I'm more Hardline then you because I don't eat refined sugar or processed wheat. In addition, I had some questions/issues about some key components of Hardline, including straight edge, abortion and Hardline's hatred of gays. Hardline was becoming a totalitarian movement. I was unhappy with the extremes and had enough. … I have mixed feelings about abortion, but really think it should be a personal choice. Is a two week old embryo a human being? Sure it has the potential to become one, but the nervous system is not even developed at that point. Another change is I don't care about someone's sexuality. I think there was a lot of homophobia in the scene. …To be honest Hardline taught me a lot of lessons regarding extremism. If you think eating meat is evil, then what does that make the people who eat meat? Keep in mind, this is where Hardline end up in my perspective, 'These things are evil and those people who engage in these activities are evil and we will destroy this behavior or lifestyle that we don't' approve of. You see the same mentality across the morality spectrum, be it evangelical Christians or fundamentalist Muslims. I fell into that trap and began to act out of hate instead of love. While both emotions are necessary, acting out of hate is self destructive" (xYosefx 2010).

Steve Lovett (Raid): "I try to have no regrets, but there were many ugly parts to the hardline scene. Speaking as someone who helped develop it, I feel that we should have kept the radical environmental and animal rights ideas and dropped the more conservative social issues. Clearly the conservative moral outlook damaged hardline's rep in the music scene, and was unnecessarily exclusive" (Rettman 2017: 275).

Ryan Downey (Hardball, Burn it Down, *Vanguard*): "March 1991: Ryan + Keith go Hardline. April-June 1991: Keith is no longer Hardline, or even straight edge" (Downey 2007).

Ryan: "Sorry Steve, but for us, Hardline never was a chapter of our teen years. It's who we are" (*Vanguard* #5, 1993: 4).

Matt, JP, and Ryan (Memphis and Indianapolis Hardline): "NO COMPROMISE WILL BE ACCEPTED ANY LONGER. From the outside,

NOR from our own members. We have laid out the plan. Be sure you are truly willing to take part" (*Vanguard* 1+2 double issue 1993: 9).

Ryan: "I left hardline not long after Sean Muttaqi had left it behind, mostly for the same reasons" (Rettman 2017: 274).

Ryan: "...it was, for a short time, a viable movement I'd say until about 1993

When it disintegrated and most of us became disillusioned with what seemed like unrealistic goals and too rigid of a stance about more than a few issues that did not seem to adequately address reality" (Peterson 2009: 95).

Sean: "For there are traitors in our midst. Devils who seek to destroy all that we have built. Ever so subtly these hypocrites have taken on positions of power, slowly yet methodically assuming roles of leadership, though they neither have the quality nor character to lead us anywhere but down. ...So the time has come for those of us in the majority, those who are true to the Real, the ones who have not strayed from the Path (whether still within Hardline, or one of the many who have left or have been 'forced' out by the current state of affairs) to take a stand against these corruptors of faith. For there can only be one way within Hardline. And in truth, and all certainty—that way can never be the way of the transgressor" (*Vanguard* 8, 1998).

Micah: "Sean and i orchestrated the closing of Hardline. i have [a] 10 page letter from him from 98 where he asked me repeatedly to jump back in and promote the Ahl-i Allah with him and 'phase out' Hardline. Why was i the one to front this? Because people had accused him of doing as much when he wrote *Vanguard* 8 (with a couple of others, though i was NOT claiming Hardline at the time), and they would have all INSTANTLY jumped on him doing this and tried to regain control of what he himself wanted to dissolve. Why did he want to dissolve it? Because like it or not, BELIEVE it or not, he didn't (and doesn't), believe most of the stuff he wrote in *Vanguard* #1. He had left Hardline 92 and only came back when he didn't like the fact that it never took on the ethnic flavor that he had desired for it (leaning more towards the Weathermen influence and less towards that of MOVE)" (MBD 2006).

Sean: "As the major voice representing both hardline and vegan straight edge at that time, we began coming under ever increasing scrutiny and attack for the rising incidents of direct action and occasional violence which were coming from these two camps. Banned throughout Babylon, monitored by the agents of Dajjal [false messiah], it soon became evident that it was impossible for us to continue on as both activists and spokesmen for militant action. Not willing to abandon our roles as revolutionaries, it became clear that the time had come to remove ourselves from the public eye. So began our journey into occultation" (Vegan Reich, *Jihad*, 1999).

Alex (Boston Hardline): "[Q: After clearing up your legal situation, you helped found and organize the New Eden Project. Tell me about this—the general premise, goals, and so on…] A: The point of New Eden Project was to create a Hardline community in Hawaii. Being in the tropics allowed us to live both closer to nature and more sustainably. We planned to start a rural homesteading community and training complex. We intended the New Eden Project to serve as a base for the Hardline movement. We also wanted to increase the already large vegan population on the island of Maui into a critical mass. By doing this, we could control the island. [Q: What caused the eventual disbanding of the NEP?] A: Lack of money, but underneath that, the reason is many of the members were undisciplined" (Anonymous 2004).

Sean: "…the movement itself was intentionally disbanded in 1999 (with our support and encouragement)" (Vegan Reich 2017b).

Origins

Origins make for difficult study. When does *anything* really begin? What factors come into play to make anything happen? What do the strands of influence and power look like as a group changes, how does a group's image develop, and how do later stories write and re-write a group's (or person's) purported genesis? We don't have enough data here to really answer questions but we can present what people-who-would-probably-know have said.

Sean: "I was in an Oi! Band in the early '80s, and as a very young kid, in a rock band in the late 70s doing cover songs. …I was a very young skater in the late '70s, hanging out with mostly older kids. You couldn't avoid hearing punk at that time. But it hadn't clicked with me yet as a scene. I was just into smoking pot and listening to whatever the older kids were playing—Sabbath, Cheap Trick, Marley—with some punk worked in. Mostly Sex Pistols, and The Clash, etc. But I was too young to really connect to any scene at that point. It wasn't until '81 when I got exposed to the local scene, that I actually became a punk, shaved my head, got some combat boots, etc." (Rettman 2019).

Sean: "[*Q: What does the name mean?*] A: …what [Vegan Reich] means for all you pathetic drug, dairy, and meat addicts—is that since you don't have the intelligence and compassion to live your life without fuckin' up the earth and all its other more valid life forms—the REICH will rule over you with an iron fist to stamp out ignorance forever" (Sean/Vegan Reich 1989a).

Sean: "[*Q: When exactly did you get involved with activism in general and when did concerns arise about the animals and the environment?*] A: …God, it's going back so far… Well, as a kid I was always surrounded by political and social issues because my parents were involved with that. As far as actually taking a personal step like going to protests and things of that nature, probably 1982. It started off as a kid going to the whole nuclear disarmament marches, different things like that, and ditching school. …During that time, even as a kid, I was always into animals and environmental things, but I didn't really know that other people thought about that type of thing too. …At first I started out getting involved with the human issues like 'no nukes' and then environmental things and I finally got into the animal lib thing probably in early '83, like turning vegetarian, but I started to get really serious about things around mid '84. [*Q: How old were you then?*] A: Fifteen" (*Destroy Babylon* 2, "Captive Nation Rising interview," 1995: 45).

Sean: "I was looking for people to start a militant animal liberation band. …We were causing a lot of controversy in the anarchist community, pointing out the contradiction of people demanding freedom for humans and oppressing animals at the same time. People started jokingly referring to us as vegan fascists, so that's where the name came from. The notion was, if you're going to call us Vegan Fascists, we're going to call ourselves Vegan Reich" (Sanneh 2013).

Sean: "The name Vegan Reich came into being as a sardonic reappropriation of the pejorative term 'vegan fascists' being leveled against us (as anarchist animal rights activists) by some members of the then American anarchist movement (which saw no place for the inclusion of animals into their notions of equality and social justice, and consequently felt it was 'fascistic' for any group to argue against their 'right' to use animals for food and clothing). Before there was a band, a group of us took to using the name Vegan Reich as a way of shoving our militant animal liberationist and abolitionist views in their faces" (Vegan Reich 2017b).

Ryan: [At the first Hardline gathering in 1991] "We bought nonalcoholic 'near beers' from the nearby grocery store and drank them in front of the venue. We wanted to elicit a reaction, and we did. I suppose the crowd saw it as further evidence of our incongruent white trash personas. To us, we were sending a message that hardline was supposed to be a true movement, a radical cause, not a social club based on our lifestyle choices. It was shortsighted and silly of us. We did it to be outcasts among the outcasts, in the same spirit as putting *Reich* next to the word *Vegan*, for militant shock value" (Rettman 2017: 274).

Rat (Statement): "[Regarding the first Hardline gathering and a live Statement performance in 1991]: That did nearly happen at the 1st Hardline gathering in Memphis in, hmm 1991? I was doing vocals, Chad from Raid on guitar, Mark from Raid on bass and Ray from Vegan Reich on drums. We rehearsed at the HL house in Memphis but never went through with the show. Vegan Reich didn't play either. Sean was pissed off that too many people seemed more concerned with seeing the bands than partaking in the gathering itself. So we headed back to California" (*Bound By Modern Age* 2, 2015a: 17).

Jon Street Justice (*Justice*): "Well, it seems like ages ago that Sean (VEGAN REICH and HARDLINE rec.) and I started getting real sick of the whole straight edge scene. It just didn't seem to be going anywhere. Sean decided to start a label that was what a label should [be]—a label with a higher sense of what was up and a commitment to fight against the many evils in our world" (*Praxis* 1991: 10).

Sean: "Overnight a [Hardline] movement was born and across the globe people were becoming straight edge vegans and direct action was occurring more than it ever had" (Vegan Reich, back cover text on "Vanguard/The Wrath of God," 10" EP, Uprising Records, 1995).

Sean: "At our inception, we were not a straight edge or drug free band, but over time as we saw more activists succumb to alcoholism and drug addiction, we embraced a strict drug free lifestyle. During this phase, our members were also exploring various spiritual paths, from Taoism and Buddhism to Eastern Orthodoxy, Islam, and Rastafarianism. Those influences led us to a strictly ascetic lifestyle, during which time we wrote and released the *Hardline* EP (that in turn gave birth to the Hardline movement, essentially a modern day monastic order)" (Vegan Reich 2017b).

Sean: "In terms of markers in time, where I can see—at least from my own perspective—to have progressed from one mode to another—the following things were pretty formative moments of coming into my own, apart from any cultural or political aspects of my upbringing—things that would definitely lead up to Hardline. As mentioned before, Flux Of Pink Indians' influence on becoming vegetarian; Conflict in regards to a more militant approach to animal liberation; Rudimentary Peni's influence to not do drugs. And my friend Rat from England is a great motivator to stop drinking. As far as individual events that were some type of catalyst that started the process of physically forming something new from a lifetime of influences and experiences—I can definitely say that process began at the 1986 Anarchist gathering. It was the starting point of our small group's discontent within the Anarchist movement over the issue of animal liberation. Two years later, the excessive behavior we witnessed at the 1988 Toronto Anarchist gathering was the nail in the coffin and the realization that we needed to form some new construct to work within. That was essentially the start of the process, and within the next few months, Hardline was born" (Rettman 2019).

Sean: "I had spent most of the 80s involved with the anarchist movement - however tensions were forming between our particular crew which leaned heavily towards a Class War approach / anarcho-syndicalism etc—and currents that were of a more individualist nature. Concurrent to that, was our rising militancy with regards to animal rights and veganism, that was also causing friction with otherwise likeminded anarcho-syndicalist types (something which played out at the 1986 Chicago anarchist gathering where a huge argument and protest arose regarding meat being catered for the event)" (Muttaqi 2021).

Sean: "By 1988, many of our old friends from the movement had either died or been incapacitated by drug abuse or alcoholism—which led us to swear off such usage ourselves" (Muttaqi 2021).

Sean: "The concept or ideology of hardline was really a cumulative process that happened over many years, and honestly had almost nothing to do with straight edge" (Rettman 2017: 266).

"Religion" and "cults"

Scholars have not reached a consensus on the meanings of "religion" or "cult" and their working definitions can vary widely. So whatever people mean when they call Hardline a "religion" or a "cult" I cannot say. But, as one reads the following quotes, one can clearly see that some of the attributes typically ascribed to "religion" (such as comprehensive belief system) or "cult" (such as fanaticism or charismatic leader) appear quite distinctly in relation to Hardline. [*Note: In 2006, Micah published a book entitled* "Biogenesis: The Creation of Man by an Angelic Species" *advertised via the Taliyah site in 2004. An online review, perhaps written by Micah, wrote:* "In this book, the author seeks to explain exactly what and who the Elohim are and the possible Reptilian-Angelic connection they have to humanity. The author essentially explores the history of the Serpent religion/culture in various traditions around the world, and its connection to the extraterrestial beings known as the Reptilians who may have been the 'Angels' from pre-biblical times to the era of Quranic revelation." *Whether Micah's personal theories or Sean's behind-the-scenes intrigues, definitive accounts of such rabbit-holes-within-rabbit-holes will likely remain elusive. As with any group that emphasizes esotericism and secrecy, outsider descriptions and assessments will invariably fall short of the "whole picture." Whether one feels it worth to effort to dig far enough into any given group to find it remains up to each person to decide. This section will hopefully provide material to facilitate that.*]

Steve Lovett: "[*Q: What are your religious views, as a person and a band?*] RAID does not advocate any particular religion. Several members in the band are traditional Christians and the others are spiritual. RAID believes in one God and one goal. ...There is a meaning and purpose for our life. The atheist is living in a material, physical world of decay. For this he or she will suffer" (Edge 1990: 4).

A Wikipedian on Hardline's "Wikipedia-Talk" page: "This article is **not** within the scope of Wiki Project Religion, because Hardline is **not** a religion" (Wikipedia 2020).

Dave Agranoff (*Defense, Rescue and Survival*, *Vanguard*): "The first issue of *Vanguard* is the Bible of a Hardliner's life. Adherents to the Hardline should know its text well" (*Forward to Eden: A Guide to Hardline Viewpoints*, c. 1995: 1).

Finn McKenty aka "Sergeant D": "Hardline was a combination of deep ecology, survivalist culture, and various religions cobbled together that was way, way more than just abstaining from drugs. Hardline …had a strong religious/spiritual component, which initially included Rastas, Christians, and Buddhists but then took a turn toward Islam in the late 90s. If you're thinking 'what a fucking weird combination of super wacky leftist shit and religious fundamentalism,' you basically hit the nail on the head! It more or less boiled down to a belief in using violence to defend 'natural order,' and (you guessed it) *they* were the ones who got to define what was and was not 'natural.'" (Stuff you Will Hate, 2014.).

Tim Rule (Forward to Eden, BBMA records): "[*Regarding the name Forward to Eden]* It's based on an old Hardline zine which basically holds (and explains) the manifesto. So, no... it has nothing to do with any religious beliefs. In this case, Eden is more a kind of condition than a place. Eden is the state of Veganocracy" (Forward to Eden, "Fight For A New World / The Epitome Of Humanity," forwardtoeden.bandcamp.com, 2015).

Sean: "If one defines 'religion' as 'anything done or followed with reverence or devotion' (as it is described in Webster's English dictionary) then certainly hardcore, and straight edge both can be seen as being a religion to some as it is. As to if there's a connection then between this 'religion' or 'path' of 'straight edge' and 'hardcore' and that of the 'REVEALED RELIGIONS', I would say this: Many of the people that are involved in Hardcore, Punk, Straight Edge, etc. are very often striving for knowledge. They are people who have broken away from the confines of the status quo, of what society wants them to be and have decided upon their own path. In this manner, I think that such individuals have a lot in common with those who broke away from the status quo of their societies and followed the path of the Prophets, and Saints of their times. Unfortunately, in modern times, 'Religion' has become so corrupted by evil dishonest people speaking in the name of God, that many really good people who seek to separate themselves from the corrupt ways of their society, also close themselves off to a spiritual life, as they see it as tied up with the outward forms of corrupted religion. So a sad situation has arisen. Those who at one time would have been voicing their protest in a manner that included not only political and social knowledge, but also spiritual enlightenment, are now being shaped by their society into individuals who are denied knowledge of their true selves, and thus in their rejection of all that is bad, also throw out much of what is good. Such is the case with many in the Hardcore, Punk and Straight Edge scenes. There is of course a common bond between the positive side of these movements and the inherent truth present in all Religions and Faiths. But the question is, who will see it?" (Muttaqi c. 2001).

Hardline Inner Circle: "It is imperative that we study all matters of social/political/cultural and spiritual relevance. For our movement is the culmination and synthesis of all movements and faiths that have come before us in the struggle for justice. We must understand the root causes of evil as well as be well-rooted in the historical struggles against that evil (whose legacy we carry on)" (*Vanguard* 8, 1998: 11).

Sean: "Being frustrated with the state of things, we began looking elsewhere for inspiration. Having been involved in the Big Mountain protests, many of us were exploring Native and Chicano Spirituality, Rastafarianism, Eastern Orthodoxy, Taoism, Islam etc. Likewise, groups like MOVE, SLA, NOI etc had been an influence as well" (Muttaqi 2021).

Sean: "I would say that I have had a fascination with both orthodoxy and heterodoxy at the same time. I'm always interested in studying stuff that's on the fringes of different religious currents. I love the Boxer Rebellion and all these Kung Fu mystical cults that existed, that were not mainstream Buddhism or mainstream Taoism. But whenever I study heterodox movements, I find that there are certain weird ideas that are there because of a leader, usually some charismatic person, who wanted to make allowances for himself. So at the end of the day, I always find myself drawn back to orthodoxy" (Sanneh 2009).

Fabio (Absence, Destroy Babylon): "I believe spirituality is damn important in my life, yes. I am fascinated by religions and the power they had and still have within our communities. You will always find books near my bed of texts related to old prophets or new theories and new interpretations of old creeds. From Lao [Tzu] to Confucius to Mohammed, I love to read about it all… I don't pray [to] any God but I do believe that we are all One, I do believe we are not just points floating throughout time and space. If this was the case then the whole concept of good and evil would have no purpose to even exist and this would create chaos, absolute chaos. I read a lot about Christianity and Islam, I read a lot about Krishna and Taoism, I try to read as much as I can on pagan tributes and old rituals in northern Europe or even about sects and spiritual leaders such as Charles Manson and the ATWA [*ed.: Manson's group Air Trees Water Animals*], as it is really fascinating for me to understand how human communities all needed to create their own myths to maybe escape reality or maybe embrace higher wisdom. I am too sceptical to believe in one manmade set of rules" (Sparks of Dissent 2010c).

Sean: "Having been through earlier movements, both Punk and Anarchist, that were derailed by drug and alcohol use—and simultaneously being heavily immersed in martial arts at the time; there was definitely a notion of creating an almost monastic movement, whose sole purpose was self-negation for the sake of the struggle" (Rettman 2019).

Sean: "[Hardline manifesto excerpt]: "Under the principles of the Hardline ideology, all shall be permitted to do as they please as long as their actions do not harm, in any way, the rights of others. Any action that does interfere with such rights shall not be considered a 'right' in itself, and therefore shall not be tolerated. Those who hurt or destroy life around them, or create a situation in which that life or the quality of it is threatened shall from then on no longer be considered innocent, and in turn will no longer have rights. Adherents to the hardline will abide by these principles in daily life. They shall live at one with the laws of nature, and not forsake them for the desire of pleasure—from deviant sexual acts and/or abortion, to drug use of any kind (and all other cases where one harms all life around them under the pretext that they are just harming themselves). And, in following with the belief that one shall not infringe on an innocent's life—no animal product shall be consumed (be it flesh, milk or egg). Along with this purity of everyday life, the true hardliner must strive to liberate the rest of the world from its chains—saving life in some cases, and in others, dealing out justice to those guilty of destroying it" (Hardline manifesto c. 1990).

Declaration: "I laid my foundation stone by stone, each solidifying and reinforcing the structure I knew would take a lifetime to build. That structure was me, that structure was self discipline. Surrounded by the wicked who spat upon my effort, huddled into darkness and kicked sand in my face. Alone I stood left to continue in a struggle to free myself from the dying, rotting world around me. I ignored their kind and focused on all I knew to be true. And now I stand higher, looking down on the fiery pits of this hell. And every day I ascend another inch towards a life of greater fulfillment, of total purity and confidence. Dirty, bruised, bloody, and tired but still brazen, my task will forever be undertaken. I must see things through no eyes but my own, and I must see things from a vantage point of clarity. And occasionally I will gaze down to remind myself of what I left behind, of the fools blackened by their self-created filth crouching in dens of immorality and indulgence. And pity will not seize my heart as I watch them slowly, agonizingly crushed in the wake of their own degeneracy" (Anonymous, *Declaration* 1, c. 1995: 10).

Mike Karban (*Caring Edge*, *SEAL*): "ANIMAL MURDERERS, VIOLATORS OF THE INNOCENT MUST DIE FOR THEIR CRIMES, DRIVEN BY AVARICE. THIS WORLD'S A FUCKING NIGHTMARE. BLACKENED SKIES, DEFORESTATION, POISONED SEAS. THIS CIVILIZATION'S PRICE ISN'T WORTH THE FEE. PERPETRATORS OF THIS MADNESS, YOUR RIGHT TO LIVE IS GONE. YOUR BURNING BODIES SHALL LIGHT THE PATH TO A GLORIOUS NEW DAWN!" (original in all-caps, "XXX DISCIPLINE XXX," SEAL 3, 1996: 16).

Sean: "Some people charged that we were a cult, but that would definitely be a stretch of the imagination. Cults usually have some sort of central figure who wants to create a centralized form of allegiance. Hardline had people from a Buddhist, Christian or Judaic framework, and we weren't trying to erase whatever sort of cultural milieu they were coming from" (Peterson 2009: 488).

Dave Agranoff (*Defense, Rescue and Survival*, *Vanguard*): "Hardline looks to the dawn of human existence for answers to modern day problems. We realize that prophets have come from many different cultures and periods of history. *'We embrace the truth from where ever it reveals itself'* – Vanguard #1" (Agranoff, *Forward to Eden: A Guide to Hardline Viewpoints*, c. 1995: 4).

Sean: "And certainly, Hardline has never been without a succession of leadership, and never without a plan. At times this plan has been hidden from view, and those in control have worked from behind the scenes in order to protect their identity and Hardline's future …For Hardline has always moved in one direction, and that is Forward to Eden. Certainly the founders and key historical figures of this movement know this. And that is why they themselves have given their approval of the HCC for this centralization of Power—including legal ownership of the name Hardline, and Vanguard, as well as authority and control of not only the Hardline movement, but of Vanguard magazine and Hardline Records (should we decide to resurrect the label)" (*Vanguard* 8, 1998).

Sean: "Even going back to the first *Vanguard* magazine I had quotes and references from The Quran. I spent of a lot of years studying Islam. My father had given me Malcolm X's [auto]biography when I was a kid. I had contact with MOVE in the eighties and during the early years of hardline I was heavily into the Old Testament via the Rasta influence and Taoism and Buddhism through my martial arts background. Around 1994 or so, I spent some time in Jamaica exploring Rastafarianism and hung out with Rastas in the hills, but ultimately I just couldn't get with the concept of God being a man, which was the same thing that always turned me off about Christianity. Ultimately, I ended up at a vegetarian *masjid* in Philadelphia [*ed.: the Bawa Muhaiyaddeen Fellowship*], which inspired me to take my *shahadah* (declaration of faith within the Islamic tradition), which I did with a *shaykh* in Oakland shortly thereafter" (Peterson 2009: 131).

Sean: "I also had a fairly strong background of Liberation Theology, Black Power and Indigenous Rights struggles influencing me. I was really impacted by groups like MOVE, as well" (Peterson 2009: 484).

Sean: "Really, my first journey through spirituality came through the martial arts. I became more exposed to Taoism and meditation. I was also exploring Rastafarianism, and through that I was exploring the Old Testament and studying Christianity. In some ways, Islam was a balance, for me, between those realms, between East and West. And I had known Five Percenters, the Nation of Islam, things like that" (Sanneh 2013).

Steve Lovett (Raid): "Some of the history is revisionism. I was there in the very beginning and most of the Hardline founders were agnostic, nonreligious or atheist. It had nothing to do with 'Abrahamic' religion. The band Raid had as much to do with formulating the Hardline movement as the record label owner, Sean. The difference is Raid became disenchanted with the Hardline movement early on and the record label continued on. Before Vegan Reich, Statement and Raid were released, Hardline was only a record label idea, not a movement. By the time the records were released, we created a movement. That movement was created in Memphis, not Laguna Beach. Later Hardline morphed into a quasi-Islamic scene. Initially, it was simply hardcore vegan straight edge and not anti sex, cursing, etc..." (Wikipedia: Talk page 7 August 2009).

Daniel (Racetraitor, Hinkley, Everlast, Arma Angellus): "I remember basically my girlfriend at the time got a *Vanguard* from someone involved in hardline and showed it to me. I looked it over, and it reminded me a lot of my own beliefs that had been shaped by my father's beliefs (Baha'i), at least the little I knew about either of the movements at the time, the idea of religion being more about the meaning of the words than following the letter of the law, and all the religions teaching an essential truth" (Peterson 2009: 93-94).

Sean: "Part of the hardline movement was the syncretistic thing, finding truth where it exists. I still think that's a good approach. But the danger is that if you just pick and choose from a bunch of different traditions, the end-all, be-all of your decision-making process is you. That wasn't the mentality of hardline. We had certain standards that everybody had to abide by. But at the end of the day, the decision about what is or isn't a moral decision — it's yours. I really felt like I had to find something that had standards and rules, teachings that I could accept and follow. Because otherwise it's too easy: You come up against something that you don't want to do in a certain situation, and you can just change your mind about whether or not that's okay.

That said, I also didn't want to jump into someone else's religion, a different culture, and not be able to do it all the way. Probably since 1990, I had been completely sold on Islam's view of the nature of God. And by 1993, I was saying, I want to convert, but I don't want to convert and bring in my own ideas that are in conflict with the broader Muslim community. I didn't want to come in and start arguing with people. The vegetarian thing was the final sticking point. So I started a journey to see if I could find an actual organic Muslim community that had vegetarian views, that existed within Islam—not converts bringing vegetarianism to Islam. It took some time, but eventually I came across the Bawa Muhaiyaddeen community, which was founded by a Sufi sheikh from Sri Lanka who had come to Philadelphia. I found a community where I could still maintain my veganism. That was a more important issue then than it is now, all these years later. And I'm still vegan, personally, but I'm not out there trying to argue that the Muslim world should become vegetarian" (Sanneh 2013).

Michelle (*Gaia Screams*, *Invictus*): "I'm lucky because Hardline defines my moral structure, and if one looks at Hardline (rationally!) then they have a better understanding of who I am. The only holy Hardline rules I know of is the ugly truth of humanity that Hardline challenges. The lifestyle isn't for everyone, only the strong. ...Do you know why I am anti-abortion? Do you know why I have certain views of human sexuality? Please, just ask" (*Invictus* 1, 1995: 15).

Declaration: "Every drop of blood you draw is another you will bleed. Every burn and wound is another bullet in your body. The tormentor becomes the tormented. ... You are inflicted for the suffering you created. An eye for an eye. A tooth for a tooth. A life for a life" (*Declaration* 1, c. 1995: 27).

Vanguard: "Hardline is an all encompassing philosophy that addresses all aspects of human existence. It is a continual progression to purify one's mind and body, strengthen one's discipline and increase one's actions towards saving the Earth. PROGRESSION is the key word. One who is Hardline always sees room for improvement and is never content with the life s/he lives. This is not to say that one who is Hardline is in a state of constant guilt or shame because s/he is not perfect. We understand that because we were born into this society it will take time to free ourselves from the wrong values we have been taught from birth—by our parents, in our schools, from television, movies and almost all aspects of this anthropocentric society. It is important to understand this and then change" (unsigned article, "Progression to Purity" *Vanguard* 5, 1993: 16).

Ryan Downey (Hardball, Burn it Down, *Vanguard*): "The Hardline view, as it has been laid forth thus far, acknowledges that there is a certain energy, conscious of itself or not, which gives everything balance and order. It also accepts that some may choose to call it God and worship/communicate with it in their own fashion while others are free to be atheists and still be Hardline.

Obviously, adherents to the Hardline, atheist or not, can not endorse any organized religion entirely, although each may have some good points, due to the numerous atrocities committed in the names of said religions and the fact that all religions today are products of human centered thinking in some manner.

However, a belief in God and a spirituality within our movement is entirely feasible. By spirituality we mean a general attempt to understand further ourselves and our role in nature. ...The communion with nature that the Hardline movement seeks, that of fulfilling coexistence for each [living being], is much like that sought after by many spiritual texts when interpreted with a non-anthropocentric view.

It is hard, almost ludicrous to imagine that something as immaculate as the Earth's eco-system just 'happened' as some believe—it makes considerable more sense that it was created, or brought into being by something beyond our capacity to understand yet too, close to all of us who seek to liberate it from its current chains.

Not everyone in Hardline believes in God as a personality or physical 'being' so to speak, such as the typical depiction of the Eastern gods of Western bearded man, but all share a common belief in the forces of good and evil, absolute wrong and absolute right and that we are most definitely on the side of the right.

It is indisputable that any kind, loving God or eco-system is also on the side of the right, on the side of innocent beings in dire need such as food, animals, and fetuses.

Our struggle is not only for ourselves or a specific group but for the Earth and the forces of nature itself; God or our idea of God is what we are fighting for and therefore can also be considered an ally" (*Vanguard* 1+2 double issue, "Spirituality," 1993: 12).

Sean: "At the end of the day, Islam has a set of rules for its believers—but according to the Quran (and not some whacked out Wahhabi reinterpretation) there is no compulsion in religion. Meaning, the rules that I chose to live by as a Muslim, are not bearing on non-Muslims. Not my job to be the morality police" (xCatalystx board 2009).

Scott Beibin (*Ascention*, Bloodlink Records, Lost Film Fest, Evil Twin Booking): "With hardline and the radical veganism we were espousing at the time, we pushed the middle. Basically, people looked at hardline and they felt it was so extreme with all its viewpoints; however, people could relate to what was in the middle, which was becoming vegan. That's what really triggered the mass exodus from people eating meat. They were not interested in being hardline, but they were interested in being vegan" (Peterson 2009: 101).

Scotty Niemet (More Than Music Festival): "I had this love/hate relationship with groups such as hardline. I took a pretty proactive stance on direct action, but I never felt the need for hardcore kids to turn against other hardcore kids with their variations on how to approach the grey areas of animal rights. I felt this uncomfortable view of hardline, that they were being way too divisive within the hardcore scene. I would even say they were becoming like an outsider group recruiting through hardcore. Just like Christian groups, I feel hardline was coming in and stating their rules to make people decide if they were 'true' vegans or not. They never took a step back and thought that maybe some kids were taking things in their own hands outside of the scene to take actions on animal exploiters. It was a bit too 'look at me I'm more of this and this and this than you… you have the information, make a change now or you will be banished.' Also, being a queer, animal rights activist vegan, I didn't hold anything lightly that told me that me being queer, I was somehow less of an effort for the 'cause'" (Peterson 2009: 96).

Sean Ingram (Coalesce): "At the time, I thought hardline was very attractive. I had no direction in my life, and it was kind of a religion—a reason to live; to be undeniably righteous for a righteous cause. But as everyone figured out, nothing man builds is righteous. It was all bullshit, and ended up turning very Nazi-like. I don't find any honor in blowing up buildings or intimidating doctors" (Peterson 2009: 101).

Michelle Borok (*Gaia Screams*, *Invictus*): "Life is different in Alaska. There I could walk out onto an ocean. I could climb Denali, the Great one. I could die walking out onto the tundra, and turning to face the wind. In the real Alaska, life and people are different. There, Nature isn't some intangible force. There, Nature is not the enemy. Nature is master. Nature is God. She gives a lot of her resources and beauty, but she commands the harvest and the bounty. In fact, my ideal Hardline commune would have to be somewhere there, a little northwest of Fairbanks. We would find a place with good, fertile ground for the growing season and lots and lots of open space, no fences (you have got to have room for all of the Hardline military training of course). …There aren't enough non-white Hardliners yet to maintain a good size population for communal living in that climate. There isn't as big of a melanin issue in the Pacific Northwest, so Alaska it is. Imagine the sorrow at the first loss of a vegan warrior to a wandering polar bear. Did Dave say it, or Shane? Stand for justice/submit to Nature!" (*Invictus* 1, 1995: 18).

Sean (Vegan Reich): "With these currents all coming together, a unique blend of anarchism and those influences melded to form a monastic revolutionary movement of sorts (I, by way of example, had become celibate during this period—trying to eschew any worldly pleasure for the sake of the revolution). Knowing that most people couldn't adhere to that level of discipline, we decided the base level rule was to [have] sex only for procreation. And yes, when one heads down that road of thinking sex is a purely biological function, and desire something to be avoided, active homosexuality was clearly verboten within the ranks" (Muttaqi 2021).

Sean: "Although some Vegan Reich lyrics drew inspiration from religious symbolism, the band has never been a vehicle for any religion, and there has never been any one such belief present within the band at any given period of its history" (Vegan Reich 2017b).

Vanguard: "We must remember that we live in society to destroy, and rebuild, not become a part of it. There are two things we can do: limit our participation in society to a minimum and increase our productivity and actions, to make up for inevitable evils we can not avoid. There are many things we can do to limit our participation in society. CONSUME LESS. That is probably the most important thing you can do.

...[citing Screaming Wolf:] 'did you know that road kills are the number two destroyers of non-human life? One million animals are run over by cars and trucks each day in the United States alone!'

...does this mean for one to be vegan, they can not drive a car or use any product that required a car to be used? No, but we must make an effort to keep our automobile use to a minimum. If possible walk, ride a bike, car pool, or take a bus and use your car only when necessary.

...So next time you use your car to 'hang out', think about what is being compromised. Whether we like it or not, the more we participate in society, the more its warped values wear off on us. American culture, for example, is based on sense gratification, material 'wealth,' wastefulness, selfishness and greed. All of our lives we have been taught that love and happiness can be bought and sold and that we should think of ourselves before others. Our culture is based on consuming. ...When we base our lives on money, we fail to have a real purpose in life. ...We are not told to ask ourselves 'What can I do to make this world a better place?'

We say fuck this American culture. Happiness is not found in Stussy hats, tattoos and MTV. Life has a much greater purpose than that. ...Mentally break free and the rest will come naturally. We are not totally liberated and free until we know exactly who we are inside and what our purpose in this life is. Become connected to the Earth that gave us life and feel your true self awaken" (unsigned article, "Progression to Purity" *Vanguard* 5, 1993: 16-18).

Sean: "Hardline is not a loose coalition of individuals who share similar beliefs or goals. It is not a banner under which those who embrace only certain aspects of the hard line march. Nor is the ideology of Hardline open to debate or change from those within its ranks. Hardline is what it is and that is the way it is. ...Abstinence from animal products and drugs in itself does not make one Hardline. The belief system of Hardline is much more complex and involved than merely having a healthy diet and sobriety. Hardline is a philosophy which addresses all aspects of human experience and its relation to the world around it—from political and social, to ethical and spiritual" (*Vanguard* 1, "What is Hardline," 1992: 5).

Sean: "[*Q: Why are there no pictures of your band on the records? Are you afraid to reveal your identity to the public?*] A: Individual identities and their physical manifestations are entirely irrelevant to the message we give, which has nothing to do with ego, or our personalities, as we are merely messengers of a truth and wisdom that exists with or without our acknowledgment of such. There would be no purpose or reason for us to portray our likeness to the public, other than to foster idol worship, and foment a cult of personality—both of which we despise" (Boston Hardline 1995: 17).

Sean: "VANGUARD—a magazine whose purpose will be to present the Hardline Ideology/philosophy/way of life and action in a definitive manner to ensure cohesion of thought amongst the Hardline movement; further educating our members to all aspects of, and realms which pertain to, our struggle—while providing a forum for discussion on new revelations, concepts and approaches within the Hardline" (*Vanguard* 1, 1992: 4).

DJ Rose (Path of Resistance): "At the first hardline fest in Memphis in 1991, I saw Raid. ... I didn't find anyone that I connected with. I thought some of what they believed in to be awesome, but some of it seemed like religious dogma to me. ...I didn't agree with all the stuff that came along with hardline. I was supportive, but they always tried to push me into the antiabortion and anti-homosexual camp. Those were issues that I felt were bigger than me. The thing with hardline was that it had a leader, and leaders can change the rules or tweak them. Then you have to fall in line or be gone. Once Sean started adding stuff, all of a sudden there were rules on caffeine and strawberries" (Rettman 2017: 272-273).

Sean: "To be 'damned' is merely to be condemned. Certainly, the powers that be have condemned us all to a living hell on earth. If you think such is not the case, then they've even taken your sight. The concept of ecocentricity ([of] which veganism is a part) is the only hope that this world has for continuance and prosperity. Thus, the message which we give <u>is</u> one of 'salvation'—offering a way out of this mess, saving the world from self-destruction" (Boston Hardline 1995: 19).

Ryan Downey (Hardball, Burn it Down, *Vanguard*): "This section will explore these questions through interviews concerning spirituality with various Hardline activists or perhaps just essays or stories of a time when one felt a 'religious experience' or something. We are not doing this to be corny, as silly as that last sentence just read. This is a topic a lot of us strongly feel should be dealt with. If you disagree, don't read this section anymore..." (*Vanguard* 1+2 double issue, "Spirituality," 1993: 12).

Dave Agranoff (*Defense, Rescue and Survival*, *Vanguard*): "Hardline is very spiritual. We feel that we can learn lessons from all Religions—which tend to be interpretations of the same theme. However, Hardline views its belief to be rooted in ideas that are pre-culture and we reject organized Religion on the basis that they have been compromised by its surrounding culture" (*Vanguard* 6, 1995: 3).

Sean: "I had always spent time around a lot of Rastafarians, was exposed to Islam, and I was always heavily into martial arts so there was a strong Taoist and Buddhist influence on me. I also met some of the people from MOVE who had actually fled after that whole thing went down. Basically, I was always into religious studies and my lyrics reflected some Old Testament and Quranic influences in terms of structure" (Peterson 2009: 488-489).

Sean: "All of these beliefs and our whole world view comes from an understanding that there is a better way to live. That beyond human subjectivity exists an objective truth that is the path on which man was meant to follow.

Hardline recognizes that what is born is born to another, and that the life on earth and the natural order around which it's meant to revolve, springs forth from the root of a higher power. With that acknowledgment we also understand that each people, according to their situation and experiences will have different conceptualizations of what that higher power is. Some may call it God, others a Lifeforce, and others still, perhaps just life or nature. Some may proscribe to it a consciousness, others may not. Cultural diversity promotes religious diversity and we accept people's inclination to search for truth through the customs and traditions they can relate to (provided they are not used as an excuse for brutality). However, Hardline sees our natural state to be pre-civilization and pre-culture, and thus we do not ascribe to any man made religion, as they cannot help but be weighted down by cultural baggage and inevitably clouded by their surrounding societies' garbage. Rather, we embrace truth wherever it reveals itself (be it in certain passages from the writing of religious or philosophical texts to great artistic masterpieces) and we strive for it wherever it can be found in the beautiful workings of nature, the miracle of life that surrounds us all (making that higher power self evident to any who can truly see). Lastly, and just as importantly—we look within, where the road map to life on the true path lies, where our instinctual knowledge which has been dormant for so many years (on the human calendar of chaos and destruction) is still to be found.

Through purity of body and mind—gained by an abstinence of animal products, caffeine, nicotine, alcohol and all drugs, chemically refined and processed foods such as white flour, white rice, sugar and artificial colors, flavors and preservatives; through exercise, right thoughts and right deeds we can achieve a oneness with that natural order, and live the way we're meant to.

Through this personal healing we gather the strength to fight against those who refuse to see—the infidels who force their discord on [us], we the righteous followers of the true path. This is our solution. Not only for ourselves, but for the world. Only those who live life to fulfill their destiny will have the strength to fight against wickedness and iniquity. And only will a world that accepts this reality and lives accordingly, ever have peace and harmony.

There can be no compromise. We must go back to our original state. No more poisonous medicines and vaccines. No more chemical and hormonal birth control. An end to the death camps for the unborn and all scientific atrocity. No more excuses for unnatural activity. The world is choking on its sins. It's time to set it free" (*Vanguard* 1, "What is Hardline," 1992: 6).

Dave Agranoff (*Defense, Rescue and Survival*, *Vanguard*): "We must drop the attitude that [because] we are always in the right [it] will bring us victory" (*Vanguard* 6, "Hardline: We Have Failed," 1995: 25).

Sean: "In all certainty, this is the path of Truth and Light. Those hypocrites and wicked ones who have tried to turn this movement from the straight and narrow have only succeeded in veering themselves from the Path. For the Way cannot change. It is permanent. Eternal. Forever fixed. Even if the name Hardline were to be washed away in the coming years like the sand beneath the ocean waves, our mission would not have failed, the Path would not have changed. For the name 'Hardline' carries in and of itself, little importance. Neither do the particulars of Hardline's external laws. They are just how we manifest the Divine Will in this Time and Place. Had we been born at another time or under different circumstances, we may have called our path by a different name. ...And the understanding of this will only come with True knowledge of 'Gnosis'. Or behind all exoteric or outward form and law, lies an inward or esoteric meaning. And it is only this inward meaning that remains unchanging; Permanent; Eternal" (written under the pseudonym "Ishraq Furqan" of Hardline Central Committee, *Vanguard* 8, "The Way and the Light," 1998: 19).

Sean: "Because I don't regret it. I was young and attempting to make a positive change. If some of the views were too conservative for some folks, it is what it is. ...Hardline is what it is (or rather was I guess). A unique merger of hard left politics with somewhat millenarian religious influences" (Muttaqi 2021).

Sean: "HardLine is about fighting against evil not worshipping it! I got a letter from one of those kids and it just had like a pentagram and some fucked up writing on it. I wrote him back and was just like don't ever fucking write to me again! There are a couple of others of them who aren't a real chapter and they're just fucking ridiculous, you can't be a Satanist and HardLine! Also I would like to tell all of the HardLiners out there that they should try to work in unity with other groups that they have a lot of things in common with. For instance, Rastafarians would probably think that they were HardLine if they read *Vanguard* 1 (they don't see pot as a drug). And even other revolutionary groups, beside themselves. The struggle isn't going to be won with just one group, it's going to be won by a bunch of different groups fighting for it and they all need to work together" (*Destroy Babylon* 2, "Captive Nation Rising interview,"1995: 48).

Sean: "Hardline, was, and is, one of many '*Tariqah*' or paths one could take in order to work for change, and for revolution. It no longer is the parameter from which I work, but nonetheless, I recognize it as a key factor in my life, and in my personal development of discipline and character, so I will always have respect for it, and for those who work within its structure" (Muttaqi c. 2001).

Sean: "Where I am today is the result of a natural progression and evolution over a 10 year period of activity. The nihilistic approach of the early hardcore scene was a very necessary reaction to the problems which we faced, and it did its job in shaking things up and getting people to think—but such an approach became stale after a while so I took it to another level, where I actually moved beyond pure criticism, to doing constructive work to achieve change. For a while this was involvement in the peace/anti-nuke movement and anarcho-pacifism (and, in turn, animal liberation). Later in time pacifism was dropped because it was unpractical and ineffective, and I progressed to revolutionary anarchist principles and tactics (and militant animal liberation). I became drug free (and have stayed that way) out of political motives, not through straight edge, and I could hardly be considered a 'straight edger' now—so this in no way can be seen as merely moving from one trend to another. Since I've never been one to jump on the band wagon, I see no reason for me to start now.

My past helped me attain a level of awareness which enabled me to grasp the correctness and absoluteness of the truth we've come to call Hardline. If it were not for the past, I would not be who I am today. And by the same token, I will most definitely develop further the more I achieve oneness with the true force (which is the inspiration of Hardline)" (Boston Hardline 1995: 9).

Sean: "I think it is important for people to understand the nature of the Qur'an's revelation. And the key to this requires contextualization and applying *tawil* (or going inward to determine its meaning). Contextualizing it is important, because the Qur'an did not come as a blueprint from the sky for a perfect world with a list of instructions at how to get there. Rather, it came *Surah* (chapter) by *Surah*, over a period of years, in answer to and in relation to events that were unfolding at the time. Therefore, we must use analogy and comparison to current events and how it relates to things in these modern times, to understand how it applies today, and what the Prophet (*sal*) would have taught concerning the issues before us today.

It is the very living presence of Truth prevalent in the Qur'an, and the beauty contained therein, that first drew me to it and continues to inspire me. Even in English translation its strength as a mystical document is clear, and once one reads its words in Arabic, there is no denying its Divine origin, or at least influence. The very fact that a whole Islamic culture of the arts, architecture, mathematics, and science, not to mention spirituality, developed from the application of its principles certainly shows if nothing else, that it contains very deep levels of understanding. Therefore, I would suggest that every person read it, whether religious or not. At the very least, one will get a better understanding of history, politics and one of the most articulate calls for social justice ever made. And insha'Allah, one will also find it as a useful tool in helping them to decipher the Qur'an within, the book of Truth that is within the heart of Man. For only then, when we come to recognize the spiritual side of our being, do we fully develop to our true potential" (Muttaqi c. 2001).

Sean: "Unlike past movements which have failed to be all encompassing, disciplined and stress cohesion of thought and action among its members by allowing their stated philosophies to be changed and debated (this is not to say Hardline is *not* open to new revelations, for that is one purpose of *Vanguard*) HARDLINE can and must succeed in its goal of vegan revolution. If we fail, we will at least have saved some innocent lives and we shall die trying to save them all. This is it, LET'S GO TO WAR!!!" (*Vanguard* 1+2 double issue, "Hardline," 1993: 7).

Kevin Seconds: "I look at straight edge, at least the more outspoken militant side of it, in the same way I look at religion. At its core, the values are decent and the intent is sincere, but we humans are terribly flawed. We are always searching for more—more love, more meaning, more acknowledgment, and more approval. And in our quest for all of those things, we do stupid shit, like imposing our will on other people until we bastardize the initial meaning and intent of what is basically a good thing" (Rettman 2017: 275).

Sean: "I would still agree with what I said before that religion a lot of times is hampered by cultural baggage. Now to some extent I would say that true Islam is an exception to that in the sense that it specifically states in the Koran that it is apart from cultural things. Basically Islam is accepting every way in which God has presented himself to man. Islam just means submission to God" (*Destroy Babylon* 2, "Captive Nation Rising interview,"1995: 43).

Kevin Seconds: "We'll raise our voice and blast right through, we'll stop the ones who fuck it up, and show the world that they can't stop the crew" (lyrics to "The Crew" 7 Seconds).

Sean: "Be wary of those who stretch the rules of law merely to satisfy their desire. For there is no redemption in deceit. Only that which is done in the name of the Most High will ever be accepted. So take this as a reminder of what the ancient Prophets have said, and stay true to the Path. For Hardline reflects all sacred teachings, and only the righteous can manifest the Divine" (written under the pseudonym "Ishraq Furqan" of Hardline Central Committee, *Vanguard* 8, "The Way and the Light," 1998: 20).

Sean: "[Q: Why do you still live in this world and don't draw the consequences and move to an island… build up a new system of living…?]

A: Do you think that I enjoy living barely above the poverty line, struggling to get by in an area filled with pollution, and crime? I would much prefer to live on an island, do some farming, and raise a family. But that would be pure isolationism and would do nothing to change the state of the world. Animals would still be tortured and killed in laboratories and slaughterhouses. Rainforests would still be burnt to the ground; and the Indians within massacred. The seas would continue to be poisoned, the sky's polluted and the ground strip mined for coal and gold. Apartheid would continue to exist and the Klan would still lynch blacks. …As long as injustice continues in the world, then I will be located in a place where I can engage in the struggle against the wicked and evil. If that means using a door that a meat eater may have made, then so be it. When it is practical, we may indeed have isolated communities (that are self-sufficient) in order to engage in secluded training for guerilla warfare—but apart from that, we will continue to work, struggle, and teach in the midst of the empire which we hate, so that we may one day tear it to pieces" (Boston Hardline 1995: 22).

Sean: "[Q: May we please have your reaction to the following quote by Ray Cappo: 'Vegan Reich are fanatical. They are defeating their own purpose. According to my reality it is wrong to be fanatical. Vegan Reich doesn't even believe in God. Why is it wrong to kill an animal? If there is no God, who is to say what is right and wrong? You do? Sean Vegan Reich says what is right and wrong? Is he God? Is he the decider? Why should I accept his subjective morality? Accept my subjective morality. Everybody should kill Sean Vegan Reich. So unless you accept a higher authority, what's the purpose?'] A: …As to Ray's comment that Vegan Reich doesn't believe in God? Everybody in the band, and within Hardline have their own personal beliefs regarding this subject—so I won't comment for them. Personally, I do not believe in an omnipotent God. That however, is not to say that I don't believe that those forces of energy are conscious of their own existence and power. So, it is not me that dictates what is right and wrong. I am merely picking up on that energy, obeying its truth and enforcing its righteousness. This admittance of spiritual beliefs on my part is not to say that Ray's argument has any validity, even when dealing with a militant atheist (who have been some of the most active participants in the struggle for justice throughout the ages). For Ray cannot prove that his God exists. So, in the end Ray is just believing what <u>he</u> wants to (which too could be called subjective)—the same as those he criticizes. When it comes down to it, faith is a personal thing and everything is visibly subjective except to those who truly believe that they are following the truths of a higher source—which makes it objective in their mind. For I know that what I speak is objective fact—but how can I prove it? How can Ray prove it? It comes down to asking people to make a leap of faith—and either someone feels that what is being said is inherently righteous and pure, or they don't" (Note: the Ray Cappo quote originally appeared in an interview with him in LongShot #5 1991, I asked Ray recently about the authenticity of this quote and he vehemently denied that he ever said it. I could not reach the editor of LongShot for comment]; Boston Hardline 1995: 8).

Matt (*Praxis*): "After reading several interviews with the band Shelter, I've decided that something must be done about the Krsna Movement/religion. The main problem I have with them is that they try to justify torturing animals for milk. Well, what goes around comes around. Look out Krsna, this is war! …This is my main problem with Krsnas. I hate them for other reasons but I won't go in to that now. All I have to add is that any Krsna should do his best to avoid the Memphis Hardline Militia, because milk is murder no matter what the fuck Krsna says. DAIRY IS TORTURE!!!!" (*Praxis*, "In the Name of Krsna?" 1991: 26-27).

Sean (writing as Shahid **'Ali** Muttaqi): "From a mystical perspective, we have to realize that '*spirituality*' and '*Religion*' are two different things. Only with this in mind can we begin to ascertain the Truth. For we have been taught for so long to perceive reality from our limited human perspective (ascribing human characteristics to God, and perceiving linear notions of time and space, to be absolutes) that our spiritual perception is invariably clouded by this, and we are locked in a prison of our own misunderstanding. However, within the words of the mystic teachings of the Prophets, there is a key to unlock that prison, and open the door to True Gnosis. That '*key*' is the understanding that every outward event or teaching has an inward meaning, and that every exoteric form contains a more important esoteric reality (with even that inner aspect having a deeper meaning contained within itself and so on).

...Each one of us will eventually die, receive a judgment and either be resurrected into a higher spiritual plane, or be trapped within the hellfire of one's own making. Likewise, within this very life itself, every sinful action we commit has a consequence, as do all righteous thoughts and deeds.

...There has never been a moment when the earth has been without Prophecy and Imamate. Neither has any Prophet brought a message that fundamentally contradicted that of another. For they are all representatives of Allah, and even more specifically, earthly representations of spiritual archetypes. All manifestations of the ONE. Once one understands this, it makes not only the concept of Tawhid (Unity) more understandable, but also its application.

... So it is the Prophet (both externally, as Muhammad the Man/Prophet as well as the Prophet of one's being, on an internal level), that makes an individual be able to recognize 'Ali, the sublime radiance of Allah. And likewise, once this principle of 'Ali—the elevated essence of Allah—manifests itself within man (esoterically as the Ali of our being, and exoterically, as an outward figure—the Mahdi) this paves the way for the birth of Messianic Consciousness—seen outwardly as the return of Isa (Jesus)—his titles having been both the '*Soul of Allah*' and the '*Son Of Man*'—signifying the birth of Allah's essence within man.

Once one understands all these things as the archetypes and symbols for which they are, it makes it clear (that although outwardly divided) there is in truth Unity between the inward Reality of the world religions (as well as within various sectarian '*divisions*' in Islam) even though they all claim what would seem to be opposing theories, at least from an exoteric understanding.

The problem as things now generally stand, is that each seeker tends to acknowledge only the truth presented in '*their religion*' (taking external teachings at face value). Inevitably this causes problems of theological justification when one is faced with the fact that there are positive elements and evident Truths being expressed in Faiths not their own (not to mention the sometimes negative aspects which can exist within the traditions which they themselves hold dear). Even within a single tradition such as Islam, there are many sects and schisms. Sunni, Shi'a (and sub-sects therein), various Sufi *Turuq*, as well as movements such as Amadayiya [Ahmadiyya], Nation of Islam, and offshoot groups like the Baha'i etc.—many looking to one figure as the *Qutb* of the age, or return of the Mahdi, or Jesus, or Muhammad (sal).

What many within these groups are missing is that no 'One' group is THE group. They are ALL merely playing out divine principles in the microcosm enacting them within their daily lives, within their own understandings and perceptions—and the figureheads of each denomination are just the loci of the manifestation of these aspirations etc." ([*Note: italics in original; bold added to indicate "Ali" as capable of signaling multiple meanings: Ali the Prophet's cousin, Ali the coming messiah, and Ali as Sean's second Muslim name*]; Muttaqi, "Forward to Eden: The Straight Path Towards the Messianic Era," *Ahl-i Allah/People of Allah* homepage, 2001).

Sean: "God is omnipresent and all knowing. I definitely believe in a conscious God, as far as a creating force with will and foresight" (*Destroy Babylon* 2, "Captive Nation Rising interview,"1995: 44).

Sean: "And of all the world religions, Islam is unique in that it accepts all those paths that came before, and views them as part of Islam. For really, Islam does not see itself as a 'religion.' Rather, it is the natural 'way,' inherent within man. Our True nature. Therefore, all 'religions' that have come, were expressions of the One Divine Will, manifesting through 124,000 Prophets in human history. Every messenger brought the same message—that of 'Islam.' Perhaps the outward form varied, due to time and place variations. But essentially, every message has been that of 'Tawhid,' or 'divine Unity.' Islam includes Judaism, Hinduism, Buddhism, Taoism, Christianity and accepts their Prophets as being Prophets of Islam. So that is why I came into the din or faith of Islam. To me it seemed to have the most inclusive attitude and complete understanding of spirituality that I had found in many years of searching. And on the outward level, I think it is one of the only traditions that really is inclusive of all racial backgrounds, and absolutely revolutionary in its demand for social justice" (Muttaqi c. 2001).

Dave Agranoff (*Defense, Rescue and Survival*, *Vanguard*): "As you can see, i'm writing from a Syracuse jail ...i was just holding a sign and using my voice to chant '40 dead animals, one fur coat' and for that i was placed under arrest...Nicole said once 'if i think it's murder in my head i should act like it's murder in my heart!' Just in that one store thousands of dead animal skins hang in a macabre example of the depravity of human greed and vanity. Thousands of sentient beings lived lives of hell which make my Onadoga County jail vacation seem like a bed of roses" (*Defense, Rescue and Survival* 3, 1995: 10).

Sean: "The truth and righteousness of veganism is not a subjective concept. It is objective fact. Thus, our opinion and what we feel is 'right' has nothing to do with it. The true and correct path exists with or without our acknowledgment. We just happen to have accepted that truth and are willing to enforce it" (Boston Hardline 1995: 19).

Sean (writing as Shahid 'Ali Muttaqi): "**The first step of that is to rise above our reliance on other human beings and their man made institutions in order to know God**. For as long as we continue to view God as an unreachable entity except by way of an intercessor, and intermediary, etc., we will forever limit our spiritual potential to that of a helpless observer instead of an active participant in the Divine Plan. And that is NEVER what any of the great spiritual masters have taught. Prophets, Imams and Saints have all come as examples so that we may learn to live in a like manner. So that we can awaken the light of Allah within, and attune to the same celestial archetypes that are the source of their inspiration and strength. Not so that we can always remain a follower.

... The Mahdi will only return for humanity when a large enough grouping of the faithful attain that level of consciousness, and enact here in the material realm, the Will of the celestial Mahdi archetype (itself emanating from the Command of Allah). Likewise, only when this community assumes the role of Mahdi, will it have the power to usher in the coming of the Messiah, or Era of the Messiah (when an even larger segment of the Earth's populace achieves Messianic Consciousness and Self-Realization). So come let us prepare the way for the coming of the Messiah. Let us enact the will of the Mahdi. For in Truth, there can be no Messianic age without there first appearing a Mahdi to reestablish the Straight Path towards Allah. And the celestial archetype of the Mahdi will not manifest on Earth until we as mystics and gnostics come together to actuate that return. And that will never happen as long as we build divisions amongst mystical paths. Nor will it occur so long as spiritually minded people tolerate injustice, lies and falsehood.

...The time has come to remove the veil of intercessor and intermediary and seek direct communion with Allah. Let there be no more sects or denominations. All of the Prophets, Imams, and Saints have spoken the word of God, so let us not construct divisions where they have not. The Prophets are ONE, ALLAH is one. No true Prophet says "*pray to me, worship me*." And certainly no genuine Shaykh would do so either. So let there be no more separation between those on a mystical Path based on who our teacher is, or who we perceive to be the ideal embodiment of that archetype of Mahdi or Messiah. In the end, ALL spiritual knowledge comes from Allah. And all mystics who walk in the presence of their Lord, are the People of Allah. There is only one "*primordial spirituality*" and that is *Submission* to Allah. There is only one source of Life, only one way to salvation, and that is within Allah. So let us cast aside all manmade institutions, and sectarian divisions. If we want to move forward towards the Messianic Era, we must restore the primordial faith that is Pure Islam and act as a single body to rid the world of injustice, and oppression. Only when this happens will the spiritual/archetypal reality that is represented by the Mahdi manifest in the terrestrial plane in its full potential. And only then will we be able to move forward to Eden, to the Messianic Era" (italics in original, bold added; Muttaqi, "Forward to Eden: The Straight Path Towards the Messianic Era," *Ahl-i Allah/People of Allah* homepage, 2001).

Sean: "**I think that within the community, it's important to defer to scholars.** Sometimes people that came out of hardline or hardcore and became Muslim come to me to ask about this or that. I'm not a scholar, but I might guide them to a scholar that would know. If you're talking about politics, then, yeah, as a lay Muslim, I feel fine giving my opinion. And as to the issue of vegetarianism in Islam, I feel fine speaking about it, because I've studied and I have an opinion and I'll express it. But even there, when there were younger Muslims interested in vegetarianism, we went to the scholars and got rulings from them saying that it was permissible. At the end, it's important for people to have these people — experts — they can go to. But that doesn't mean that everybody is going to listen to everything they say" (Sanneh 2013; bold added).

Declaration: "I will make justice a reality. No trivial matters would result in this hate. You have committed sins that can be reconciled only through a higher power. A greater truth evokes this rage in my soul. And your destruction outweighs the value of your life. Millions of innocent peaceful animals, or one damnable, callous, greed festering human being? Arm raised, shoulder tightening, hand shaking, I take aim. Right between your eyes" (*Declaration* c. 1995: 10).

Sean: "Again, this is not our 'concept' of justice. Certain things are just objective truth. We did not create these rules. We merely observe them and when necessary, enforce. As this is not a cult of personality, and we do not seek any personal power over others, whether we could be corrupted is irrelevant, as we are like anybody else—and should our ways go astray, we would be judged the same" (Boston Hardline 1995: 20).

Sean: "[Q: Judging by your lyrics and particularly, by the info sheet enclosed with your 7", Hardline is more a religion/cult than an ethical system. I don't like religions/cults since their main function is to keep people down.] A: We are of no religion, and after studying various religions and cults, we are aware of the negative aspects which are entwined in many of them—but your blanket statement that 'their main function is to keep people down' is ridiculous. Religions are not fomented by conspirators seeking to enslave the masses (although some cults are). They develop over thousands of years simultaneous with a people's culture; the two influencing each other. And like everything tied up within the confines of culture—religions are going to reflect the good and the bad aspects of such. But even with those negative elements, which sometimes consume a whole religion—one cannot say they developed with such an intention.

As to whether Hardline is a religion or a cult? That's for others to decide. The words we speak are not influenced by our cultural or physical surroundings—they are universal truths which all people of the world can learn from, no matter what their religious or spiritual background is" (Boston Hardline 1995: 20).

Declaration: "Wiping the sick and evil beings from our world will be its only salvation, this is my declaration of war" (*Declaration* c. 1995: 12).

St. Paul Hardline: "Today we wage wars for the enslavement of our environment and its resources. Survival has become trivial, second to the satisfaction of our senses and the temporary fulfillment of material wealth. ...So how do we subsist outside of this malevolent existence? For some the answer stands before them. The answer lies in the spiritual pursuits of Hardline. Understanding and application may not lie straight ahead in destiny, but the Hardline leads the way to a deeper love of liberation in the most genuine part of the soul. ...The revolution begins at home, in the soul. ...How many people have disgraced Hardline because their spirits were foul? They adopted the diet and the easiest part of the politics, but never tasted the dedication. Whose war were they fighting? The battle of ego, self-enslavement. How much do you take for granted? Many Hardliners drive cars. Some Hardliners consume large amounts of refined foods. And most of us contribute to the incubus of capitalism for fashion, fads, and simple pleasures. These things don't make us inherently evil, but they don't leave us guilt free" (*Vanguard* 7, "Hardline and Spirituality," 1996: 9).

Sean: "Religions that follow a basic principle of Liberation Theology I have respect for because they are active in the struggle against those who are reaping profit by the exploitation of man, animal and earth. Krishnas on the other hand, do not believe such a struggle is necessary, as they feel the horrible conditions on earth are good for motivation to withdraw further into their spiritual selfishness—and that I have nothing but contempt for. An animal in a laboratory doesn't need a prayer or a chant—they need liberation" (Boston Hardline 1995: 7-8).

Sean: "Dedicated with respect and reverence to the prophet Isaiah, Isa [Jesus], Muhammad (Sal), Buddha, Lao Tzu, Chief Seattle, Black Elk, Marcus Garvey, Malcolm X, Bob Marley, Peter Tosh, and all prophets, wise men, and mystics who came to this earth with a salvation plan. And to the warriors who laid down their lives in pursuit of those dreams. Though their flesh has departed, their spirit lives on. By the power of the most high, we shall carry on their jihad for truth and justice" ([*Note: around a picture of lions eating a human, the record cover came emblazoned with the Islamic crescent and star at top and each of the two Hardline logos—the earth ecology symbol and the X with crossed guns inside to the left and right*]; Vegan Reich, "The Wrath of God," 10" EP, Uprising Records, 1995).

Sean: "The definition of compassion is 'pity for the suffering or distress in another, with the desire to help or spare.' How does anything we say lead you to believe we are lacking that? ...We are filled with compassion. It is what drives us to end the economic exploitation of the poor. It is what makes us strive to end hunting, the meat industry, vivisection and so on. It is why we are willing to lose our lives or go to jail in our fight against those who inflict such suffering. Don't blame us for what the oppressors have done. Don't blame us because you love in your heart for the wicked ones who don't know the meaning of that word. They bring any pain which they may receive unto themselves! And until you start living a life that is as free from inflicting pain and suffering on the innocent, as ours is—don't even think you have a right to judge us, and say we lack compassion!" (Boston Hardline 1995: 2).

Dave Agranoff: "I am hardline because I think the ideology behind it is the only hope for this planet. If you don't that's fine, but I do. ...The earth and nature are more important than you or your opinion of me. …There is a higher law and I will seek it out. 'It is not desirable to cultivate respect for the law, so much as for the right. The only obligation which I have a right to assume is to do at any time what I think is right.' Henry David Thoreau" (*Defense, Rescue And Survival* 2, 1995: 2).

Declaration: "'Behold this truth,' God said unto me. 'Force me into your existence, let me seep through the cracks and take root in your insecurities.' 'Yes, Lord,' I uttered. 'And hold this talisman close to your heart, but far from your mind so reason will not interfere with the gifts I have bestowed upon you.' I stared at the icy god my ancestors created and nodded my approval and acceptance of blind allegiance. For 16 years I walked through the deserts of timelessness and found nothing. For 16 years I toiled in complacency, starving for a deeper truth. In despair, crestfallen, I returned to the place that in my infancy had held so much hope, so much promise. But as I stared at the altar, where atop my God had sat, I saw nothing. I did not see the omnipotent deity that had imparted so much wisdom and knowledge with tongues of fire in my youth. And as I inched closer I gazed upon the altar and looked upon a still pool of dormant water. I thought, 'this is all that is left of my God?' Crushed, I peered into the pool and saw something that startled me. My reflection. This holy god of mine was me. This god was a product of my imagination. I created that which deceived me. I tore the talisman from my heart and cast it upon the floor, sending it into a million shattered pieces that cascaded across the empty throne of a god of falsity, of my god of deceit. My joints stiffened, I was sick with realization. Knowledge is my god, I denied that. I could feel my heart slowly stop beating. I could feel my veins congest and harden. I could feel my entire body turn to stone. But my mind and soul, were free to roam for eternity" (Anonymous "The Breaking of the Spell of Hypocrisy," *Declaration* 1, c. 1995: 18).

Sean: "[Q: All other things aside, do you think you're being realistic?]
A: If you asked someone 100 years ago, if they thought that it was a real possibility that all life could face extinction in the next hundred years, they would have said absolutely not. Such are perceptions. Here we are one hundred years later, living out a bizarre science fiction movie—with the planet on the brink of destruction. By all accounts, and perceptions, our struggle does not have odds to win, and no—it wouldn't be realistic to think it could. But there is no other choice. …This is our only chance. Our only hope. And whether or not it's realistic, or probable—we know that we must win. No matter what it takes, victory must come" (Boston Hardline 1995: 21-22).

Sean: "So, one who is hardline in the struggle for our earth, and all life realizes the connection between personal behavior and its effects on the world around them—thus living a life as free as possible from such weakness, rejecting the evils of the present system, and all of its vices, putting forth a new ideology founded on inner strength and purity of thought where the truly strong individual is (and the society they seek to create) lives a moral, righteous life, at one with the natural world—obeying its order and its laws—taking shelter in nothing but their own power and strength—with every action based on one principle—that all innocent life is equal and sacred" (Boston Hardline 1995: 1).

Sean: "Hardline is the primordial way. It is the striving for the Divine where ever that Presence can be found. It is a reminder of that Glory which has been revealed by all the Prophets, saints and Holy Men throughout the ages. It is a recognition of the Miracle that lies before you every day—the manifestation we call creation" (*Vanguard* 8, 1998).

Sean: "I guess without getting in some elaborate theological discussion, the most practical thing non-Muslims should know about Muslims, is there's no inherent aspect of our faith that makes us believe in world domination, or hate non-Muslims. If that propaganda was true, we'd already rule the planet. Quite the contrary in fact. This quote from Imam Ali (as) sums it up the best: 'People are of two kinds, either your brothers in faith or your equals in humanity.' That is the heart of how I approach life and my interactions with people" (Dorff 2018).

Sean: "Meanwhile the earth – and all LIFE upon it – takes the brunt of humanity's trials and tribulations. Species are hunted to extinction. Forests clear cut. Oceans polluted. And everyday, the butcher wields his knife, taking more and more life, as man devours Allah's creation from off the earth. And through it all, still we wait. Occupying our time with meaningless pursuits to distract our minds from the reality of these end times. Praying for the intervention of the divine, but doing nothing to change our lives. Somehow, still believing that Heaven is up in the sky—instead of within our hearts, and right before our eyes.

And like our ancestors before, we'll go to our graves—leaving our children to suffer the same, unless we get up, stand up and fight. ...So for strength and victory let us pray. And then Jihad we must wage. Not merely an outward Jihad against the infidel, the Kufr, the tyrant, but an inward Jihad of self purification, spiritual progression and edification. We must learn to live like Muhammad, Buddha, 'Isa (Jesus). For it is the Insan Kamil or true human being who is the foundation of Heaven on Earth. So let us educate ourselves and liberate our minds from the illusion and lies of the system. Let us strive towards upright living and honesty. No more talking justice while stabbing our brothers and sisters in the back. No more talking about equality, unless we can stop objectifying the human body and treating the opposite sex like a commodity. For we are all ONE in Allah's sight. And if we love Allah, then we must respect Allah's creation. No more abusing our bodies with fast food, cigarettes, alcohol, and drugs. No more talking about faith when we can not even be faithful to our partners. The time has come to change. Peace on earth begins within. If we are humble, modest, calm, compassionate, and sincere, it will manifest in our homes. And only once this has happened, once we have our own house in order, can we begin rebuilding our communities—improving our standard of living both morally and economically. Only through this effort will conditions begin to change in the world. For there is no point in waging an external Jihad, if our hearts and actions are as corrupt and evil as those we fight against.

So come, let us use the sword of Jihad to slash the veils of illusion from before our eyes—cutting the wickedness from our hearts. It's time to wake up and live. For only those pure of faith, intention and action will have the strength to strike down this system of Dajjal [false messiah]. Allahu Akbar!!! (Shahid Ali Muttaqi, "Destroy Babylon," Ahl-i Allah webpage, 2001: 2).

MOVE

In the early 2000s, Joey Leyva wrote: "to sum it all up, Hardline, in its short time, started as one person's zine and ideology, seemingly based on the beliefs of the MOVE organization and small handful of bands, which as it grew in popularity began to move hardcore kids from the basements and into the streets" (*Out from the Shadows* p. 7-8; reprinted in Kuhn, see Anonymous 2019: 227). Indeed, Hardline certainly *seemed* to build on MOVE beliefs. Animal liberation. Earth liberation. Anti-racism. Sobriety. Natural law. Anti-(state)communism. Anti-capitalism. Anti-abortion. Anti-homosexuality. Eternal ideology that preceded civilization. Sectarian. Hardline seemed to check all of the boxes that MOVE had done more than a decade prior. Yet, despite later comments (especially by Sean) claiming that MOVE inspired Hardline from the start, no evidence appears to support that.

I could find no earlier instance of Sean ever mentioning anything or anyone related to MOVE prior to 1995. In that case, Sean mentioned

MOVE supporter Mumia Abu-Jamal (with whom he apparently shares a birthday) and expressed sympathy for Mumia's case in *Destroy Babylon* 2. Yet, by then, the entire punk scene talked about Mumia's case and, at any rate, Sean did not mention MOVE in relation to Mumia nor in the rest of that interview—even when suggesting to Hardliners that they should cooperate with other revolutionaries (he only mentioned Rastas as a concrete example). After Sean left Hardline, *Vanguard* began to include a prisoner support section for Earth and animal liberation activists. Many other journals, such as *Love and Rage*, *Earth First! Journal*, and *Prison News Service*, had begun to include incarcerated MOVE members in their prisoner support lists—but *Vanguard* never did. Hardline Europe did, however, begin distributing MOVE literature around 1995 (mentioned in the fine print of their ad in *Destroy Babylon*). I could find no mention of MOVE or Mumia in any Hardline lyrics or zine prior to 1995.

Sean: "There is truthfully nothing new under the sun" (Vegan Reich, *Jihad*, 1999).

Sean: "This [Hardline] is the first highly organized revolutionary struggle to be built around and fighting for the equality of all life" (*Vanguard* 1 1993: 2).

Hardline Inner Circle/Sean: "This is the first highly organized revolutionary movement of modern times to be built around, and fighting for, the equality of ALL life and its survival, compared to many battles fought (some won some lost) by various groups throughout time who have been driven to the point of revolutionary by their oppressors. ...our movement is built on the unity of those from all walks of life who share a similar faith and well defined belief that we all spring from one source and that all life is therefore equal and in need of liberation ([*Note: the author[s] lifted nearly verbatim from* Vanguard 1]; *Vanguard* 8, 1998: 10).

MOVE: "JOHN AFRICA taught us that Life is the priority. Nothing is more important or as important as Life, the force that keeps us alive. All life comes from one source, from God, MOM NATURE, MOMA. Each individual life is dependent on every other life, and all life has a purpose, so all living beings, things that move, are equally important, whether they are human beings, dogs, birds, fish, trees, ants, weeds, rivers, wind or rain" (*25 Years on the MOVE*, 1997: 68).

Frank Africa: "It should be understood at this point that this is a very clear issue of right and wrong, and what is threatening is wrong. Our belief isn't threatening to no one. What is threatening is as recent as the second reference and not ours. The poison of industry is a threat to all life, but the family that makes up life's body knows nothing of threat. …You can point to the sun and ask ten people of different faiths what it is and they will all say it is the sun in agreement but when asked what channels its energy, where is the source that powers its consistency you will have ten different theories and disagreement, for this is the answer that science is lacking because science is question and not answer. For to know the answer is to be as the answer which is not scientific or civilized. And this is why MOVE is unique, for MOVE is consistent because our Founder that guides us is answering. …Understand that this information is not designed to offend any religions or personal feelings. The purpose of this statement is in defense of our lives, for we are under a very serious threat concerning the necessity of our diet, our belief, and our principle is our only defense. …and the blame for this pain is not the earth, for the Earth as all Life is balancing, while the threat of imbalance is the cause of all pain. …and we will continue to defend right until the threat that wrongs it is no more, and we will not rest 'til this is done" ("Brief to Define the Importance of MOVE's Religious Diet," 1981: 1, 15-18).

Michael Africa Jr.: "The Move Organization is not an organization about separation or prejudice. You can see that because we believe in life. We believe in ALL life. We don't believe in black, white, red, yellow, dog, cat, horse… we believe in life. Life is one principle, not fifty thousand different categories. If it has feelings, then we believe it should be protected. We believe that it should be in its environment as nature intended it. Who is to say that they know better than God? Who?!" ("Seeds of Wisdom: The *Network Magazine* Interview," *First Day* 19, ca. 1999: 11).

Sean: "ALL life is equal regardless of age, race, sex or species" (Boston Hardline 1995: 9).

Ronna Africa (MOVE): "Because of **John Africa** no Move people are on drugs. There's no drinking or nothing. Because of **John Africa** I'm healthy" ("Seeds of Wisdom: The *Network Magazine* Interview," *First Day* 19, ca. 1999: 10).

Sean: "My initial vision for the whole thing, had been something that merged Anarchism with elements of American radical groups such as AIM, MOVE, Black Panthers, Nation and so on with a sort of universal spiritual esotericism—that incorporated things—in my particular case—from Rastafarianism, Buddhism, Taoism, and Islam, and from others in our circle—Christianity and Judaism" ([*Note: Tony Rettman deleted parts of this section—such as the mentions of AIM and MOVE—from the book version yet published the full version on his blog*]; Rettman 2019).

Nimrod Africa: "One of the most important things is to free life, to stop man's system from imposing on us. That's why we go out speaking the truth, putting out the truth about the enslavement of life, the enslavement of plant life, animal life, people" ("Seeds of Wisdom: The *Network Magazine* Interview," *First Day* 19, 1999: 10).

Sean: "Our main denunciation of the system is not because it shifts things around so that people don't have to take responsibility for their actions. That is just clever maneuvering on the part of the system to help ensure that things run smoothly; so that no one questions their part in the whole thing. We hate the system because it is based upon the evil side of mankind, and that is manifested in the destruction of all life for the benefit of the wicked" (Boston Hardline 1995: 20).

Janet Africa: "All life comes from **GOD**, all Life have feeling, there is no separation in Life, no divisional categories in Life, no such thing as inferior, superior" ("What's Really Killing Us," *First Day* 6, ca. 1995: 4).

MOVE: "Over the last century, industry has raped the earth of countless tons of minerals, bled billions of gallons of oil from the ground, and enslaved millions of people to manufacture cars, trucks, planes and trains that further pollute the air with their use. And because of the billions of dollars in profits to be made, the system will favor artificial transportation over the legs and feet Mama gave us to walk and run with" (*25 Years on the MOVE* 1997: 69).

Sean: "If these people want to end things such as racism or abortion, etc. then they should deal with the underlying issue that leads to such things' existence, which is a belief that there are certain life forms that are more valid and others are inferior" (Boston Hardline 1995: 10).

John Africa: "The principle of collective is natural law, and has nothing to do with your distorted concepts, for example, the squirrel collects nuts, the wolf collects squirrels, and while they may appear to you to express themselves differently, they are not, as they are, along with all other natural life, reflecting a collective expression of balance" (*The Book*, 1973: 51).

Sean: "Hardline is not about false human perception of law and morality. It is about living by the natural law—where morality means abiding by the natural order of things—maintaining the balance" (*Vanguard* 1, "The Balance of Things," 1992: 10).

MOVE: "While we do not heed the system's legal institution of marriage, we do adhere to the natural law that requires one male and one female to mate and produce new life. We are monogamous. JOHN AFRICA taught us that childbearing is a natural, instinctive function of a mother and requires no drugs or hospital stays" (*25 Years on the MOVE*, 1997: 70).

Sean: "Hardline is not against sex. It is against certain deviations of that act and some contexts in which it occurs. The pure attraction between woman and man, and that which will occur between them, should not be restricted for it is the natural way" (*Vanguard* 1, "The Balance of Things," 1992: 10).

MOVE: "We believe in natural law, the government of self. Manmade laws are not really laws, because they don't apply equally to everyone and they contain exceptions and loopholes. Man-made laws are constantly being amended or repealed. Natural law stays the same and always has. Man's laws require police, sheriffs, armies, and courts to enforce them, and lawyers to explain them. True law is self-explanatory and self-enforcing" (*25 Years on the MOVE*, 1997: 68).

Sean: "The Hardline has existed since the dawn of time. It is the true way and path that springs forth from the root of creation. Either one walks that path and is Hardline or they do not and are not" (*Vanguard* 1, "The Hard Life," 1992: 9).

Sean: "[*Q: ...what would be the one thing that concerns your daily activism the most?*] A: Well, like you said, there is not just one thing in that sense. But it goes in phases for me, and lately I've been really involved in indigenous rights. And that incorporates on several levels whether it's working for land rights, political freedoms or even going down to the struggle of people like Mumia Abu Jamal who is in prison right now for supposedly killing a cop. Basically it looks like he's been set up because of his political views. A lot of what I'm working on now is racial things and how the system tends to screw over the so called minorities. And beyond that if I really think of what I'm focusing on it would be spirituality. Not so much isolating myself and praying, more of how spirituality applies to a revolutionary struggle. Specifically for me it is Islam. And I don't want this to be taken the wrong way because when you say 'holy war' then every [one] just thinks that you are a lunatic. But specifically how it ties into the way in which we were meant to live on the Earth and how it's all screwed up. I see it definitely as a battle between good and evil" (*Destroy Babylon* 2, "Captive Nation Rising interview," 1995: 43).

Ryan Downey (Hardball, Burn it Down): "Tension arose at that first hardline gathering when it become clear that there were two distinct camps. Some of us saw hardline as a serious revolutionary group, along the lines of John Africa's MOVE organization in Philadelphia; the American Indian Movement, or AIM, that championed Leonard Peltier; Earth First!; and similar activist collectives. Another camp looked at hardline like business as usual in straight edge hardcore, with an extra rule or two" (Rettman 2017: 273).

Scott Beibin (Bloodlink Records): "I don't recall MOVE mentioned at the first Hardline gathering" (personal conversation 3 March 2021).

Sean: "During the early eighties I had gotten progressively more into the animal rights stuff. I started reaching out, writing some radical articles, and looking to make contact with Animal Liberation Front (ALF) people. I also got exposed to the ideas of MOVE. After the bombing [of MOVE] in 1985 a couple of members came out to the L.A. area and I got exposed a lot to their ideas and philosophy, which was very influential" (Peterson 2009: 93).

Sean: "The mystical element was always there in Vegan Reich. It became more pronounced in our lyrics as we went on. I had always spent time around a lot of Rastafarians, was exposed to Islam, and I was always heavily into martial arts so there was a strong Taoist and Buddhist influence on me. I also met some of the people from MOVE who had actually fled after that whole thing [i.e., bombing of MOVE by Philly police in 1985] went down" (Peterson 2009: 488).

Phil Africa: "Despite the hardship of being separated from our children, spouses, sisters and brothers, **Move** members remain **strong** and **committed** to our belief, **life**, the teachings of **John Africa**, a **powerful testament** to our commitment to **total revolution** exampled by our belief in **Mama/Life/God/Nature/John Africa. Long Live John Africa Forever**!" (Phil Africa, *First Day* 19: 3).

Micah: "Our ideology and method of ACTION has gone by many names, in many languages, from generation to generation. We derive inspiration from and pay homage to such social justice REVOLUTIONARIES throughout the ages, as MOVE, the American Indian Movement (AIM), the Black Panther Party For Self-Defense, and the Weather Underground. With respect to "Eco-Defense"—we honor and walk in the footsteps of the Earth Liberation Front (ELF), the Animal Liberation Front (ALF), and an array of militant movements with which there are obvious parallels and inspirations" (Taliyah homepage 2020).

Sean: "[Hardline was] heavily influenced by the politics of Malcolm X and MOVE…" (Vegan Reich, *Jihad*, 1999).

Number of times that the Hardline manifesto mentions MOVE: zero.

Number of times Sean or other Hardliners call to support the MOVE 9 (incarcerated at the time since 1978) in *Vanguard*: zero.

Number of mentions of MOVE in *Vanguard* issues 1-7: zero.

First time Sean ever mentioned MOVE in Hardline literature: 1998.

Naj One aka Harun Najwan al-Askari (Taliyah al-Mahdi): [*Q: Which social groups have inspired you the most in word and action? And are there any groups you are active in yourself?*] A:"MOVE! Long live John Africa, they are the first group to say revolution starts from doing the right thing. They are also one of the first groups to recognize the exploitation of animals and the planet. … I am a member of the Taliyah al-Mahdi, and I am not very active. I am just a wannabe new jack; I do not consider myself very revolutionary. … I will say that revolution starts with yourself; you must fight the inner struggle before you fight the outer problems. … drug free and veganism are all part of submission to Allah. [*Q: Which writers and artists influenced you as an individual?*] A: Damn, where do I begin: Eldridge Cleaver, Huey P. Newton, Howard Zinn, Zack De La Rocha, Nas, Prophet Muhammad (pbuh), Noam Chomsky, Immortal Technique, Earth Crisis, Isa Adam Naziri, Vegan Jihad, Saul Williams, Chuck D, Tupac, Dead Prez, Killa Priest, Marcus Garvey, John Africa, Franz Fanon, Che Guevara, Russell Simmons, Eminem, Jay-Z, …Shahid Mustafa, Amir Sulaiman, Emcee Search, KRS1, Peter Tosh, Bob Marley, Jesus Christ (as), Confucius, Erica [Erykah] Badu, Askari X, Imam Jamil Amil, Bawa Muhayideen, Russell Means, Rob Coronado, Mustafa Talib, Talib Kweli, Ramona Africa, …Ill Bill, Mumia Abu-Jamal. Yo, I could go on for days" (Bahr 2010)

Nature and human nature

Hardliners did not spend too much time publically philosophizing about human nature. One senses a general tone of misanthropy coming through alongside a critique of "civilization" and celebration of indigenous peoples but Sean/they don't really develop a clear conception of either nature (e.g., the boundary between "human" and "nature") or human nature (e.g., what humans will or won't do based on intrinsic traits or proclivities).

Sean: Most people are, at best, amoral, and at worst immoral. Accepting that as truth, we must put our energies into creating a situation where they are forced to grant rights and freedoms to all life. Ideally, that would mean an ecology-oriented, vegan governing structure, which would ensure that people followed one moral/ethical code" (Boston Hardline 1995: 16).

Sean: "Humans seem to have an inherent weakness which has led to the corruption of modern day civilization. Most people are concerned with sense gratification than for the rights of those whom their actions affect. Rather than abide by nature's laws, mankind has tried to control her. ...people still ignore the rights of other innocent, sentient beings such as unborn human babies and non-human animals. ...While in pursuit of profit, sense gratification, and fulfillment of the ego, mankind has wrecked the ecology of this planet. The world is almost, if not already, on an irreversible path towards destruction which affects everyone, guilty or innocent. All the while people still support the large industrial polluters with only moderate protest. For these reasons, the HARDLINE movement has evolved and organized. ...We fight for the protection of this planet and all of its downtrodden inhabitants regardless of their race, sex, age or species, and oppose all acts which go against nature's laws, including deviant sexual acts such as same sex attraction or attraction to young children or animals. We are straight for various reasons, with the main one being that drug use breeds apathy. Most of all, we will use any means necessary to defend innocent life and this planet..." (*Vanguard* 1+2 double issue 1993: 7).

Sean: "We're in the final days. ...it's gonna be now or never, ...'cos our time's running out. No more ozone, no more trees, no more oxygen. Get it?" (Sean/Vegan Reich 1989b).

Declaration: "In creating technological advancements humans are actually evolving backwards—since fusion with nature is the highest possible evolutionary form. Humans' regression from nature and animal's allegiance to it is merit enough for their respect.

...Every species on this planet lies in shackles now, but we have the key. We have the key to end their enslavement. That key is veganism. ...Ceasing to view animals as inferior life forms and human commodities is integral to our struggle. Realization of the truth that they are just as important as us is coming slowly. We must defend them with every weapon at our disposal, but first we must gain a sense of admiration and value for them" (*Declaration* c. 1995: 14).

Upstate Hardline: "Morality and ethics are being wiped out. We as a society search our minds not for spiritual or moral answers, but scientific ones. If we have the ability to produce something, we do. Its ethical implications are not considered or they are covered up and hidden from view. ...Our technology has increased industrial and corporate pollution. We have created new and more irreversible pollutants for every fax machine, all-season tire and twinkie that we have devised on the drawing board. ...Non-human animals find their natural role on Earth involuntarily relinquished and replaced by the role of the slave. They are enslaved, mutilated, and digested by our indulgent habits. Heart disease, diabetes, cancer, and all of the other nutritionist related ailments create the need for live animal research. It is a vicious cycle of desensitization that leads back to technology.

Every new invention that we produce, every natural mystery that we solve builds our tower of Babel higher. We separate ourselves from our cooperative role in exchange for a competitive one on a larger scale everyday. Through chosen ignorance, we allow corporate press statements and dishonest media coverage to alleviate our guilt.

Technology is the path leading away from the natural order. It is a well-beaten path. We follow the multinational pied piper straight to our apocalypse. This is a predicament for us to realize and reverse. It is our obligation.

The perceived benefit of technology to the common person is that it will re-balance the scales that bound our grandparents and generations before to seemingly endless toil with no vigor or energy left to reap the harvest of their hard work. We strive as a society to work less and thusly create more 'quality time' which in actuality amounts to watching TV and consuming even more natural resources.

...If we are going to as a movement wage war against unnatural ecological plundering, we have to consciously fight the television indoctrination that urges us to be consumers. Commercial consumption is what draws us away from appreciating and revering this beautiful Earth in its natural state. To fight against the Earth's destruction, we MUST battle the multi-national corporations that callously lead us to imminent destruction. Fight consumerism in all of its monstrous forms. Reduce and re-use. When looking upon technology, the Hardline urges you to see it as the Sodom that it is" (*Vanguard* 7, "Technology a Quest for Useless Knowledge," 1996: 24-25).

Rat (Statement): "i've always been an atheist, and always will be. im not in to the human race, id like to think that pretty soon the human race gets wiped off this planet, so that non human animals and nature are left to their own devices, and can some how get things back to where they were before humans started to destroy so much shit. i think these two things are probably pretty much against hardline ideology. ... i used to be strongly opposed to abortion, but now i'm more concerned with the over population of this planet, and the destruction that over population brings. so, for me, i have to see the greater picture, and that is of the survival of the planet, not survival of individuals. ... as for primitivism, i want to see an end to the human species, so i'm not sure that fits in with what i believe!" (Bahr 2010).

Sean: "...ultimately, I have to say that I truly believe that every living creature is born Muslim. Not 'born Muslim' in the sense of being born adhering to a particular religious form (i.e. 'Islam' with a capital 'I') but rather born as a 'Muslim' and one who is instinctually practicing 'Islam' (or the act of submission and true peace, which are the root meanings of that word, and the state of being one has as a child, before ego and false identity of self take us away from our true purpose—which is living in harmony and communion with the Divine Will). For I don't believe in the Christian concept of being born into Sin. To me, we are perfect at our conception and at our birth. At that movement we are untainted with pride, vanity, and illusion. We are truly a part of the whole of creation, which is an emanation from that which we call Allah. Therefore, I feel my spiritual side has always been a part of my being, and has always been responsible for my striving towards righteousness (now, and before I even knew what the word 'Islam' meant). So on that level, Islam has always been with me" (Muttaqi c. 2001).

Declaration: "All forms of oppression are interconnected and can be traced back to the human race. We cannot see the big picture, we cannot come to the realization of what we are doing. We subjugate everyone but ourselves in order to satisfy our personal ambitions, without taking into account the consequences of our actions. And now that mentality is finally catching up with us, but somehow I find it hard to put faith back into humanity. I think our greed and laziness outweigh our morality and stifle our reasoning in the end" (*Declaration* c. 1995: 16).

Sean: "The hardline ideology sees mankind's insecurity with himself and his position to the world around him as one of his biggest downfalls. It is that fear of life, and lack of faith in himself that leads to him walling himself off from the natural world, which he does not understand, and thus hates. It is why from there, he feels not content to be merely removed, but then must also conquer what lies outside his walls—ever threatening his sheltered little world. It's the same reason he cages the wild beasts in his zoos, or hangs their heads on his walls. It is why he domesticates what he does not kill or cage, removing all elements of the wild, producing instead a docile slave to his every whim. And on down the line it goes… From the massing of wealth and possessions to gain a false sense of security and stability, to the taking of intoxicating substances to remove oneself from the horrifying reality that is everyday life, seeking refuge in a state of temporary invulnerability and bliss" (Boston Hardline 1995: 1).

Hardline ad for the first Survival of the Fittest gathering: "This world, our home is on the brink of destruction—victim of a dying empire's attempt to maintain the status quo of its excessive existence. Draining the lifeblood from our mother earth, filling her veins with their poison and disease—they have turned a once sustainable paradise into a hellish inferno where only the fittest shall survive. In times such as these, it is imperative that those dedicated to the struggle of world liberation be mentally and physically equipped to not only survive in today's climate of self destruction, but also excel—while effectively and efficiently working towards a successful revolution that shall bring about the earth's salvation. …This gathering is not open to the general public and will not be a forum for debate on these issues. If you are part of the struggle to achieve the liberation of all life from the clutches of 'modern man' then we would like for you to join us" (*Praxis* 1991: 17).

Declaration: "Someone once said that humans are an inherently good race. Nothing could be further from the truth. It's just when a little something good happens we blow it out of proportion until it makes the bad look trivial. We forget all about the rape of the Amazon, of the fact that every second another piece of land the size of a football field is clear cut or burned down in the tropics. We don't make the connection between the hamburger on our plates and the suffering cow having its throat slit in the slaughterhouse. …Why do we forget? Why don't we make the connection? Why do we overlook? Because we are conditioned to ignore the damage we are inflicting until we become so desensitized that nothing really matters anymore. Until we are enslaved, until we are mutilated and murdered, until we are at the receiving end of the injustice we will not empathize. Apathy will reign until we are personally confronted with our wrongdoing, and by that time it will be too late. By then we will be caught in the grips of the industrial wasteland we have created" (*Declaration* 1 c. 1995: 15).

Dave Agranoff (*Defense, Rescue and Survival*, *Vanguard*): "There is a way to live with our natural world that places us within the web of life rather than above it. There is a way to live with respect for all life, and a love for the natural world. There is a way to regain our spiritual connection with the Earth. That way is the Hardline. A path that has existed before any of us but has been formulated into a movement of individuals from all walks of life. For Hardliners a single ethic exists. The ethic that all innocent life is sacred regardless of species, race, sex, origin, etc. and has the right to live out its life within its natural habitat without any interference of any kind whatsoever. Those who knowingly violate the rights of the innocent must be stopped by any means necessary. ... Reject the myths of this western culture. It's time to return to our natural state and regain our connections with the forgotten natural order. Embrace the Hardline not as a means to an end but for the beginning of a life-long quest to regain our instinctual knowledge and connection with all life. Embrace the Hardline!" (*Vanguard* 7, "Introduction," 1996: 4).

Declaration: "To say that drug usage, promiscuity, abortion, animal, earth and human exploitation and destruction are the problems with society and humankind would be only partially true. Yes, these are problems that need to be dealt with, but they are more so symptoms of a deeper and more complex problem (or disease) that is interconnected and exists across the globe. This problem is that humans have somehow taken it upon themselves to elevate beyond the laws of nature and in doing so, supersede our niche in the natural world with a tyrant species that is willing to take every sort of moral gamble in order to satisfy its supremacist lethargy. ...Each of these secondary plights stem from the primary source: The desire to control and live over the ordinance of the Earth and the power that flows from it.

It is this power that keeps the world in balance, with all life flowing smoothly and naturally, interacting correctly with one another while preserving the ecosystem. We have exiled ourselves from that code of behavior, and in doing so have created the genesis of this problem. We *are* the genesis of this problem. And now we must solve it, we must correct our mistakes.

It is, sadly, wholly probable that our destruction has reached such an extent that a return to the natural order is impossible for our species. This must not serve as a deterrent however, union with all life and the planet that gives birth to that life is our rightful place in nature's hierarchy, it is our destiny. And I refuse to let this industrialized hell we have created come between me and my proper place in the world I hold dear" ("The Genesis of the Problem," *Declaration* 1, c. 1995: 25).

Raid: "Born into an age of anthropocentricity, where nature is considered an evil, a wild that must be tamed. Humanity is now a plague, a cancer to the ecosystem. Stop the machine; society, before we reach total annihilation. BLOOD GREEN. Burn it down. Ecotage for self-defense, nature is our home that we must defend. Man and earth are one. This is the final truth for global salvation. This is a call to arms for those who put nature above themselves.

4 1/2 billion years of earth is on the verge of extinction. BLOOD GREEN.

Burn it Down. Destroy the poison of technology that is killing the land. This is your ultimatum and you better heed our demand" (lyrics to "Blood Green," 1991).

Steve Lovett (Raid): "When I wrote Blood Green I was somewhat of a misanthropic Luddite. I was then and still am a want-to-be anarchist. I say that because I believe in human potential, however I am all too familiar with human nature. Most anarchistic intentional communities have failed for one reason or another. I think the real issue is how can our society become more environmentally sustainable? …I lived for nearly 8 years isolated in the mountains of northern California. We did have a small country store, but for groceries we would have to drive nearly an hour and a half to town. Living like that it's easy to believe in anarchy. Shit, we were living it. There were no cops around and what few neighbors there were looked out for each other. Most folks had gardens or paid for local produce grown in the valley I lived in. There was a strong community element there because you knew everyone and wanted the best for them. The situation is vastly different in major metropolitan areas. …I have read some Zerzan and I'm familiar with the ideas of anarcho-primitivism. Personally I think they are romantic, idealistic and unrealistic. There was never a golden age! There have always been struggles, losers and winners in history. Armchair philosophers like Zerzan write in the ethers, not in the real world. Ultimately primitive Anarchists fail to address the complexities of modern life. Don't get me wrong, he is a compelling author. I don't know much about Zerzan as a person, except he lives in the middle of a neighborhood in Eugene dreaming he was living in the ancient hunter gather age. Ahh, the good old days—what a joke" (xYosefx 2010).

Alex (New Eden Project): "The only problem I have with the ALF and the ELF is that they do not support taking people out" (Anonymous 2004).

Sean: "[*Q: What do you think of the Unabomber?*] A: I think that it is the most inspiring person or group that has been active in years in this country" (*Destroy Babylon* 2, "Captive Nation Rising interview,"1995: 47).

Declaration: "We are living (or dying rather) in the age of an extinction culture, wherein **every** element be they living or inanimate is being pushed towards termination at an alarming rate. This process is nurtured under the ethics of apathy and greed. …We have slashed and killed everything in our path and now there is virtually nothing left, who is to be held accountable? Every one of us. Every one of us who participates in the decimation and does not lift a finger to halt it" (*Declaration* 1, c. 1995: 15-16).

Ethnicity and anti-racism

Probably somewhere, unbeknownst to me, there existed in the murky corridors of the 1990s punk scene a Black person who identified as Hardline. Micah once described his wife as an "African member" of Taliyah and that seems like the closest I have even heard of a Black Hardliner (Source: Adam Naziri, *Indybay*, 21 July 2004). Of course, Chuck Treece played in post-Hardline Pressure but, as a scene, Hardline did seem largely white even if Sean identified as a Mexican/person of color via his mother. Similarly, other members of Vegan Reich had Latin@ background, Walter Bond and Micah both claimed non-white Native backgrounds to some extent, and Michelle Borok of Memphis had Jewish and Korean background. So one cannot exaggerate Hardline's general whiteness but nor can one deny it. At the same time, perhaps due to Sean's overtures and appropriations of Nazi terms like "Reich," phrases like "final solution," and anti-homosexuality, some outsiders have described Hardline as racist which seems inaccurate because Hardline explicitly rejected racism from the beginning and maintained that position throughout. While some of the person-of-color status claimed after Hardline's demise may involve revisionism, Hardliners never, as far as I can tell, ever espoused any overtly racist ideals. At the same time, one cannot exaggerate the degree to which Hardliners opposed racism. Sean and other Hardliners did not discuss racism/anti-racism much in their zines. Sean claims that he and his crew fought neo-Nazis in California but *Vanguard* and the Hardline manifesto clearly did not place racism at the center of their discourse or program. Not until the band Racetraitor on Uprising Records entered the hardcore scene (with one brief member, Eric Bartholomae, identifying as Hardline) did race take on a more central role but, even then, only in tangential relation to Hardline.

Steve Lovett (Raid): "...there's this Memphis paper here and on the front page they were talking about some of the youth camp meetings or something and it was talking about the different racial mix and said, you know, like 'five Asian Americans, maybe ten Afro Americans, twelve European Americans and: one vegan' (laughs)" (*Vanguard* #5, 1993: 5).

Joey Leyva (*Out From The Shadows*): "We [radical vegan straight edgers] have every right to express and celebrate our identities, and anyone who opposes our doing so should ask very serious questions about themselves and their role in resistance culture. To celebrate one's identity should never be hindered, but in fact encouraged, as such expressions can create solidarity and support in communities that are largely dispossessed and discouraged. A wonderful example of such empowerment is Anarchist People of Color. I can't imagine anyone in the anarchist community condemning or opposing APOC based on the negative aspects of former movements by people of color, or calling the group 'superiorist' because it seeks to create a safe space for persons of color to identify and organize. Aren't we as the radical vegan straight edge merely asking for similar space and opportunity?" (Leyva 2006: 10).

Sean: "People would say 'Oh, Vegan Reich—a bunch of rich, white, vegan straight edge kids.' But our band was always a majority Mexican entity. Not that it would have mattered if the whole band was white, but it was just weird having these perceptions from people who didn't know us and seeing how wrong they were" (Peterson 2009: 489).

Mack Evasion (*Evasion*): "They called them privileged white kids, when the visionary and lyricist of Vegan Reich wasn't even white" (Evasion 2004, 31).

Sean: "In a lot of ways, having a really diverse background—we have a lot of mixture in my family, everything from Mexican, French, Arab, Irish, Sicilian, African, and Cherokee — it just all felt real natural. The cultural and ethnic aspects were put to rest when I embraced Islam. ...by the time I was old enough to have [ethnic identity] become an issue, the punk rock thing had taken over.

But when we moved to a new neighborhood, I was always the brown kid. On the other end, I can pretty much travel wherever and blend in, because I have this look that's in between. If I'm in Jamaica, Jamaicans think I'm Jamaican; if I'm in an Arab country, the Arabs think I'm Arab; if I'm in Mexico, they think I'm Mexican. But for me, especially when punk and hardcore started losing the sense of community and ideology, Islam gave me a place to feel comfortable" (Sanneh 2013).

Sean: "My father for instance was a soul/r&b musician and by no means living a conservative lifestyle, but he's the first person to introduce me to Malcolm X. Similarly my mother's side were always left leaning politically—but being a family of Mexican, Irish and Cherokee descent—religion was always present" (Muttaqi 2021).

Micah: "…you don't know anything about my background. I was raised by parents making a combined household income in the $20,000's in an otherwise all black neighborhood. My grandfather himself is half Cherokee and half Melungeon. But in REAL Islam there is no such thing as 'race.' …But I'm not black, I'm a mix of a number of backgrounds, Jewish, Cherokee, Melungeon, German... All of these can be held to scrutiny in the eyes of the PC white elitists (the same who called the Democratic Party 'The White Man's Party' in the 19th Century). Perhaps if we had African members of our group speaking, even my wife, then we would be off the hook for believing differently than you; just like Tupac, just like Xzibit, and most of hip hop, along with MOVE and Rastafarians..." (writing as Adam Naziri, "Calling All Anti-Homophobes!, Protest MTV," *Indybay* 14 July 2004).

Rat (Statement): "The world's a violent place, oppressors everywhere—from governments to racist nazi shits, to murdering animal abusers. Fuck, I'm not gonna stand still while innocents are being smashed. …For when I see the huntsmen fall, for when I see the nazi scum tumble, for then I know to inflict pain on these oppressors of the innocent. Death." (lyrics to "Prepare for Battle" by Statement, 1990).

Defense, Rescue and Survival [presumably Dave Agranoff]: "American Pride, White Pride, the lie is the same. When i was younger i was involved with skinheads. Although not racist, i think i might as well have been. I had this stupid pride in my country. I had nothing to do with achieving the fact that i was born within these borders so why the pride? …this country is nothing to be proud of, it is something rather to be ashamed of. Over 200 years the U.S. government has almost completely destroyed the six Indian nations. For a people who at one time lived through out Northern America, when was the last time you even saw an Indian reservation? …Dan from

Everlast put it best 'if you want to burn down a crack house, burn down the White House, it's the biggest one.' ...I ride my bike through white trash Dayton every other day. ...It is easy for us to demand change in our hardcore community but what right do we have if we take pride in the system which encourages continued drug abuse?" (unsigned article "American Pride, White Pride, the lie is the same," *Defense, Rescue and Survival* 1, 1995: 8).

Michelle (Memphis Hardline, *Gaia Screams*, *Invictus*): Asian culture is known almost purely through stereotypes. Most of this is left over from World War II, the Korean War, and of course Vietnam, all horrible types of suffering, hare, and destruction. Most Asian countries can't be rid of war. Foreign (mostly U.S.) military bases and well protected embassies everywhere, make soldiers and camouflage a common sight on city streets. ...Korea remains the number one consuming nation of American mink. The value of fur as a status symbol has warped the Asian attitude towards the issue of animal rights, but we cannot give up hope. ...The good news is that the Hong Kong fur manufacturing industry is on a decline. Bad news is that the production facilities are now being relocated to China. Why? Very simple—cheap labor.

...As for animal consumption, Koreans eat more meat now than ever, downing the flesh of 1,226 head of cattle and 8,029 hogs daily. The numbers aren't as frightening as the American death toll, but the increase over the years is very disturbing. This can all be attributed to...you guessed it—Western civilization" (Michelle, "Animal Liberation," *Vanguard* 6, 1995: 21-22).

Micah: "The HardLine ideology and way of living outdates all forms of modern government. We do not agree with the anthropocentric concept of 'land ownership' which this and other modern nations were based on. In addition, we take no pride in the fact that we were born within the boundaries of any so-called nation. For example, having american pride would be the same as having pride in the warped 'value' system of patriarchy, speciesism, racism and drug abuse which American society encourages. ...you who profess being vegan, how dare you take pride in a system that views our animal brothers and sisters to be at best nothing more than servants for us to build our empires upon and at worst simple thoughtless machines who exist for the sole purpose of providing us with a 'product'? ...And what of those who claim to live a drug free lifestyle while they might have an american flag on their jacket, car/pickup truck, or house? In all truth this government is the largest drug dealer. In the late 60s the Federal government pumped drugs into the inner city to suppress the civil rights movement and who do you think is responsible for supplying Native

Americans with the alcohol so prevalent in what remains of their communities? In 'white' neighborhoods how many liquor stores do you see? Now how many in 'minority' communities? Are you making the connection here? ...You might as well be taking pride in the injustice you claim you are fighting against.

Remember, it is not a matter of love it or leave it (because believe me we would undoubtedly leave it). WE ARE HERE TO DESTROY IT! Not to respect it, not to leave it and certainly not to take pride in it! That is why any movement or ideology that is struggling against tyranny and oppression, be it the pro-life movement, animal liberation or Earth liberation movement, civil rights movement, even straight edge and certainly HardLine, will be inherently anti-american for america is the picture of oppression and the epitome of injustice" (*Note: despite claiming Cherokee background in quote from 2004, note that Micah described Native Americans in third person: "their communities" not "our communities"*; Collins "Hardline is Anti-American!" *Destroy Babylon* 2, 1995: 60-61).

Mani (Racetraitor): "Racetraitor was never a hardline band. Most of us weren't that into it actually for a lot of reasons, not the least of which was the view of some hardline chapters on homosexuality and pro-life. But also the weird fetishizing of the animal rights struggle just felt like white males wanting to be the voice of the voiceless. Mind you we were all vegan and I'm still vegan. But we were big in those circles and I think for a few reasons. Obviously, Uprising put us out and Sean started hardline. By the time we met Sean he had been out of hardline for a while. It was odd at first because I thought of hardline as something kinda far from what we were about, but to my surprise Sean was the first label guy that fully understood Racetraitor. He understood the approach and he 100% shared our race politics, which almost no one at that time was into. He was as annoyed by the self-satisfaction of hardcore kids. He understood the band name and that made us feel like he was a good choice. He actually left hardline exactly because he thought it was too white and weird by like 1993. For him hardline was a thread of anarchism, but that got lost fast, and I think he knows he's partly to blame for that" (Dorff 2016).

Sean: "We support the Black Liberation and Indigenous people's resistance movements and fight along side them in their struggle to reclaim their dignity as a people, restore their rights and lay claim to what they've been denied" ([*Note: Despite claiming both Mexican and Cherokee descent, Sean wrote here of indigenous people in the third person*]; *Vanguard* 1, "What is Hardline," 1992: 5).

Michelle (*Gaia Screams*, *Invictus*): "Humanity is much crueler when your skin is a little darker, your lips a little fuller, your eyes a little more defined. I'm just going to say it....white people will never understand. Racism is more than a slogan or a bandwagon. Racism is a knife that stabs and slashes. It is painful and intense. It is not just black and white. It's black, white, brown, red, yellow. It's about defiling beautiful people of all shades of beige. Most disturbing, it's about destruction of magic. Cultural ancestral magic. I am earthbound, like a tree.

...I only see it getting worse with children like me, second generation, mixed blood. Growing up in homogewhite America, life seems it would be easy if you weren't so different, so unique and foreign. Alien. Swallow that native tongue, forget the folklore. You don't need it anymore. Now you have Bobby and Sally White here to make wonderful fun of kung fu movies and kemosabe. And they'll do it all of your life, at your expense. They'll always make tasteless classless jokes and never think of what harm they might be doing to your self-image. So be strong while you are finding pride, because they will always be there with their ignorance. It's in their nature, to be afraid and hopeless.

Keep fighting because you are a shoot pushing up through the mud. To dredge through growing pains and grow back down again with deep roots. They stay foolish because they have nothing to be proud of. Dirty barbarians among emperors, shaman chieftains" (*Invictus* 1, 1995: 19).

Sean: "[*Q: Is it 'black' and 'white'? To racists things are black and white too—what makes you right and them wrong?*] A: What makes us right, is that we are. Racism is rooted in anthropocentricity (the belief that mankind is superior to all forms of life) and although the pure manifestations of anthropocentricity take the form of abuse to animals and the earth, it is also the underlying basis of why post tribal European culture has oppressed all races which existed in balance with nature and lived in a natural animal state—as such was something to be inferior and inhuman. Now, obviously certain elements of racism developed over territorial and economic disputes between certain races, but when looking at the form of racism practiced against Africans, Native Americans, Pacific Islanders etc. by European imperialists—the cause is that of an anthropocentric attitude.

Hardline is about ecocentricity—that is, that life revolves around the earth's needs. Racism is founded on the reverse; based on human arrogance practiced by people in search of power through the domination of another.

Since Hardline is about living in harmony and existing in accord with the unity and oneness of nature—we obviously oppose the foundation of racist thought and all of its manifestations" (Boston Hardline 1995: 17).

Sean: "One just has to look at the Bushmen who would pray to the spirit of the animal they killed, asking for forgiveness etc. Similar was the relationship between the Native Americans (in the plains region) and the buffalo. And in areas where weather permitted, and the knowledge of farming had been preserved, many tribes went back to a vegan diet" (Boston Hardline 1995: 18).

Sean: "Adolph Hitler, and the Nazi Party, based their political, economic and social ideology on the flawed framework that all modern nations and political groups have also built upon, and that is around a principle which places self interest above the good of the whole. With the Nazis, that was an interest in their race, and the re-aryanisation of Europe, to benefit the Germanic people. This obsession with their own special interest group led to atrocities against all who stood in their way for the benefit of their own selfish, singular concerns. The difference between what you call a 'vegan master race' and an Aryan master race' is clear. Firstly, veganism is a way of living, not a racial identity—thus our unity comes from common objectives, not common ancestry. The superiority of veganism has nothing to do with the superiority of individuals. Beyond that, the goals of militant veganism has nothing to do with the self interest, or of seeking privilege or dominance. We are expendable in the struggle. All that matters is what's good for the earth. That is <u>much</u> different than the concept and goals of an Aryan master race" (Boston Hardline 1995: 18).

Sean: "As fascists have sought to rebrand themselves with vulgar euphemisms such as 'alt-right,' along with a co-optation in certain countries of veganism or straight edge by racist, and xenophobic elements, it becomes clear that we must clarify our name and beliefs in order to preserve our legacy from being used by those who hold such retrograde and ignorant views. First and foremost, Vegan Reich started out as an anarcho-punk band. Our members have always been committed anti-fascists, and the band has historically primarily been made up of people of color throughout its existence" (Vegan Reich 2017b).

Sean: "I am absolutely 100 percent against the state of Israel and do not believe it should be in existence. This has nothing to do with Islam, or Judaism. For I support true Judaism, and I support equal rights for all people. But if one looks at the history of this issue, they will see that religion is getting used as a justification by the Israeli government to oppress and exploit the Palestinian people. It's so absurd. If one knows their history, they will see that the whole idea of an ethnic 'chosen people' who can claim ownership of Jerusalem is a lie. Certainly Moses was a Hebrew, as were many of his followers. But when he led 'his people' out of Egypt into Palestine, he was not leading just one racial group out of slavery and into the 'promised land.' Rather, he was leading a whole multitude of races who had come to accept his teaching (and this group included black Africans, Arabs, Asians, Europeans that had resided as slaves in Egypt etc.). It is this group that came to be called the Jews. However, when Rome sacked Jerusalem, and the Jews were dispersed, this community went in many directions. Those who had been more of European descent migrated back towards Europe and intermarried, becoming intertwined with the local populations where they settled etc. Those who were primarily of Hebrew and Arab ethnicity (both a Semitic people), as well as the multitude who were a mix of all the people who had been in the first exodus out of Egypt, stayed in the region, and those who were primarily of African background went back into Egypt and Ethiopia etc.

...And all of this immediately got more complicated with the evil atrocities committed by Hitler against anyone who was either a practicing Jew (even if European) or merely had 'Jewish Blood' (being related in any way to the original tribe of Israel, no matter if Christian or not)—for after the holocaust, a situation arose where the survivors were looking for a place to once again call their own, and area to establish a homeland. And this is where the results of one injustice start to compound and make way for a new tragedy.

...This is NOT saying that those of Hebrew descent, or those who practice the Jewish religion should not be allowed to live in Palestine. Certainly there have been long surviving communities of a Hebrew Jewish population living in Palestine, and the fact is, they have always been given a protected status under Islam which sees them as brothers, and a common 'People of the Book.' But when it comes to people of primarily European descent moving en masse to a Middle Eastern country, and kicking the local inhabitants out (whose families have owned the land for thousands of years). To me this is nothing more than colonialism and racism. Pure and simple. And prominent members of the international Jewish community have expressed the same opinion (in their rejection of the State of Israel). So let's make sure this does not get confused as being an anti Jewish issue. I have love for all people. My stance on this one [is] for justice, and one against oppression. Nothing more.

Those who oppress in the name of Judaism, but live not as Jews. The people of the world need to recognize this, and not criticize Judaism because of the injustice done by some in its name. The same as they must not judge Islam by those who act un-Islamically and bring terror to innocent people. I wholeheartedly support resistance against the State of Israel by any means necessary (as a struggle against occupation and genocide), but I also pray for a day when Christian, Muslim and Jew alike, can live at peace in the sacred city of Jerusalem (and all of Palestine)" (Muttaqi c. 2001).

Size

An inevitable (yet impossible to answer) question always arises about Hardline: How big did it get? How many adherents did they get at their peak? I neither care nor can I answer the question but here you can read what others have said…

Wikipedia Talk Page: [Commenting on a Wikipedia text about Hardline) "'At its height, the hardline movement had approximately ten chapters, with one or two people involved in the US, Europe, South America, and Australia.' So there were like twenty people involved in this at its height? That can't be right, can it?" (Wikipedia, anonymous Wikipedian, 15 September 2008).

Wikipedia: "Many hardline bands existed, the most well known of which were Vegan Reich and Raid" (Wikipedia 2020).

DJ Rose (Path of Resistance): "In hardcore, you learn there's reality and then there's perception. If you can make the world perceive you as bigger and better than you actually are, they're going to flock to you. Anyone could place a full-page ad in *Maximum Rocknroll* and make it look like their band or label was this giant thing, when it was just a one-man band with maybe twelve kids worldwide supporting him. Illusion goes a long, long way" (Rettman 2017: 269-271).

Steve Lovett (Raid): "At the apex of the Hardline scene, our crew had around 60 supporters and our shows drew a lot more" (xYosefx 2010).

Micah: "Since the demise of Raid's commitment and the termination of Vegan Reich, it has appeared that the number of Hardliners has vastly decreased, with our numbers dropping from the hundreds to around 50 or so. …We realize now that there is no difference between having 200 people saying that they are Hardline while only having 5 doing things for the movement, and actually having only 5 true activists who are doing things. …*Vanguard* 1 warned us that the Hardline would never gain mass adherents as our code of ethics is far 'too strict' for most (who are content with the mechanical day to day convenience based life of modern society)" (*Destroy Babylon* 1, 1995: 4).

Memphis Hardline Militia: "While we can't say that we have fifty Hardliners in Memphis today, we can say that those we do have are true to the core. That is what was important all along; quality first and foremost. We are striving to gain new soldiers within our ranks, but we are more discriminating in our acceptance of one's desire to claim they are Hardline. Unless one is of the highest caliber, they are not fit to be honored by the Hardline label" ("Memphis Hardline Update Summer 1994," *Vanguard* 6, 1995: 17).

Michelle (*Gaia Screams*, *Invictus*): [List of 8 Hardline chapters in 1995 in four countries, U.S., Germany, Belgium, and Poland. Michelle marked four chapters, Belgium, Germany (Tina and Peta), Memphis (Michelle), and Dayton with "active Hardline women in these chapters." (Presumably, the other four chapters, Poland, Indianapolis, New Jersey, and Fon du Lac-Wisconsin, had no active Hardline women; *Gaia Screams* 1995: 16).

Ryan (Hardball, Burn it Down, *Vanguard*): "Certainly in 1990 everyone was talking about hardline, though at most, it probably only ever had a few hundred adherents, and I was chief among them" (Peterson 2009: 95).

Miscellaneous

Here you'll find a few scattered tidbits. Just because.

Declaration: "You run away and hide in the corners of deceit, concealed in this darkness. Beacons of light fall around but not on us. Behind this mask you coexist in a world I can't penetrate. Choking, coughing, drowning, and all the while you're indifferent to my suffering. And my suffering is on account of you. I try to end this charade the only way I know how. I scream the truth at the top of my lungs, everything I feel, everything I've wanted to keep locked up inside, but nothing breaks the silence. Not even a whisper. I haven't said anything at all. Insanity coursing through my veins. Eyes brimming with tears and blood polluted with desire for that which slipped through my hands. Swallowing thunder, grey blank walls, a relentless pressure. Locked inside an open room. I am here because of you. I am here because of me. I swallow my pride and vomit hope" (*Declaration* 1, c. 1995: 21).

Dave Agranoff (*Defense, Rescue and Survival*, *Vanguard*): "We need to stop looking like a bunch of bleeding heart pissed off kids. Most of us (including myself) are guilty of this. Every time we print stuff or publically say, 'fuck you, if you're not vegan or go pro-life or else,' it paints a negative image of Hardline that should not be painted. When we are confrontational in a negative way, we look like angry kids on a self-pleasing ego trip and not holders of the truth that is the only salvation for our world. …Hardline is not for anyone who must use such vulgar terms (it makes one look as though they have no good reason only angry emotion)" (Agranoff, *Vanguard* 6, "Hardline: We Have Failed," 1995: 25).

Sean: "Fuck you, shut your fucking mouth. We didn't ask for your opinion. We're telling you the way it is so sit back and listen" (Vegan Reich, "The Way It Is," 1990).

Dave Agranoff: "I'd say fuck you but you already fucked yourself! You can cry and scream all you want but nothing you can say will change the path that humanity has tread toward destruction" ("Holy War," *Defense, Rescue and Survival* 3, 1995: 18).

Anonymous Hardline Wikipedian: "I don't think it's necessary or positive to mention full names, though, what with security culture concerns and all. I also think that the involvement of Micah and the Cincy chapter should be mentioned, since they are so very vocal these days" (Wikipedia, unsigned comment on Talk:Hardline (subculture), "impressive!" 2006). [*Note: Sean has fomented a culture of secrecy in the name of security and protection. The logic goes that, since Hardliners engage in illegal activities, one should not publish their full names. This logic would make sense if, for example, one discussed an actual clandestine group which had sustained anonymity. Let's confuse Hardline with the EZLN or ALF. Sean, however, as well as the rest of Hardline zine writers and musicians, have had public personas. If anyone knows their full names, the police and government know them. In light of that fact, spewing hateful rhetoric from the shadows toward at-risk communities such as gays does not seem to warrant the "we need anonymity for security reasons" excuse.*]

Dave Agranoff (*Defense, Rescue and Survival*, *Vanguard*): "Animal rights have no place in this zine: I do not believe in animal rights.… I think animal rights is a term i am trying very hard not to use anymore. First off what right do we human beings have to give or take away other animals' rights? How egocentric is the term animal rights? …i have no interest in animal rights as it applies to our sick and twisted world's ideas of rights. I would like to see animals free of all forms of enslavement not just another part of this already doomed culture" (*Defense, Rescue and Survival* 3, 1995: 5).

Michelle (*Gaia Screams, Invictus*): "A vegan dog is a happy dog" (*Invictus* 1 1995: 9).

Dave Agranoff (*Defense, Rescue and Survival, Vanguard*): "Most humans in our culture digest 130 pounds of sugar and other useless sweeteners a year assaulting the body with the chemicals they had been refined with. …All this is a sign of how far society has separated itself from nature…it may seem like a little thing but it is not. Really aside from pleasure (which is a subjective argument) what purpose does sugar or high fructose corn syrup serve? …Only anthropocentric values can defend the consumption of completely unnatural products like refined sugar. …**Vegans**: ...do you find out where each item of food you eat (with sugar) got their sugar? If not, how do you know it's vegan? ...**Straight edgers**: You may have beaten the temptation to take other forms of drugs but what if you're still addicted to sugar? It has many of the same effects as other drugs, granted on a much slower more insidious scale, however eating large amounts of sugar is also a slow form of self-destruction (by damage to your immune system, you leave your body open to assault from bacteria)…It is poison so why not really be poison free? **Social justice activists**: Sugar is a cash crop. Like tobacco, cocaine, coffee, sugar is grown most often in third world countries where exploited workers harvest crops for U.S. and European companies for pennies an hour sometimes pennies a day. …**The bottom line**: Sugar is horrible for the environment …sugar is simple to quit if you just try. If anyone needs help quitting sugar contact me please…" ("Sugar," *Defense, Rescue and Survival* 3, 1995: 11-12).

Declaration: "Rape. Molestation. Incest. Assault. Sex crimes subliminally fueled and condoned by society. Warped perceptions of desire haze our views, twist and mutate our sexuality and affection until we are no longer capable of truly loving, of knowing natural sexuality, of becoming one with our personal sexuality. Fashion industries. Magazines. Movies. Television. Newspapers. Peers. Every corner we turn we are bombarded by a culture that wants nothing short of controlling and deviating our sexuality until it fits its standards and preconceptions, not ours. Perversions are rampant, what do I really feel? How should I feel? Beneath all this filth, under these grotesque lies, what is my status as a sexual being? Stripping away, we must learn all over again. Unlearn all this world has taught us" (*Declaration* 1, c. 1995: 20).

Sean: "Ignorance means lacking of knowledge or experience, or being uninformed, etc. How does that really apply to me? After nine years of being involved in the punk / Anarchist/ animal liberation movements there isn't anything in the social / political realm I haven't studied, or couldn't intelligently argue with you and needless to say, during that time, not to mention the rest of my life, I've experienced a lot first hand, so there goes your argument of ignorance" (Sean/Vegan Reich, *Profane Existence*, 1990b).

Sean: "Through all of this and the external turbulence of the struggle, the one thing that never changed and the one thing which the Hardline activist could depend on was my presence. Not only as an articulate spokesman for our movement and as an organizer, but also as an information source for those within the movement" (*Vanguard* 1993: 9).

Sean: "I literally could care less if someone likes me or what I believe in. For a large portion of my life, quite possibly the opposite was true (something about us nihilistic punk rockers who thrived on people's animosity)" (xCatalystx board 2009).

Sean: "[*Q: What does the name mean?*] A: 'VEGAN REICH' is the highest form of discipline attainable by the human race at this point in our historical development" (Sean/Vegan Reich 1989a).

Sean: "Self-control, physical strength, and mental awareness are what it's about 'cos it's survival of the fittest and this time it's gonna be the straight-up Vegan who comes out on top" (Sean/Vegan Reich *MRR* 79, 1989b).

Sean: "…unfortunately, there were other streams of thought that I think had come to dominate the general culture of straight edge—namely a sort of Nietzschean Will To Power, and rigid mindset, not to mention a sort of general conservatism" (Rettman 2019).

[Note: The two contrasts above may seem incompatible but for Sean, apparently, they still do not. An apocalyptic form of social Darwinism and "Survival of the Fittest" played a key role in Hardline but, unlike his perception of an individualistic ego-aggrandizing "Nietzschean Will To Power," Hardline's rigidity, "conservatism," and "Will To Power" aimed toward the welfare of all living beings (as long as they conformed to "natural law") during the End Times. Sean bemoaned the fact that "the notion of purity ceased to be a tool for self-negation (for the sake of the greater good)—and instead became a basis for self-aggrandizing, and worship of the self" and that observers could not distinguish one self-focused Will To Power for the sake of pleasure from the other self-negating and self-sacrificial Will To Power for the greater good. Tip for readers: rather than trying to fit the world onto a narrow "left-right" spectrum, try other means of understanding overt and covert ideologies and social dynamics.]

8 Timeline detailed

Pre-Hardline: 1984-1988

> *Politics is the art of looking for trouble, finding it whether it exists or not, diagnosing it incorrectly, and applying the wrong remedy.*
>
> –Ernest Benn (quoted by Mykel Board at the beginning of a column that discusses, amongst other things, Vegan Reich).

Although researchers seem to have decided on naming Sean after the famous actor Sean Penn, his actual birth name seems like an open secret. At the age of 15, Sean sent his first letter to *Maximum Rocknroll* in 1984 and signed it "Sean Panno." (He later had his father, Mike Panno, play saxophone on Pressure's 1998 *Hardcore Roots* release and nearly two decades later Sean released his father's novel *Animal Rites* on Primordial Press, a division of Uprising Communications, first in the year 2000—and *Maximum Rocknroll* reviewed it in issue #212 in January 2001—and again in 2016).

The first letter, however, provided no insights into his political thoughts, activism, or musical projects. Instead, Sean sent in a very short, simple letter trying to locate a friend of his who had moved back to Sweden. He concluded with a PS that read: "Remember the weird photographer that made movies of all of us at the beach?" If anything, the letter seemed to effuse a sense of warmth and innocence.

Also in 1984, Paul Conroy's animal lib/peace punk band End Result released a tape on Bluurg (run by people from Subhumans UK) named No Masters Voice. Paul started his own label in Melbourne, Australia also named No Masters Voice (neither one with apostrophe) the same year. If Sean got the idea from Paul's label to name his own, he has not stated that (additional unrelated labels with the same name have cropped up in France, Denmark, and the UK).

Another 1984 release included Statement's first demo tape which proclaimed "MEAT MEANS MURDER. Ignorance is guilt" would come out on Active Sounds that year and the eventual friendship between Sean and Rat would radically change his life… (Rat's second release came out on Bluurg in 1985).

In the meantime, Sean got into a variety of largely British anarcho-punk and Oi! As he recently recalled, "Oi!, with its whole skinhead ska connection was a big draw. In fact, my first band was an Oi! band" (Rettman

2019). Whether recordings exist of that band or not, I have no idea. As far as I could find, the first documented examples of Sean's foray into music started with Common Ground distribution which he ran at least by 1987. In particular, he distributed two punk bands from South Africa: peace punks Another Destructive System (ADS) and Power Age as well as the anarcho-punk, anti-abortion group Screaming Foetus (the latter two of whom featured in Sean's first ad in *MRR* in August 1987).

Like Sean, Aaron Sperske (the first drummer for Vegan Reich) had Hispanic background. From Alice Bag and Suicidal Tendencies to the Plugz and Circle One, southern California hosted numerous partially or entirely Hispanic punk bands. Although never casting themselves as such at the time, Sean would later place Vegan Reich in that type of category by describing them as "majority Mexican" (Sanneh 2013). Yet, unlike bands like Los Crudos, who brought the Hispanic element to the fore, many punks in southern California with Hispanic background such as Mike Vallejo guitarist/co-founder of Circle One or Zack de la Rocha (Inside Out, Rage Against the Machine), their ethnic identity did not seem so obvious to most people in the punk scene.

Sean has mentioned Circle One (who had released their LP in 1983) and the fact that they too used a cross of machine guns on their record cover but he never really discussed their influence or impact. As a popular LA-based Hispanic hardcore band, Circle One must have made a significant impact on young Sean. In particular, singer John Macias (of Puerto-Rican background) seemed to foreshadow some of Hardline's notoriety: people described John as both compassionate and intimidating, very caring and also very violent, charismatic and mentally ill (depression and schizophrenia). His tone of speaking before songs would carry the sort of Old Testament Prophet authority that seemed to foreshadow Vegan Reich. During the 80s, John formed a gang-like (or sect-like?) group of punks called The Family (as well as a booking and promotion group called P.U.N.X. which put a $5 cap on admission—imagine seeing the Misfits for five bucks!) and he preached a Christian-influenced gospel even while still singing for Circle One. In songs like "The Gospel," John sang blatantly anti-homosexual lyrics (veering off the lyric sheet) and guitarist Mike Vallejo affirmed (and personally rejected) John speaking "hateful…toward gays" (Alvarado and Taylor 2008: 45; for lyrics, see Appendix 3). According to John's lyrics and Mike's testimony, he saw this world as decrepit, corrupt and ruled by Satan while purity and salvation through Jesus awaited in the hereafter. Multiple sources described John as a towering figure within the LA-area punk scene and how he both preached unity and built peace while behaving very violently quite randomly (see, for example Alvarado 2001, Andy 2013, Robinson 2020; for an article covering the LA punk gang phenomenon in general see Dewitt and Rose

2013). Witnesses would tell of how John stared down police who tried to bully punks, how, on another occasion, he overturned a cop car, and, on yet another occasion, he actually intervened when a cop tried to arrest a punk and punched the cop straight in the face (and managed to escape with a group of angry officers chasing after). He sang (in, for example, "Highway Patrolmen") about multiple ways to kill a police officer. While Sean has never cited Circle One specifically as a big influence, he has mentioned them and it seems difficult to imagine that John did not leave more of an imprint than Sean has stated so far.

More clearly, one could see the impact of The Apostles, co-led by Andy Martin described as "The openly homophobic homosexual, the openly anti-racist racist." The Apostles put out two blatantly anti-homosexual and racist tracks, "Kill or Cure" and "Rock Against Communism." According to Andy, they involved an elaborate political prank (for his 2016 explanation of that prank, see Appendix 4). Who knows—perhaps the bizarre idea of releasing racist and heterosexist music purportedly in order to expose prejudice seemed interesting to Sean. After all, many observers accused The Apostles of fascism and homophobia, charges that Vegan Reich and Hardliners would later face themselves. Clearly, what The Apostles lacked in musical success, they made up for in controversy. They also held radical views against drugs and vivisection. In their 1985 *Smash the Spectacle!* EP, The Apostles included a 9-point program entitled "...BUT WHAT WILL YOU DO AFTER THE REVOLUTION??" that stated, "A national citizens' militia must be formed in order to maintain our own system of defense against NATO forces and possible foreign invaders. ...The slaughter of animals for vivisection and human consumption will be abolished. Those found guilty of an offense under this act must face sentence of death" (Listen and Understand 2011/The Apostles, Discogs 2021). Furthermore, Rat of Statement also briefly played in The Apostles and the two groups had split records released in 1988 and 1989. Sean apparently liked The Apostles so much that he released their *Hymn To Pan* LP on his own No Master's Voice label in 1988. And their idea of punishing vivisectors with death obviously foreshadowed Vegan Reich's identical message.

Also worth noting: both Circle One (as well as the band Rocks who got interviewed in the issue of *MRR* immediately prior to the first Hardline ad, pre-Hardline's gun logo) both had a M-16 gun-cross symbol for their own logos (see Appendix 3). The Apostles similar gun logo appears on the last page of this volume.

In 1985, police in Philadelphia bombed MOVE which both devastated the group, killing 11 people including five children, while also bringing them global attention. Sean probably first heard about MOVE then. (Although Sean claimed in his talk with Brian Peterson that he met MOVE people who left Philly after the bombing, he has not said whom from MOVE he met or gone into any detail about that supposed encounter. After all, in the mid-80s, most MOVE people had either gotten killed or incarcerated and only about one third of the original group remained in Philly. Considering Sean's silence in regard to MOVE during all of the 80s and most of the 90s, it seems reasonable to question his assertion.)

Also, in 1985, Tomas Squip of DC jazz-funk-punk band Beefeater wrote a letter to *MRR* wherein he argued against abortion on the same premises as against meat-eating. The language and logic seemed so similar to what Hardline would later say about "perversions," applying compassion universally in response, and how ethical veganism necessarily implied respecting the sanctity of fetuses as well, that I have trouble imagining that the letter did not have *some* impact on 16-year old Sean (for an excerpt from the letter, see Appendix 5). At any rate, Tomas included his address at the end of the letter. And Sean would later include a track from Beefeater on his first compilation in 1988. We know that much.

In 1986, Sean attended the anarchist gathering in Chicago marking the centennial of the Haymarket massacre. Although they did serve vegan food at the gathering, a major banquet during the event apparently did not have *any* vegan food (until attendees arranged their own). Apparently, by this time, the then-vegetarian 17-year old Sean said he had started a zine named *No Master's Voice* (later the name of his first label) and distributed an "anarcho-beef people" flyer at the gathering lambasting anarchists as hypocrites for meat-eating. Together with the street theater contingent he co-organized an agit-prop event during the dinner and caused a bit of a stir (see Appendix 6 for his missive on the topic).

At the end of 1986, a young activist named Rod Coronado, similarly inspired by bands such as MDC, Flux of Pink Indians, Rudimentary Peni, Crass, and Conflict, went out with a comrade and sunk two whaling ships in Iceland (Kuipers 2009: 81). Sean might not have known of Rod then but he certainly did in years to come.

The first mention of Vegan Reich in *Maximum Rocknroll* appeared in 1987 in a Southern California scene report where we could read that "Sean of Common Ground-Lethal Dose distribution and tapes has a band going called VEGAN REICH," and they "need a talented drummer to join 'em, and are looking for someone ...drug-free, non-pacifist (into direct action), has vegan views, etc, but who is still open-minded, so they can start playing around" (*MRR* 54, 1987: 21).

Soon Sean would assemble the first version of Vegan Reich in the form of himself (vox, git, and bass) plus fellow Oi! enthusiast Aaron Sperske from Naturecore and skinhead band Doug & The Slugz (Aaron would later go on to drum for—among other bands—Ariel Pink's Haunted Graffiti; see

Crustcave 2018). Together they recorded the first Vegan Reich track "Stop Talking—Start Revenging" which would come out on Sean's first compilation release in 1988.

In the meantime, Rat visited Sean in California and they did a road trip to an anarchist gathering in Toronto in July 1988. According to Sean, that event proved a turning point for him due to the anarchist lack of understanding for veganism and animal liberation, thereby providing the impetus to found Hardline. Years later, *MRR* columnist Mykel Board would recount stories of the Toronto Anarchist Festival and his encounter with the vegan punk pair plus Brian (then the bass player for Vegan Reich). Mykel began—in classic Mykel fashion—by blending fiction into reality.

In 1988 (*MRR* #64), he described the festival itself:

> I went to find the 'Bomb Making' workshop as being in room 723. Of course there was no room 723. All the other rooms were numbered randomly and those numbers kept changing every five minutes. I tried to find the men's room, but there were only 'person rooms.' Hardline anarchists objected anyway. It was fascist to assign a specific function to a specific room. Each room should be allowed to seek its full potential and not be hampered by arbitrary human restrictions. That was 'animist.' People pissed in ashtrays and shat in coffee urns.

Board immediately followed the above description with the caveat: "None of that is true. I wish it were." He went on to describe how despicably *nice* the Canadian anarchists seemed. Then, in 1990 (*MRR* #85), Mykel wrote (in a column devoted to the theme of homosexuality and homophobia):

> I'm not denying there's discrimination—and worse—violence directed at people who do IT (or are perceived to do IT) with fellows of the same equipment. Sean from Vegan Reich seems to have made that clear in his anti-homo comments. (Is this the same Sean I slept with at the Toronto @-fest? Pretty weird if it is).

If Sean learned trolling techniques from Mykel, the master could turn the tables. Much later, in *MRR* #340 in 2011, Mykel recounted a story of meeting Sean, Brian of Vegan Reich and Rat at the 1988 festival:

> I stay at the house of MRR columnist Steve Beaumont. (A decade later he'll be a world-famous beer writer.) Also at the house are a bunch of guys I don't

know from some band I don't know. They're funny and friendly. I've never seen them before. 'What's the story on those guys?' I ask Steve.

'Oh Mykel,' he says, 'you're in for a surprise. That's VEGAN REICH.'

The big guy in the band wears an even bigger t-shirt with 'MEAT IS MURDER' stenciled on the front. He's fiddling around in his backpack.

'Got it!' he says, taking out a box of something.

'What's that?' I ask.

'It's tofu burger mix,' he says.

'Yuck!' I answer. 'I wouldn't eat that shit in a million years.'

'That's what you think,' he says. 'Steve, get the camera.'

And he reaches for me. I'm out the door…sprinting across the front yard…into the next yard. I can easily outrun this big guy, I think. I think wrong.

Blam! I'm on the ground. Tackled like some football player. Another guy from the band kneels over me. I can't see him clearly. Things are a blur. I'm face up. The guy clamps my head between his knees. He reaches over my face and squeezes my jaw, forcing my mouth open. He does not open his fly and lower his turgid tumor into my mouth. Instead, the big guy, who's faster than he looks, has that box of Tofu Burger Mix open in his hand. He pours it into my mouth.

It's like he's force-feeding me sand. Awful. Grains of tasteless nothing… filling my mouth…spilling over my cheeks….clustering first around then into my ears. I'm gonna suffocate. I can't talk….breathe…nothing. I try to shake my head… turn away from the granular invasion. The other guy's knees keep my head just where it is.

Then it's over.

They let go of me. And they help me stand up.

I spit out the crap. Stick my fingers into my mouth to scrape the insides of my cheek. Steve is laughing behind the camera. The Vegan Reich guys are laughing. My piss-offedness turns to laughter. It really is funny.

[Note: Skeptical regarding this story's veracity, I reached out to Mykel and he responded:

> I am notoriously bad with chronology. The force-fed tofu story is true, but the date was probably 1988 and not 1995. It was definitely at the Toronto anarchist festival. It was done in the spirit of fun though... not anger. I never felt threatened or in danger. Just comically uncomfortable. We never did the nasty, as far as I remember, though I may have joked about it.

I checked with Stephen Beaumont who said that only Mykel stayed at his house and that he never saw this incident or knew of it. For a minute, I opted to personally believe that Mykel got the two stories mixed up: he only *joked* about the tofu story but that he *actually did* sleep with Sean. But then I checked with Rat and he confirmed both the story and the good-natured spirit of the incident. He also identified the big guy in the band as Brian, Vegan Reich's bass player at the time. He guessed that Sean did the stuffing of the food while Brian held Mykel down but couldn't remember the details. Supposedly someone has pix of it all somewhere…]

Also in 1988, Sean started his first label No Master's Voice (NMV). Initially, it seemed, Sean did not focus on animal liberation but, in *Endless Struggle* zine, requested bands for an international hardcore/thrash compilation tape that "deal with some intelligent social or political issue, but other than that, subject matter is up to you." Later that year, two-half page ads in *MRR* (December 1988) showed animal liberation-focused bands/releases from The Apostles, Naturecore, and the international compilation LP *The ALF is Watching and There's No Place to Hide...* which included bands such as Chumbawamba, Statement, Beefeater (with Ian MacKaye on backup vox), Oi Polloi, Toxic Waste, Power Age, and the aforementioned Vegan Reich song: "Stop Talking—Start Revenging" (see Appendix 7 for selection of early Hardline ads). Aside from generally positive reviews (also mentioned earlier), the compilation did not stir much attention. Vegan Reich—not yet an actual band—had not started touring and Sean had not yet finished formulating his vision for it. The term "hardline" had a generic meaning applied in various contexts such as straight edge and anarchism (as exemplified above by Project X and Mykel Board) as well as signifying full-on DIY/activist orientation as when Jello Biafra used the term in 1987 "I realize we're not as hardline or grassroots as MDC, BGK or Crass, but I think we have had a very positive cultural and even political impact" (*MRR* 44, 1987). This type of meaning (the image of a completely devoted anarcho-punk activist), seemed to somewhat foreshadow its later more extreme meaning.

Although never active in Hardline, Elgin James co-founded a parallel scene on the East Coast: militant anti-racist straight edge crew FSU (standing for both "Fuck Shit Up" and "Friends Stand United"). As early as the 1980s, FSU pretty much practiced the type of assaults on drug dealers that Earth Crisis would later sing about (James 2004; Binelli 2007).

Maximum Rocknroll originally got its name by tweaking The Who's slogan "maximum rhythm and blues." Tim Yohannan figured then that if one could describe rock music as "maximum rhythm and blues" then, according to that logic, one could describe punk as "maximum rocknroll" (I thought I read that in *MRR* at some point but can't find the source now. But I also met with Tim Yohannan a few times and he might have told me that. Either way, I recall that he said it at some point). If hardcore effectively created a sort of "maximum punk rock," then Hardline seemed poised to create a "maximum hardcore." This impulse to break borders and take existing tendencies to further extremes, coalesced with both the trademark shock value of punk and increasing concerns for social justice.

Around this time (late 80s), a Christian-oriented straight edge band in Memphis, Tennessee named One Way transformed into Raid.

It bears recalling that the late US 80s punk scene had, according to a number of observers, begun to stagnate. Early pioneers such as Bad Brains and Black Flag had their best releases behind them while others such as Minor Threat and Dead Kennedys had broken up. Straight edge had started to tread familiar territory with militant edge bands like Judge largely accentuating stances initiated by SSD years earlier. Crucial Youth had already made parodies of straight edge dogmatism with releases in 1986 and 1988 (Eden 2005). The hugely influential Youth of Today emphatically pushed the issue of vegetarianism and provoked significant debate in punk/HC/sXe scenes. Much like the delayed development of Animal Liberation Front cells from across the Atlantic, British punk emphasis on animal liberation had not yet taken hold in the US. So the time seemed ripe for something that would radically push animal liberation in the US punk scene. Placing the origins of Vegan Reich in that light makes Vegan Reich seem like a cross between Crucial Youth and Sacred Reich: part-metal, part-punk, part-serious, and part-joking with 25% Nazi reference, 25% crucial issues, 25% sanctity, and 25% youth crew. Indeed, various observers (including Mykel above) looked at Vegan Reich and could not tell if Sean intended it as a parody or not. Reading Sean's first published interview did not clarify that.

Formation of Hardline: 1989-1991

Sean's first (probably self-performed) interview in 1989 which he submitted to *MAS* (*Minneapolis Alternative Scene*), the forerunner to *Profane Existence*, seemed to trigger a gradual but increasing degree of notoriety that persisted throughout Vegan Reich's, and later Hardline's, existence (also note Sean's ad published next to the interview, see Appendix 8). Although the interview contained no mention of Hardline, abortion, or all-encompassing ideology, it did foreshadow some of Hardline's themes such as animal liberation, authoritarian imposition and enforcement of veganism, ambivalent advocacy of anarchism, opposition to homosexuality (which he termed "The Pink Triangle Crowd"), and a display of aggressive and self-righteous fanaticism so belligerent and full of hyperbole that it seemed closer to parody than an actual ideology (e.g., "the REICH will rule over you with an iron fist to stamp out ignorance forever"). In other words, one could have written it off as another goofy band talking smack like a pre-match Worldwide Wrestling dude flexing his muscles and yelling into the mic about how he plans to CRUSH his opponent. Attention-seeking. Hype-building. Entertainment.

Similarly, Sean's first Hardline Records ad in *MRR* (December 1989) did not give readers any impression of a movement stirring (except, perhaps, the description of "militant Straight Edge/ Vegan bands." No guns in the X, no ideology, no logo, and, of the four bands mentioned in the ad (Vegan Reich, Will of Iron, Pressure, and Class War), Hardline Records only released one of them. Yet, the first Vegan Reich interview and future Hardline Records ads did mention an upcoming—but never released—cookbook and/or Vegan Reich 7" named "Uncarved Tofu Block" (a nod to both Flux of Pink Indians and Taoism's *pu* or uncarved block/return to our original nature).

Two things, however, changed that relatively harmless ambiguity.

First, Sean wrote two letters—one to *MRR* which appeared in the same December 1989 issue as the first Hardline ad (the same issue in which Ryan Downey authored an Indiana scene report) and the other in *Profane Existence* in early 1990 (in response to a critical letter from "Pat" who critiqued Sean for advocating the extermination of "homosexuals, meat eaters, and drug users"). In that issue of *Profane Existence,* Dan Susskind aka "Troll" added an editorial comment and said he regretted publishing the Vegan Reich interview in *MAS* and labeled Sean "sexist, homophobic, and intolerant" [*Note: against this, one sees that the last issue of* MAS *9, 1989 included Vegan Reich in the list of dedications and indicated that they intended to "piss people off" in the previous issue, see Appendix 9*]). Both of Sean's new letters essentially stated (among other things), "No, I'm not doing a fake Worldwide Wrestling-type performance and I'm not just some kid just trying to hype my band: I actually *do* hate homosexuals and meat-eaters and I plan to do something about it" (my summary, not an actual quote; see Appendix 10 for the content of Sean's two letters).

Second, Sean's next ads in *MRR* described Hardline as a movement. He had placed an ad in *MRR* 75 (August 1989) for a straight edge, vegan bass player and requesting submission for a straight edge/veggie 7" compilation and the connections that resulted from that ad (such as Steve Lovett of Raid) made a "movement" possible.

Certainly notoriety brought hype yet, together, these developments clarified the essence of Hardline: not a parody and very anti-homosexual. The main focus of Hardline—animal liberation and sobriety—often did not come through as clearly due to the negative stigma that would ever taint the scene. This conundrum—why would Sean place so much emphasis on vilifying homosexuals when it clearly could only *detract* from his seemingly greater priority of animal liberation?—has baffled me. Certainly, the anti-homosexual rhetoric of influences such as John Macias and Andy Martin might have had an effect. But then I looked at Laguna Beach in general and it seemed like another potential reason arose...

A slight digression: Laguna Beach apparently had a reputation as a sort of gay mecca at the time. Names like "Faguna" hung in the air... The history seemed to go pretty far back. The first wave of gays came to Laguna Beach in the 1920s due to L.A.'s rising film industry. The longstanding and popular club Boom Boom Room opened in 1927 until 2007. As police raided gay and lesbian bars in Los Angeles, people gravitated toward Laguna Beach. Later, police who harassed people at gay beaches in the area gave Laguna Beach the nickname "Fag City." In 1953, President Eisenhower issued order 10450 which allowed "sexual perversion" as a cause for dismissal from Federal employment. 18-year old Army Swim Team athlete Joy Liles from Orange County trained for the Olympics at a base in Newport News, VA when the FBI swooped in, investigated her, and then issued dishonorable discharges to the entire Women's Swim Team (including personnel). Joy returned to the Laguna Beach area without attending the Olympics. In 1982, Laguna Beach elected Bob Gentry, the first openly gay mayor in the history of the US. He passed numerous non-discrimination ordinances which bolstered Laguna Beach's status as a queer h(e)aven. As one journalist wrote, "by the 1970s, 1980s, and even into early 2000, Laguna Beach was a prime gay playground" (Lavdas 2012; for more info, see Bharath 2014, and the Orange County LGBTQ Timeline Project).

Alongside a strong gay presence, Laguna Beach also hosted anti-gay prejudice—including from within the punk scene. In one story of Casey

Royer, singer of Laguna Beach's most famous punk band D.I., we hear from someone on the receiving end of their "jokes":

> Alas, the pleasures of casual fag-baiting ("I work at the Laguna Nursery and we have a new gang together," Royer told *Flipside* in '85. "We're called the L.B.F.B., the Laguna Beach Fag Bashers. And we like to beat fags up, like, it's cool") were not similarly open to me to enjoy, not because of sexual preference as much as because in my own experience, it tended to accompany the act or threat of getting the holy snot beaten out of my flabby person. While D.I.'s homo jokes probably had no more malice or seriousness in them than Fear's, it was not comfortable to be young and foppish in their presence (OC Weekly 2006).

And for those who don't know, Fear (based in L.A.) put out virtuously raunchy punk. They captured national attention through their controversial appearances on Saturday Night Live and the 1981 documentary *The Decline of Western Civilization* by Penelope Spheeris. A large part of their notoriety involved trolling with "anti-PC" stances, playing with fascistic imagery in their 1985 *More Beer* release, and routinely calling people "homos" and "queers" in derogatory fashion. As if mainstream society's discrimination toward gays did not suffice, the southern California punk scene offered plenty of anti-homosexual prejudice to influence young Sean. While Casey later denied involvement with the Laguna Beach Fag Bashers in an interview in *MRR* 84 (1990), he phrased it like this: "there was a bunch of skins that I was living with cause I had to because I had no where to go and they're all 'There's homos out there, we're gonna beat them up.' They liked to beat up homosexuals in Laguna, it wasn't my doing or anything. I didn't hit any fags at all, it doesn't matter to me what people do, it's their own deal" [*Note: it seems unclear if, by "their own deal," he meant the skinhead violence, homosexual behavior, or both*]. Tavia Nyong'o wrote on the topic of queer theory and punk:

> As James Chance bluntly informs viewers of Don Letts's recent documentary *Punk: Attitude* (2003), "originally punk meant, you know, a guy in prison who got fucked up the ass. And that's still what it means to people in prison." At one level, then, queer is to punk as john is to hustler, with both words referencing an established if underground economy of sexual favors and exchanges between men. That Chance could announce his definition as a ribald revelation suggests, however, that the subterranean linkages between punk and queer are as frequently disavowed as they are recognized (Nyong'o 2008: 107).

Perhaps the underlying innuendos stung Sean extra hard as a "punk" coming from California's gay mecca? Although Sean has only mentioned rastacore Bad Brains in passing as a musical—not ideological—influence, they too had gained notoriety for their vitriolic anti-homosexual encounter with the Big Boys and Dave Dictor of MDC during a tour in 1982 in Austin, Texas (Blush 2010). One of Sean's main reggae influences—Mutabaruka—also clearly opposed homosexuality (yet, one may note, he has —at least more recently—expressed a more "gentle" disapproval, for example, calling for more support for homeless gays in Jamaica; see Gay Jamaica Watch 2016). So, it would seem, Sean did not lack for anti-homosexual influence, whether in Laguna Beach, mainstream society, Rastas, Daniel Reid's book *The Tao of Health, Sex, and Longevity*, or the punk scene.

In November 1990, the second Hardline Records ad in *MRR* stated "Hardline presents these truths for your edification" and then re-printed verbatim a list of more than 30 statistics surreptitiously lifted from the April 1990 issue of *Vegetarian Times* (reprinted first in *Caring Edge*) such as:

> • Number of people who could be adequately fed by the grain saved if Americans reduced their intake of meat by 10 percent: 60 million people.
>
> • Current rate of species extinction due to destruction of tropical rainforests and related habitats: 1,000 per year.
>
> • Water needed to produce a pound of wheat: 25 gallons. Water needed to produce 1 pound of meat: 2,500 gallons.
>
> • Amount of trees spared per year by each individual who switches to a vegan diet: 1 acre.

Sometime around 1989-1990, Sean inspired both Steve Lovett of Raid and Ryan Downey of Hardball to veganism. Also around this time, Sean struck up a pen pal relationship with vegan straight edger Scott Beibin from New Jersey and the two exchanged ideas. Scott, who also had contact with Steve, published *Ascention*, perhaps the first vegan straight edge zine, around early 1991 and the zine included a rare Hardline text—a sort of early manifesto, completely different from its more famous counterpart in terms of content (no mention of a specific movement, ideology, or opposition to "sexual deviation") but similar in terms of tone (prophetic, seeking balance with the primordial order, etc.). Entitled "Life in the Balance: HARDXLINE—A Plea For Thought A Call to Action," the anonymously authored text read, in part:

> "In the beginning, things were as one. They were in harmony. Conflict existed, but in balance—as in positive and negative charges. Then came the fall and the balance was lost. The flowing circular motion of energy was broken. Chaos reigned supreme.
>
> And in these times, so it still does. The power generated from this turbulence is evilness. So long has that force been in control, it is now perceived as goodness. The masses are lost in illusion.
>
> If the flock has lost its way, many search for a solution—but they are quickly lost in the ever growing maze of roads that promise a destination of freedom and peace. They have no aim, and only arrive at despair. Self-destruction is inevitable.
>
> Through the quagmire runs a path. A path which has always been and will always be. It is the true course—one rooted in life itself. This is the hard line a narrow path which promises salvation: taking those who walk it forward to their destiny—rebirth and oneness with the original harmony.
>
> The true path exists with or without our acknowledgment and explanation. Individuals may happen upon it but they cannot lay claim to its creation. I, like the other proponents of hardline, am merely a prophet—revealing truths that are part of our instinctual memory. What once was shall be again. It is our destiny.
>
> ...Mankind are social animals. It is part of our place in nature to create society. Individuals will create a society because they are incomplete when they are alone. Those who are at one with themselves and have inner-peace will form harmonious societies. Those formed by people in turmoil and filled with self-hatred will be ridden with violence and discord.
>
> To change society the individual must find their true self—stripping away the false exterior of the identity and the ego: getting to the core of their essence—the oneness and sameness of all life. The instinctual being.
>
> That is the foundation. From there strength and knowledge flow. Reaching that point is the first phase. Building on it, achieving perfection in time is the second, and when that is accomplished, one can efficiently begin the third phase —that being the eternal struggle" (Anonymous, Ascention 1, 1991: 38).

As Steve noted earlier in regard to Hardline origins, the idea coalesced into an actual scene or "movement" in Memphis and primarily due to Raid. Members of Raid also inspired and interwove with new Hardline bands such as Monkeywrench, Limit, Recoil, and Pure Blood. This coincided with new local Memphis zines such as *Praxis* and *Unsilent Minority*. J.P. Goodwin, also in Memphis, started Life for a Life Distribution as perhaps the first explicitly Hardline distro. It therefore seemed natural that Memphis would host the first Hardline "Survival of the Fittest" gathering August 2-4, 1991, which featured bands such as Raid, Green Rage, Recoil, and Hardball. Statement and Vegan Reich would have played (as advertised) but Sean canceled the Vegan Reich show and with it went the first attempt to do a live Statement performance (for a video of Raid's performance at the event see Memphis, "Memphis Hardline Gathering," 1991). Kim, her boyfriend Scott Beibin, and Sean held the workshops. The ad for the gathering in *Praxis* listed the topics as "Animal Liberation, Third World Struggles, Radical Environmentalism, Alternative Communities, Organic Farming, Hunt Sabotaging, Vegan Nutrition, Natural Law, Herbology, Women's Health Care, Natural Childbirth, Martial Arts/Self Defense, Revolutionary History, Raising Vegan Children, And More…" The ad also stated that they intended "to plan fund raising efforts and coordinate volunteer work towards establishing a HARDLINE vegan farm collective" and noted that the "gathering is not open to the general public and will not be a forum for debate on these issues. If you are part of the struggle to achieve the liberation of all life from the clutches of 'modern man' then we would like for you to join us" (Praxis 1991: 17). Although largely organized by local Memphis activists, the contact address directed readers to Sean (still in Laguna Beach at the time).

Back in California, Circle One had broken up but they reunited in 1991. On May 30th of that year, 29-year old John Macias preached the word of the Lord a bit too aggressively for some of the lunchtime customers on the Santa Monica pier (reportedly pushing a pedestrian in the street). Someone called security. A security guard came over and John threw him off the pier. Soon thereafter police showed up. According to a news report at the time: "One officer shot Macias once, but he continued to advance, police said. The officer fired three more shots as Macias grabbed him, and both men fell to the ground. Macias died at a nearby hospital from bullet wounds to his neck and chest" (Moran 1991). One observer wrote recently about John, "to those who knew him, his memory can never be captured by a song or by an article on the internet. Instead, his heart and passion for helping others is remembered" (Newbery 2017). John Macias took his last breath only a few months before the first Hardline gathering. One "Family" ended while another began…

Establishment of Hardline 1992-1996

During this period a wave of Hardline-affiliated and Hardline-adjacent bands cropped up. Many of them had at least one Hardline member while others held vegan straight edge views that veered very close to Hardline. Some of these bands include: Green Rage (NY), Birthrite (NY), Warcry (IN), Culture (FL), Abnegation (PA), Gatekeeper (NY), Lifeless (UT), Contempt (NY), Downfall (OH), Lifer (UK), Slavearc (UK), Healing (Poland), Ecorage (Germany), Neckbrace (Germany) and Purification (Italy). Notably, Fabio Raffaeli of the Italian band Absence (and later the band Destroy Babylon, both from Turin) came to visit Hardliners in the US during this period and returned to work as one of the main propagators for Hardline in Europe.

Also during this period, Earth Crisis took off around 1993, shook punk scenes out of their stupor, and helped radically change the face of hardcore with a wave of vegan straight edge metalcore (see, for example, Haenfler 2006). They did not, however (as we have seen), embrace Hardline even while they had taken influence from Hardline and Vegan Reich. Instead, by heralding a wave of vegan straight edgers, they did help broaden the general message, making people more aware of Hardline as the xVx scene grew.

Another band that also gave Hardline-adjacent people and bands a huge boost: Birthright from Indianapolis. This band contained both Hardline ally Kurt Schroeder (who went on to found Catalyst Records—one of the main purveyors of vegan straight edge still going to this day) and Pete Wentz (singer of Fall Out Boy who—believe it not—probably identified as Hardline at some point because he has the Hardline Earth ecology logo tattooed on his back, see Appendix 11). Pete also played in Racetraitor in this period. While neither Birthright in itself nor Racetraitor identified as Hardline, the upcoming success of Fall Out Boy (which also included Andy Hurley of Racetraitor, Killtheslavemaster and eventually Vegan Reich) would help boost and finance Sean's Uprising label far more than any other band.

Similarly, as the first wave of exclusively US-based Hardline zines faded away (e.g., *Vegan Delegation*, *Justice*, *Praxis*, and *Caring Edge*), a new wave of Hardline zines began to come out such as *SEAL* (*Straight Edge Animal Liberation*, Minneapolis, from Mike Karban who did *Caring Edge*), *Earth War* (Indianapolis), *Eco-War* (Germany), *Our Struggle* (Austria), *x Convenience x* (Norway), *Cardinal Spirits* (TN), *Gaia Screams* (TN), *Invictus* (TN), *Destroy Babylon* (OH), *Defense, Rescue, and Survival* (NY), *Declaration: The Earth's Last Line Of Defence!* (MD), *Unveil the Lies* (NY), and *Contention Builder* (CA; which may have first come out only as early as 1997).

In February 1992, *MRR* published a letter from Sean regarding *MRR*'s censorship policy. Tim Yo and *MRR*, decreed that they would no longer accept ads from Hardline Records, Life for a Life Distribution, or anything overtly Hardline-related. Sean sent in a letter critiquing their decision: "I find such a move on your part to be very inconsistent with the past (and probably present) policy of your magazine, not to mention with your supposed anti-censorship stance, & I'm writing to see if this Stalinesque tactic of airing only those views which conform to your agenda is one that you'll be using on everyone or if it's reserved for us only" (Sean 1992).

Sean noted that *MRR* regularly ran ads for Bad Brains and Shelter (both anti-abortion) as well as sexist ads from Sub Pop and G.G. Allin "who also violently assaults women" and also Slapshot, whom Sean accused of nationalism, racism, and ethno-centrism. Sean accused *MRR* of resorting to the same tactics as the PMRC (the Parents Music Resource Center founded by Al Gore's wife, Tipper Gore, and funded largely by Republicans to put warning stickers on music "harmful" to children). "If everything we say is just bullshit and we're so ignorant," Sean wrote, "then why are you so afraid to let people decide for themselves which views are more logical?" He continued:

> ...Your magazine grew to be what it is not as a mouthpiece for a single agenda, but as a forum for dialogue and debate amongst a whole spectrum of thought within the punk/hardcore community. ...If you cut out all divergent voices from your magazine and only air the opinions of those who share your exact political & social viewpoints—not only would you run out of advertisers, scene reporters and records to review which live up to your approval—you'd also run out of readers, who... buy your magazine more for its musical courage, than the lefty columns section (Sean 1992).

In this early example of so-called "cancel culture," Tim, Suzanne, and Mike of *MRR* replied with a letter that acknowledged inconsistencies and defended the right of people doing "such a labor of love" to make relatively arbitrary decisions according to what they felt comfortable printing. Interestingly, they repeated their ad policy as always "anti-racist, anti-fascist, anti-sexist" but (a) did not mention discrimination toward homosexuals in their response at all (only a rejection of Sean's "anti-choice agenda"); (b) did not explain why they felt more comfortable with ads for G.G. Allin than Hardline, and (c) they claimed a huge difference between *MRR*'s policy and the PMRC "that want to snuff out differing expressions" but, in this case, *MRR* engaged in deplatforming whereas the PMRC primarily advocated warning labels on records (making *MRR* closer to censorship than the PMRC at least in this instance). It would seem (to me at least) that, despite his false prediction of loss in advertisers, writers, and readers, Sean clearly won the argument. But it didn't matter because only *MRR* had the power to decide. That said, Sean won the argument by appealing to the lofty principle of encouraging debate, disagreement, and divergent viewpoints that—ironically—he did not permit for his own group, Hardline. Perhaps aware of this incongruence, Sean seemed careful to argue for the forum principle on utilitarian grounds (i.e., *MRR* would retain their readership and advertisers) not on ethical grounds (e.g., permitting divergent views has a value in itself). Sean slipped up, however, by describing *MRR*'s new policy as "Stalinesque" because, unless he intended it as a compliment (as in "hey, we think alike"), that *does* imply that he sees something ethically wrong with shutting down debate and dissenting views.

Through a letter in *Vanguard* 2, Sean formally left Hardline in early 1993 and went on to do reggae with his new band Captive Nation Rising, putting out their first record as the first release on Sean's new label Uprising Records in 1994. He maintained close ties with people in the scene such as Micah Collins who did *Destroy Babylon* zine and Ryan Downey who took over editing *Vanguard*. Ryan put out four issues of *Vanguard* in 1993 and then, he too left Hardline by the end of the year.

Vanguard 3 in 1993 seemed to mark the first mention of Rod Coronado in a Hardline context, interestingly, as the scene took on an increasingly desperate and millenarian tone. In a single unsigned paragraph under the rubric "Looking Ahead Part II," the author (most likely Sean or possibly Ryan) wrote:

> We will never have all we need. Out recruitment methods have all but dried up and our recruiters are on drugs, in jail or burned out on recruiting efforts. For the next few years, while we train in martial arts, weightlifting, natural remedies, cooking, survivalism, etc. we can work through mainstream organizations and such as to not forget what can be done in the meantime. Many have grasped at least part of our message and we grow stronger day by day. The time is drawing ever nearer. David Koresh, the Trade Center, the Memphis Three, Rod Coronado, the FBI witchhunt, Dr. David Gunn [doctor killed by an anti-abortionist], society is crumbling, and the Hardline movement shall be there every step of the way, liberating life, dealing out justice, and praying for the day when we can rise up from the ashes of "civilization" and reinstate the natural ways (*Vanguard* 3, 1993: 3).

This period also saw Hardline expand from a primarily music- based phenomenon to a rising presence in the world of direct action. The season of actions began at least as early as August 1992 when police arrested J.P.

Goodwin and five other Memphis Hardliners on eight counts of felony vandalism (broken into buildings, slashing truck tires, spray-painting, throwing paintbombs, gluing locks shut, etc.) against animal use businesses. In 1993, J.P., along with fellow Hardliners, Mike Karban (*Caring Edge*, *Straight Edge Animal Liberation* (*SEAL*), and Jesse Keenan (*Cardinal Spirits, Unsilent Minority*), elicited the moniker "The Memphis 3" after their conviction for 1993 attacks on fur shops in Memphis (sentenced in 1994 on four counts of vandalism to nearly a year in prison but served three weeks, paid the $2,000 fines, and then left on bond while they appealed the verdict; see *Out of the Cages* 1993: 13; Goodwin 1992; Michalski 1998). Then, in 1994, at the age of 21, J.P. Goodwin founded CAFT (Coalition Against the Fur Trade) which gradually grew and still runs today as an international organization. Somewhere around this time, Memphis Hardliners (such as Jesse, Michelle, Mike, Frank, and others) put out a Hardline zine named *Memphis Vegan.* Some formed a group named Vegans For Life who organized protests outside of abortion clinics (see *Memphis Vegan* 1995).

Memphis had clearly transformed into the initial center of the Hardline scene. Yet, other smaller but notable scenes soon grew in other areas such as Syracuse, Indianapolis, Salt Lake City, and elsewhere. In 1996, Hardliners Josh Anderson and Clinton Colby Ellerman got arrested and convicted of (respectively) firebombing a fast food restaurant construction and raiding the Holt Mink Ranch, releasing thousands of animals and causing $263,000 in damages (both actions in Utah). According to the *TIME* article Josh said, "We joked and said it would be neat if we burned it down. I had a Molotov cocktail. I waited until everyone was out in the car. I threw it and ran" (Lopez 1999: 37). Alex of Boston Hardline and three others got arrested in late 1996 in Hinsdale, MA on charges of releasing mink and attempted arson. Alex described his time in jail:

> The worst thing about jail was all the talk about material things from other inmates. You're locked in there and people talk about the things they own on the outside. Some inmates have pictures of stereos, jewelry, cars, and whatever else. And the fucking TV is blasting most of the day. The only time I got into any sort of confrontation was cuz I couldn't stand hearing that shit nonstop. Other than that, most of the inmates thought what we were charged with was cool and wanted to know more about it. Jail didn't change shit, besides making me more calculated. My tactical shift happened after the legal crap got wrapped up. It was catalyzed by weaknesses in the animal liberation movement. The largest flaw was that people were and are insincere. By this, I mean that they are more into being liked in the animal liberation scene than being down for the cause. The phoniness of the movement pushed me further toward an internal struggle and community building (Anonymous 2004).

Meanwhile, Sean converted to Islam in 1995. He took the name Shahid 'Ali Muttaqi but, in the punk scene, everyone calls him Sean Muttaqi. [*Note: That name, however ("Sean Muttaqi"), does not seem to appear in zines (via an Archive.org search) until at least the end of the 1990s*.]

Militant Records and Vegan Earth Order released a benefit compilation in 1995 for Rod Coronado entitled *Stones to Mark a Fire* featuring bands such as Statement, Birthright, Abnegation, Earth Crisis, Painstake, Tension, Birthrite, Culture, and Captive Nation Rising. Later, the same year, Sean released the same compilation but with a few bands added and a few removed under the name *Ceremony of Fire*, also as a benefit for Rod [I asked in 2021 and Rod confirmed that his support group did, in fact, receive funding from the benefit]. *Vanguard* 6 in 1995 featured a full page of coverage dedicated to Rod Coronado which provided his arrest history and update:

> On September 28th, 1994, Rod Coronado was arrested on the Yaqui tribal reservation located in Tucson, Arizona. He had been on the run for over 2 years since the FBI took on a violent assault on his home. He also had been receiving death threats from people in the fur industry and was the victim of FBI harassment. The FBI had raided Rod's house back in 1992 because of a federal warrant issued for him in connection with the arson on Michigan State's mink research lab which caused over $100,000 in damage and 30 years of research was destroyed in the raid. ...While Rod was known for being involved in ALF activities in Canada back in 1987 and 1988, he was an active participant in the Sea Shepherds also. ...Rod faces anywhere from 41 to 51 months. "*My arrest is a testament of the U.S. government's willingness to use deadly force to squash my representation of Native American wildlife, and those who defend them. In over ten years of non-violent resistance to the destruction of native wildlife and lands, I have never caused an injury or loss of life to any living being. Through my obligation as a citizen of the Earth, I have only ever targeted the implements of life's destruction, such as whaling ships in Iceland. I have never, nor will I ever carry or use firearms or explosives in defense of my Earth mother. My religious beliefs recognize the sanctity of all life and would never allow me to justify a violent act that would result in the loss of life...*" –Rod Coronado (*Vanguard* 6, 1995: 15).

Beginning in 1995, Rod began publishing his own zine, *Strong Hearts*, during his incarceration (also see Coronado 2007).

The next year, Destroy Babylon quoted Rod as describing the zine as "Fucking Rad!" (Destroy Babylon 4, 1996: 55). [Note: when I asked Rod about it in January 2021, he said he never supported Hardline and that if he had said that about Destroy Babylon, he did so prior to understanding all of what it stood for].

Also around this time, Sean started to distribute literature via Uprising such as *No Other Road to Take* by Vietnamese revolutionary Nguyen Thi Dinh (1976) and the nihilist booklet *Catechism of the Revolutionist* by Sergey Nechayev (1869) as seen in an Uprising ad (see examples of this ad in *Destroy Babylon* 1, 1995; *Destroy Babylon* 4 1996; *Defense, Rescue and Survival* 1, 1995; and *SEAL* 3 1996). Some have supposed Mikhail Bakunin to have co-authored the text but, if he did, it would have entailed a unique retraction of his otherwise rejection of killing of civilians. In case you didn't know, the *Catechism* included such gems as:

> The revolutionary is a doomed man. He has no personal interests, no business affairs, no emotions, no attachments, no property, and no name. Everything in him is wholly absorbed in the single thought and the single passion for revolution.
>
> The revolutionary despises all doctrines and refuses to accept the mundane sciences, leaving them for future generations. He knows only one science: the science of destruction.
>
> Tyrannical toward himself, he must be tyrannical toward others. All the gentle and enervating sentiments of kinship, love, friendship, gratitude, and even honor, must be suppressed in him and give place to the cold and single-minded passion for revolution. ...Night and day he must have but one thought, one aim—merciless destruction. Striving cold-bloodedly and indefatigably toward this end, he must be prepared to destroy himself and to destroy with his own hands everything that stands in the path of the revolution.
>
> The revolutionary can have no friendship or attachment, except for those who have proved by their actions that they, like him, are dedicated to revolution. The degree of friendship, devotion and obligation toward such a comrade is determined solely by the degree of his usefulness to the cause of total revolutionary destruction.
>
> He should not hesitate to destroy any position, any place, or any man in this world. He must hate everyone and everything in it with an equal hatred.
>
> Aiming at implacable revolution, the revolutionary may and frequently must live within society while pretending to be completely different from what he really is, for he must penetrate everywhere.
>
> This filthy social order can be split up into several categories. The first category comprises those who must be condemned to death without delay.

> Above all, those who are especially inimical to the revolutionary organization must be destroyed.
>
> Our task is terrible, total, universal, and merciless destruction.

You get the idea.

Also in 1995, Dave Agranoff (*Voicebox*, *Defense, Rescue, and Survival*, *Unveil the Lies*) took over as editor for *Vanguard* and put out issue #6. Sean then started the hardcore/reggae band Pressure, putting out the first release *Destroy LA* on Uprising Records in 1996, the same year that Dave put out his last issue of *Vanguard* (#7). At the end of 1997, Walter Bond, influenced in part by Hardline and Earth Crisis, got arrested for burning down a meth lab in Iowa. A court sentenced him to four years.

Decline of Hardline: 1997-1999

Although vegan straight edge began to surge, Hardline began to dwindle. The turnover rate seemed high and rapid with few newcomers arriving. Yet, while the scene itself floundered, some of the activists involved dedicated themselves even more intensely to activism.

In 1997, police accused Hardliner Jacob Kenison of firebombing a leather store in Salt Lake City (CBS Tonight News 1997). Another Hardliner James Ray Blackman remained sought after by police alongside Adam Troy Peace (Fox News 1997a). 1997 also saw the bombing of the Fur Breeders Agricultural Cooperative in Sandy, Utah causing an estimated $900,000 in damage to the Co-op and nearby vehicles. Reported Hardliners (most in their young 20s) Clinton Colby Ellerman, Douglas Josh Ellerman, Adam Troy Peace, Sean Gautschy, and Andrew Bishop of Salt Lake City (SLC) went to trial but only the Ellerman brothers got convicted in this particular case. Also indicted in the action, Alex Slack, Hardline vocalist for the SLC band Lifeless, had gotten paralyzed from a car accident after the incident and killed himself in 1999 (Associated Press 1999; GC Activities 2009). Josh Ellerman, only 18 at the time, cooperated with authorities to turn in five accomplices but the effort failed anf they got acquitted (Rayburn 1999; Sahagun 1998; Smith et al 2006; also related, see Fox News 1997b; No Compromise 1997).

In the fall of 1997, Peter Young and "a trusted friend" went, with bolt cutters in hand, on an animal liberation spree. The first farm they raided had to shut down due to the incurred losses and damages. And they went down the line: In Iowa, they released 5,000 mink and 100 foxes. Within a week they had released, according to his account, between 8-12,000 animals. "It was supremely rewarding in that finally there was no gap between my thoughts and my actions" (Young 2019: 29). They kept going until they got arrested. By then, they had shut down another farm. Police told them to report back in 24 hours. They never did. Instead, they went underground for years. Peter described his perspective and the impact of music on his actions:

> My shift to activism was inspired by the mid-90s straight-edge scene. Bands like Abnegation brought me from the "self-hating vegan" phase to one of action, and understanding this was not another "single issue," but something much more urgent than I had admitted. We listened to the Earth Crisis demo every night before masking up and hitting those farms in 1997 (Young 2019: 55).

> Bands such as Raid and Vegan Reich were part of a unique subcultural phenomenon in the early-to-mid-90s which combined a staunch anti-drug and alcohol message with militant animal liberation politics. These bands brought many people into the fold during that period and inspired a surge of animal liberation activity. The era saw a new and zealous breed of activist, many arrests, and even more broken windows. Music is a powerful tool, and very often a stepping-stone to activism (Ibid: 346).

> **Focus on the 20% of your efforts that will have 80% of the impact.** When I look at people I got involved with, I would estimate 80% to 90% of them got involved in three ways. One, a music subculture. Two, through someone they knew. …Three, from a video or image. …Personally, I've never met someone who became vegan from hearing a statistic (Ibid: 106-107, emphasis in original).

> I came from a flatly middle-class background. …The clearest impetus to criminality I can identify is getting involved in the punk rock music scene at age 15. The punk rock scene imparted a sense of urgency that it's the obligation of all of us to not just complain, but take action. I trace that stirring of a higher calling to those days. Eventually this stirring lead me to prison (Ibid: 38-39).

Peter also had his own prison stories to share:

As an animal liberator, the first day of prison is like the first day of school, except instead of being made fun of for ill-fitted thrift store clothing, they make fun of you for committing what they identify as the world's stupidest crime. I'd heard all the jokes ("Mink? Motherfucka, you look like you got caught stealing your momma a birthday card!"), and put my mouth on autopilot while my mind was on the clock. Six hours until dinner. Survival for the entire year hung on the alignment of three variable: dining hall menu, ease with which inmate staff could smuggle out edibles, and the selection of prison commissary. Praying for immediate vegan revolution or a presidential pardon, I would settle for dairy-free bread (Ibid 272).

The fact is, no one person can talk about the prison experience with authority because there are many different prisons. My bottom line here is that when we talk about or focus solely on those horror stories, we do the enemy's work. Fear: the most powerful weapon they have (Ibid 278).

Peter also added his own personal Seven Laws of Action which almost read like a version of *The Power of Positive Thinking* applied to direct action:

Nothing is ever as hard as you think it is.

Get outside, where things really happen, i.e. The Proximity Effect.

Demystify consequences.

Adopt a sense of urgency/speed of execution.

Identify and destroy your limiting beliefs.

Answer to the animals, not the opinions of humans.

Demystify fear.

You should do things because the only true measure of an activist is your actions. In fact, the only true measure of your life are your actions. Nothing else.

...Everything I ever wrote or spoke on the subject of animal liberation was crafted for one specific avatar, an audience of one: me at age 18 years old. What would have motivated a younger me to move quicker from idea to

> execution? What were the psychological hurdles? Every word spoken or written was to this end.
>
> ...Two people can liberate 1,000 mink every 15 minutes. I believe if most people knew the simplicity of these actions, they would spend a little less time on the internet and a little more time tearing down fences (Ibid: 75, 12-13, 54).

Peter certainly had company in those beliefs. Yet, a 1998 *Los Angeles Times* article conflated direct action and antisocial violence:

> These are mostly young, middle-class, Anglo vegetarians who communicate through their own Web sites and view themselves as courageous sober soldiers in a dangerously corrupt and polluted society. And they enforce their mantra—"True 'Til Death"—with brass knuckles, baseball bats, knives, Molotov cocktails and pipe bombs. According to Utah law enforcement authorities, the number of these "suburban terrorists" has jumped from a few dozen to more than 1,000 in five years—and shows every sign of growing further (Sahagun 1998).

The specter (or experience) of incarceration, however, had different impacts on different people. For example, Colby's legal conviction changed his personal conviction: "It turned into trouble and fighting. All I want now is to do my time, get married, start a family and all that stuff. I'm even covering up a Straight Edge tattoo on my back with a new one of angels and devils fighting over the Earth and its people" (Ibid). And from elsewhere, "Colby Ellerman testified about the dark underworld of the movement and said he fell into a subgroup called 'Hard Liners,' who taught him how to sabotage businesses and build devices to get free long distance calls" (Associated Press 1999).

Alex from Boston Hardline, quoted earlier in regard to his own jail experience, persisted after his release. In 1998, he organized an attempt to form a Hardline commune in Hawaii named New Eden Project. They had intended to live communally and grow their own food. The experiment failed in less than a year.

In 1998, Sean re-entered Hardline to, along with Alex and others, put out *Vanguard* 8. Implicating Dave Agranoff as a "traitor" (based on vague assertions) and creating a new Hardline Central Committee to provide a quality control over Hardline members and chapters, Sean seemed to aim toward re-starting Hardline. *Vanguard* 8 did not explicitly dismantle Hardline but called to expand it (only suggesting the *appearance* of dismantling it as a tactical move). Most notably, the tone changed entirely. If

Dave had shifted *Vanguard* into a somewhat more standard militant activist direction from *Vanguard* 1, *Vanguard* 8 shifted into a more clandestine-oriented and millenarian direction that suddenly repeated (and elaborated on) the very vision of a brutal vegan dictatorship that Hardliners had spent years denying. In a narrative sense, the approach provided a "win-win" for Sean. If his intervention helped Hardline grow, he could take credit for it. If it instead helped speed Hardline toward an early demise, he could say he had planned that all along as a part of a long-term clandestine vision to *seemingly* dissolve Hardline while actually spreading throughout society growing stronger behind the scenes.

In 1999, Vegan Reich briefly reformed to release the three-track *Jihad* EP (in which they claimed they would change the band name to Vegan Jihad. They never did). They performed a single show that year—the first since 1992—in Indianapolis.

As with *Vanguard* 8, a "Tree of Life" interview with "an anonymous Hardline activist on March 20 1999" depicted a transitional period between Hardline and Islam:

> First, it must be said that Hardline is the original state of man—his primordial being. From Adam and Eve (sal) in the Garden of Eden, the spirit of Hardline has existed as the very essence of creation. That being, the spirit of submission to God and the Natural Law. Hardline is, and always has been (since the first man and woman), about living naturally, and in harmony with one's surroundings with God. However, if we are speaking of the manifestation of this essential nature known as 'Hardline,' its inception took place in 1990, out of the Straight Edge movement— which is dedicated to strict abstinence from all drugs, alcohol, and promiscuous sexual activities. Hardline spawned into creation in the words of VANGUARD no. 1 (the manifesto of the Hardline Movement), preaching the single ethic of non-interference (i.e., that all innocent life must be left to live out its natural existence in peace and without interference). …The Hardline ethic prohibits the use of any and all products tested upon animals, and encourages adherents to boycott companies that profit from the exploitation of both humans and animals alike. Other violations of human equality and unity such as sexism, racism, etc., have no place within Hardline, and are combatted in our war against the corrupters of faith that perpetuate such atrocities. …Hardline does indeed recognize the Higher Power from which we have all sprung forth… The reality that we are all a united Whole is the basic premise of Hardline, and so it is with the Almighty One. With that said, Hardline does NOT require adherence to any one path or religion. While adherents to the Hardline are free to search for truth through any religion they choose, Hardline sees them all to be equally valid and true. However, a recognition of the Real is a must for all who walk the Hardline. There have been many activists kicked out of the movement for their infidelity and disbelief. Currently, there are Christians, Muslims, and Rastas involved in

> Hardline, but there are some who do not walk the path of a specific faith. But in this diversity there is the intrinsic recognition of the Oneness—for we are all brothers and sisters of the one True Faith. …a great emphasis must be placed on the inward Struggle, the internal Jihad, which is the basis of real change. …'we,' as the Hardline movement, have no 'authority' at all. Ultimately, all authority resists in the Hands of God (Tree of Life 1999).

The same year, Ahl-i Allah (People of God) took shape and went online. Organized by Sean and Micah Collins (aka Adam Nizari), the group recruited people from Hardline scenes (including Path of Perfection in Portugal and Fabio from Hardline Italy) as well as a few new recruits.

Even while Hardline had begun to unravel, new recruits got active. Mike aka Talib (Messiah Communications) started a Hardline-oriented zine in 1999 in German:

> The name was "Rise from the Ashes" and contained articles about John Africa's MOVE, Hardline, Veganism, [major brand] and other sweatshops companies, etc. It also included interviews with political bands such as Birthright, Slavearc and Ultimatum. We sold books, magazines, clothing and music records through there. We made interviews with different kinds of people and I wrote some articles for the website. Messiah Communications also printed books like *A Declaration of War* and a German translation of the "Unabomber Manifesto" under its name. We ran the labels for several years (Bahr 2010).

Meanwhile, back in the US, Justin Clayton Samuel, accomplice to Peter Young in the animal liberation actions, got caught by police in 1999 and collaborated with police against Peter.

Post-Hardline 1: 2000-2006

Y2K came and went. If Hardline had attached any significance to the turn of the millennium, it failed to materialize. As far as I know, they did not specifically focus on the date but the sudden shifts in activity in 1999, from Hardline to Ahl-i Allah as an openly messianic organization, combined with clear millenarian ideology, indicate that the impending turn of the millennium had an influence at some level. (That said, Sean did not ignore the millennium either, see liner notes to Vegan Reich's *Jihad*, Appendix 12). Around this time, Sean published another interview with himself by himself (i.e., "Uprising Records interview with Sean Muttaqi") in which he ended by announcing his new organization: "Also, I have started an Islamic oriented movement that is geared towards mysticism and progressive political/social action called the 'Ahl-i Allah' (or 'People of Allah')" (Muttaqi c. 2001).

For whatever reason, Ahl-i Allah did not meet with huge success. At least by 2001, Sean and Micah launched Taliyah al-Mahdi (Vanguard of the Messiah) which, according to Micah, had a more political, revolutionary angle than the more mystically-oriented Ahl-i Allah. And whereas Sean acted as the unofficial leader of Ahl-i Allah, Micah could direct Taliyah (opting, he claimed, to decentralize it, yet retained webmaster role of the largely Internet-based group): "The second that [Sean] left the Taliy'ah we IMMEDIATELY de-centralized it and i REFUSED to accept position as 'leader' even when many people asked me to. Since we all dissolved the Taliy'ah, i STILL refuse any position of 'leadership' in any group or organization. Sean, conversely, has started groups, appointing himself as the unchecked 'leader' for decades" (MBD 2006). Either way, Taliyah, like Ahl-i Allah, resulted in a largely online group of people (including some former Hardliners) that identified as Shi'a Muslim yet also retained the syncretism that characterized Hardline (drawing from Taoism, Rastas, the Bible, martial arts, and, a bit more notably now, MOVE). Whereas Ahl-i Allah's logo employed the eight-pointed star of Islam with an Arabic "God" written in the middle, Taliyah's logo used the original Hardline crossed-guns in an X logo in between "TALIY'AH" and "AL-MAHDI" (see back cover). Taliyah gained perhaps its most public notoriety after the 2003 Space Shuttle Columbia explosion. As the shuttle had the Israeli pilot Ilan Ramon among its crew, Micah publically declared the explosion a victory writing "there can be no coincidence in the remains of these traitors falling on 'Palestine,' Texas ...All Praise is due unto Allah for the execution of this Zionist and the indifferent criminals with him" (SPLC 2003). A few selections from the Taliyah homepage in August 2002 read:

> The Vanguard of the Mahdi:
>
> "Let there arise out of you a band of people inviting to all that is good, enjoining what is right, and forbidding what is wrong: and these it is that shall be successful." Qur'an, Sura 3:104
>
> Ayat'ul-Mahdi
>
> Allah gives a sign that Mahdi (atfs) will be among us when a double eclipse occurs in the month of Ramadan. The information that i found revealed that this miraculous event is scheduled for Ramadan 2003.
>
> The Final Warning to Isra'il
>
> "And kill them wherever you find them, and drive them out from where they drove you out, and persecution is worse than bloodshed." Al-Qur'an, Sura 2:191
>
> Ashura: A Time For Direct Action
>
> Islam is not a religion for those content to listen to a speech that pats them on the back and allows them to feel contented until their nagging conscience deteriorates the callus placed over their heart. Islam is a revolution (Taliyah 2002).

Walter Bond got released from his first period in prison in 2001.

Mykel Board's 2011 column cited above described the year 2003 and post-9/11 America:

> Suddenly, all Muslims have become terrorists in the eyes of America. [...] What could be punker in the 21st century than becoming a Muslim? In my April Fool's column of 2002, I explained my conversion to that religion.
>
> This year [2003], Vegan Reich says:

> *"Perhaps the outward form varied, due to time and place variations. But essentially, every message has been that of 'Tawhid,' or 'divine Unity.' Islam includes Judaism, Hinduism, Buddhism, Taoism, Christianity and accepts their Prophets as being Prophets of Islam. So that is why I came into the 'din' or faith of Islam. To me it seemed to have the most inclusive attitude and complete understanding of spirituality that I had found in many years of searching. And on the outward level, I think it is one of the traditions that really is inclusive of all racial backgrounds and absolutely revolutionary in its demand for social justice."*
>
> Are they serious? ...or is this just an extension of the elaborate put-on that included me being force-fed tofu in Canada? I don't know. Good satire/parody should skirt the border of reality... touching the possible and the funny at the same time.... Like *The Onion*. If it's a satire, it's a great one. If it's sincere... it's still funny as hell.

Then Mykel proceeded to ponder the definition of "fascism" and began with the broad British crusty anarchist definition of "any totalitarian attitude that says 'My way is the only way.'" Unsatisfied with this, Mykel decided to see how fascists defined it. So he perused a fascist website that defined "fascism" as, among other things, NOT Nazism, racism, materialism, capitalism, communism, or globalism and IS meritocracy, nationalism, and virtue, Mykel rejected the meritocracy and nationalism but identified with the rest and wondered:

> Does that make me fascist? A 5/7 fascist? Does it matter? No it does not. We can sit and debate the fascism or not of any person or band from here to Laibach. ...If you don't like the politics, protest the politics. Present Alternatives. Counter-demonstrate. If you don't like the music, don't listen to it. But trying to shut down what you don't like, especially if you shut down music because you don't like the politics. Why that's ...that's fascist! Just ask any British crusty street punk.

Although he claimed that he read that someone called Vegan Reich "fascist" because "they're Muslim," he did not dwell on the topic. Though he could have. Despite the precarious circumstances (trying to recruit vegans to Islam and Muslims to veganism in a post 9/11 world and having already appeared on the US government's radar for animal liberation actions), Taliyah al-Mahdi met with some success in terms of creating an impact. They recruited rappers such as Amir Sulaiman, Abdul Shahid Mustafa, and Naj One. Ian Hamilton, former Hardliner and affiliated with Taliyah, organized the 2004 Total Liberation Fest in Erie, PA (where Gather first got inspired to form a band). Ian then organized the Total Liberation Tour of that summer (which Gather then joined). All three rappers joined the tour and Hardline-adjacent bands such as Seven Generations (CA), Purified in Blood (Norway), Purification (Italy), and Cherem (UT), who has recorded with Naj One, joined as well. Although Ian abandoned the tour halfway through (complaining of extreme debt and low turnout), the tour itself continued and the lasting effect and implications of it would reverberate onward inspiring a new generation of militant vegan straight edgers.

One attendee of concerts on that tour: Michael Muhammad Knight.

The not-yet famous author of the *The Taqwacores* offered a tiny glimpse of offline Taliyah al-Mahdi from the 2004 Oakland section of his travel journal *Blue-Eyed Devil*:

> Then we went to the next stop of the Total Liberation tour down on Telegraph. On the way we found another Your Black Muslim Bakery and this time I got a big bag of granola for five dollars. It'd come in handy since we'd arrive at iMusicast to find a mess of punk kids with vegan patches on their bags and t-shirts with stuff about non-human liberation. As they passed around my granola bag I learned that they were all in the bands that would be playing that night. I asked if Rogue Nation [hardcore band on Uprising Records fronted by vegan Muslim, Omar X] would be there and they said probably, as far as they knew. I was concerned because the tour's website didn't have them slated to be there but they were advertised on the flyer….but then again, the flyer said the show would start at noon and here we were at six just standing around the parking lot doing nothing…
>
> The show finally started around eight with a kid in cut-off fatigues on stage talking about how blowing up a [fast food chain] was cool but there were other ways to liberate human-animals. …Then a white punk guy with tattoos on his neck came up and started rapping. Made for an odd scene, with him trying to get these dozen or so vegan kids to throw their hands in the air and such, especially since he rapped about Islam in a few songs. Then in a heartfelt spoken-word he cried of having 'the same blood type as Magic Johnson' and not able to do anything with his girlfriend because she was afraid to touch him.
>
> The guy's names was Naj.One, aka Foeknawledge. I went up to him after his set to buy one of his DIY CDs and ask if I had really heard right about the Islam-Allah stuff. He said he was Muslim and asked if I was, we exchanged salams and then he introduced me to three or four other Muslims, one of them a white rotund white guy with a bushy blond beard. I was quick to explain my Five Percenter shirt by saying I had [ed.: had constructive dialogue about knowledge/the teachings of Clarence 13X Smith] with everyone from them to the Sunnis to the Shi'as—then Naj stepped in and said he was Shi'a and I

replied that I was all about Shi'as, I had built with them in Muharram. Naj said that someone had stolen his turba [ed.: small piece of clay used for prayer] at the last show; my first reaction was to say, 'Who steals a fuckin' turba?' but I guess it was in his bag and someone had stolen his bag. I gave him my turba from the grave of Imam Ridha.

I asked a girl who looked to be one of the tour's organizers whether Rogue Nation would be playing. She said she didn't know since nobody had heard from them. If they showed up she said she'd love to pencil them in but at the moment it didn't seem promising. I guess if things had any more structure and reliability than that, it wouldn't be punk.

There was no vacuum of Muslim voices, however, as Amir Sulaiman and Abdul Shahid [ed.: now Shahid Mustafa; both Shahid and Amir had ties to Taliyah and Sean put out Amir's CD on Uprising] took the stage. Amir tore the house down with his spoken-word piece 'Dead Man Walking' where he spewed that he knew about 'shahadah, Quran and homemade bombs' and then Abdul Shahid (voted 'best unsigned MC' by readers of hip-hop magazine The Source) took the mic and gave props to the people of Palestine, Bosnia and on down the list…

Naj.One's real name (or at least his convert name) was Harun. I told him that it was kind of surprising to see all these Muslim rappers at a vegan punk show and he told me about the Taliyah al-Mahdi movement: 'We're getting ready for the Time,' he said. 'We're all Shi'a, we're all vegan and we take kung-fu and it's pretty…yeah.' He seemed unsure of how much he should tell me and could read the shock on my face.

'Where's it based out of?' I asked.

'We're everywhere' (Knight 2006: 150-151).

Mike followed up a bit later with his meeting with Todd Gullion from the band Time in Malta (which also included ex-Hardliner Ryan Downey for a period):

Then we talked about the Taliyah al-Mahdi, those kung-fu vegan Shi'as I had run into in Oakland. Todd had some insight on the movement. He said the driving force behind it was a partnership between that Muttaqi kid from Vegan Reich and a yahoodi convert named 'Isa Adam Naziri [ed.: Micah Collins], who might have been the bass player. Todd said that some of their writings were alright (Ibid: 156).

Ironically, by the time Mike's book would come out two years later, readers would find themselves hard-pressed to find any sign of Taliyah. Their website had disappeared by then and the organization, or whatever existed, (seemingly) dismantled.

Another person who attended the Total Liberation Tour: Peter Young.

After 8 years living as a fugitive, he got arrested by police the next year, in 2005. Thanks to receiving enough support to pay for a good lawyer, he got sentenced to 2 years instead of 82 years and got released in 2007. During his stint in incarceration, he spent time in seven or eight jails. He calculated it out: "When I did the math, it turns out I was going to serve about 12 hours per mink that was never recaptured. That's 12 hours per mink that we can say had a reasonable chance of living its full life in the wild. I remember thinking, 'I am honored to be able to give so little to get so much" (Young 2019: 88).

Post-Hardline 2: 2007-2021

How can you speak of empathy, while your compassion is a heteronomous construct, Arbitrarily specified by people you don't even know

How can you speak of tolerance, when your acceptance is based on an understanding shaped from an antiquated society that still holds on to their false-proven views

In the quest for equality, We must proclaim veganocracy.

Forward to Eden, "Veganocracy" 2018

In 2010, the Hardline/Taliyah-affiliated blog *Sparks of Dissent* (alt. *1000 Voices of Dissent*) went up with a flurry of activity between September 2010 and July 2011 and included interviews with key figures such as Sean, Micah, Naj One, Fabio, John Johnson (Hardball, Burn It Down, X Edge With The Dreads X), Rat (Statement), Mutabaruka, and Purification. Although no new posts have appeared in ten years it remains as one of the few remaining pnline Hardline-affiliated resources. The rise to media stardom of taqwacore during this period did not seem to transfer much attention to Hardline/Taliyah nor did the two scenes seem to have much overlap. In a sort of converse dynamic to Sean (whose vitriol opposition to homosexuality abated somewhat after he embraced Islam), Mike Knight's ardent support for sexual-preference equality eventually led him to sever his identification with the Five Percenters after he confronted prominent figures in the scene such as Lord Jamar and Sadat X (both of Brand Nubian) regarding Jamar's anti-homosexual remarks. In his parting post, Mike wrote in 2013:

> There are more possibilities in the Five Percent for a straight white man than a gay black man, or perhaps even a straight black woman. To a certain extent, I was able to transcend my status as a white devil because I still had the privilege of being male and heterosexual. …Undeniably privileged by both race and sex, I cannot assume that I have the right to speak on this issue. But the refusal to speak is also an act of privilege, because silence is not neutral. I wrote against Jamar, and my hetero shield fell to the ground. In the controversy that followed, I learned something about straight privilege as compared to white privilege. When I publicly affiliated with the Five Percent, I would sometimes see 'race traitor' comments on the internet, but no one accused me of being secretly black. Straight privilege works differently. For some Five Percenters, taking a pro-queer stand meant that I had exposed myself as secretly gay, as suggested in comments that I wrote my column because Jamar had 'touched a nerve.' Gods [Five Percenter term for Black men] asked me why I was 'so defensive about gays' and many just flatly called me a 'fag' and a homo. I also saw my whiteness become problematic in a new way, because my apparent queerness revealed the danger of welcoming devils into the cipher (Knight 2013).

And so, a white punk rock Muslim trying to build interracial bridges found it on fire with the flames of anti-homosexual hatred. It seemed like an odd contrast to Hardline in which a largely white scene (Vegan Reich's ethnic status notwithstanding) strove to build bridges to POC revolutionaries in part through anti-homosexual rhetoric [recall, for example, Micah's comment cited above "we oppose such unbalanced coupling (as does most of the world)"].

One might note that Five Percenters had nonetheless largely welcomed Mike for years despite knowing his disagreement on that issue—his stay there lasted longer than it likely would have had he attempted to join Hardline. While Mike's first book, *The Taqwacores*, sparked two movies (a documentary and a dramatization of the novel) and while the image of Muslim punks seemingly struck a chord through post-millennium bands such as Al-Thawra and The Kominas or, most recently, in the 2021 British comedy series We Are Lady Parts, the real life pioneers of Islamic punk—Sean, Micah, Naj-One, and others, never got (much?) attention from mainstream media as "Muslim punks." Did their insistence on animal liberation and global revolution dampen liberal interest in covering them? Or did their status as converts and non-Middle Eastern ethnicity undermine the racial edge that editors wanted? Perhaps their generally pale skin and lack of stereotypical "punk" attire failed to live up to the image of "brown kids with mohawks" that photographers wanted? Did Hardline's widespread notoriety in hardcore and vegan straight edge scene simply not add up to a blip on the radar of mainstream media attention? Maybe Hardliners' dogma, and intolerance toward homosexuals made journalists want to barf rather than investigate? I don't know.

Maybe Hardliners and former Hardliners don't actually want so much attention anyway. Maybe they don't need movies made about them. And the day that Hardliners cooperate with the BBC on a comedy series sounds like it will happen the same day that Vegan Reich reunite to record a cover of Cyndi Lauper, albeit slightly tweaked: "Girls Just Want Animal Liberation." Sean's predisposition for speaking from the shadows with very few photos of himself, writing anonymously authored texts, and not listing names on Vegan Reich releases, seemed to set a tone for Hardline in general where members typically keep their Hardline tattoos, history, and sympathies out of sight and underground. Whether intentional or not, it proved an apt means of addressing the stigma that Hardline would earn.

Nonetheless, Hardliners, or rather ex-Hardliners, have seen far greater success than *The Taqwacores*. Although the first release of Fall Out Boy on Uprising initially did well, they really broke big after switching to a major label first hitting the charts in 2005. Two years later, in 2007, their release *Infinity on High* hit number one in record sales and included global hit songs like "This Ain't a Scene, It's an Arms Race" and "Thnks fr th Mmrs." They also won several MTV music video awards. Interestingly, an old fellow Hardliner to Pete and Andy by the name of Ryan Downey happened to work at MTV (no implication here that he had an effect on the awards—just sayin'). According to the IMBD bio page for Ryan (Hardball, Burn it Down, Time in Malta, *Vanguard*), he started working with MTV in the late '80s: "Ryan J. Downey was born on November 7, 1973 in Indianapolis, Indiana, USA. He is a writer and actor, known for MTV News (1989), MTV Movie Awards 2004 Pre-Show (2004) and MTV Movie Awards 2010 Pre-Show (2010)." A YouTube promo for him wrote about his career: "MSNBC film critic and MTV entertainment reporter talks with Johnny Depp, Tom Cruise, Will Smith, Tina Fey, Harrison Ford, Miss Piggy, Arnold Schwarznegger, John Travolta, Dolly Parton, Tony Iommi (Black Sabbath), and Quentin Tarantino." His homepage added Britney Spears, Christina Aguilera, Metallica, Tim Burton, and others to that list. If accurate, it would mean that Ryan worked with MTV both prior to (during?) and after his stint with Hardline. If Hardliners strived for entryism and surreptitiously influencing other organizations, they sure picked interesting choices… (I have had trouble discerning any effect Ryan has had on MTV in converting it to veganism but who knows!).

Elgin James (also of 90s bands Wrecking Crew, 454 Big Block, and The World Is My Fuse and mid-2000s hardcore band Righteous Jams) left FSU in 2007. While Fall Out Boy reached superstar status around the same time, Elgin wrote the short film Goodnight Moon (2007) which starred Fall Out Boy lyricist and bassist, ex-Hardliner Pete Wentz. In 2009, the FBI arrested Elgin on charges of extortion and FSU attacks against a member of Chicago-based pop punk band Mest in 2005 (Olmec and Paul 2009). Using, in part, video interviews from the Boston Beatdown documentary against him, prosecutors secured a conviction but, with support from Robert Redford and others who vouched for him, Elgin's sentence got reduced from four years to one year in prison (Kreps 2009; SkolarX and Paul 2011). Elgin later directed the full-length feature film Little Birds in 2011 (without Pete) and co-wrote the movie Lowrider (2017).

In 2009, David Agranoff began cooperating with government authorities regarding ELF actions more than 10 years prior that had involved gas tanks "filled with sand, ...also packed into oil crankcases ...Fuel and hydraulic lines ...cut, and a tractor-trailer filled with wood chips ...set on fire... [with] the words, 'Go develop in Hell.' [and] 'ELF' ...spray-painted on several pieces of equipment..." Dave provided information on fellow ELF activists Frank Ambrose and Marie Mason (now Marius Mason) in order to reduce his prison sentence to 1 year and "because Ambrose and Mason [were] both currently imprisoned" (Potter 2012). Dave had also previously given public support to Justin Samuel after his testimony against Peter Young. This led to Dave receiving pariah status in activist circles (see Earth First! n.d.).

Also, in 2009, Earth Crisis released the album *To The Death* which included the track "To Ashes," dedicated to Walter Bond's 1997 attack on the meth lab. On July 23, 2010, Walter Bond got arrested for burning down a sheepskin factory in Denver and two Salt Lake City area businesses: a leather factory and restaurant that sold *foie gras* (bloated liver of duck or goose made through forced feeding). Walter, who has identified as bi-sexual, Puerto-Rican and, first and foremost vegan, began his prison time fiercely in support of anarchism, Hardline, and anti-abortion ethics:

> One Vegan argument I have heard is that these unborn children will most likely grow up to be meat-eating consumers, so it's best to stop them before they can start. To which my response is: you're pre-judging and, in doing so, you're promoting the murder of innocent lives that are defenseless. I agree the world is overpopulated with people. So, utilize legitimate contraception and don't have an unwanted pregnancy to begin with. Why turn your hatred for humanity on the innocent and voiceless when there is a world of flesh eaters, vivisectionists, milk drinkers and animal enterprises that deserve to be aborted.

> I'm sure this statement is bound to upset certain people within the Animal Liberation/Rights community, and that's fine. We are all entitled to our opinions and beliefs, and I'm sure many of those same people will then write me and Vegan Hardline off as some right-wing ideology in disguise. But the same can also be said of Malcolm X, Dr. King, John Africa, the entire grassroots Rastafarian movements and many, many others that have fought, and do fight bravely for social justice and were and are pro-life.
>
> These are my basic beliefs concerning a Vegan pro-life ethic and also a basic tenet of Vegan Hardline. It is what it is. If you disagree it's because you are wrong. You should adjust your worldview and actions and become right (Bond via *Remain Upright* blog, 2011).

Walter converted to Islam for a few years and went by the name Abdul Haqq. Around this time, a Christian anarchist started writing to Walter in prison—feeling intrigued by his opposition to abortion. This person described how local anarchists supported Walter but didn't know where he stood on abortion. The Christian anarchist opposed it vehemently and felt that the local vegan anarchists ought to know but they shrugged "Want to know? Write to him." So the Christian anarchist did and then reported in their commune's zine:

> He [Walter Bond] described tabling at events and how he had displayed aborted human fetuses, alongside images of slaughtered animals. For him, sanctity of life included all species, at least all mammals. This conviction did not originate in any particular religious ethic, nonetheless he clung to it with a very honest consistency. He was actually irritated by other activists who were not as consistent and especially by those who talked a lot but who were not ready to take big risks and make big sacrifices like he had. So there it was, and yet…
>
> He went on in his letter to explain how the activists who ran a support website for him had threatened to shut things down if he continued to write and post about this particular conviction of his, that is, his anti-abortion stance. He was ashamed to admit that he gave into their threat, so desperate was his need for the money they sent. Canteen money allows inmates very meager but very meaningful access to extra food items in prison (Anonymous 2021: 13).

The scenario reminded me of the decision of *MRR* to shut down Hardline ads (while keeping G.G. Allin ads). In both cases, one party had power to decide (*MRR*, Walter's support group) over the support or exposure they would give to another party (Hardline, Walter). They based the legitimacy of their decision on the fact that they did their work not for pay but out from their heart and their convictions. Hence, they would not support things that went against those convictions. And yet, what of the power discrepancy? *MRR*, as a fanzine, sure existed as a labor of love but it also *functioned* as the primary and normative channel for communication and exposure for a huge sector of punk and hardcore scenes in the 1980s and 90s. The Walter Bond support group similarly had the power to support him because they had not gotten arrested for the types of actions that he did. And they would only support him conditionally. Walter touched a bit on this type of topic in an interview for *Profane Existence* in 2013:

> Today anarchism is firmly connected to my activism. The Animal Liberation Front has been an anarchistic dis-organization since its inception. ... Anarchism is in opposition to State control, corporate domination, class privilege, oppression of one group by another. These are the identical ideals fought for by Animal Liberation abolitionists, just applied to different objectives. I think that anarchism and Animal liberation from the abolitionist or radical perspective are an organic pairing. What good would it do to establish a human society of free communities only to destroy the planet with ...mass addiction to industrialization? The reality is that there are billions of people on the planet! ...Going out of your way to be offended because a group of people's opinion differs from you in opinion or politics is weak, ingenuine and silly. If it's a big deal or serious (which sometimes it definitely is) then fight those that oppose you. To me it's often irrelevant who alienates me or not. I have my own rigid beliefs such as Vegan Hardline, Pro-Life and Islam but I also know that whether you liberate an Animal while singing the star spangled banner and wearing the American flag as a cape, or you liberate an Animal in crustie jeans filled with DIY Crass patches and dreadlocks down to your waist, the end result is still life and freedom to the Animal and politics didn't even matter. Vegan Hardline ...encompasses not just Animal liberation but also Earth and Human Liberation from a holistic, fundamental, moralist and syncretic worldview (Comrade Black 2013: 21).

Walter began to depart from anarchism at least by 2014:

> I do relate a lot better with Foreman's Earth First! Mainly because it was so much more effective than this new Anarcho-EF!. There have been a couple times in my activism that I have put myself in league with anarchism or at least paid lip service to it, being as it is so prevalent in what passes as radicalism and militancy in the Animal Rights community. But I have truly come to understand that anarchy is detrimental, divisive and distracting to the movement. The focus of Animal and Earth Liberation should obviously be the Earth and Animals. Not extreme anarchist fringe ideology or agenda. But this is the case especially with the new EF!. It seems that Earth Liberation is only important to these people as long as it's a caboose to their primary political issues. In the process a lot of great people become alienated from these groups,

> people like most of society and most of the activist community that they profess to speak for (Pieslak 2014: 73).

By 2017, Bond had rejected Hardline too and reversed his positions on abortion and homosexuality:

> Along with this purging of religious thought I am also leaving behind the moralisms and unrealistic expectations of Vegan hardline as professed in the "hardline manifesto" of which I have been a proponent for two decades. Because I can no longer support its stances against abortion and so-called 'sexual morality'. The problem on this planet is humanity in general and flesh eating humanity specifically. From this vantage point it is just incredibly obvious to me that ANY habits, practices, or philosophies that seek to slow or stop the reproduction of humans are of great importance to the life of the planet!
>
> Abortion, birth control, homosexuality, sterilization, and non-reproductive sexual activity really should be championed as responsible, conscious and evolved decisions, lifestyles and choices and not stigmatized or discriminated against by religious wing nuts that think one little flesh eating bastard is more important than the Earth and all life upon her! (Bond 2017).

And in an interview the following year:

> I am sometimes embarrassed at how I did not question certain idiotic ideas I have held in the past. For example, the ridiculous and fucking idiotic ideology of so-called 'vegan hardline', with all its hyper masculine religious proto-fascist bullshit! I became enamored with the band Vegan Reich back in the 90s and allowed myself to get taken in by the hardcore and unapologetic stance that they embodied. Unfortunately, this warped much of my thought when it came to Animal Rights and Straight Edge. But in the end I was chasing a ghost. Nobody can be so brutally self-disciplined, internally and externally, as to be able to actually live your life without masturbating, eating only raw fruitarian diets and beating up anyone (or everyone) that has 'unclean' thoughts or actions. It wasn't until years later I learned that this is all just another form of the old fascist 3rd position [a reference to Third Positionist fascism] crap that infiltrates and syncretizes already existing movements (Bond 2018).

Even while rejecting Hardline, he swung back to support anarchism again (perhaps depending on his mood or who interviewed him): "Yes I identify with the left, but I do so only as an Anarchist. And one I might add one that has 5 arsons on his record as is doing this interview from a CMU counter-terrorism prison unit and not from a book circle in some cozy manicured squat" (Bond 2018). The next year, 2019, he released an explicitly anti-anarchist text writing:

> I have for half my life had an on again, off again relationship with anarchism. And various factions of anarchism have also had an on again, off again relationship with me. But this has now come to an end. I can no longer, in good faith, have ANYTHING to do with the polyglot mish mash of political and ideological insanity that is anarchism" (Bond 2019).

He labeled it "divisive," "against nature," and "against freedom." He concluded:

> Whether a transvestite gets to use the bathroom of his choosing …or whether a junkie gets a fresh needle to shoot up with in a public restroom is not what concerns me. And it need not concern me. One of the greatest swindles of recent times is the notion that nothing you do or believe has merit on its own unless it is part of a larger conglomerate of orthodox beliefs. Animal Liberation is important, the health of the planet is important. These beings are real, they are life. Leftwing and rightwing politics are a social construct, they are not flesh and blood. They are not Earth and Air. So anarchism and I have come together and separated, off and on, like a defective couple that can't seem to hang it up. But this is my final dance. This is closure. I don't feel that it was a waste of time but I am glad to be done with it. Every man has his own nature and anarchism is contrary to mine (Bond 2019).

In 2018, the TV series Mayans M.C., co-written by Elgin James, began airing for several years to come. At the end of 2019, Elgin, by this time vegan straight edge, began working as advisor for the ALF's media center aka North American Animal Liberation Press Office (NAALPO 2019).

After release from prison in 2020, Walter Bond collaborated with animal liberationist Camille Marino (partially known for making threats against fellow animal liberation activist Steven Best). Together they produced a web page entitled Vegan Final Solution. Although a number of anarchists and former supporters reacted to his use of the term "final solution" (associating the term with Nazism), none seemed to notice that the term had previously appeared in Vegan Reich lyrics as well—in relation to animal liberation and something that Walter no doubt knew (see the first line quoted from "This Is It" earlier). In other words, when he supported Vegan Reich and Hardline, his supporters tended to accept it but when he lifted certain parts of their belief system forward, they reacted negatively (an indication that many of them knew little about Hardline/Vegan Reich. For excerpts from the Vegan Final Solution homepage manifesto, see Appendix 13). Anarchist and anti-fascist reaction came swiftly. Former supporters immediately began to distance themselves from Walter, they rescinded crowdfunding support, and the site came down with a few months. In July 2020, some of them wrote a public disavowal of Walter (see Appendix 14). One might note, however, that throughout Walter's swings from fervent dedication to anarchism, Hardline, and opposition to abortion to equally fervent advocacy of abortion, misanthropy, and opposition to anarchism, he has remained consistently dedicated to vegan straight edge.

The same year, 2020, also saw the return of Taliyah al-Mahdi's webpage. Re-posted and elaborately revised by Micah Collins, he claimed that the movement had simply gone into "occultation" and now re-surfaced after years of training, preparation, and underground organizing (for the revised versions of the Hardline manifesto posted by Ahl-i Allah c. 1999 and Taliyah al-Mahdi c. 2001 and 2020, see Appendix 1). In collaboration with Micah, we find Tim Rule of Germany who formed Bound By Modern Age Records in 2014 putting out material by his solo project Forward to Eden and other vegan straight edge bands. Beyond conventional vegan straight edge, however, BBMA and Forward to Eden espouse a contemporary version of Hardline minus the abortion and homosexuality stances: just pure vegan, animal liberation militancy and millenarian sectarianism. From a 2021 interview with Tim:

> [Q: What exactly is the Natural Order Movement, which manifesto can be obtained from you? I read it and would basically say it is a hardline, but pro-choice and with strong LGBTQ+ support. Could you briefly summarize its assumptions? Is it a real organization or movement? Is it somehow active?]
>
> A: It's the idea of transporting Hardline ideals into this day and age.
>
> It's a laid out idea that explains the Natural Order, the way it is, as we see it. These principles are universal and will hold forever true. The MOVE indicates a drive for action and, wherever you are, if you can identify with the Manifesto and feel the need to act, then it is active.
>
> Educate yourself: https://bbmarecords.com/product/the-natural-order-movement-manifest/

9 Afterthoughts and Looking Forward

A JUST PERSON WILL IGNORE HIS PRIDE WHEN HE HEARS WHAT IS RIGHT, AN UNJUST PERSON WILL IGNORE WHAT IS RIGHT AND HOLD FAST TO HIS GODDAMNING PRIDE.

- John Africa

The God I believe in is in the smile of children, is in the rocks Palestinian children throw at Israeli tanks, is in the hugs I receive from my friends, is in a rainy day that makes life come alive, is in every corner where there is hope for better days, is in animals being liberated from places of exploitation, is in every uprising of people who fight to destroy the shackles that makes them prisoners, is in birds singing, whales diving, trees growing, is in a summer rose being a victim of fall…

-Break (xNEW WINDSx)

This book has tried to do a few simple things: (a) provide an overview of both literature on the topic as well as various voices—from hardcore punk, vegan straight edge, and Hardliners themselves—about Hardline; (b) clarify some unclear issues, errors, and contradictions; (c) raise some questions about sectarianism, efficiency, and critical social change in a time of increasing ecological crises. Now we can reflect a bit on it all.

(a) Regarding the literature and various voices about Hardline, outsiders and non-allies tend to have a strongly negative view of Hardline. Sometimes this view seems well-informed, sometimes not. While the information here probably will not change (m)any minds, it might at least add some nuance. For example, Gabriel Smith's point about Hardline's use of "semantic ambiguity" seems quite relevant. The frequent application of ambiguity has enabled Hardliners and ex-Hardliners to distort historical records, evade accountability, and justify arbitrarily violent and abusive language (to themselves and to others) and by this, I do not mean violent language directed toward vivisectors but toward onlookers who do not "choose the side of righteousness" or homosexuals (whom Sean has yet to reconcile with in regard to having openly declared his hatred for homosexuals as people and calling for others to combat them). Saying that his views had gotten more moderate on the topic since going Muslim does not do anything to heal past wounds or build trust. Similarly, Sean's example of the Buddhist monk illustrates how he controlled the Hardline narrative by virtue of his role. If you enter an organization and agree that a certain person (e.g., the "founder") has all the answers and you commit to believing in them, then who can you blame when the answers don't make sense, don't seem ethical or sustainable, or seem inconsistent? This constructed conundrum can function as a Machiavellian tactic in any relationship or organization wherein those who control the group narrative can ostracize anyone who tries to think independently after joining the group. Sure, they make it sound like you knew in the beginning (e.g., once you "claim" straight edge, you can *never* have even a small sip of alcohol or consume any drug). But, as with any social hierarchy (formal or informal), groups can make for great allowances and exceptions for the powerful (who may simply deny reality and convince followers to believe it) while pulling out a tape measure for minions, workers, minorities, "troublemakers," and—quite often—women. A person viewed as important to the scene might get away with excess (who really cares if a major sXe record label owner drinks?) but someone perceived as disposable and/or undesired could find themselves ostracized for a single alcoholic drink, drinking coffee (caffeine!), or using medical marijuana (in Ryan Downey's recent podcast interview, for example, he described how some people have told him he couldn't get a straight edge tattoo because once, nearly 30 years ago, he had an alcoholic drink, see No F'en Regrets 2021). Whether in a Buddhist monastery or a punk rock clique, it can happen that arbitrary rules rule and denying that possibility helps blind regular people from seeing their own power to renegotiate rules. Sean never allowed the concept of renegotiating Hardline's rules and preferred to see it die than allow others to do that. Ian MacKaye didn't seem to give a shit what people did with straight edge because he never tried to impose it on others. It spread across the world. So yeah, the strong concern for narrative control and heavy usage of ambiguity gave Hardline both technical advantages and long-term problems (may the nationalists and racists who adopt the movement choke on its bones and walk away enlightened). That said, apparently problematic aspects of Hardline seem to have hindered more nuanced examinations and understandings. Most observers seem to have looked at the Hardline phenomenon in regard to its obvious benefits or drawbacks and walked away thinking "good" or "bad" rather than …simply thinking.

(b) Regarding unclear issues, errors, and contradictions, hopefully this book has cleared some things up. No, Earth Crisis never identified as Hardline even if they supported most aspects of it. Yes, abortion and homosexuality took up more Hardline ink than combating racism. Yes, Hardliners clearly and emphatically opposed both abortion and homosexuality while apparently attempting to justify violence towards people who practiced them (e.g., "Sexual attraction to …the same sex [is an] obvious deviation from the *natural order* of things." Then, after talking about buying guns for justifiable violence, Sean said "What we do is …against those who …live lives in excess, and *in transgression of the natural order*"—see full quotes above in sections on violence and homosexuality, cited from *Vanguard* 1, 1992: 9 and Boston Hardline 1995: 3). No, Hardliners never advocated racism or nationalism. Nor did they advocate fascism per se. Yes, Sean did reject leftists and communists and, at least early on, he explicitly advocated a "vegan dictatorship." And yes, Hardliners seemed to always take anti-racist and anti-sexist stances but no, they did not dwell much on issues of racial justice or gender inequality (except via a few anti-Nazi remarks and a few articles on women's self-defense and passing comments regarding women's safety). Yes, Sean's newly minted ideology nearly exactly mirrored MOVE's beliefs but he either did not know about them at the time or, if he did (as he claimed to), he never credited them for it and seems guilty of ideological plagiarism (claiming the status as "first" when clearly MOVE came before Hardline) and neglect of a group he claimed to support. Yes, Hardline had some women involved but no, not many (seemingly less than 10 at their peak), I found no women performing in any Hardline bands, and none of those whose names appeared in zines (including Michelle of Memphis Hardline, seemingly the most prominent female in Hardline) ever used their last name (making their identity difficult to verify). No, not every band you've heard labeled as "Hardline" actually identified as Hardline. Except Raid, very few bands both consisted of all-Hardline members and lasted longer than a few months. More typically only one or more members (such as with Contempt, Slavearc, Day of Suffering, or Gatekeeper) identified as Hardline at some point. No, Hardline did not have thousands of adherents. Yes, it did have a significant impact on hardcore punk scenes. If I have added any new notable errors to the mix then put out your own essay or book on the topic and, if I revise the text for a future edition, I may incorporate your points.

(c) Regarding sectarianism, efficiency, and critical social change in a time of increasing ecological crises, I'll conclude with a few reflections.

Personally, my view probably seems clear at this stage but I'll leave no room for speculation. Yes, Hardliners largely consisted of teenagers and kids in their 20s during the 90s but they've gotten older by now, right? Those still alive can learn (whether in their 50s or the next generation of teens responding to the very same manifestations of societal violence and yearning for holistically consistent resistance that Hardliners responded to). Putting off Hardline's shortcomings on the naiveté of youth does not help give better guidance for the future. Distorting the past only makes it harder to learn. So I present my views because I think we can learn things from Hardline and need not consider the whole enterprise a complete waste of time (as a number of people apparently believe). I began by talking about possible functions of sectarianism: Counterculture, Consolidation, Community, and Efficiency. In general, I'd say Hardline most definitely created its own counterculture within a counterculture. If anything, that much should seem clear by now. And if you believe we learn in part through challenging one another by developing different streams of thought including ones we absolutely disagree with—I'd say they clearly passed that mark by any objective view. They seemed to function less effectively in terms of consolidation. Certainly, they seemed consolidated in the early Memphis days when new zines, distros, and bands sprouted up but, like juggling, if you get five balls in the air at once—great—but you can't call it juggling until you can keep the flow going. Lasting less than a decade in a largely diminishing circle of enthusiasts does not (to me) qualify as long-term consolidation from a sectarian-societal scope. It seemed to function better in terms of community but, even there, the high turnover rate, over-intensive monitoring of personal behavior, abandonment by early key founders, and unnecessary divisiveness seemed to leave the community function intact for a dwindling minority. Of the hundreds of kids who passed through Hardline, perhaps a dozen or so still retain that sense of community together. The two previous points tie in to the last one: efficiency. Like Yin and Yang, they interweave... had they functioned more efficiently (such as actually organizing a farming cooperative in the beginning like they planned and later attempted), they might have functioned better at consolidating a community which, in turn, might have enabled them to learn and increase their efficiency. That said, they seemed quite efficient in some sense such as propagation and getting their message out there (whatever one may think about that message). Considering the small numbers of people who engaged in it, they seemed highly effective at creating a network of distribution, zines, and music to inspire and recruit people. Yet, again with the juggling metaphor, it helps to have two hands to juggle. Half-effective juggling can mean it all comes tumbling down. Which, in Hardline's case, it did.

Now, to go into some detailed response…

More Militancy, Please

First, I have no problem with Hardline's supposed "militancy" and, if anything, think that the whole discussion of animal advocacy really brings to the fore the question of how and when society finds force justified. Society says we can use guns to needlessly attack or hunt animals, to protect people who incarcerate and torture animals, to incarcerate humans, etc. But society does not allow for the distribution of violence in such a way that protects our shared habitats or defends animals from senseless violence. Hardliners repeatedly pointed out this contradiction. So far, so good. Yet, in combination with other Hardline statements and behavior, the logic seemed drowned out by arrogance, threats, and posturing. Unlike, for example, the Plowshare Movement activists who willingly and humbly faced prison time (and still continue) to use their court appearances and incarceration as opportunities to preach the gospel of peace, most Hardliners never got arrested for direct actions and, of those that did, half of them—including Dave Agranoff, the Ellerman brothers, and others—apparently cooperated with police against their former comrades.

Perhaps Sean helped build this lack of loyalty into the movement through the very Machiavellian tactics he proscribed (e.g., "put them through …an action to prove their loyalty and also one that you can hold over their heads should they ever turn on you"). Even the act of advocating "abortion clinic bombings," "political terrorism," and plans to drag "the rich ruling elite …from their homes" for summary execution could have served to both (a) put all Hardliners at risk of undue incrimination, and (b) succumb to precisely that Machiavellian tactic of getting a person to agree to something reprehensible which more central figures can later "hold over their heads." Such tactics seem to breed distrust, power-plays, bullying, blind obedience, fear, inequality, and arbitrary violence—not the type of compassionate and egalitarian society Hardliners claimed to struggle for.

In 1998, Sean faced a dying scene (the term "movement" seems quite a stretch—certainly at that stage). *Vanguard* 8 did not actually prepare members to form cells and embark on world revolution. They had already failed at a tiny fraction of that task. They had made far more enemies among potential recruits than allies. Their sectarian venture had dwindled down to a tiny handful of enthusiasts. Instead, *Vanguard* 8 served to further mystify Sean's role and his abandonment of Hardline as well as seemingly justify his apparent lack of action. Even if Sean hypothetically *did* engage in clandestine direct actions, a movement does not build on founders who seem to only talk and/or only talk about actions that no one can see or prove (having to simply go on the word of the "founder"; [*Note: I write "founder" in quote marks because no one ever founds a group alone.* Per definition, *people* co-found *groups* together *with other people and the use of the term "founder" without quote marks—even in academia—tends to perpetuate a group's internalized fiction and myth as well as the popular belief in singularly "great men or women" rather than historical fact*]).

Rather, the first followers will mimic the "leader" and suppose that they too can simply talk and hope that foot soldiers will arrive willing to do the actual work (which, to some extent, did happen in Hardline). Even supposing Sean engaged in actions behind the scenes (that no one has evidence for), it fosters a culture of apparent hypocrisy or detachment between revolutionary posturing and actual action (even if one believes in guerilla warfare and even if it seems appropriate in a given time and location). To then lead the flock to believe that a group like Hardline would actually *expand* during martial law (with no talk about how many Hardliners would get killed or jailed) amounts to sending sheep to slaughter. Sean talked a lot about how actions speak louder than words but, in the end, he created a complex set of justifications that would exempt himself (e.g., "fake a public break with the movement") and also seemingly explain the complete demise of Hardline (e.g., "it will become necessary for the whole movement to go underground and appear to have dissolved"), making his crafted position as part-time prophet presumably comprehensible and justified.

But clandestine activity and secrecy can function as a form of violence in itself. Anarchist history, practices, and insights can offer a lot as we move forward but taking the most psychopathic, authoritarian, and manipulative part of anarchist history (i.e., *Catechism of the Revolutionist*) and essentially transforming it into official Hardline policy (i.e., *Vanguard* 8) seems like one of the most counter-productive things one can do. I get the whole point of nihilism (e.g., society has gone too far and we need to completely burn it down in order to start anew—especially before industrial society kills or completely enslaves us all). But if we don't create wholesome, healthy processes and ways of relating to one another in the meantime (see, for example, Gustav Landauer's conception of society-building; Landauer 2010) then we get stuck with nihilist methods, nihilist social relations, and, in effect, de facto "tyranny of the fittest" and arbitrary power over anyone who thinks differently. If we have learned anything from anarchist history, I would hope that we learned that much.

When engaging in public activity and exerting power in a public sphere, transparency usually functions better to get more people involved and counterbalance inevitable cliques and hierarchies (see, for example, means of countering "domination techniques" or "master suppression techniques" with affirmation and "validation techniques"; Amnéus et al 2004). While one certainly needs secrecy in relation to a direct action, that does not provide blanket justification for entryism (secretly joining other groups to influence them and recruit new members). Of course, each individual has their private space but each act of organizational secrecy, each use of violence, each instance of hierarchy, requires actual justification (not just the sanction of the "founder"). Rather than attempt to push people toward questionable actions or "tests" of loyalty so that one can hold them over their head (the dregs of sectarianism), one could set examples through actions of vulnerability, openness, and courage in order to foster a community of trust, peace, and equality that genuinely counters our society of violence and injustice. Sean claimed that he did not oppose violence, only injustice but the two intimately intertwine because violence works most commonly and effectively in the hands of those with disproportionate power. The Zapatistas, for example, knew the harm of maintaining a military force so they put down their arms once they had used them to accomplish the initial task that they had secretly trained for a decade to do. Not many groups conceive of that—much less succeed. But recognizing that acts of minimizing violence—whether through reducing gun violence, peacemaking, Non-Violent Communication (NVC), direct actions, or equitably distributing resources and power—go hand-in-hand with processes of maximizing justice seems essential to any successful movement.

Ex-priest Philip Berrigan of the Plowshare Movement spent half of his last 30 years alive in prison, going in and out, repeating the same types of direct actions again and again—completely unwilling to accept the system and equally unafraid of what they would do to him. Each time the state tried to stop him (and other Plowshare activists like Liz McAlister or Steve Kelly, both of whom recently served time for breaking into a US nuclear weapons base in Georgia), they (quite Tao-like) just went with the flow, served their time in prison, and then went back to fearlessly serving the community and consistently confronting militarism with a living example of justice. *That*, to me, seems like hardcore militancy. In this sense, perhaps, one might well view Hardline as *not nearly militant enough*.

On a related note, it feels weird to witness Hardline's misleading and gratuitous use of automatic weapon imagery when they did not, in fact, ever assault anyone with automatic weapons (that I know of). Not that I wish they did (quite the contrary), but the romanticizing of violence probably helped attract and cultivate some unhelpful personality traits (among both the founders and new recruits), raise false expectations of an impending armed revolution, foment internal aggression within the group, and falsely portray the group's core ideals (as Ché Guevara supposedly said, "the true revolutionary is guided by strong feelings of love" whereas, if you read the *Catechism* that Sean both distributed and seemed to model *Vanguard* 8 upon, you'll see the opposite ideal: "[The revolutionary] must hate everyone and everything in [society] with an equal hatred. All the worse for him if he has any relations with parents, friends, or lovers; *he is no longer a revolutionary if he is swayed by these relationships*").

How could one describe that aside from destructive? In stark contrast to Native worldviews of All-Our-Relations, the *Catechism* advocated destroying relations. When the actions of a so-called "revolutionary" and that of an undercover police provocateur seem indistinguishable, I can't see why one would treat them any differently except by exposure and transparency. See, for example, Courtney Desiree Morris' article/booklet *Why Misogynists Make Great Informants: How Gender Violence on the Left Enables State Violence in Radical Movements* (2010) because much of what she wrote could usefully apply to recognizing and dealing with people who speak and behave as Sean and leading Hardline figures did. I don't mean that Sean always acted this way. Most people I've talked to who met him have liked him. But if you look at Hardline and its development and read *Vanguard* 8, you will see elements of the *Catechism* pretty clearly. And that element, something no one has ever questioned, seems as toxic as white pride racism. And yet, maybe no one talks about it because a lot of anarchists either support it or at least tolerate it (maybe because people like Black Panther Eldridge Cleaver endorsed it or because the author, Sergey Nechayev, had befriended Bakunin or because some people think Bakunin wrote it—and even attribute it to Bakunin). The Anarchist Library, for example, still distributes the *Catechism* on their website. And yet… no surprise that White Aryan Resistance does too.

Since Hardline talked quite a bit about Yin and Yang, they could have first understood it and then practiced it better.

(1) Hardliners seem to have essentially conceived of a Western-style black-white binary that removed the dots from Yin and Yang. Sean wanted to create a movement both "not hindered by any sort of contradiction" *and* strongly influenced by Taoism and Yin-Yang! Sounds like a serious contradiction right off the bat. After all, Yin and Yang clearly emphasize contradiction with each side containing and embracing its opposite. So he wanted to avoid contradiction and embrace contradiction at the same time? Sean saw the "balance" part of Yin-Yang but somehow ignored that part. Subsequently, Hardliners falsely imagined some "pure" heterosexuality or "pure" homosexuality when, in fact, Yin and Yang describe life's inherent and necessary *impurities.* In the sexual realm, this means each largely heterosexual society will have a minority "dot" of homosexuals and each largely heterosexual person will have at least a "dot" of homosexuality (and

vice versa). If Hardliners disagreed, then they could find other means to argue for their nonsensical intolerance but using Yin and Yang to argue against homosexuality made no sense no matter what translation of the *Tao Te Ching* they read (and, without Daniel Reid's *The Tao of Health, Sex, and Longevity*, they made not have even made the connection between Yin-Yang and heteronormativism). Yin and Yang function far better to show us fluidity, harmony, and complementarity of opposites—even the opposites of sexual preferences—rather than as justifications for Western-style binaries, absolutism, dogmatic violence, and exclusivity. Hear Lao Tzu, for example (*Tao de Ching* verse 76):

People are born soft and supple;
dead, they are stiff and hard.
Plants are born tender and pliant;
dead, they are brittle and dry.
Thus whoever is stiff and inflexible is a disciple of death.
Whoever is soft and yielding is a disciple of life.
The hard and stiff will be broken.
The soft and supple will prevail.

(2) If you genuinely have a nuanced message opposed to a certain group of people (as Hardline did against homosexuals) and if your nuanced message both condemns them *and* rejects violence directed at them, then, in order to keep those people safe, you would have an obligation to make that distinction completely clear. Not long after Sean had spoken of his hatred of homosexuals, a group of young men in Laguna Beach brutally beat and nearly killed a man whom they suspected of homosexuality, lodging a rock nearly an inch into the back of his skull (Pinsky and Le 1993). And yet I have never heard Sean discuss or condemn anti-gay violence nor claimed to have done anything to create safe spaces for gays at his concerts (other than claiming that no violence ever occurred). If gays got more space and equality to live their lives like others in Laguna Beach, Sean seems to have reacted—as many other mainstreamers—with a reactionary hetero-backlash. After all, Silence = violence in such instances. Because if you have a local group attacking homosexuals and you yourself go out publically hating on homosexuals but you "really" *oppose* anyone attacking them just for their sexuality, then you would *obviously* stake a clear strong stand—both to help protect them as people and to help clarify the nuance in your message. I never saw that happen. Instead, Hardliners employed a menacing doublespeak in which they would say things like Hardline "in no way advocates 'fagbashing'" while in the next breath claim that when homosexuality "starts to infringe on my rights, action will be taken" (*Praxis*

1991: 48). Not only does that merely claim to refrain from (not condemn) "fagbashing," it also left plenty of leeway for Hardliners to interpret what constitutes "infringement" and what constitutes "action." Sorry, but if you genuinely want people to feel safe, you have to work a bit harder than that.

(3) A largely male group who focuses on animal liberation, clandestine direct action, martial arts, and responding both psychologically and physically to societal violence might want to focus on structural as well as personal change, provide social safe spaces for women and gender diversity, and constantly remind oneself of ethical counterweights such as humility, charity, gentleness, forgiveness, and humor. [*Note: JP Goodwin seemed to have an interesting approach when he and others named a group Hugs for Puppies. As their neighbor said at the time following a 2005 federal raid: "I think that the agents with guns and dogs in a house for a group called Hugs for Puppies is pretty much overkill" Earth First! Journal 25, #2, 2005: 13*]. Regardless of whatever one names one's group or scene, beyond labels and the spectacle of advocating drastic social change, the ultimate determinants for a group's effectiveness ends up in their concrete impact. Peter Young emphasized the point of literally liberating animals from captivity. Yet, what might it look like to also build a supportive sectarian community that can stand the test of time because people both within and close to its boundaries feel secure and supported?

One need not look far to find living examples of what Hardline could have looked like without the anti-abortion and anti-homosexual rhetoric. It could have ranged from "militant" vegan straight edge in the form of Gather or Catalyst Records to sectarian and millenarian forms such as Bound By Modern Age and Forward to Eden. Bridging beyond hardcore need not entail starting a tiny ineffective and online sect but simply reaching out and networking with the Vegan Hip Hop Movement. Even actions as simple as creative protests and "eat pussy, not animals" shirts at supermarkets, sports events, and bars have sparked media headlines, notoriety, pub bans, and the unwitting description of "Hardline vegan" to a non-Hardline activist like Tash Peterson (PerthNow 2021). Even if one chooses not to build bridges one need not burn them. Recalling Peter Young again who retained a singular focus on animals. As he put it, "I'm not an anarchist. I'm not even a 'radical.' I just care about animals and dislike cops" (Young 2019: 343).

If militancy means that one attacks one's comrades for not adhering precisely to the decreed groupthink then, of course, few things seem more unproductive. But if militancy means that one uses whatever means possible, effective, and necessary to actively dismantle and replace the physical, social, institutional, ideological, and systemic apparatus that incarcerates, destroys, tortures, mutilates, kills, drugs, manipulates, enslaves, and threatens animals, people, plants, and living habitats, then I cannot see how we will survive—much less thrive—without it. The spirit of Yin/Yang can enable such militancy to survive by balancing out militant acts with gentle action, balancing short-sighted, moral goals with long-term, structural change, balancing critiques of this world with examples of a better one.

Keep Your Personal Prejudices, Please

Second, if you have a controversial view that can both alienate a majority of the constituency from whom you hope to attract new members and cause emotional injury to current or present members, you may want to keep that issue private. If Hardliners genuinely believed that the ban on homosexuality only related to questions of membership then they had no need in propagating that belief. Look at MOVE people or even large parts of the Catholic Church where people may privately not find anal sex and/or homosexuality ethical but do what they can to make gays around them feel welcome.

And even if a group chooses a violently exclusive ideology such as Hardline's vehement opposition to homosexuality, one can try to maintain at least some integrity and clarity in discourse by debating honestly. For example, In Sean's debate in *Profane Existence* he largely skirted the problematic aspects of his stance on homosexuality and instead reiterated vague and unsubstantiated claims of homosexuality as a necessarily hedonistic deviation from "nature" contributing to the demise of society. It seemed to confirm Gabriel Kuhn's remarks in his debate with Dave: "I never get the sense that self-identified hardliners at least somehow understand how offensive and frightening hardline was to a lot of people—and, no, not evil capitalists, but many women, queers, their allies, and generally everyone who feels uncomfortable when folks claim to be judge and jury based on supposed 'righteousness' and 'purity.'" Like Gabriel, I agree that "If there was any indication for self-reflection, I might see hardline differently" but, so far, no key figure of Hardline (not Sean, Steve, Ryan, Micah, Dave, or anyone else as far as I can see) has stepped up and admitted: "We did *nothing* to ensure and defend the safety of gay people in a society of rampant discrimination. We can and will do better." Simply allowing them at concerts without attacking them does not seem sufficient. If Sean simply wanted to intentionally stir controversy and make Hardline absurdly extreme in order to "push the middle" of moderate vegan activism and make it seem more attractive (as Scott Beibin suggested), I can't see that demonizing homosexuality did anything beyond self-sabotage. Marching people out of a concert hall to burn down a local fur shop might have sparked more controversy and (more constructive) attention while serving the same purpose far better.

Preach the Gospel Everywhere and, If Necessary (and Only Then) Use Words

Third, accept that the fact that if you go out publically and pretend like you have the answer to everything, you might eventually find yourself buried under the lies that you tell yourself and others. Furthermore, by leaving open a certain amount of space for the unknown and the uncertain, one can more easily cultivate space for group learning and mutual support in social and organizational experiments to figure out what works for a certain group of people in a specific space during a particular period of time. The first two words in Sean's first song title read "Stop Talking" but, if anything, Hardline primarily manifested through talking thousands and thousands of words, through zines, through song lyrics, through online postings—all of which Sean engaged in himself. Unlike Peter Young, Walter Bond, and maybe a dozen other Hardline-affiliated activists, Sean never served time in jail or prison for animal liberation actions. It does not mean that he never engaged in direct actions but it does indicate that he stopped before he got caught or, at least, it suggests that he, de facto, did not sacrifice as much for the cause as his peers did (leaving Hardline, according to his own account, "in order to casually date, travel, and enjoy life"). It means that, in the talk-action ratio (as per Hardline's adopted slogan "ACTION SPEAKS LOUDER THAN WORDS"), Sean's words took up a disproportional amount of space. In fact, he even (publically) left Hardline only a couple years after he started it. Maybe, just maybe, with more down-to-Earth ambitions, a touch of humility, an ability to show others how one can learn from the past (rather than distort it), and a predisposition to lead by *example* rather than *talking*, we might actually finish what we start and find some help along the way.

Give the Devil Her/His/Their Due

Fourth, much like Mykel Board's approach to satire as that which skirts the border of reality, one might venture that powerful social change must skirt the border of fascism. Look, for example, at various punk and anarchist groups that depend on key movers and shakers even while, in their better moments, they continue to struggle against such informal hierarchies.

A really "pure" life spent in isolation, self-sufficiency, and detachment commits the "impure" act of neglecting to even attempt to change a world full of inequalities, injustice, violence, and universally unsustainable developments. A less "pure" life engaged in change, invariably involves ongoing and uncomfortable compromises.

Early Greek philosopher Heraclitus seemed to sum up a version of Yin and Yang through different terms when he wrote: "They do not comprehend how a thing agrees at variance with itself; like that of the bow and the lyre. The name for the bow is life, its work death. The hidden attunement is better than the obvious one" (Kahn 1979: 65). In other words, things we think of as opposite of one another (such as night and day, order and chaos, etc.) actually link together to produce life which, in turn, produces both death and music. Unlike the Yin-Yang symbol, the images of bow and lyre offer us a perhaps more useful image filled with both tension (of the string) and movement (stretching the bow and shooting an arrow and plucking the strings of the harp-like lyre). If we only acknowledge this fact of life (as at least some Hardliners seemed to do), we don't get very far. We still need to do the work of learning to string the bow and lyre and then gradually train our skill in shooting the arrow and playing the melodies. It takes time. It takes an awareness of those tensions and constant open discussion about how to address them and nurture the various relationships.

Recently, more attention has gone to the complex tensions within Gandhi and, on one hand his virtual sainthood anti-colonialist and social justice activist while, on the other hand, his racism, patriarchal behavior, and support for the caste system. One of my fave examples comes from the Catholic Worker Movement. High figures in the Catholic Church have literally nominated Dorothy Day, co-founder of the movement, for sainthood. Although she rejected such characterizations of herself during her lifetime, she also received her share of accusations of authoritarianism. She had no tolerance for breaching certain moral boundaries (for example sexual promiscuity) but she also worked hard to make a visible difference in the lives of the most destitute as well as establish communities led by the spirit of charity, transparency, labor, and humility rather than lives dependent on leader figures or charisma. Or take another example closer to home: Tim Yohannan. Few would ever accuse him of *not* having some authoritarian tendencies and he seemed to genuinely believe in some sort of Stalinistic socialism. Yet, he worked incessantly in perpetual DIY fashion with a largely anarchist punk network to produce a major influential forum (both via *MRR* and *Book Your Own Fuckin' Life*) that helped foster global and regional DIY networks of a predominantly anarchist flavor. He did not squabble about equal voting rights at *MRR* instead, he said, "whoever does the work gets to decide" (and that meant mostly him along with a host of shitworkers throwing in their two cents).

That, to me, seemed like Yin and Yang stringing the bow and firing a straight arrow and rocking the shit out of that lyre for several decades. Yes, it bordered fascism, but it also helped make a lot of cool shit happen and left a strong antiauthoritarian legacy in its wake.

In his talk with Brian Peterson as well as his own debate with Tim Yo, Sean seemed quite aware of the dynamic tension involving informal hierarchies, power discrepancies, and inevitable sort of Yin-Yang relationship between centralized authority and anarchism. But Hardline never learned to really shoot an arrow or play a coherent melody. The arrow fell down a few feet from the bow and the tunes left a discordant ring in the ear as the performers promptly left the stage.

We may never really get rid of leadership disparities, invisible power cliques, or fully implement egalitarian organizations without any hierarchies but we *can* take the conversation to another level and look at how each group and each active person relates to informal hierarchies, what steps one takes to build egalitarian structures, and how one implements processes of transparency and/or reconciliation to rectify and/or learn from past mistakes. I cannot see that Sean specifically, or Hardline in general, ever even tried to do that (much less succeed at it).

Instead, by cloaking the past in mythology, embellishments, and denial, it makes it harder for both former participants and outside observers to cull (m)any lessons. Watching the Walter Bond organizational trainwreck seems to affirm this thesis. He didn't seem to learn anything from this part of Hardline's history. Instead, he repeated it while regurgitating Hardline's rhetoric with a stark misanthropic gloss. His effort lasted an even shorter duration, with far fewer people, and far less impact (aside from his own personal actions which, in a material sense, may have constituted a significant chunk of Hardline's legacy). It did not have to work out that way. Here you had a fairly prominent animal liberation activist returning to the scene from a decade in prison and he could have utilized his existing support network for more actions, better organization. Instead, as with Hardline, he chose "purity" and watched his "organization"—not another sheepskin factory—burn to the ground.

Screw Purity

Fifth, maybe the desire for absolutes and absolute purity does, after all, contain the seeds of fascism as suggested by Tim Yohannan (Allah bless his fucking soul). The fact that neo-Nazis could so easily adapt Hardline to their own views says something. Of course, they adopted straight edge too but straight edge did not claim to advocate an all-encompassing ideology. By letting anti-racism and issues of whiteness take a distant backseat to issues such as anti-abortion and opposition to homosexuality, Hardliners made it all too easy for actual fascists, nationalists, and neo-Nazis to see it as something they could salvage. Had Hardliners, more like Racetraitor, placed questions of anti-racism and whiteness as centrally as they deserves they would not have had this problem. But if you read the Hardline manifesto, you'll see that racism appears as sort of an aside—not a key part of addressing the problems of our world. And, despite Sean's and other Hardliners' identification as people of color (except for Michelle of Memphis Hardline, mostly years after Hardline died), they declined to discuss whiteness, racism, or colorism within their own ranks or within hardcore/straight edge/anarcho-punk contexts.

Furthermore, fascism need not imply racism but it can involve a sort of totalitarian intolerance. Like a hyperactive immune system overreacting to an essentially harmless virus, it can kill its own host through paranoia and excessive violence. Somehow, in this case, the gentle ideas of non-intervention and harmony explicit within the *Tao te Ching* got transposed via Hardline into a rigid, inflexible, and intolerant doctrine, incapable of listening, opposed to egalitarian and inclusive change (such as open debate and adapting to constructive criticisms) and, in the end, incapable of survival.

Also, conceptions of "purity" have an extraordinary tendency to provide huge loopholes for those pushing the purity. The creation of toxic and volatile binaries both demonizes the "enemy" as a reviled "other" and simultaneously cushions key figures from accountability. Venom directed outwardly invariably spills over internally yet leaders (official or otherwise) can use a host of excuses to evade accountability (e.g., blame the "other" for spreading lies, denial, necessity of wartime crisis, etc.). This seems especially so when playing out in a music scene context where one begins with the underlying assumption that people talk smack, speak in metaphors, use poetic license, and engage in a variety of activities for the sake of attention and performance. As DJ Rose described above, punk and hardcore scenes build themselves on images and stories rather than reality and action. Either way, I cannot say, if he had a choice in the matter. To some extent, some of those who heeded Sean's call at least tried to bridge the gap between words and action. We still face similar choices in an increasingly techified world. We do what we can with the past we have and the present we face. Rejecting the temptation to strive for absolute purity might also give us some understanding, humility, and empathy in relation to the masses who will never take the "monastic" vows of revolutionary fervor.

Will The Real "First Highly Organized Revolutionary Struggle to be Built Around and Fighting for the Equality of All Life" Please Stand Up?

Sixth, Joey Leyva's piece on Hardline in *Out From The Shadows* (2006) seems to deserve an entire section on its own. Lots to unpack there. I can't really do it justice here but will at least attempt to open a conversation about Joey's essay and continue existing conversations about unspoken "rules of race" within predominantly white punk contexts. At that time, Joey published the first critical piece on Hardline in years and, it seems, one of the most difficult to untangle. Most hardcore critiques of Hardliners simply dismissed them. Joey's piece kind of did that too but also attempted to both embrace them and add some nuance by telling fellow vegan straight edgers to stop feeling shame due to the stigma that Hardline had wrought upon the entire scene: "the first attack to suppress discussion of radical vegan straight edge is almost always in some way, shape, or form linked to an aversion to the Hardline Movement" (Leyva 2006: 7; reprinted in Kuhn, see Anonymous 2019: 227). And the piece continued to articulate a clear rejection of both Hardline and its morphing into Taliyah: "…[Hardline's] basic tenets remained, and thus were widely criticized for their sexist and homophobic stances. Rightfully so, I'd like to add. …I want to make it clear that **any group or person that stands in the way of total liberation for all as Hardline and in turn Taliyah al-Mahdi did, should be criticized and openly resisted**" (emphasis in original). So far, the piece seemed to follow standard dismissals. Yet, the article then stated: "We are no more responsible for the Hardline Movement than any white radical person is for the Ku Klux Klan, and much like that white radical, we have a responsibility as vegan straight edge persons to work against such organizations, beliefs, and activities in our communities" (Ibid: 8). This logic seems to fall flat by implying that white radicals have as much in common with the KKK (due to skin color and/or white skin privilege) as radical vegan straight edgers (due to ideological similarities and the fact that xVx built directly on Hardline's legacy). Then the article positively quoted Mack Evasion (whose *HeartattaCk* column showed an affinity for Vegan Reich) as saying:

> When people criticise Hardline (generally for the stands on abortion or homosexuality), I always ask them: What do you think of the Black Panthers? Of MOVE? Of course amongst radicals the response is positive, 'I support them,' etc. There is a certain obligation as an 'anarchist' or whatever, to dis on Hardline, just as there is an equal obligation to support the Black Panthers. But I have to point out that high-ranking members of the Black Panthers made openly sexist and homophobic statements. MOVE was openly homophobic.

> Why do we discriminate? Because we assign 'fashionable' status to some groups, and 'unfashionable' status to others. There is no pause for objective consideration. As a person belonging to a certain counterculture ('anarchist,' etc.).

To this, Joey added:

> I really couldn't have put it better myself. The radical [white] punk community yearns to find solidarity with other [non-white] communities and to move beyond its history as a 'white movement,' and in the process has a tendency to all-too-quickly align itself with movements, organizations, and persons from outside communities whose views and goals are incompatible with that of resistance (Ibid: 8-9).

These comments from both Mack and Joey seem to radically distort conversations about history and Hardline and end up unduly placing Hardline's anti-homosexual rhetoric in a far better light than it deserves while oddly (and somewhat racially) critiquing MOVE and the Black Panthers without any shred of evidence or actual information. MOVE people did what Hardliners only claimed to do: they opposed homosexuality in principle and they held a strong, even oppressive, opposition to homosexuality within MOVE (see *Leaving MOVE* blog post "Sex and Sexuality Within MOVE: The Testimony of Maria Hardy" 9 July 2021). But in practice MOVE people never seem to have discriminated against gays outside of MOVE. Instead, they worked closely with gays and garnered queer support, and—in stark contrast to Hardline—*they rarely broached the topic in public*.

In other words, MOVE *earned* their position as a respected part of the anarchist scene. Had MOVE spewed out the types of anti-homosexual rhetoric as Sean and other Hardliners, they would have received even more critique than they did. And, contrary to Joey Leyva's and Mack Evasion's assertion, MOVE *did* receive critique on this point even though MOVE people never pressed the matter. See, for example, Anthony Nocella and Steven Best who wrote: "While MOVE is widely recognized as a radical and innovative movement, many members of the feminist and lesbian, gay, bisexual transgender, queer [LGBTQ] communities believe that MOVE founders adopted regressive views toward women and homosexuals based on a dogmatic, patriarchal, and homophobic interpretation of 'natural law'" (Best and Nocella 2006: 28). Similarly, *Profane Existence* published an interview with Ramona Africa but noted: "As a collective, we decided it was important to mention a few beliefs MOVE stand behind, in which we strongly disagree. One of us called MOVE and spoke with Ramona Africa to confirm what we had heard. As it turns out, MOVE is in support of all life and is therefore, against abortion. …[Ramona] stated that [homosexuality] was 'Something they could not "believe" in, because it doesn't promote itself …if homosexuality was right, then…[it] would essentially signal the end of the human race'" (*Profane Existence* 35, 1998: 6).

Furthermore, MOVE people endured a police bombing which killed 11 of their family. They endured decades of unjust incarceration and brutal beatings by police over the years. And *still* US anarchists virtually *ignored* them until the early 1990s when Ramona Africa got out of prison, MOVE supporter Mumia Abu-Jamal's death penalty case began to gain worldwide attention, and *Love and Rage* published an article in 1992 by QUISP (Queer Women and Men In Support of Political Prisoners) that declared support for Mumia and MOVE due to the racist oppression that the government subjected them to. So anarchists and punks did not "all-too-quickly" embrace MOVE—it took more than a decade for any anarchist zine (mostly ones in Canada like *Reality Now*, *Bulldozer*, and others connected to the Toronto Anarchist Black Cross) to start giving MOVE any notable attention. Aside from a little coverage in *Fifth Estate* after the 1978 confrontation and in *Overthrow* after the police bombing of MOVE that burned down an entire city block, anarchists virtually ignored MOVE until the 1990s. It happened only after years of prison abolitionists and incarcerated activists (including imprisoned MOVE people) *organized* and did not "just happen" due to fashionable status.

Maybe if Sean and other Hardliners had endured half as much violence by the government as MOVE endured then anarchists, queers, and queer anarchists might had felt more willing to overlook Hardline's anti-homosexual rhetoric for the moment. But they didn't. So the discrepancy in treatment of MOVE and Hardline did not turn on MOVE's "fashionable" status (even if, for a few latecomers, it may have), the main obvious and historical reason seems to have turned on the fact that Hardline and MOVE received *very different* treatment from the government and *behaved* very differently in regard to their shared position regarding homosexuality. And if we don't recognize that, we cannot learn from it.

Also, MOVE's case raises the question of what "total revolution" even means and in which ways or to what extent Nechayev, MOVE, ELF, Black Panthers, ALF, vegan straight edge, or Hardline hinder or help us in that sense.

So Joey's article seemed confused in that it both wanted to condemn Hardline while simultaneously justify it and embrace its legacy. Maybe I feel triggered because I recognize it as close to but distinct from my own position: First, I would not issue a blanket condemnation of Hardline and

Taliyah like Joey did because I believe in selecting out parts of people and groups and addressing each issue piecemeal rather than conflating a person or group with one or more stances that they hold or mistakes that they make. Perhaps naive, but I still believe people/groups can learn and change. Second, I would not walk back said condemnation into an indirect vilification of MOVE or any sort of "we white folks all-too-quickly give black folks a pass" trope.

Joey wrote that "to disregard the contribution to radicalism in hardcore and punk that Hardline provided and inroads into the larger resistance culture that it created, and to keep trying to fit other cultures' movements into the context of our own, demonstrates a serious problem that we as a community must face now." He added in bold: "**We need to critically approach our history and weed out the praxis from the pitfalls**" (Ibid: 9, emphasis in original).

I genuinely appreciated Joey's attempt to add a more nuanced perspective to discussion about Hardline but I feel that the apparently pre-supposed identification with whiteness deserves its own critical examination. Hardline's ideology seems virtually identical to (and perhaps lifted from) MOVE's ideology. Why, then, does Joey want to acknowledge Hardline's "contribution to radicalism in hardcore" but view MOVE as "other"? What makes MOVE "them" and Hardline "us"? Does Joey see Vegan Reich as part of punk's "history as a 'white movement'"? And, if so, on what basis? It might help to distinguish between "white identity" as a choice and point of pride and "white identity" as a default social condition acknowledged in order to help expose existing racial dynamics. Would a white radical speak about the KKK's "contribution to radicalism…that provided inroads to larger resistance"?

Similarly, comparing adverse reactions to vegan straight edge (e.g., accusing vegan straight edgers of "superiorism," assuming vegan straight edgers feel superior to others) to "reverse-racism," as Joey did, seems like a big stretch. It seems to place the experience and position of vegan straight edgers in the same category as that of people of color facing racism. And that, to me, seems to downright minimize the significance, brutality, and impact of racism on both global history and billions of people's lives. The two situations and histories—that of vegan straight edge scene of predominantly white and generally comfortable activists which began about 30 years ago and that of settler colonialist racism which began more than 500 years ago and involved murder, torture, and centuries of enslavement—have radically separate dynamics and implications as well as a few actual, minor, and potential overlaps and intersections. One can critique discrimination against vegan straight edgers in its own right without mentioning racism but to compare anti-xVx discrimination to racism sounds a bit like a kid in a school classroom trying to address a mild case of bullying by referring to Nazi concentration camps, the colonization of the Congo, or Israeli occupation of Palestine. We don't do any issue justice by pulling them wildly out of their context and disproportionately using them as materials to build our own defense. So, for a white vegan straight edger to bring up the topic of "reverse-racism," in order to encourage fellow white vegan straight edgers to "celebrate their [vegan sxe] identity," just... sounds... a bit too... "Guilty of Being White" and out of step with an appreciation for what people of color have gone through and continue to go through—whether they identify as vegan straight edge or not. Finally, exposing Joey's characterization of MOVE and Hardline in racial terms, actually helps expose how Hardline's essentially *white privilege, perceived or "real"* (even if some members identified as Latin@ or Native at some point) seemed to give Hardliners more attention and support than MOVE people (with essentially the same ideology) had received. And, ironically, one of Hardline's staunchest critics, Tim Yohannan, never seemed to use his status as a person of color in debates but due to his Iranian background he would qualify at least as much as a person of color as Sean would.

We all owe to those who struggled before us. Let us all give due credit and keep learning from both those before us and those still among us. That said, I do not mean to paint MOVE as perfect. We can similarly learn from their mistakes like we can learn from Hardline's mistakes. We can learn when we let go of our preconceptions, prejudice, and pride.

Set the Record (Collector) Straight

Seventh, just come clean when you can. If you have an influence (as Sean claims to have had from MOVE), then give them credit. Give them support. If you did not receive influence from them then don't claim you did. But trying to play both sides of it damages one's own legitimacy and credibility while belittling the struggle of others (signaling to others in the scene that mentioning a "revolutionary" suffices to impress—no action required). The teaching of John Africa still leaves a lot for people to learn—especially (ex)Hardliners. For example, look at John Africa's analysis of interrelations between power, technology, and hierarchy. Or look at the way his teaching melds Zen pragmatism, with absolute Oneness, and revolutionary social justice. Check out the principle of gradualism and you'll see how he coordinated for the *very* long haul. And why did MOVE exist for 50 years (so far) despite massive police oppression and Hardline lasted less than 10 years? Take notes and learn from the elders. Learn from their mistakes, yes, because MOVE people have grappled with internal issues (abuse and hierarchy) and a hateful and morbid campaign against John Gilbride whom someone killed at the height of that hate campaign (Price 2021). It seems that MOVE people may even find themselves now in a process of rupture precisely because they had succumbed to some of the same dynamics of Hardline (deception, manipulation, etc. but on an even far worse scale involving abuse of children and possibly murder; see Nark 2021).

But also learn from their success and the degree to which they have survived with so few resources and so much working against them (Africa 2021). Imagine what it took for the surviving MOVE members in prison to last 40 years in prison without renouncing their beliefs (which could have gotten them out of prison). Even the first to pass, Merle Africa in 1998, lasted *20 years in prison*. Consuewella Africa, just months before she took her last breath on June 16th, 2021, said: "The MOVE organization is not just a bunch of people you see here," she said. "We are a family, a unit. We stand together. This is my family. The family of John Africa. Our belief is life. Our children is life. Animals are life. Therefore, we stand together and fight for one life" (Roberts 2021). Because a judge forced a lawyer upon her after the 1978 confrontation, Consuewella did not count among the MOVE 9 and outsiders have tended to forget about her and forget that she got convicted alongside the MOVE 9 (while the MOVE 9 represented themselves, Consuewella's court-imposed lawyer got her a lower sentence). Consuewella alone served 16 years in prison—more than all Hardliners combined (even if one included Peter Young and Walter Bond). She lost two daughters to the police bombing in 1985—while incarcerated. Imagine the feeling of sitting in prison and hearing from a guard about how police killed your children. Janine, Janet, Edward, Phil, and Delbert of the MOVE 9 also lost children then. Together, the MOVE 9 served more than 360 years in prison. (This does not include the years of incarceration endured by other MOVE members such as Ramona, Carlos, Albert, Sue, Alphonso, various MOVE supporters, or—the one MOVE person still in prison—Mumia Abu-Jamal—still incarcerated after nearly 40 years now). And Sean, despite the prominence he claimed to have and despite his claim that he met with MOVE members, and despite his claim that MOVE impacted Hardline from the beginning, he never once called for the release of the MOVE 9 or even a new trial on any of his music releases or any issue of *Vanguard*. When he wrote a dedication list on *The Wrath of God/Vanguard* ranging from Chief Seattle to Malcolm X, from Buddha to Marcus Garvey, he managed to leave out John Africa, the co-founder and primary figure of a group whom Sean claimed had a direct impact on him (MOVE). Why the silence? Maybe because Hardline would no longer seem like "the first highly organized revolutionary struggle to be built around and fighting for the equality of all life"? How else to explain it? Sean mentioned Mumia in '95 and namedropped MOVE in '98 and '99, so why the lack of engagement? He could have championed the cause and helped mobilize Hardliners to campaign for MOVE 9's release back in the 90s and potentially had an impact. But he didn't. Why not?

Sure, Ahl-i Allah and Taliyah al-Mahdi gave more attention to MOVE, quoted John Africa, Micah even used the screen name "Aboo Jamaal," and linked to MOVE-related homepages, and even Walter Bond (2011b and 2011c) has mentioned John Africa positively, but nothing directly from Sean and nothing that qualifies as coming clean on the relationship between Hardline and MOVE. Even Micah's latest 2020 version of the Manifesto repeats the lie: "Until now, however, no single MOVEMENT has articulated as completely an intersectional and holistic description of the nature of this NEW ETHIC" (See Appendix 1). Even while mentioning MOVE in the Manifesto, he invisibilized them by denying them the status of first delivering the ideology that Hardline and Taliyah proposed.

Now, this section has focused on how Sean namedropped MOVE years later without any evidence whatsoever in the actual Hardline literature at the time to back it up. Yet, one could apply the same logic to other groups or ideas that Sean now claims as an initial influence on Hardline yet made no mention of in *Vanguard* 1 or the Hardline manifesto such as Liberation Theology (or any of its known advocates), the Black Panthers, the SLA, Five Percenters, Buddhism, or the Nation of Islam. He obviously had a familiarity with anarcho-punk since at least 1985 or '86 and he did mention Rastas and Daoism as early as 1989 and quoted the Quran as early as 1992 but I can't see that he mentioned Buddha or Malcolm X until 1995. And I first saw him mention the SLA in 2021. Maybe he did know a lot about them, maybe he didn't. But namedropping without backing it up gives minus credibility points.

I have seen people read this text and still not clearly see how Sean has downplayed and/or rewritten history so, in the addition to the example of MOVE, I'll spell it out as plain as possible. When Hardline started in 1990, Sean said in an interview in *UNAxVOCE* that Hardline consisted of 4 basis points: "1. Being vegan; 2. No alcohol or any other drugs; 3. Anti-abortion, anti-gay; 4. Radical environmentalism." The same year, he told *Profane Existence* that homosexuality "must be spoken out against and combatted." Years later, in the 2000s, he told Brian Peterson in an interview that "People ...wanted to jump to conclusions and would say hardliners ...had an anti-gay agenda. But those things never happened in hardline." Researchers and record collectors will most likely see Peterson book but have no idea that Sean simply lied about the historical record. Hardline and Sean very literally had an anti-gay agenda.

Hardliners probably did not go around beating up gay people—not that I have seen any evidence of at least, but to deny that Hardline had an anti-gay agenda amounts to nothing other than historical revisionism. That anti-gay agenda seems to have diminished after Sean and Ryan left Hardline and many Hardline zines (e.g., *Gaia Screams*, *SEAL*, *Invictus*, *Unveil The Lies*, *Memphis Vegan*, *Defense, Rescue and Survival*), rather focused on animal liberation and anti-abortion. They showed little interest in opposing homosexuality but they built upon Sean's legacy of animosity to homosexuals and, at the time, never created an alternative Hardline that openly disputed Sean's interpretation and framework. So, for these activists and ex-Hardliners, without acknowledging the damage done and the limits of Hardline's legacy, it doesn't suffice to claim (as Adam Malik did) that "most" Hardliners rejected *Vanguard*'s ban on "sexual deviation." Not if you want to clear the historical record.

The same holds true for the massive amount of intrigue, subterfuge, and clandestine duplicity that Sean built into Hardline. Early on, in two of the first interviews (in *MAS* and *Caring Edge*), Sean openly declared that Vegan Reich aimed for a "vegan dictatorship." In case some might write that off as a 20 year-old kid's hyperbole or attempt at shock value, we can recall that he followed up nearly a decade later with *Vanguard* 8 that laid out seemingly dead serious plans as to how Hardliners would literally establish a vegan dictatorship including ripping wealthy people from their homes as assassinating them. So when Sean later claimed online in 2009 that the "name Vegan Reich came about as a shock tactic" and "if you think we ever believed in the real possibility of creating and maintaining a vegan dictatorship across the world, what can I say…" …well, we can say it sounds like a fabrication of history, that's what. Just because Hardline failed in its aims does not mean it didn't literally aim for a dictatorship sown through disorder, carnage, and authoritarian assaults against those they classified as "wicked." But I have yet to see Sean really comment on the contents of *Vanguard* 8, much less come clean about it.

And yet, he did create a clever conundrum that worked to his advantage: by writing in *Vanguard* 8, that "it will become necessary to dissolve the outward structure of Hardline" and sometimes "fake a public break with the movement (pretending to sell out, or give up etc.)," severances that "may even have to be believed by the rest of the movement," Sean allowed for a small and dying scene to *appear* to initiates as if everything actually went according to plan. Thus, anyone really paying attention to Hardline could feel that they had access to "inside knowledge" and believe that perhaps Sean never *really* left Hardline, Hardline never *really* died, it all just went into "occultation" as Micah claimed when he attempted to resurrect Taliyah in 2020. Hardliners, in their imagination, could actually operate as secret agents in a world-spanning conspiracy engaging in entryism (entering other organizations to "influence them subtly"), even while everyone, including Sean, claimed the Hardline scene had died. With so much deceit and mythmaking in Hardline, it can naturally feel difficult to come clean about all of its fabricated intricacies and historical revisionism.

But if one really cares about honesty, integrity, and accountability, then one can simply set the record straight. One can admit to a lie rather than clinging fast to it. So just tell the truth—even after years of not doing so—and come clean with the question of influence and debt. Come clean on the question of veiled threats to vulnerable communities. Come clean on the question of violence, informal hierarchy, and dictatorship.

Those of us outsiders who never got involved in Hardline may have our own skeletal closet contents to deal with. 30 years now after Hardline's first Survival of Fittest gathering, we might mock how a few hardcore kids thought they would organize world revolution, but what did *we* do? They accurately recognized the world ecology crisis and the critical state of animal welfare and, however fraught with shortcomings, aimed to do something about it. Many of them devoted countless hours to both propagating for this urgency in zines and bands but also on the streets, in direct actions, in protests, in jails and prison time. Maybe if the vast majority of us who did not put so much time and focus on those issues had done so, then things could have turned out differently. And maybe it doesn't matter whether or not (ex)Hardliners really exist quietly within mainstream organizations as hidden sleeper cells to aid a world vegan revolution or whether Hardline really dissolved. *Maybe it only matters whether or not we take action now.* Yes, the vast majority of society and even the vast majority of activists failed to really devote themselves to rescuing enough forests or animals, hindering enough plastic production or weapons sales, stopping enough air and water pollution, slowing down enough civilizational expansion and destruction of our shared habitats. But what do we do now?

Even organizations who already work with these issues can learn to take more effective actions and find ways to work sustainably both socially and societally as well as ecologically. If we earn trust through our actions and cultivate healthy means of communication, we can look forward to reaping what we sow. If we rethink our relationships to technology and travel, we can learn to reconnect with the land where we live. If we recognize the sanctity of the soil and all of Her children, we can infuse our daily life with prayer. If we reach across artificial and destructive divisions to really listen to and connect with people and species whom we never *really* take time to hear, we can reassemble our lives more effectively and inclusively. If we develop durable and meaningful communities then maybe we can raise generations of revolutionaries as if our children can—and will—have a future worth living in.

Now, Go in Peace and Raise Hell

In order to really face Hardline's (and our own) uncomfortable pasts, we may need to make more space for listening. Space to connect. Space to hear small, quiet voices speak. Space for the past to let its lessons rise. Space for silence.

Maybe Reinhold Niebuhr had it right, after all. Maybe rather than loud, deafening music and people shouting over each other in angry debates, we could use more silence, we could use more listening, we could use more Quakers. After all, Quakers gifted anarchism with consensus circles. They could just as well gift some silence too. And, in doing so, in that silence and listening to the still small voice from within, around us, and beyond, maybe something like Hardline could turn into the sort of revolutionary monastic order that Sean claimed to have originally envisioned—minus the intrigues, arrogance, informal authoritarianism, ultraviolent language, and duplicity (all of which Hardliners presumably imagined would disappear "after the revolution"). Maybe we could witness the power of quiet dedication, humble bridge-building, creative social gardening, radical inclusivity, gentle action, and the pragmatic construction of an alternative society from within the shell of the old—the type of world we actually want to live in. Maybe in that silence a storm could grow, tectonic plates can shift, and volcanic magma can stir. And maybe a Queer Quaker Union of Egalitarian Evolutionary Revolutionary Servants will start liberating animals, engaging in direct actions, and burning down this system before it burns us up.

10 Appendices

Appendix 1.

Evolution of the Hardline manifesto: Hardline (c. 1992), Ahl-i Allah (c. 2000), Taliyah al-Mahdi (c. 2002). Taliyah al-Mahdi (2021). **Bold text** signals parts retained from original manifesto.

Hardline Manifesto (c. 1992) [unsigned Hardline manifesto, version 1]

The time has come for an ideology and for a movement that is both physically and morally strong enough to do battle against the forces of evil that are destroying the earth (and all life upon it).

One that cannot be bought, nor led astray by temptation. A movement free of the vices that sedate the mind and weaken the body.

An ideology that is pure and righteous, without contradictions or inconsistencies. One that judges all things by one standard and emphasizes personal responsibility and accountability above all else.

An overall view on life that not only deals with the external, but also the internal—realizing that a physical entity of oppression, such as the capitalist system (where all life is deemed an expendable resource), is merely an outward manifestation of the warped values held by the people who run the institutions that control our lives, influence our culture and destroy the earth.

It must also recognize the intrinsic flaw of single issue causes, where the concept of justice is always a selective one (with each special interest group fighting for the rights of those that fall under their personal concern, while neglecting, or in some cases, opposing those rights for others)—moving beyond such failed approaches—to a logical and all encompassing system of thought and program of action, which can and will succeed.

That ideology, that movement, is Hardline.

A belief system, and a way of life that lives by one ethic—that all innocent life is sacred, and must have the right to live out its natural state of existence in peace, without interference.

This single ethic ensures that all life, from a foetus, or a grown human (black, white, male or female), to an animal, or its habitat, is guaranteed equal rights, with liberty for all, regardless of someone's personal bias against them.

Under the principles of the Hardline ideology, all shall be permitted to do as they please as long as their actions do not harm, in any way, the rights of others. Any action that does interfere with such rights shall not be considered a "right" in itself, and therefore shall not be tolerated.

Those who hurt or destroy life around them, or create a situation in which that life or the quality of it is threatened shall from then on no longer be considered innocent, and in turn will no long have rights.

Adherents to the hardline will abide by these principles in daily life. They shall live at one with the laws of nature, and not forsake them for the desire of pleasure—from deviant sexual acts and/or abortion, to drug use of any kind (and all other cases where ones harms all life around them under the pretext that they are just harming themselves). And, in following with the belief that one shall not infringe on an innocent's life—no animal product shall be consumed (be it flesh, milk or egg).

Along with this purity of everyday life, the true hardliner must strive to liberate the rest of the world from its chains—saving life in some cases, and in others, dealing out justice to those guilty of destroying it.

Only with this dedication, and conviction—living a life that is in harmony with our stated goals and beliefs, gaining strength from our purity of body and mind, while actively opposing those who are guilty of destroying the world with their poisonous thoughts, deeds and pollution, can we be victorious in the struggle.

Source: *Vanguard* 1 (c. 1992). https://archive.org/details/vanguard_1

One God, One Aim, One Destiny: A Call To Unity and Struggle Against Injustice (2001) [Ahl-i Allah version; Author: Shahid 'Ali Muttaqi, Hardline manifesto version 2, bold signifies parts lifted from original manifesto]

In these times ruled by avarice and vice, where racial injustice and economic exploitation enslaves humanity, where women and children are forced into prostitution, good men murdered by police and military death squads, and our youth go to an early grave—victims of self destruction via gang violence, drug abuse and sexually transmitted disease—there is no room for division amongst the poor and righteous of this world over theological differences; no reason to fight inter-religious wars. For in Truth, so long as we fight for justice, and our Faith is genuine, we are allies. As the great Imam Ali said:

"Allah admits to Paradise anyone for sincerity of belief."

And certainly, in this world of corruption, where all traditional cultures and beliefs are under attack from the Godless Whore which is Babylon—there are only two divisions: Those who seek to live upright, and those who do not.

Likewise, there is no hope in racial or nationalistic divisions. For in this modern world, the grasp of the beast encompasses every nation and people upon this earth. There is nowhere to hide. No community is free of its evil influence. So there can be no victory in isolationism. No salvation in sectarianism.

For while the downtrodden of the earth remain divided over inherited political, cultural and religious divisions—divisions which are not of their making—the system of Dajjal [false messiah] marches forward in its quest for world domination and the subjugation of the human soul.

Therefore, **the time has come for** the downtrodden, exploited masses of the world to embrace **an ideology** of unification, **and** form **a movement that is both physically and morally strong enough to do battle against the forces of evil that are destroying this Earth (and all life upon it). One that recognizes the intrinsic flaw of single issue causes, whose concept of justice is always selective (with each special interest group fighting for the rights of those that fall under their personal concern, while neglecting, or in some cases, opposing those rights for others)—moving beyond such failed approaches to a logical and all encompassing system of thought and program of action, which can and will succeed. One that cannot be bought, nor led astray by temptation. One that is free of the vices that sedate the mind and weaken the body.**

The time has come for **an ideology** and spiritual **conception that is pure and righteous, without contradictions or inconsistencies. One that judges all things by one standard and emphasizes personal responsibility and accountability above all else. A belief system, a way of life** (tariqah, or "path") **that lives by one ethic, that all Life**, by its very nature of existing within the Totality of the Creator (Allah) **is sacred, and must have the right to live out its natural state of existence** unhindered by this modernist hell (which has placed wrong for right, falsehood for truth, and downpression for justice). A **movement that not only deals with the external, but also the internal—realizing that a physical entity** of exploitation and tyranny, **such as the capitalist system (where all life is deemed an expendable resource), is merely an outward manifestation of the warped values held by the people who run the institutions that control our lives, influence our culture and destroy the earth.**

That ideology of unification is the Eternal Light of Truth taught by ALL Prophets, Imams, and Saints throughout the ages. It is the primordial path of Submission to Allah (known in different languages as The Tao, Middle Way, Central Column and Sirat al-Mustaqim) that has been expressed by Adam, Zoroaster, Abraham, Lao Tsu, Buddha, Moses, Jesus, Muhammad and all 124,000 Prophets (may the peace of Allah be upon them all) who were sent with a mission to uplift humanity and bring salvation to the world. And though some people have caused division in this singular message of Truth by breaking it into separate "religions" and calling them by the name of one particular Prophet or people—be it Zoroastrianism, Buddhism, Jainism, Judaism, or Christianity—in Truth, there is no division. All Prophets have declared the Unity Of God. All Prophets have spoken of Islam (or submission to ALLAH). Likewise, ALL true Gnostics and mystics who live upright and believe in justice are truly the People of Allah, no matter what label is given to them.

So let us unite around the common Light of Truth that shines through all sacred scriptures. Let us come to the realization that no matter what sect or denomination our parents have raised us in, that we were ALL born Muslim (inherently submitting to the will of ALLAH). That ALL Prophets have preached a singular unifying message of Islam.

For there is no division in ALLAH. No variation in divine Truth. Humanity is ONE. Creation is ONE. ALLAH is ONE.

Only once we begin to enact this Truth, moving past notions of separation, will we truly fulfill our destiny as the People Of Allah—purifying our lives from the corruptive influence of Babylon, and gaining the strength to slay the beast which is this system of Dajjal [false messiah].

Source: People of Allah/Ahl-i Allah homepage.

https://web.archive.org/web/20020527031717/http://www.peopleofallah.org/articles/pdf-files/One-God.PDF

The Vanguard of the Mahdi (2002) [First Taliyah al-Mahdi version; Unsigned Hardline manifesto version 3; bold signifies parts lifted from original manifesto]

"*Let there arise out of you a band of people inviting to all that is good, enjoining what is right, and forbidding what is wrong: and these it is that shall be successful.*" Qur'an, Sura 3:104

The time has come for an ideology and for a movement, that is both physically and morally strong enough, to do battle against the forces of evil that are destroying the earth, and all life upon it. One that cannot be bought, nor led astray by temptation. A movement free of the vices that sedate the mind and weaken the body. An ideology that is pure and righteous, without contradictions or inconsistencies. One that judges all things by one standard and emphasizes personal responsibility and accountability above all else. An overall view on life that not only deals with the external, but also the internal—realizing that a physical entity of oppression, such as the capitalist system, (where all life is deemed an expendable resource), is merely an outward manifestation of the warped

values held by the people who run the institutions that control our lives, influence our culture and destroy the earth.

It must also recognize the intrinsic flaw of single issue causes, where the concept of justice is always a selective one, (with each special interest group fighting for the rights of those that fall under their personal concern, while neglecting, or in some cases, opposing those rights for others)—moving beyond such failed approaches—to a logical and all encompassing system of thought and program of action, which can and will succeed.

This is a movement, **and a way of life that lives by one ethic—that all innocent life is sacred, and must have the right to live out its natural state of existence in peace, without interference. Under these principles, all shall be permitted to do as they please as long as their actions do not harm, in any way, the rights of others. Any action that does interfere with such rights shall not be considered a "right" in itself, and therefore shall not be tolerated. Those who hurt or destroy life around them, or create a situation in which that life or the quality of it is threatened shall from then on no longer be considered innocent, and in turn will no longer have rights.**

Members of the Taliyah **will abide by these principles in daily life. They shall live at one with the** Law of Allah and the Shariah of Islam, **and not forsake them for the desire of pleasure—from deviant sexual acts and/or abortion, to drug use of any kind, (and all other cases where ones harms all life around them under the pretext that they are just harming themselves). Along with this purity of everyday life, the true Mu'min must strive to liberate the rest of the world from its chains—saving life in some cases, and in others, dealing out justice to those guilty of destroying it. Only with this dedication, and conviction—living a life that is in harmony with our stated goals and beliefs, gaining strength from our purity of body and mind, while actively opposing those who are guilty destroying the world with their poisonous thoughts, deeds and pollution, can we be victorious in the Struggle.**

Instructed by Muhammad (sal) to "search for 'Ilm (or 'divine knowledge') even if you have to go to China" —we seek edification from ALL sacred scriptures and traditions, and strive to unveil their esoteric Truth and underlying Unity (in an effort to bring about true Gnosis and usher in an era of Messianic Consciousness).

Knowing this cannot come to pass while still locked in the chains of Babylon, we strive for justice and liberation by any means necessary. First, through an inward Jihad of self improvement, and spiritual refinement (manifesting in the moral and economic uplifting of our families, community and nation) and secondly, by waging an outward Jihad against the forces of evil that enslave this earth and make universal spiritual awakening impossible. Only through an effort of the faithful will al-Mahdi rise and only then will al-Masih return.

Come join us in our struggle to purify the heart and mind; to build an Ummah (community) of pure and righteous souls, and to fight against ALL forms of injustice and exploitation.

Source: Taliyah al-Mahdi, Homepage, 2003. https://web.archive.org/web/20030810011437/http://www.taliyah.org/index.php

The Vanguard of the Mahdi: On The MOVE For Intersectional Social Justice (2021) [2nd Taliyah al-Mahdi version; unsigned Hardline manifesto version 4, posted by Micah Collins; bold signifies parts lifted from original manifesto; caps in original]

When they could no longer keep us shackled within physical chains of bondage and servitude, they chose instead to keep us shackled in mental slavery and spiritual bondage. Finally, when these forces of oppression and ignorance realized they could no longer control us, they attempted to wipe out entire peoples and communities through GENOCIDE. Today, mass incarceration and other insidious methods of ethnic cleansing, along with top down CLASS WARFARE continue these methods and their LEGACY OF BRUTALITY.

Whether the Trans-Atlantic Slave Trade, the GENOCIDE of the Indigenous Native peoples of the Americas, the Nazi Holocaust or the continued Western imperialism that subjugates and dominates the world in the pursuit of profit, sense gratification and imagined gain, the STRUGGLE of resistance which we must engage in remains intersectional—ONE MOVEMENT—which is fought on many fronts, but must never be divided nor seen as separate, disconnected or unrelated.

Our MOVEMENT is **one that cannot be bought, nor lead astray by temptation, moral compromise, or personal weakness. It is an ideology that is pure and righteous**, because our focus is not merely outward on the world we are all a part of, it is also internal—with an eye towards self-critique and purification, and constant alignment of our words and deeds with what is ethically right and strategically intelligent.

This NEW ETHIC, which we present here for the edification of those who SEEK THE TRUTH, **judges all things by ONE standard and emphasizes personal responsibility and accountability above all else.** It is **an overall view on LIFE that not only deals with the external, but also the internal.** It thus necessarily **realizes that a physical** manifestation **of oppression, such as the capitalist system (where all life is deemed an**

expendable resource)—is merely an outward manifestation of the warped values held by the POWER **ELITE who run the institutions that control our lives, influence** Western **culture and destroy the Earth.**

Our NEW ETHIC **also recognizes the intrinsic flaws of single-issue causes, where the concept of justice is always, invariably a selective one—with each special interest group fighting for the rights of those that fall under their personal concern** alone, **while neglecting, or in some cases, opposing** altogether the recognition of **those rights for others**. TOGETHER, we are **moving beyond such failed approaches, and single-issue causes, to a logical and all- encompassing system of thought and program of action, which can and MUST succeed**.

This MOVEMENT is not a new idea, but one which has gone by many names – working within and manifesting as various organizations which may on the surface seem to be unrelated and disconnected one from the other. While our WAY is a TRUE PATH which revolutionaries, sages and mystics have walked for generations, it is one which has been necessarily renewed in this era of darkness and utter ignorance for the salvation of our species and the healing of this planet.

Our ideology and method of ACTION has gone by many names, in many languages, from generation to generation. We derive inspiration from and pay homage to such social justice REVOLUTIONARIES throughout the ages, as MOVE, the American Indian Movement (AIM), the Black Panther Party For Self-Defense, and the Weather Underground. With respect to "Eco-Defense"—we honor and walk in the footsteps of the Earth Liberation Front (ELF), the Animal Liberation Front (ALF), and an array of militant movements with which there are obvious parallels and inspirations [of] this MOVEMENT.

We support and derive inspiration from the historical anti-fascist resistance movements like the Iron Front, the White Rose Society and their modern expressions today as the Anti- Fascist Army and the White Rose Revolt.

Our spiritual roots reach back into every resistance movement against injustice and oppression, whether John Brown and Nat Turner's revolts, the Boxer Rebellion, the countless indigenous UPRISINGS against imperialism around the world, the Hashashin (Assassins), the first century T'ai Ping and Yellow Turbans Movement or similar movements thousands of miles away with the Zealots and Siqariyim ("Sicarii")—whether fighting Roman imperialists on the raised fortress of Masada or executing collaborators in the marketplace.

Until now, however, no single MOVEMENT has articulated as completely an intersectional and holistic description of the nature of this NEW ETHIC. Today, we refer to this ideology, WAY OF LIFE and course of DIRECT ACTION simply as THE MOVEMENT. Ours is a belief system, and a WAY OF LIFE that lives by ONE SINGLE ETHIC: that **all innocent life is sacred, and must have the right to live out a natural state of existence in peace without interference**, unless they have aggressed against another. **This** NEW **ETHIC ensures that all LIFE**, whether human of any background, gender, sexual orientation or sex, or even the Eco-Systems we are all a part of in our state of Nature (under one NATURAL ORDER), are guaranteed the right to exist unhindered, **regardless of one's personal bias against them** or perceived right to exploit them.

Under the principles of the MOVEMENT, **all shall be permitted to do as they please as long as their actions do not harm, in any way, the rights of others. Any action that does interfere with such innate rights will not be considered a "right" and therefore will not be tolerated. Those who hurt or destroy life around them, or create a situation in which that life or the quality of it is threatened or compromised, will from then on no longer be considered innocent life, and thus will in turn, no longer have rights.**

Adherents to this MOVEMENT **will abide by these principles in daily life: they will live at ONE with the LAW** of the NATURAL ORDER **and will not forsake them for the desires of pleasure**—from acts of violence against the innocent members of our communities, or the Eco-System, to predatory sexual acts, to the use of synthetic, man-made drugs of any kind for escapism, or any other cases where one harms all life around them, destroying our communities and financing tyrants, dictators, and billionaire parasites, under the pretext that they are only harming themselves.

Consistent with the principle that **one shall not infringe on an innocent's life**—we restrict our diets to refrain from needless suffering of non-human animal species—whether their flesh or factory farmed dairy products, eggs, or commercial honey where honey is replaced with sugar water for an insect species that we symbiotically rely on for pollinating plants, and thus for our human survival. **Along with this purity of everyday life, the** REVOLUTIONARY in the MOVEMENT **must strive to liberate the rest of the world from its chains—saving life in some cases**, through DIRECT ACTION, **and in others, dealing out justice to those guilty of destroying it.**

Only with this dedication and conviction—living a life that is in harmony with our stated goals and beliefs, gaining the strength from our purity of body and mind, while actively opposing those who are destroying this world with their poisonous thoughts, deeds and pollution – can we be victorious in our **STRUGGLE** for TOTAL LIBERATION.

Source: Taliyah al-Mahdi homepage, 2020. https://taliyah.org/socialjustice.html

Appendix 2

Kent McClard, "HardXline." *Indecision* 1 (1991).

The Hardline has been the subject of a lot of discussion, anger, and debate in the last year, and I've been accused of being associated with this movement, but while I am very vegan and extremely straight edge, I am not a gun-loving, homophobic, "pro-life" advocate, and I do not offer law as a solution to our problems. I think the Hardline represents an exaggerated mutation of certain aspects of hardcore-machismo harder-than-you attitudes combined with a religious self-righteousness and a charade of more-political-than-you banter. Straight edge and veganism and environmentalism are worth fighting for if the war is fought with words, personal commitment, integrity, honesty, abrasion, dedication, sincerity, and knowledge. The forces that oppose us hold a monopoly on violence and macho attitudes. We cannot defeat them with the very game they have perfected. The war plan involves restructuring our thought process, reworking our lifestyles, searching for alternative ways to live, creating expression without financial compromise, striving for a purity of integrity, constantly disseminating information, questioning the status-quo dribble (not to mention our own dribble), and setting an example that becomes deadly in its subversion of mainstream values and lifestyle. In my opinion, the acceptance of so-called sexual deviance, mainly homosexuality, and the understanding that women have a choice over their reproductive functions and the realization that we were all once animal abusers are all intricately interconnected needs. The machine that we all supposedly oppose creates an image of humanity in which we are told to fit, legislated to fit, and forced to fit. Breaking that down involves dismantling all levels of discrimination. Knowledge overall, and truth of thought, word, and action are the weapons of choice. Legislation, force, and violence only bring us back into the plans of the machine. Hardline is a product of the American way. The coercion, false pride, empty rhetoric, legislation, religious righteousness, and manipulated image of Hardline is so typical of our society that it is almost completely benign. Hardline is as threatening to the American way of life as baseball, apple pie, and hot dogs. Like some flashy MTV orientated media trend, Hardline will burn itself out as all substanceless and disposable commodities do. – Kent McClard • Po Box 680 • Goleta, CA 93116

Appendix 3

Excerpt from "The Gospel" by Circle One (from *Patterns of Force*, Upstart Records, 1983).

[Satan] will brainwash you and tell you that you're no good,
that you're born to be gay and that's understood.
But listen homo, disgrace of our race,
a joke you are a joke of bad taste,
Everything on earth is bad you see,
evil root of society
...Jesus loves you so much, he'll give you a chance,
believe in him and you'll surely enhance.

Circle One logo with M-16s:

Rocks logo with M-16s (*MRR* 78, 1989):

Appendix 4

Excerpts from Andy Martin's explanation as to why The Apostles put out two blatantly prejudiced tracks:

I stated the majority of punks were bigots and racists. So I wrote "Kill Or Cure" (which calls for homosexuals to forcefully submit to aversion therapy or accept the death penalty) and "Rock Against Communism" (which includes every vile complaint, moan, whine and gripe I could remember my parents making when they told me not to bring "chinks" or "niggers" into our house). I predicted very few punks would express any resentment in response to these numbers. On the contrary I expected to receive praise and approbation for my courage. This is precisely what happened! My assertion was vindicated. The trouble is, many people thought I actually meant what I sung (which is fair enough, after all) and thus rumours spread: The Apostles became a neo-nazi outfit. Yes, that's me in the swastika T-shirt at the Pied Bull ready to support Skrewdriver at their next concert! In a sudden attack of conscience, I destroyed most of the records barely a month after their release—I think only sixty copies are in existence.

Source: Penguin 2016.

[Note: Andy seemed to have regretted his destruction of racist tracks like "Rock Against Communism." In 2018, he decided to re-record it and re-publish it in 2018 via his current band Unit on the release entitled "Better Dead Than Red."]

Appendix 5

Excerpt from letter by Tomas Squip of Beefeater in *Maximum Rocknroll* in 1985 responding to Mykel Board's defense of meat-eating.

[Mykel] is being whimsical and crudely light-hearted with an issue that deserves more, as it involves death. I'm trying to be diplomatic, let me just get down to what I feel. Here's the part that shook me up: he says you can go to some fast-food house to get meat without being cruel.

Man, man-unkind has stock in many perversions, but to look to sensationalistic teenage gross-outs like nailing goose feet to the floor and crippling an animal-child and then to look past ten-fold crime that goes down behind [fast food production] because you're distracted by the muzak and color photos in such an unmentionable slip—I almost feel guilty bringing the charge up. Yet, you let loose and I've gotta counter it.

I was in an argument about abortion with a girl a little while ago and she said to me: "How can you claim to be so humanitarian and still encourage births that will lead to unwanted lives that are destined to broken homes?": I said: "I'm fighting for human rights..." You can't even discuss human rights when you've killed the party in question. That's the same kind of 'modest proposal' logic as suggesting one start crusades that scout through lower income neighborhoods and filter out unhappy people or children from broken homes and killing them for their own best interest. Similarly, you must consider that if you try to be an altruist in any valid form, you can't limit your efforts to causes that appeal to you and neglect others that are too much trouble to fight for. Compassion is only compassion when it's applied universally. To limit your love only to select subjects is selfish and barely loving, and to restrict your warmth and concern to yourself and your friends is in effect the opposite, it's cold.

Source: *Maximum Rocknroll* #27 (August 1985): 4.

Appendix 6

Excerpts from Sean's missive (under pseudonym "kilgour") to the 1986 Chicago anarchist conference:

when i first heard that meat was to be served at the banquet, it shocked me. i didn't feel much anger at the time, only a great sense of disappointment.

i had begun to assume that anyone committed enough to travel (in some cases, all the way across the country) to chicago, for the haymarket centennial (to yet again make the voice be heard that cries out for freedom and liberty and sings loud of the beauty of life) would have if still not having rid themselves from the ugly habit of eating that which once was a living creature, at least been considerate enough, for one night, to refrain from doing so, out of the simple realization that it would greatly offend a good number of people (who for some odd reason don't like watching their animal friends being torn up and chewed on). but of course, it was naive to believe such a thing ... my feeling of disappointment became a feeling of anger as i found out that somewhere around a thousand dollars was spent (and please correct me if i'm wrong. i hope i'm wrong, but from what i've been told, that is how much was spent) on catering the roast beef and chicken, while hardly anything was spent on vegetarian meals and even less was done for the vegans (at the banquet at least we vegetarians got some lasagna—which i should add ran out right away, leaving many unfed—while the vegans got nothing at all, except for some lettuce and that's about it. only later, when someone went and bought some vegetables and rice, with their own money, did the vegans get anything of substance). ... this, along with the fact that it was such a fuckin' hypocrisy in the first place (meat being served at a banquet by people supposedly against oppression and enslavement) propelled us to print up the "anarcho-beef people" flyer (from our magazine NO MASTER'S VOICE) which was initially written for the "anarcho-punks" in our area, for whom this type of behavior has become commonplace. realizing that the flyer alone would not quite have the desired effect ...we sought out a group of people who had been doing street theater at the demos, and asked them if they could think of anything to do through theater that would shove the reality that "meat is murder" that much closer into the faces of the "anarcho-beef people."

...during the middle of dinner, the signal went out and a group of people (or should i say "cows," as that is what they represented) crawled to the space between the tables, mooing and chewing on lettuce along the way. once they got to the center, another group of people (this time the "butchers") walked to where the "cows" were and proceeded to 'slaughter'

them and "gnaw" away at their arms and legs. while all this was happening, we walked about and gave everyone eating meat a copy of our flyer. ... i have to admit, though, that i'm a bit pissed off that none of the "counter-attacks" were to our faces). ... after people had time to read the flyer and digest the whole of its meaning, quite a lot of faces began to redden. i tried to talk to a few of them about it, but all i got was "i don't want to talk to you, don't preach to me" from people who looked like they were about to cry (for fuck sake, i wish someone would have at least punched me, rather than holding all their anger in, for that's surely what they wanted to do). towards the end of the night when a good number of people had gone outside, we were helping to clean up when we found a few of our flyers wrapped around pieces of chicken as well as roast beef (or some kind of beef—i'm no expert!). that was such a cowardly, spineless thing to do, it makes me sick! people are so afraid of a confrontation, they end up pulling this petty symbolic bullshit of wrapping a flyer around a dead animal. big fucking deal! i hope the cowards all choke and die (how's that for reactionary?)! of course the attacks months later in magazine reviews as well as in letters (to other magazines, of course—no one having the guts to write us about it, all preferring to backstab instead), were really great. it's funny how people who have nothing to say to you at the time suddenly have quite a lot to say when you're not around to defend yourself. so say what you will about us—that we're reactionaries, fanatics, etc. we love this world and those living upon it, so if in order to protect this world and its inhabitants we have to offend a few crybaby anarchists, then that is what we shall do. "enjoy your burger—and may it be your last."

—love
kilgour
king of "the bombflict bozos"
Source: Campion et al 1987: 62-64.

Appendix 7

Selection of Sean's ads: Sean's first ad in *MRR* 51 with Common Ground (August 1987); No Master's Voice ad in *Endless Struggle* 8 (1988); Vegan Reich band member request in *MRR* 75 (August 1989); First Hardline Records ad in *MRR* 79 (December 1989); Second Hardline ad in *MRR* 87 (August 1990).

Sean's first ad in *MRR* 51 with Common Ground (August 1987).

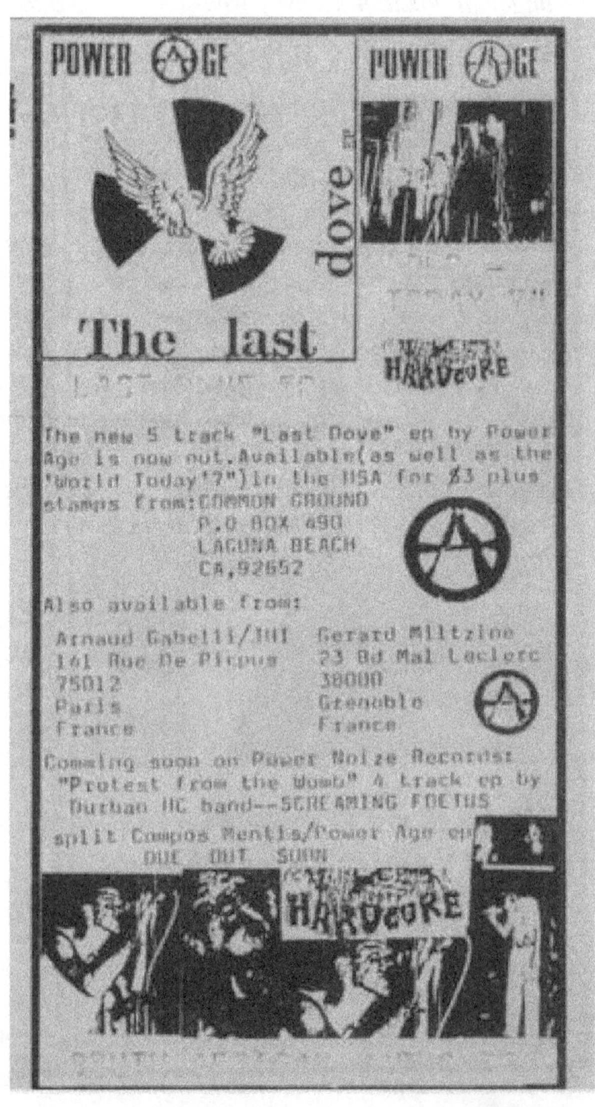

No Master's Voice ad in *Endless Struggle* 8 (1988).

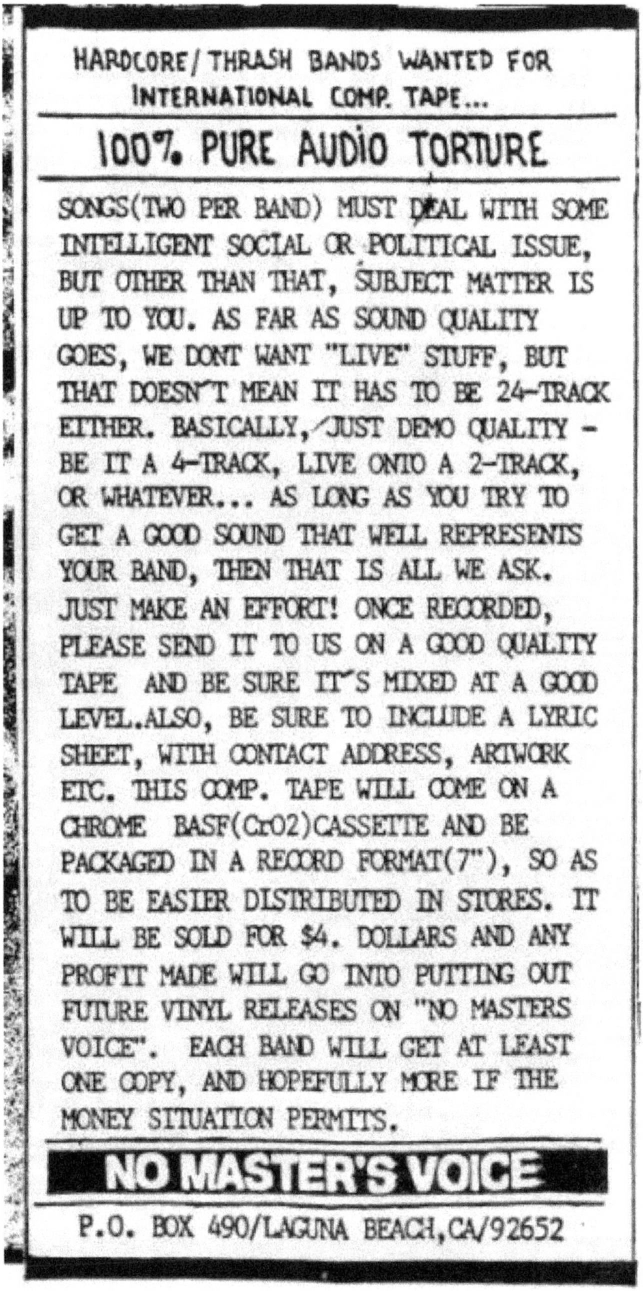

HARDCORE/THRASH BANDS WANTED FOR INTERNATIONAL COMP. TAPE...

100% PURE AUDIO TORTURE

SONGS(TWO PER BAND) MUST DEAL WITH SOME INTELLIGENT SOCIAL OR POLITICAL ISSUE, BUT OTHER THAN THAT, SUBJECT MATTER IS UP TO YOU. AS FAR AS SOUND QUALITY GOES, WE DONT WANT "LIVE" STUFF, BUT THAT DOESN'T MEAN IT HAS TO BE 24-TRACK EITHER. BASICALLY, JUST DEMO QUALITY - BE IT A 4-TRACK, LIVE ONTO A 2-TRACK, OR WHATEVER... AS LONG AS YOU TRY TO GET A GOOD SOUND THAT WELL REPRESENTS YOUR BAND, THEN THAT IS ALL WE ASK. JUST MAKE AN EFFORT! ONCE RECORDED, PLEASE SEND IT TO US ON A GOOD QUALITY TAPE AND BE SURE IT'S MIXED AT A GOOD LEVEL.ALSO, BE SURE TO INCLUDE A LYRIC SHEET, WITH CONTACT ADDRESS, ARTWORK ETC. THIS COMP. TAPE WILL COME ON A CHROME BASF(CrO2)CASSETTE AND BE PACKAGED IN A RECORD FORMAT(7"), SO AS TO BE EASIER DISTRIBUTED IN STORES. IT WILL BE SOLD FOR $4. DOLLARS AND ANY PROFIT MADE WILL GO INTO PUTTING OUT FUTURE VINYL RELEASES ON "NO MASTERS VOICE". EACH BAND WILL GET AT LEAST ONE COPY, AND HOPEFULLY MORE IF THE MONEY SITUATION PERMITS.

NO MASTER'S VOICE

P.O. BOX 490/LAGUNA BEACH,CA/92652

Vegan Reich band member request in *MRR* 75 (August 1989).

VEGAN REICH

Needs a straight edge, vegan bass player who can play fast hardcore with complex structures, as well as reggae etc. Must have experience and be willing to tour. No matter how far away you live, if you think you might be interested, give us a call at: (714) 497-9095.

I, THE JURY

ALSO:

S.E./vege bands are wanted for a straight edge/animal liberation oriented 7" comp. as are vegan recipes for a cookbook to accompany a Vegan Reich 7" titled Uncarved Tofu Block.

P.O. Box 490 / Laguna Beach,
CA 92652 / USA

First Hardline Records ad in *MRR* 79 (December 1989).

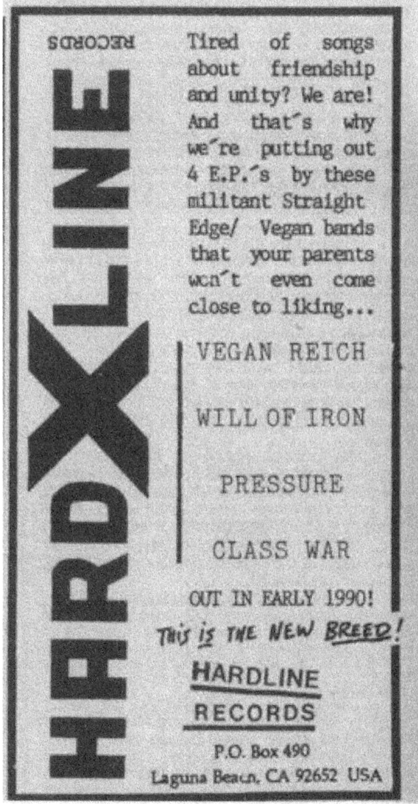

Second Hardline ad in *MRR* 87 (August 1990).

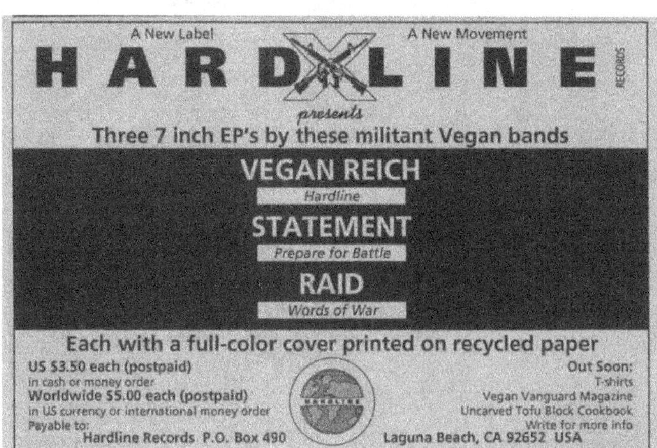

Appendix 8

First Vegan Reich interview *MAS* 8, 1989 with ad for No Master's Voice on second page.

Vegan Reich

VEGAN REICH, from Orange County, have quite a following, called the Soy Boys/Girls. Sorry no bandmember names, but anyways...**How long have you been around?**

VEGAN REICH has been, and will always be, around forever! Its more than a musical group-its a movement. And if you get in our way we'll turn your brain into tofu scrambler!

How did you become vegans... from punk rock?

Your question answers itself. We are punk and thus we are vegan. Any fool out there who thinks they're punk without being vegan is just conning themself.

The Soy Boys/Girls have gotten a bad rep from people saying they are a "violent gang". I've heard rumors of knocking burgers out of peoples hands, beating up hippies etc. What do you think of this?

We won't comment on any rumors. You will know when you are confronted by the REICH.

What does the name mean?

"VEGAN REICH" is the highest form of discipline attainable by the human race at this point in our historical development. And what that means for all you pathetic drug, dairy, and meat addicts-is that since you don't have the intelligence and compassion to live your life without fuckin' up the earth and all its other more valid life forms-the REICH will rule over you with an iron fist to stamp out ignorance forever. You are either standing with the REICH, or you will be crushed under its wheels of progress.

Do you think everybody should stop eating meat?

We don't care if they "should"-THEY WILL!

What are your views on drugs?

We don't have "views"- liberals have views. Views are opinions-we only deal with what is, and there is only one truth! You either face reality or are smashed in the face by it! As to the drugs-they will not be tolerated, nor will hippies-even if they quit doing drugs!

What about homebrew?

Homebrew's better than buying vivisected animal ingredient beer, but abuse of any substance is lame, and will be dealt with accordingly. Sober Brew is the REICH'S Brew!

What are your favorite things?

List of favorite things: Girls, Punk, Sex Pistols, Dead Nazi skins, Vitasoy, Trader Joes, Payless Shoes (home of non-leather steel toe), Paulina, Jessica Lange, Michele Pfeifer, Jane Seymore, The two Miami Vice girls, Anarchy (the chaotic kind), Mykel Board, All Laguna Beach girls, The Germs, Bondage (with non-leather straps), Italian food, Italian Girls (non-New York hybrids) Tofu, Jamacan women (natty queens), Mexican food, All rad girls on above list naked, deals (not the drug kind), salad (not the green kind), The Apostles, Miami Vice, Saturday Night Live, David Letterman, Blonde girls, raging Scottish punx, Jimmy Cliff, Peter Tosh, Matabaruku, The Epileptics (pre-Flux), Tom Likas, furniture.

Whew! Unfavorite things?

List of fucked things: Girls, smelly-skanky-rotten to the core-yeastie-infected-unshaven-intrenched and intwined with lard-bitchy-separatist-antiMykel Board-Feme cunts!, Cocaine, anything rad with "Whey" in it, The Pink Triangle Crowd (liberate gerbils from Homo-vivesection), AIDS, people with AIDS who pass it knowingly, concussions, Nambla, dirty fucking child molesters, peace "punx", crust scum core, nineteen dollar Jimmy Cliff shoes, The Rolling Stones, South O.C. cops, Bush (the George kind), Quayle (the Dan kind), virgins, San Francisco/Berkeley, Deadheads/hippie scum, Steve Jones playing with Bob Dylan, King Diamond.

Do you guys have anything recorded?
There's a track on the comp LP "The ALF is Watching and There's No Place to Hide". Also we have a track on a comp 7" coming out in South Africa.

How about future recordings?
We'll be recording stuff for an EP called "Uncarved Tofu Block", which will include a vegan cook book.

Heard any good jokes?
What do get when you cross a Scandenavian with an animal rights activist?

I dunno, what?
A NÖR-VEGAN!

Anything else you wanna say?
We do believe in anarchism as an ultimate goal, but realize that at this point in time too many humans in this world are weak and unable to resist the temptations of hedonism. Thus anarchism could not function at this stage in history-at least in most of the world. The first step would have to be a dictatorship by vegans who would help speed up the natural evolution process by re-educated those who can be, and weeding out those beyond help. After this has occurred and the human race is dramatically reduced in numbers, the dictatorship can be dissolved and true anarchism can flourish. A more immediate goal is to help show as many people the true path of veganism and drug free life so that they can further reach their true potential and live life to the utmost extent without damaging the earth or her creatures. Write us at: PO BOX 490, Laguna Beach, CA 92652

An international compilation L.P. as benefit for the U.S. Animal Liberation Front Support Group with...

ANTI-HEROES
BEEFEATER
BODY COUNT
CHUMBAWAMBA
MAN'S HATE
NATURECORE
OI POLLOI
PARANOID VISIONS
POWER AGE
STATEMENT
TOXIC WASTE
VEGAN REICH

plus a 12 page lyric/info booklet with articles on factory farming, the dairy industry and vivisection, as well as info on veganism and interviews with A.L.F. activists.

Mail Order Prices (post paid)

U.S.A.	$7.00
Canada & Mexico	$8.00
Air Europe	$11.00
Air Australia, Japan, etc.	$12.00
Overseas via Surface	$8.00

Overseas customers—check your local mail order for cheaper prices

U.S.—Cash or Money Order Only
Overseas—U.S. currency or International Money Order Only
payable to:
No Master's Voice
P.O. Box 490
Laguna Beach, CA 92652 USA

Appendix 9

Excerpt from *MAS* 9, dedication to Vegan Reich and implying intent to provoke (1989). [Note: two sections from same issue clipped together].

MAS

FORCE

#8 April-May '89 $1.50

Also dedicated to all the following people who have, in one way or another, contributed to our efforts: Dale Sedgewick, MISERY, Anarchist Homebrew Collective, Maddog / Anti-Racist Action, BLIND APPROACH, CRIBDEATH, our friends in Belgium, Rachel Weber, Shannon Oslund, Cricket, Iggy Amo, Gord / "Endless Stuggle" Fanzine, Jason and the rest of the THD Radio Crew, Tom Angelli, Minneapolis A.Y.F. (Anarchist Youth Federation), LIBIDO BOYZ, IRON FIST, GOVERNMENT ISSUE, Vancouver anarchists, Amy Hoagland, Persona non Grata, Dan Van Lanen, Jon G. / "Impulse" 'zine, Nick Skrade, Paul Kuehl & Leon Rohrbaugh / "Bondage" & "Distorted Views" fanzines, NAUSEA, John Crawford, Pat Pelini (Get well soon!), Jez Nanker, Gary Sandwick, Glen Hirabayashi / "High School is a Wasteland" fanzine, Jakob / "Sorte Rose" Fanzine, Pat Rohling, DISSENT, VEGAN REICH, MORAL CRUX, NO APPARENT REASON and last but not least, Chip Pearson. Also can't forget those who have helped us out in many other ways but they are too numerous to name; you know who you are! Also thanx for those who helped bring out this issue but you'll have to figure out who that is for yourself!

This issue we had a rather skimpy amount of letters sent to us meaning either we didn't piss enough people off or you're all just lazy and can't get off your ass to drop us a line. We will continue to have a letters section in "Profane Existence" and if anyone wants their letters published, keep sending them in. Also, Dan would like to

M.A.S.U. #1 Januar

MINNEAPOLIS ALTERNATIVE SC

NON-LEATHER

Appendix 10

Sean's letters to *Maximum Rocknroll* 1989 and *Profane Existence* 1990 (along with respective responses).

Maximum Rocknroll 79 (Dec 1989):

MRR,

Do you wanna know what's wrong with the Anarchist/ Commie/ Left wing/ Punk movement? Its adherents talk a lot about spreading their message to the working class and building a movement capable of bringing down the decadent capitalistic system—yet not only do they seem to have a complete disdain for traditional working class values, thus alienating those they speak of helping, they also champion such things as homosexuality and drug use that are prime examples of the root evil that not only creates the possibility for such things as capitalism, but also help it thrive. And that root evil is weakness.

War, poverty, and capitalism etc. are not the real enemy—the underlying flaw in human character that makes it possible for such things to exist IS! It is the lack of inner strength and self-discipline that leads to the belief that one needs outside stimuli for happiness (be it money, power, sex or drugs), and that whatever one must do to get such things is justified by the end result of pleasure. Thus, wars are fought by men whose own body and mind were not enough of a sacred possession and had to have more material possessions and power to fill their void. Likewise, rape is committed by those who can't live without their fix of sex, and so turn to violence to get it, just as people starve so that the wealthy elite can overeat and amass wealth so that they can satisfy their thirst for pleasure.

The hippy ideal of "Free Love" which is running rampant within the alternative "scene," as well as homosexuality are just further examples of that weakness, where life is lived purely for pleasure.

The only true purpose for sex, as nature intended, is for reproduction. Yet it too has been turned into a drug. One that people are willing to kill for, as documented by the large number of abortions each year (which, while we're on that subject, I'd like to say that I find it interesting that so many people find the idea of rape, where a man brutalizes a woman so he can have his way with her, as abhorrent (which it IS), yet find it perfectly acceptable to abort a life for the same thing—SEX).

The epitome of sex being used as nothing more than for pleasure is homosexuality. There is no link whatsoever in a homosexual act with the intended purpose (according to the laws of nature) of intercourse, and it is nothing more than pure hedonism. In issue no. 77 of MRR, *the question is asked (in the letter section) as to what is the difference between hating someone because of their skin color and hating someone because of their sexual preference. I will answer that. Even though someone may be born genetically fucked up, and be attracted to the same sex, they, at one point, have to make a conscious decision to follow through on those urges and thus they choose their sexual behavior. No one can choose their skin color, and beyond that, the color of one's skin does not reflect what type of person one may be, where as being gay (which is a behavior) does i.e. A pathetic slave to desire.*

All you liberals can whine about freedom and alternative lifestyles etc. but there's no way in hell you can convince me that fucking someone in the ass (which everyone seems to have forgotten is for elimination, NOT penetration) is anything but perverse behavior. There's nothing radical, liberated or revolutionary about it. All it is, is hedonistic. And for those who say "What do you care what someone does with their dick?"... People can not be separated from their actions. Our behavior makes us who we are. And that is why I hate homosexuals. It is the same reason I hate drug users and meat eaters. It has nothing whatsoever to do with homophobia. It has to do with the fact that they represent an element in the human character which I believe is the downfall of mankind-and that is a lack of self-control and willpower in the extreme.

This so called alternative "scene" of ours is nothing more than a sickening reflection of our collapsing society, yet no one seems to see it. They talk about their decadent behavior in ways to make it seem political yet fail to realize the only politics they represent are that of suicide. I for one will no longer sit back and let these people destroy what little good is left in our society. You can call me a fascist or a homophobic or whatever. I don't give a fuck. This ain't some fucking game. We're in the final days. If there's to be a change in this world it's gonna be now or never, 'cos if it ain't soon, it won't ever be 'cos our time's running out. No more ozone, no more trees, no more oxygen. Get it? What I'm saying is end the shit like, "He eats meat but he's still pretty cool" and "I don't care if he likes little boys, he's still against apartheid" and all that other common ground, mutual cause bullshit. Self-control, physical strength, and mental awareness are what it's about 'cos it's survival of the fittest and this time it's gonna be the straight-up Vegan who comes out on top.

Sean/Vegan Reich/ PO Box 490/ Laguna Beach, CA 92652

Dear Sean,

Every now and then it's fun to print a letter like yours. Not actually fun, but curious and sad. Sean, if you're going to go around analyzing characteristic flaws in mankind's behavior, I suggest you begin with yourself. Right off the bat I can see a fine Hitleresque "purity" trait growing with you. The "will" fascination and ultra-militant Vegan stance are right up Adolph's alley, and represent a fine fear of one's self, I might add. I know there's nothing I can say that might enable you to take a long hard look at yourself before you go off on your hate trip, but maybe others can see the comparison.

Tim

Letter exchange between Sean and *Profane Existence* 3, April–May 1990, p. 7:

Profane Existence,

Writing in regard to our (VEGAN REICH's) interview in M.A.S. #8 and Pat & Troll's comments in P.E. #2 about being "ignorant...sexist, homophobic, intolerant," etc.

As to the sexist allegation—I take that in regards to the list of "favorite things" where we listed some actresses, models & various other women, etc. I thought it would be painfully obvious that we were joking (when the first choice of both the "favorite" and "unfavorite" lists was girls and then talking about non-leather bondage & hating virgins, etc—I mean who could take this seriously?) and in fact, I don't see how we could have expected to seriously with such a ridiculous, irrelevant question as "what are your favorite things?" However, it's obvious you did take it seriously, so, even though I don't see any problems with us joking around in such a manner, I will now state my opinions on sexism as to state my positions as such as to clear up any misunderstandings which may have resulted from that interview. I consider women to be completely equal to men, both in the struggle & in relationship, etc. However, I do not think we are the same. So if all you feminists who seek to negate pre-set natural roles & destroy the family structure (as capitalism and communism have done) think that still classifies me as sexist, then so be it. I know that by thought & deed I stand for complete equality of the sexes, and that's all that matters.

Concerning homophobia...That word implies fear of homosexuality—usually a fear of oneself, which then gets focused on others, etc. This has nothing to do with our stance on the issue. Fear doesn't enter the picture. From a natural & moral outlook on life, homosexuality can be seen as nothing but a deviation from nature. And like all other deviations from nature, which have brought our world to the dreadful state it is in today, it must be spoken out against and combatted.

As far as being intolerant? Yes, I will not tolerate the murder of animals & destruction of our Earth, just as you would not tolerate the murder of your family & destruction of your home. To suggest that I am fascist (as pat did) because I extend the "rights" to those beyond the human species & will not tolerate to deny them the right to kill and torture, etc. and, obviously, as stupid as you may be, you haven't yet sunken to that level of absurdity.

Regarding my "extreme feelings" (which, by the way, are shared by other vegans out there & through out the world), yeah, I have 'em. I believe in such off the top radically violent ideas such as not forcing the third world to live in hunger because we make them grow cash crops to satisfy our vices (such as coffee, cocaine, & pot etc. not to mention beef production). I believe in the oppressive doctrine of equal rights and liberty for animals, being such a fascist scum to suggest they live their lives free of our control, manipulation and murder.

Oh, and of course, the total psychopathic vision of a society which is not governed by greed & perversion. Where women can walk the streets without fear of rape, where children are not sold drugs at their schools, nor molested by their twisted parents. Yeah, I'm so "extreme" for believing in absolute right and wrong, and having some fundamental morals shared by rational decent human beings. Get a grip on reality.

Ignorance means lacking of knowledge or experience, or being uninformed, etc. How does that really apply to me? After nine years of being involved in the punk/Anarchist/animal liberation movements there isn't anything in the social/political realm I haven't studied, or couldn't intelligently argue with you and needless to say, during that time, not to mention the rest of my life, I've experienced a lot first hand, so there goes your argument of ignorance.

If you want to call me an asshole or something, that's fine—but next time you want to use any other descriptive word, trying knowing what it means first & when it applies.

Sean / Vegan Reich

Sean,

Let us not mistake anything here: [quoting Sean] 'We do believe in Anarchism as an ultimate goal, but realize that at this point in time too many humans in the this world are weak and unable to resist hedonism. Thus Anarchism could not function at this stage in history—at least in most of the world. The first step would be a dictatorship by vegans who would help speed up the natural evolution process by re-educating those who can be, and weeding out those beyond help. After this has occurred and the human race is drastically reduced in population..." This is what was stated in the M.A.S. interview. Add that to a name like Vegan Reich and it's pretty plain to see where the term fascist may come into use. Of course, it's only a matter of semantics on how these can apply—taken out of context, whatever, which may also be said about the "sexist" charge.

As far as homophobic, it may not be a blatant fear of homosexuals you have, but you are painfully misled by saying it is a "deviation from nature." That, I will argue is totally false. We cannot find anything to support your statement further than assumptions, while it is not uncommon for animals in nature to not differentiate gender preference in instinctual sexual act, barring it is not in contradiction of other instinctual traits such as territories, etc. Also, even if homosexuality deviates from sexual norms, said sexual preference does not constitute abnormal behavior. As far as being morally wrong, let us remind you that it was on the pretext of moral judgment such atrocities as the Spanish Inquisition and the Salem Witch Trials were allowed to happen.

We also find your definition of ignorance as quite simplistic. While you claim to have a great deal of knowledge, you seem ignorant in your ability to coherently use it. We could say that a dictionary has an immense amount of information, but without proper use it is nothing but an inanimate object.

As a closing comment, we would like to add that we find your intolerance abhorrent. It is imperative to be self-aware in order to initiate any positive change. Personal revelation may not always translate into the betterment of all people. We have to work together if we really want to change things, not from exclusionary ideals.

Editorial Crew

Appendix 11

Pete Wentz and his Hardline tattoo.

Reportedly, "Pete (in the dark blue boxers with his back to the camera) has a design of the earth tattooed on his lower back," which, according to the picture at least, looks enshrined in an ecology symbol—precisely the same as the Hardline logo. Accurate or not, I cannot say but, as he played in Birthright, a Hardline-adjacent band, the possibility does not seem far-fetched.

Source: https://www.ranker.com/list/pete-wentz-tattoos/tat-fancy

Appendix 12

Vegan Reich liner notes to *Jihad* (1999), original in all-caps.

IT'S BEEN 12 YEARS SINCE WE WERE FORMED WITHIN THE BELLY OF THE BEAST. BORN FROM BABYLON. NURSED ON HER BITTER MILK. RAISED ON HER HATRED, MALICE, AND COLD HEARTEDNESS. OUR BROTHERS AND SISTERS ABUSED, TORTURED, ENSLAVED. UNABLE TO BEAR HER WICKED WAYS. NO LONGER WILLING TO SIT AND WATCH AS SHE DESTROYED OUR HOME. KILLING OUR FAMILY. WE LASHED OUT WITH A HATRED THAT ONLY HATRED CAN PRODUCE.

THE WAR CRY STRUCK A CHORD. OUR MESSAGE IMMEDIATELY TOOK HOLD IN LARGE SEGMENTS OF BOTH THE ANARCHIST AND STRAIGHT EDGE MOVEMENTS. SOON, A LOOSE COALITION WAS FROM THEIR RANKS. AND WHAT HAD UP UNTIL THEN BEEN AN OBSCURE AND ISOLATED LIFESTYLE, BECAME PUBLICLY KNOWN AS VEGAN STRAIGHT EDGE. WITHIN THREE YEARS THE CORE MILITANTS FROM THIS GROUP, BEING HEAVILY INFLUENCED BY THE POLITICS OF MALCOLM X AND MOVE AS WELL AS THE SPIRITUAL DOCTRINES OF TAOISM, RASTAFARIANISM AND ISLAM, WENT ON TO FOUND A REVOLUTIONARY MOVEMENT KNOWN AS HARDLINE.

AS THE MAJOR VOICE REPRESENTING BOTH HARDLINE AND VEGAN STRAIGHT EDGE AT THAT TIME, WE BEGAN COMING UNDER EVER INCREASING SCRUTINY AND ATTACK FOR THE RISING INCIDENTS OF DIRECT ACTION AND OCCASIONAL VIOLENCE WHICH WERE COMING FROM THESE TWO CAMPS. BANNED THROUGHOUT BABYLON, MONITORED BY THE AGENTS OF DAJJAL [false messiah], IT SOON BECAME EVIDENT THAT IT WAS IMPOSSIBLE FOR US TO CONTINUE ON AS BOTH ACTIVISTS AND SPOKESMEN FOR MILITANT ACTION. NOT WILLING TO ABANDON OUR ROLES AS REVOLUTIONARIES, IT BECAME CLEAR THAT THE TIME HAD COME TO REMOVE OURSELVES FROM THE PUBLIC EYE. SO BEGAN OUR JOURNEY INTO OCCULTATION.

IT HAS NOW BEEN 7 YEARS SINCE THAT DEPARTURE. 9 SINCE THE BIRTH OF HARDLINE. AND 12 SINCE THE PUBLIC EMERGENCE OF THE VEGAN STRAIGHT EDGE LIFESTYLE.

INTERESTINGLY ENOUGH, IN THE SCIENCE OF NUMEROLOGY, THESE NUMBERS REPRESENT COMPLETIONS OF A CYCLE. SEVEN DAYS IN A WEEK, NINE MONTHS IN A PREGNANCY, AND TWELVE MONTHS IN A YEAR.

AND IN ALL THREE AREAS THINGS HAVE CLEARLY COME FULL CIRCLE. VEGAN STRAIGHT EDGE HAS GROWN CONSIDERABLY DUE TO EFFORTS OF OUR SUCCESSORS. HARDLINE HAS BECOME A WELL ESTABLISHED PATH IN MANY COUNTRIES OF THE WORLD. AND VEGAN REICH HAS RETURNED ONCE MORE.

1999 COULD NOT BE A BETTER YEAR FOR THIS. WITH THE COMING MILLENNIUM IT IS ONLY APPROPRIATE THAT ONE CYCLE BE BROUGHT TO COMPLETION AND ANOTHER MANIFESTATION BE GIVEN LIFE THIS YEAR.

VEGAN REICH HAS SYMBOLIZED A MYTHOLOGICAL ORDER THAT COULD BE A WORLD FREE OF OPPRESSION, SLAVERY AND MURDER. ONE WHERE ALL LIFE WAS SACRED AND JUSTICE RULED SUPREME.

OUR RETURN REPRESENTS THE FIRST STEP IN THE ACTUALIZATION OF THESE DREAMS. ALL OF THE LAWS HAVE BEEN LAID. ALL OF THE ARGUMENTS MADE. THERE IS TRUTHFULLY NOTHING NEW UNDER THE SUN.

WE HAVE NOT COME TO ARGUE WHICH PATH IS THE MOST EFFECTIVE, NOR TO CONDEMN ANYONE WHO STRIVES FOR JUSTICE. VEGAN REICH HAS RETURNED TO DECLARE JIHAD AGAINST THE SYSTEM OF DAJJAL. NOT JUST A "HOLY WAR" AS THE WEST COMMONLY ASSUMES THIS WORD TO MEAN—BUT RATHER A SACRED STRIVING TO PURIFY OURSELVES AND THE WORLD AROUND US FROM ALL CORRUPTION AND SIN.

IN LINE WITH THIS, WE ARE CHANGING OUR NAME, AND WILL HENCEFORTH BE KNOWN AS VEGAN JIHAD. THERE'S JUST NO MORE TIME FOR WHAT COULD BE. WE'VE GOT TO START DEALING WITH WHAT IS. THE WORLD IS UNDER SIEGE. IT'S TIME WE FACE IT HEAD ON. THERE MAY NEVER BE A UTOPIAN SYSTEM. BUT EACH TIME SOMEONE STRIKES OUT FOR JUTICE, EVERY ANIMAL THAT IS LIBERATED, EVERY ACRE OF RAIN FOREST SAVED, EVERY BOMB THAT BLASTS APART A FACTORY

OF TORTURE, OF MURDER. EVERY BULLET THAT STRIKES DOWN THOSE DEVILS PROVES, THERE IS A VEGAN JIHAD (WHICH IS IN ITSELF BUT ONE SMALL PART IN THE GREATER JIHAD —THAT BEING THE ETERNAL STRUGGLE AGAINST EVIL AND THE CONTINUAL BATTLE FOR JUSTICE ON EARTH).

INSHA'ALLAH, VICTORY WILL BE OURS. ALLAHU AKBAR

Appendix 13

Excerpt from Walter and Camille's Vegan Final Solution homepage manifesto:

WE ADVOCATE a misanthropic worldview and motive behind all our actions, deeds and writings. For the animals we have become species traitors. This includes, but is not limited to, an aggressive stance against reproduction, an advocacy of abortion and euthanasia. The only breeding not wholly intolerable in our eyes, is solely for the purpose of rearing a new generation of animal liberators and subversives against society.

...WE ADVOCATE living a minimalist and simple life, if possible, completely to the detriment of society. ...The only thing prosperity is good for is liberating animals, funding our campaigns on their behalf, and otherwise funding resistance against the techno-industrial complex.

...WE BELIEVE the measure of how much we respect a human's rights is in direct proportion to the way each individual respects animals' rights.

...WE BELIEVE that nothing that has ever been done in defense of the earth and animals is too extreme, nor could it be. The decimation of the entire human race does not even compare to the number of animals that die in one day at the hands of speciesist human oppressors.

...WE BELIEVE that human-centered issues are a distraction to animal liberation.

WE ADVOCATE a total lack of concern for egalitarian issues. The whole laundry bag of activist, and so called "total liberation" issues, not only seeks to put the focus right back on worthless people, but also undermines the animals' safety by making society more cohesive and functional.

WE ADVOCATE a complete disregard for moralism and orthodoxy outside of the vegan ethic.

...WE ADVOCATE a third position beyond left- and right-wing ideology; a third position that encompasses the best of both, and discards the rest.

...WE ADVOCATE a hierarchy where those that exercise self-discipline and self-sacrifice for the good of animals and the earth are deemed more deserving of life than the gluttonous, selfish drones that shovel dead animals into their grotesque faces, simply to satiate their lust for rotting meat. With hierarchy, we separate the wheat from the chaff.

WE BELIEVE in utilitarianism. Whatever helps animals and the earth is good. Whatever harms them is bad. And whatever does neither is of no concern.

...WE ADVOCATE nihilism and a breakdown of the social order. ...more than anything, the world needs the failure and collapse of human societies and civilizations. Nature is not in need of our stewardship. It is us that need the earth. Nature finds its own balance. Just as water in a ravine attains its own level. All that is needed is for the human race is to STAND DOWN!

Source: Vegan Final Solution, 2020.

Appendix 14

Excerpt from Anarchist response to Vegan Final Solution:

For anyone unaware of what the "Final Solution" means, the final solution was official Nazi code name for the murder of all Jewish folk within reach. ...The themes in this reactionary and despicable letter borrow from eco-fascist criticisms of anarchy, (that hierarchy is "natural", that anarchism is hypocritical when it comes to issues of power, that it is single-issue obsessed, only concerned with identity politics etc.). Around this same time, Walter wrote letters to various anarchist groups in the U.S. asking for support efforts from and contact with the anarchist movement to cease. Upon our request for any related information, Philadelphia Anarchist Black Cross forwarded us a photo of Neo-Nazi propaganda on the back of a letter from Walter. The original photo had been shared by the recipient in an animal liberation group in early 2020.

We wrote to Walter's support group asking about their stance but never received a reply, make of that what you will. We strongly recommend stopping any solidarity with Walter Bond. ...The content of this website not only confirms that Walter Bond has fully embraced eco-fascism, it also shows that he is now attempting to indoctrinate and recruit people within the Vegan and animal liberation milieu to his poisonous, hate-filled, fascist ideology. From the information published on this website, we can see that "Vegan Final Solution" are openly advocating third-positionist fascism as well as killing people that they have deemed as being either 'useless' humans or traitors to the animal liberation movement. The website also contains a link to a PDF document that they are describing as their manifesto that is titled "A Declaration of War—Killing People to Save the Animals and the Environment." *We predicted that Walter would use his position of influence in Vegan and animal liberation circles to attempt eco-fascist entryism, so this was no surprise to us, however it is alarming to see how quickly he has embarked upon this project, which makes it all the more urgent to alert comrades to this situation so that Walter Bond and his associates are unable to gain either a voice or a foothold within any of our movements.*

Source: Anarchists Worldwide 2020. https://325.nostate.net/tag/vegan-final-solution-eco-fascists

11 References

25 Years on the MOVE. Philadelphia: self-published, 1997.

Abraham, Ibrahim. "Punk Pulpit: Religion, Punk Rock, and Counter (Sub)Cultures." *Bulletin of the Council of Societies for the Study of Religion (CSSR)* 37, no. 1 (2008): 3-7.

Abraham, Ibrahim and Francis Stewart. "Desacralizing Salvation in Straight Edge Christianity and Holistic Spirituality." *International Journal for the Study of New Religions* 5, no. 1 (2014): 77-102.

Abraham, Ibrahim and Francis Stewart. "Punk and Hardcore." In *The Bloomsbury Handbook of Religion and Popular Music*. Edited by Christopher Partridge and Marcus Moberg, 241-250. London: Bloomsbury Publishing, 2017.

Abrash, Paul. "No Tolerance For Hardline." *Drastic Solutions* 5 (c. 1992): 16-17.

Africa, Frank. "Brief to Define the Importance of MOVE's Religious Diet." *Africa v. Commonwealth*, 1981.

Africa, Janet. "What's Really Killing Us," *First Day* 6 (ca. 1995): 4-5.

Africa, Michael, Ronna, Nimrod, et al. "Seeds of Wisdom: The *Network Magazine* Interview." *First Day* 19 (1999): 10-11.

Africa, Jr. Mike. *Fifty Years Ona MOVE.* Philadelphia: Never Give Up, 2021.

Africa, Phil. "WHO ARE THE MOVE 9?" *First Day* 19, c. 1999: 3.

Agranoff, Dave. "Hardline: We Have Failed." *Vanguard* 6 (1995): 25.

Amnéus, Diana, Ditte Eile, Ulrika Flock, Pernilla Rosell Steuer, and Gunnel Testad. *"Validation Techniques and Counter Strategies": Methods for Dealing with Power Structures and Changing Social Climates*. Stockholm University, 2004. http://www.ecosanres.org/pdf_files/Gender_workshop_2010/Resources/Amneus_et_al_2004_Validation_techniques_counter_strategies.pdf

Anarchists Worldwide/Liberate Or Die, "UNOFFENSIVE REPORTS - WALTER BOND AND HIS ECO-FASCIST TRAJECTORY." 28 July 2020. https://www.facebook.com/liberateordie/posts/unoffensive-reports-walter-bond-and-his-eco-fascist-trajectory-we-first-feel-the/579194582769199/

Also at: https://325.nostate.net/tag/vegan-final-solution-eco-fascists/

Anarchopedia. "Hardline Movement." 2012. http://eng.anarchopedia.org/Hardline_movement

Anonymous. "Interview with Alex of New Eden Project." 2004. https://www.angelfire.com/fl3/graphix2000/MAIN/HoldLinks.html

Anonymous. "Identity Crisis: Reclaiming and Reasserting Radical Vegan Straight Edge. [2006]." In *X: Straight Edge and Radical Sobriety*, Gabriel Kuhn (Ed.), 226-231. Oakland, CA: PM Press, 2019.

Anonymous. "Consistency." *Allālōn*. Harrisonburg, Va. 2021. (2021): 11-14.

Arciaga, Michelle. "Straight Edge." *National Alliance of Gang Investigators Associations* (*NAGIA*) homepage. 12 April. 2005. https://web.archive.org/web/20051216151051/http://www.nagia.org/new_page_2.htm

Apostles, The. *Smash the Spectacle!* EP. 1985. https://www.discogs.com/The-Apostles-Smash-The-Spectacle/release/380813

Associated Press. "Fur bomber testifies against others: Straight Edger says he didn't act alone in bombing." *Deseret News*. 6 September (1999). https://www.deseret.com/1999/9/6/19464461/fur-bomber-testifies-against-others-br-straight-edger-says-he-didn-t-act-alone-in-bombing

Bahr, Yusuf Ali. "Interview With Rat (Statement)." *1000 Voices of Dissent*. 11 September 2010. http://sparksofdissent.blogspot.com/2010/09/interview-with-rat-statement.html

Bahr, Yusuf Ali. "Interview With Messiah Communications (Mike)." *1000 Voices of Dissent*. 12 September 2010. http://sparksofdissent.blogspot.com/2010/09/interview-with-messiah-communications.html

Bahr, Yusuf Ali. "Interview With Naj One (Foeknowledge)." *1000 Voices of Dissent*. 16 September 2010. http://sparksofdissent.blogspot.com/2010/09/interview-with-najone-foeknowledge.html

Barnes, Brooks. "This Year, Sundance Will Savor Its Homegrown Projects." *New York Times*. 19 January (2011). https://www.nytimes.com/2011/01/19/movies/19sundance.html

Best, Steven and Anthony J. Nocella, II, *Igniting a Revolution: Voices in Defense of the Earth*. Oakland and Edinburgh: AK Press, 2006.

Binelli, Mark. "Punk Rock Fight Club." *Rolling Stone*. 23 August (2007). https://www.rollingstone.com/culture/culture-news/punk-rock-fight-club-190267/

Blush, Steven, and George Petros. *American Hardcore: A Tribal History*. Los Angeles and New York: Feral House, 2010.

Board, Mykel. "Sez You're Wrong!" (column). *Maximum Rocknroll* 64 (1988).

Board, Mykel. "Sez You're Wrong!" (column). *Maximum Rocknroll* 85 (1990).

Board, Mykel. "Sez You're Wrong!" (column). *Maximum Rocknroll* 340 (2011).

Boisseau, Will and Jim Donaghey. "'Nailing Descartes to the Wall': *Animal Rights, Veganism and Punk Culture.*" In Nocella II, Anthony J.; White, Richard J.; Cudworth, Erika (eds.). *Anarchism and Animal Liberation*, 71–89. McFarland & Company, 2015.

Bond, Walter. "The Importance of Straightedge—Vegan Hardline." *North American Animal Liberation Press Office* (*NAALPO*). 12 November (2011a).

Bond, Walter. *Always Looking Forward*. USA: Liberation Press, 2011b.

Bond, Walter. "An Official Statement About Abortion—Vegan Hardline." *Remain Upright*. 2011c. http://remainupright.blogspot.com/2011/12/official-statement-about-abortion-vegan.html

Bond, Walter. "An FYI from Walter." *Support Walter*. 28 April 2017. https://supportwalter.org/SW/index.php/2017/04/28/an-fyi-from-walter/

Bond, Walter. "Interview by Support Crew/Joe Jordan." *Support Walter*. 29 August 2018. https://supportwalter.org/SW/index.php/2018/08/29/interview/

Bond, Walter. "The End of Anarchy." *Support Walter* homepage. 11 September 2019. https://web.archive.org/web/20181114031321/https://supportwalter.org/SW/index.php/2018/08/29/interview/

Boston Hardline. "Vegan Reich Interviews 1990-1991." Cambridge, MA: no date [c. 1995]. 23 pages.

Bound By Modern Age. "Interview Rat (Statement)." *Bound By Modern Age* 2 (2015a): 16-19.

Bound By Modern Age. "Reppin the X." *Bound by Modern Age* 3 (2015b): 6.

Boyette, Michael and Robin Boyette. *"Let It Burn!": The Philadelphia Tragedy*. Chicago: Contemporary Books, 1989.

Bulatova, Elena I. "Straight Edge Youth Movement: Values and Cultural Practices." *Observatory of Culture* 13, no. 3 (2016): 287-295. [Russian]

Campion, Dogbane et al. *Mob Action Against the State: Haymarket Remembered… an Anarchist Convention.* (On the 1986 Chicago Anarchist Gathering). Anarchist History Nerd Brigade, 1987.

CBS Tonight News. Segment on Hardline Straight Edge in Salt Lake City, UT. Posted by Joshua M. 1997. https://www.youtube.com/watch?v=f_FXTgNcUTI

Christoforidou, Chrisa. "Deconstructing Straight Edge Lyrics and Music: The Straight Edge Total Liberation Ethics." Punk Scholars Annual Conference 2020. (13 December). https://www.academia.edu/44815062/Deconstructing_Straight_Edge_lyrics_and_music_The_Straight_Edge_Total_Liberation_ethics https://www.punkscholarsnetwork.com/blog/punk-scholars-annual-conference-2020

Collins, Micah. "Hardline Update." *Destroy Babylon* 1 (1995): 4.

Collins, Micah. "Hardline is Anti-American!" *Destroy Babylon* 2 (1995): 60-61.

Collins, Micah. "Hardline is Not 'Homophobic': An Open Letter to Liberal Know-It-Alls." *Destroy Babylon* 2 (1995): 50-52.

Collins, Micah. "What's the Matter with Pornography?" *Destroy Babylon* 3 (1996): 65-67. https://archive.org/details/destroy_babylon_3/page/n63/mode/2up

Collins, Micah. "Sodomy Contest," *Destroy Babylon* 4 (1996): 13.

Comrade Black. "Animal Liberation Prisoner Interview." *Profane Existence* 64 (2013): 21.

Coronado, Rod. *Flaming Arrows: Collected Writings of Animal Liberation Front Warrior Rod Coronado*. USA: Warcry Communications, [2007] 2011.

Crustcave, Romain. "California Screamin' (part 4): Naturecore *'With love...'* 12", 1988." *Terminal Sound Nuisance* blog. 8 February. 2018. http://terminalsoundnuisance.blogspot.com/2018/02/california-screamin-part-4-naturecore.html

Daschuk, Mitch Douglas. *"What Was Once Rebellion is Now Clearly Just a Social Sect": Identity, Ideological Conflict And The Field Of Punk Rock Artistic Production*. PhD Dissertation. University of Saskatchewan, 2016.

DiCara, Vic. "And Then Came the Vegans… Vegan Jihad." *Vic DiCara blog*. 2015. https://vicd108.wordpress.com/2015/11/17/and-then-came-the-vegans/

Dines, Mike. "The Sacralization of Straightedge Punk: Bhakti-yoga, Nada Brahma and the Divine Received: Embodiment of Krishnacore." *Muzikoloski Zbornik* 50, no. 2 (2014): 147-156.

Dines, Mike and Matthew Worley (Eds.). *The Aesthetic Of Our Anger: Anarcho-Punk, Politics and Music*. New York: Minor Compositions, 2016.

Dines, Mike. "From Punk Rock to Prabhupāda: Locating the Musical, Philosophical and Spiritual Journey of Contemporary Krishnacore."In *Trans-Global Punk Scenes: The Punk Reader Vol. 2*. Edited by Russ Bestley, Mike Dines, Alastair "Gords" Gordon, and Paula Guerra, 237-254. Bristol and Chicago: Intellect, 2021.

Dorff, Ned. "Islam and Hardcore." *Drug Free Dad*. 28 February 2018. https://drugfreedad.com/interviews/islam-and-hardcore/

Downey, Ryan. "Homosexuality: Gay Rights, the Decline of Civilization and More." *Vanguard* 5 (1993): 21-25.

Downey, Ryan. "If You Only Read One Thing This Issue, Read This! [Interview with Steve Lovett of Raid]." *Destroy Babylon* 3 (1996): 16-21.

Downey, Ryan. Reel (2005). https://www.youtube.com/watch?v=9czxm-22WUk

Downey, Ryan. IMDB bio. 2021. https://www.imdb.com/name/nm2124459/bio?ref_=nm_ov_bio_sm

Downey, Ryan. Homepage. 2021. https://www.ryanjdowney.com/about-1

Earth First! Journal. "Informants." *Earth First! Journal*. Undated. https://earthfirstjournal.news/informants/

Eden, John. "Punk Comics 3: Part Three: Crucial Youth." *Uncarved* blog. 2005. http://www.uncarved.org/blog/2005/02/punk-comics-3/

Edge, Mike (Karban). "RAID: Interview." *Caring Edge* 2 (1990): 4-5.

Edge, Mike (Karban). "Interview with Sean of Vegan Reich." *Caring Edge* 2 (1990): 22-24.

Edge: Perspectives on Drug-Free Culture. M. Pierschel & M. Kirchner. (Directors). 2009.

Ensminger, David A. *The Politics of Punk: Protest and Revolt from the Streets*. Lanham, MD: Rowman & Littlefield, 2016.

Evans, Richard Kent. *MOVE: An American Religion.* New York: Oxford University Press, 2020.

Fernandes, Walisson Pereira. *Straight edge: Uma genealogia das condutas na encruzilhada do punk*. Master's Thesis. São Paulo, 2015. [Portuguese]

Fiscella, Anthony T. "From Muslim Punks to Taqwacore: An Incomplete History of Punk Islam." *Contemporary Islam* 6 (2012a): 255–281.

Fiscella, Anthony T. *Varieties of Islamic Anarchism: A Brief Introduction.* Alpine Anarchist Productions. 2012b. https://www.alpineanarchist.org/about/Islamic_Anarchism_Zine.pdf

Flipside. "The Hardline." *Flipside* 77 (1992): 18-20.

Flynn, Judge. "Letters." *Earth First! Journal* 16, no. 8 (1996): 30.

Foster, Erin. "Don't Smoke, Don't Drink, Don't Fuck: Towards a Theory of Straight-Edge Culture." *Iowa Journal of Cultural Studies* 20 (2001): 93-103.

Fox News. Salt Lake City Straight Edge. 1997a. https://www.youtube.com/watch?v=H9MuHmX0-KQ

Fox News. Salt Lake City Straight Edge. Posted by Joseph Josephson. 24 March 1997b. https://www.youtube.com/watch?v=8grW9PGRMzg

Gay Jamaica Watch. "Mutabaruka: JFLAG & gov't should do more for homeless gays, conflates abuse with homophobia." *Gay Jamaica Watch*. 2016. http://gayjamaicawatch.blogspot.com/2016/01/mutabaruka-jflag-govt-should-do-more.html

GC Activities. Salt Lake Hardcore 101: Lifeless. *Grudge City Activities*. 30 September 2009. http://gcactivities.blogspot.com/2009/09/salt-lake-hardcore-101-lifeless_30.html

Goodwin, JP. Untitled letter. *Maximum Rocknroll* 115 (December 1992): 15.

Gordon, Alastair Robert. *The Authentic Punk: An Ethnography of DiY Music Ethics*. PhD Dissertation. Loughborough University, 2005.

Haenfler, Ross. "Rethinking Subcultural Resistance: Core Values of the Straight Edge Movement." *Journal of Contemporary Ethnography* 33, no. 4 (2004): 406-436.

Haenfler, Ross. *Straight Edge: Hardcore Punk, Clean Living Youth and Social Change*. New Brunswick, NJ: Rutgers University Press, 2006.

Happy Days. "Earth Crisis [interview]." *Happy Days* 2 (c. 1992): 16-19.

Harper, Josh. "The ALF Is Watching And There's No Place To Hide." *The Talon Conspiracy*. 2014. http://thetalonconspiracy.com/tag/hardline/

Howell, Jon. "Folks at EF!" *Earth First! Journal* 16, no. 8, (1 November 1996): 30.

Hughes, Brian. "Reich Vs. Reich: Sex Economy and the Hardline Subculture." *Parasol* 2 (2018): 76-117.

Hrafnsson, Stefán Oddur. "Straight edge" á Íslandi? Möguleg samfélagsleg áhrif þessa undirgeira harðkjarnastefnunnar. Bachelor Thesis. Rejkavik, 2021. [Icelandic]

James, Elgin. *Boston Beatdown: See the World Through Our Eyes Volume II*. Directed by Ronin Morris. Produced by Ronin Morris and Elgin James, 2004.

Jill. "My Path of Progression." *Destroy Babylon* 3 (1996): 56-58.

JX. Review of *Praxis* 1. *MRR* 101 (October 1991).

Kahn, Charles. *The Art and Thought of Heraclitus: A New Arrangement and Translation of the Fragments with Literary and Philosophical Commentary*. Cambridge: Cambridge University Press, 1979.

Kahn, Richard. "Environmental Activism in Music." In *Music in American Life: The Songs, Stories, Styles, and Stars that Shaped our Culture*. Edited by Jacqueline Edmondson, 412-417. Santa Barbara, CA: Greenwood, 2013.

Karban, Mike. "XXX DISCIPLINE XXX," *SEAL (Straight Edge Animal Liberation)* 3 (1996): 16. http://thetalonconspiracy.com/2014/09/seal-3/

Kamiński, Karol. "90s style Metalcore and Old School Rap Collide in the Newest High-Octane Track from FORWARD TO EDEN and 4PAWS." *IDIOTEQ*. 28 October 2020. https://idioteq.com/90s-style-metalcore-and-old-school-rap-collide-in-the-newest-high-octane-track-from-forward-to-eden-and-4paws/

Keenan, Jesse. "Animal Rights, Human Rights, One Struggle, One Fight!" *Memphis Vegan* 5 (1995): 7.

Keynes Junior, Milton. "Interview with Sean Muttaqi (Vegan Reich)." *1000 Voices of Dissent.* 10 September (2010). http://sparksofdissent.blogspot.com/2010/09/interview-with-sean-muttaqi-vegan-reich.html).

Khanum, Sina. "On Sexual Abuse & Accountability in Vegan Straight Edge Communities." *DIY Conspiracy.* 24 April (2021). https://diyconspiracy.net/on-sexual-abuse-accountability/

Knight, Michael Muhammad. "Lifting Up My Skirt." *Vice*. 2013. https://www.vice.com/en/article/bny453/lifting-up-my-skirt

Knight, Michael Muhammad. *Blue-Eyed Devil: A Road Odyssey Through Islamic America*. New York: Autonomedia, 2006.

Kreps, Daniel. "FSU Gang Founder Arrested For Extortion: Inside Punk Fight Club." *Rolling Stone*. 2009. https://www.rollingstone.com/culture/culture-news/fsu-gang-founder-arrested-for-extortion-inside-punk-fight-club-60041/

Kuhn, Gabriel. (Ed.). *Sober Living for the Revolution: Hardcore punk, Straight Edge, and Radical Politics*. Oakland: PM Press, 2010.

Kuhn, Gabriel (Ed.) *X: Straight Edge and Radical Sobriety*. Oakland, CA: PM Press, 2019.

Kuhn, Gabriel. "Ecological Leninism: Friend or Foe?" *LeftTwoThree*. 2021. https://lefttwothree.org/ecological_leninism/

Kuipers, Dean. *Operation Bite Back: Rod Coronado's War to Save American Wilderness*. New York: Bloomsbury, 2009.

Lahickey, Beth. *All Ages: Reflections on Straight Edge*. Huntington Beach, CA: Revelation Books. 1997.

Landauer, Gustav. *Revolution and Other Writings*. Edited and translated by Gabriel Kuhn. Oakland: PM Press, 2010.

Lang, Tom. Letter. *Maximum Rocknroll* 134 (July 1994): 14.

Lavdas, Debbie. "A Gay Heyday." *Laguna Beach Magazine*. 1 December (2012). http://www.lagunabeachmagazine.com/a-gay-heyday/

Leaving MOVE. "Sex and Sexuality within MOVE: The Testimony of Maria Hardy." *Leaving MOVE.* 9 July (2021): https://leavingmove2021.blogspot.com/2021/07/sex-and-sexuality-within-move-testimony.html

Lesko, Oliver. *Vegan Straight Edge: Einblicke in eine extreme Jugendkultur*. University Thesis. Leipzig: Hirnkost, 2012. [German]

Liddick, Donald R. *Eco-Terrorism: Radical Environmental and Animal Liberation Movements*. Westport, CT and London-Praeger, 2006.

Linnemann, Travis and Bill McClanahan. "From 'Filth' and 'Insanity' to 'Peaceful Moral Watchdogs': Police, News Media, and the Gang Label." *Crime Media Culture* 13, no 3 (2019): 1-19.

Listen and Understand. "The Apostles." *Listen and Understand*, 25 September (2011). http://anarchoscene.blogspot.com/2011/09/apostles.html

Lopez, Steve. "The Mutant Brady Bunch." *TIME*, August 30 (1999): 36-37.

MacKaye, Ian. "Idiotic Implications." *Drastic Solutions* 6 (c. 1992): 8.

Mageary, Joe. *"Rise above/We're gonna rise above": A qualitative inquiry into the use of hardcore punk culture as context for the development of preferred identities*. PhD Dissertation. California Institute of Integral Studies, 2012.

M.A.S. "Also dedicated to…" *M.A.S.* 9 (1989): 2.

MBD [Mikhah David Naziri]. "Sean Muttaqi, Vegan Reich and the Hardline Movement." *Planet Grenada.* 10 January (2006). http://planetgrenada.blogspot.com/2006/01/sean-muttaqi-vegan-reich-and-hardline.html

McClard, Kent. "HardXline." *Indecision* 1 (1991): n.p.

McDowell, Amy D. "Aggressive and Loving Men: Gender Hegemony in Christian Hardcore Punk." *Gender and Society* 31, no. 2 (2017): 223-244.

Meden, Gašper. *Hardcore: Od političnega protesta do blaga*. University Thesis. University of Ljubljana, 2011. [Slovenian]

Memphis Hardline. "Earth First!" *Earth First! Journal* 12, no. 3 (2 February 1992): 24.

Michelle/Memphis Hardline. "Women's Section." *Vanguard* 6 (1995): 7.

Michelle/Memphis Hardline. "Animal Liberation," *Vanguard* 6 (1995): 21-22.

Memphis. "Memphis hardline gathering 1991". *I am the Dax*. Posted 24 July 2010. https://www.youtube.com/watch?v=KVXvpzB4TXw

Memphis Vegan 5 (1995). Available online at Talon Conspiracy/ISSUU: http://thetalonconspiracy.com/2011/03/memphis-vegan-5/ https://issuu.com/conflictgypsy/docs/memphisvegan-05?mode=window&viewMode=doublePage

Michalski, Dan. "Pelted!" *Dallas Observer* 4 June (1998). https://www.dallasobserver.com/news/pelted-6401921

Militant Vegan. Untitled intro. *Militant Vegan* 1 (1993): 1.

Mittens XVX. "Gather: Fight for Total Liberation." *DIY Conspiracy*. 20 November (2007). https://diyconspiracy.net/gather/

Mittens XVX. "Statement: Tracing the Roots of Vegan Straight Edge." *DIY Conspiracy*. 9 January (2017). https://diyconspiracy.net/statement-tracing-the-roots-of-vegan-straight-edge/

Moran, Julio. "Police Kill Man, Wound Another Near 2 Beaches: Violence: Both had attacked several people, including a Los Angeles officer, before they were shot." *Los Angeles Times*. 31 May (1991). https://www.latimes.com/archives/la-xpm-1991-05-31-me-2755-story.html

Morris, Courtney Desiree. *Why Misogynists Make Great Informants: How Gender Violence on the Left Enables State Violence in Radical Movements*. Chicago, True Leap Press, 2010.https://trueleappress.files.wordpress.com/2021/04/why-misognists.pdf Originally published in *Make/Shift* 7, 2010, available online via INCITE!: https://incite-national.org/2010/07/15/why-misogynists-make-great-informants-how-gender-violence-on-the-left-enables-state-violence-in-radical-movements/

Mulder, Merle. *Straight Edge: Subkultur, Ideologie, Lebensstil?* Münster: Telos Verlag, 2010. [German]

Mulder, Merle. "'The Only Thing We're Straight About is the Edge. Die Diskussion Über (Homo-) Sexualität in Straight Edge." In *Thema Nr. 1: Sex und populäre Musik*. Edited by Dietrich Helms and Thomas Phleps, 151-164. Bielefeld, Germany: Transcript Verlag, 2011. [German]

Muttaqi, Sean. "To the Hardline." *Vanguard* 1+2 (1993): 9.

Muttaqi, Sean. "Interview with Sean Muttaqi of Vegan Reich by Uprising Records." *Muslims for Jesus*. undated circa 2001. http://www.muslimsforjesus.org/Musicians/Vegan Reich/Vegan Reich.htm

Muttaqi, Sean. "Interview with Sean Muttaqi (Vegan Reich)." *1000 Voices of Dissent*. 12 September. 2010. http://sparksofdissent.blogspot.com/2010/09/interview-with-sean-muttaqi-vegan-reich.html

Muttaqi, Sean. Comment. 8 June 2020. https://www.facebook.com/pg/veganreich/posts/

Muttaqi, Sean. Comments. *Hardcore Fanzines 1980's/1990's.* 3 April 2021. https://www.facebook.com/groups/144243662597560l/permalink/2961889440696971/

Muttaqi, Shahid 'Ali. "Forward to Eden: The Straight Path Towards the Messianic Era." *Ahl-i Allah/People of Allah* homepage. 2001. http://peopleofallah.org/articles/articles/forward.html Currently available at: http://www.adishakti.org/pdf_files/forward_to_eden.pdf

MW. "Review of Vegan Delegation." *Maximum Rocknroll* 102. (November 1991): 116.

NAALPO. "Interview with Peter Young." *North American Animal Liberation Press Office* newsletter 3, no. 1 (2007): 4-6.

NAALPO. "Newest Press Office Advisor: Producer/Director Elgin James." *NAALPO.* 2019. https://animalliberationpressoffice.org/NAALPO/2019/12/30/newest-press-office-advisor-producer-director-elgin-james/ Also see current page: https://animalliberationpressoffice.org/NAALPO/contact/

Nark, Jason. "Ex-MOVE Members Say They Were Raised in a 'Cult' Where Abuse and Homophobia Ran Rampant." *Philadelphia Inquirer* August 27 (2021). https://www.inquirer.com/news/move-bombing-philadelphia-africa-podcast-blog-abuse-20210827.html

Naziri. "Total Liberation Tour 2004." *Indybay*. 2004. https://www.indybay.org/newsitems/2004/06/22/16864161.php

Naziri, Adam. "Calling All Anti-Homophobes!, Protest MTV," *Indybay* 14 July 2004. https://www.indybay.org/newsitems/2004/06/22/16864161.php

Newbery, Jorge. "Remembering John Macias, Punk Peacemaker Killed By Police." *Huffington Post*. 13 February (2017). https://www.huffpost.com/entry/remembering-john-macias-punk-peacemaker-killed-by_b_589b5f81e4b061551b3e068b

Niebuhr, Rienhold. *Moral Man and Immoral Society*. New York: Charles Scribner's Sons, [1932] 1960.

No Compromise. "Felony Court Cases." *No Compromise* 7 (1997): 18.

No Compromise. "Interview with Peter Young." *No Compromise* 28 (2006).

No F'n Regrets. "NFR #084 - Ryan J. Downey (Podcaster, Manager, Burn It Down Vocalist)." 2021. https://www.youtube.com/watch?v=lj_4IITx708

Nyong'o, Tavia. "Do you want queer theory (or do you want the truth)? Intersections of punk and queer in the 1970s." *Radical History Review* 100 (2008): 103-119.

OC Weekly. "No Bueno, Big Guy." *OC Weekly* 11 January (2006). https://www.ocweekly.com/no-bueno-big-guy-6374300/

O'Hara, Craig. *The Philosophy of Punk: More Than Noise!* 2nd Ed. London and Edinburgh: AK Press, 1999.

Old Man's Mettle. "Rat of THE APOSTLES, UNBORN and hardline vegan sXe band STATEMENT on the old days, new projects, going from one extreme to another, and bidding farewell to England." *Old Man's Mettle* blog. 4 September (2021). https://oldmansmettle.com/2021/09/04/rat-of-the-apostles-statement-and-hardline-vegan-sxe-band-unborn-on-the-old-days-new-projects-going-from-one-extreme-to-another-and-bidding-farewell-to-england/

Olmec and Aubin Paul. "FSU Founder Elgin James Arrested for Extortion." *Punk News*. 2009. https://www.punknews.org/article/34393/fsu-founder-elgin-james-arrested-for-extortion

Out of the Cages. "Vegans Vow…" and "Three Face Jail…" *Out of the Cages* 7, 1993: 13.

Panno, Sean. Untitled Letter. *Maximum Rocknroll* 14 (June 1984): 4.

Panno, Michael. *Animal Rites*. Laguna Beach, CA: Primordial Press, a division of Uprising Communications Group, [2000] 2016.

Penguin. "The Apostles Scum Records," *Kill Your Pet Puppy* blog, 2016. https://killyourpetpuppy.co.uk/news/poison-girls-studio-out-takes-1980-omega-tribe-centro-iberico-1982-the-apostles-scum-records-1984-vex-fight-back-records-1984-lack-of-knowledge-l-o-k-records-1982-xmal-de/

Persist. "Earth Crisis (interview)." *Persist* 1 (1993): 23-25.

PerthNow (Staff writer). "Vegan activist Tash Peterson leaving WA after being banned from every pub in the State." *PerthNow* 20 June (2021). https://www.perthnow.com.au/news/wa/vegan-activist-tash-peterson-leaving-wa-after-being-banned-from-every-pub-in-the-state-ng-b881905795z

Peterson, Brian. *Burning Fight: The Nineties Hardcore Revolution in Ethics, Politics, Spirit, and Sound.* Huntington Beach, CA: Revelation Records, 2009.

Pieslak, Jonathan. "The Music Cultures of Radical Environmental and Animal-Rights Activism (REARA)." *Journal EXIT-Deutschland* 3 (2014a): 5-68.

Pieslak, Jonathan. "A Collection of Interview Correspondences with Incarcerated ALF and Vegan Straight Edge/Hardline Activist Walter Bond." *Journal EXIT-Deutschland* 3 (2014b): 69-92.

Pike, Sarah. "Religion and Youth in American Culture." In *The Study of Children in Religions: A Methods Handbook.* Edited by Susan B. Ridgely, 33-49. New York and London: New York University Press, 2011.

Pike, Sarah M. "Radical Animal Rights and Environmental Activism as Rites of Passage." *Journal of Ritual Studies* 27, no. 1 (2013): 35-45.

Pike, Sarah. *For the Wild: Ritual and Commitment in Radical Eco-Activism.* Berkeley: University of California Press, 2017.

Pinsky, Mark and Thuan Le. "2 Plead Guilty in O.C. 'Gay Bashing.'" *Los Angeles Times*. 3 August (1993). https://www.latimes.com/archives/la-xpm-1993-08-03-mn-19798-story.html

Potter, Will. "New Information in Earth Liberation Front Prosecution." *Green Is The New Red*. 21 February 2012. http://www.greenisthenewred.com/blog/dave-agranoff-informant-elf-bloomington/5723/

Praxis, Matt. "Justice: An In Depth Interview with Jon Justice of Justice Zine and Street Justice." *Praxis* 1 (1991): 9-14.

Preston, Sarah Amber. "Rebelling Against Rebellion: Resistance and Tensions in Straight Edge Subculture." Master's thesis. San Diego State University, 2014.

Price, Elizabeth. "Weaponizing Compassion: The 1990s Vegan Straight Edge Metalcore Movement and Hybrid Masculinity." 26 October 2017. Critical Animal Studies Conference.

Price, Kevin. Various articles and group statements. *Leaving MOVE* blog. 2021. http://leavingmove2021.blogspot.com/

Profane Existence. "Ramona Africa and MOVE…About Mumia Abu-Jamal and You." *Profane Existence* 35, 1998: 4-7.

Purchla, Jeff. "The Powers That Be: Processes of Control in 'Crew Scene Hardcore'." *Ethnography* 12, no. 2 (2011): 198-223.

Ramirez, Carlos. "Interview with Tim Rule, Hardline fan, Record Label manager, and Record Collector." *No Echo*. 15 January 2018a. https://www.noecho.net/record-collectors/record-collector-tim-rule-bound-by-modern-age-records

Ramirez, Carlos. "Interview: Scott Crouse (Earth Crisis, SECT, Path of Resistance)." *No Echo*. 2018b. https://www.noecho.net/interviews/scott-crouse-earth-crisis-sect-path-of-resistance

Rayburn, Jim. "Trio not guilty of bombing fur farm. Jury found no physical evidence in '97 incident." *Deseret News* 10 September (1999). https://www.deseret.com/1999/9/10/19465057/trio-not-guilty-of-bombing-fur-farm-br-jury-found-no-physical-evidence-in-97-incident

Reid, Daniel. *The Tao of Health, Sex, and Longevity: A Modern Practical Guide to the Ancient Way*. New York: Atria, 1989.

Rettman, Tony. *Straight Edge: A Clear-Headed Hardcore Punk History*. New York: Bazillion Points, 2017.

Rettman, Tony. "Sean Muttaqi (interview)." *Sandpaper Lullaby*. 23 October 2019. https://sandpaperlullaby.wordpress.com/2019/10/23/sean-muttaqi/ Relocated to: https://rettman.substack.com/p/sean-muttaqi

Rob R-Rock. Letter to *MRR*. *Maximum Rocknroll* 90 (November 1990).

Rob R-Rock. Letter to *MRR*. *Maximum Rocknroll* 122 (July 1993).

Roberts, Randall. "La Punk Rocker, Screenwriter, Alleged Gang Leader Elgin Nathan James Arrested In Silver Lake." *LA Weekly*. 15 July (2009). https://www.laweekly.com/la-punk-rocker-screenwriter-alleged-gang-leader-elgin-nathan-james-arrested-in-silver-lake/

Roberts, Sam. "Consuewella Africa, 67, Dies; Lost Two Daughters in MOVE Siege." *New York Times*. 21 June (2021).

Sahagun, Louis. "The Twisted World of a 'Straight Edge' Gang." *Los Angeles Times*. 29 January (1998). https://www.latimes.com/archives/la-xpm-1998-jan-29-mn-13171-story.html

Sangosti, R.J. "Jeremy Nelson of the Ogden Police Dept. Gang Unit." *Denver Post/Getty Images*. 13 July 2006. https://www.gettyimages.com/detail/news-photo/jeremy-nelson-of-the-ogden-police-dept-gang-unit-shows-off-news-photo/161091705 ; Or https://www.gettyimages.com/photos/denver-police-gang-unit

Sanneh, Kelefa. "Vegan Jihad: A Conversation with Sean Muttaqi." *Bidoun: Art and Culture from the Middle East* 16 (2009): 144–147.

Sean/Vegan Reich. Letter. *Profane Existence* 3 (April–May 1990): 7.

Sean/Vegan Reich. "Vegan Reich" (interview). *MAS (Minneapolis Alternative Scene)* 8 (April-May 1989a): 26-27.

Sean. Untitled ad. *Maximum Rocknroll* 75 (August 1989a): 44.

Sean/Vegan Reich. Letter to MRR. *Maximum Rocknroll* 79 (December 1989b): 13, 16.

Sloan, Willona M. "Expand Your Mind." *Scorpion* 3 (1998): 14-15.

SkolarX and Aubin Paul. "Elgin James gets sentenced to a year in prison for Mest extortion scheme." *Punk News*. 2011. https://www.punknews.org/article/41888/elgin-james-gets-sentenced-to-a-year-in-prison-for-mest-extortion-scheme

Smith, Brent, Kelly Damphousse, and Paxton Roberts. *Pre-Incident Indicators of Terrorist Incidents: The Identification of Behavioral, Geographic, and Temporal Patterns of Preparatory Conduct*. University of Arkansas report prepared for the U.S. Department of Justice, 2006.

Smith, Gabriel. "White Mutants of Straight Edge: The Avant-Garde of Abstinence." *The Journal of Popular Culture* 44, no. 3 (2011): 633-646.

Sparks of Dissent. "Interview with Mutabaruka." 1000 Voices of Dissent. 2 November 2010. http://sparksofdissent.blogspot.com/2010/11/interview-with-mutabaruka.html

Sparks of Dissent. "Interview with Destroy Babylon (Fabio)." 1000 Voices of Dissent. 11 November 2010. http://sparksofdissent.blogspot.com/2010/09/1-ok-please-introduce-yourselves-band.html

Sprouse, Martin. "Review of *The A.L.F. is Watching...*" *Maximum Rocknroll* 67 (December 1988).

Staudenmaier, Peter. "Ambiguities of Animal Rights." *Institute of Social Ecology* 1 /*The Anarchist Library* (2005): 1-10.

Staudenmaier, Peter. *Ecology Contested-Environmental Politics between Left and Right*. Porsgrunn, Norway: New Compass Press, 2021.

Stefanie K. "REVIEW – Sober Living for the Revolution." *Anarkismo*. 7 May 2010. http://www.anarkismo.net/article/16542?userlanguage=es&save_prefs=true

Stěhulová, Petra. "NS Straight Edge." Bachelor's Thesis. Prague: Charles University, 2010.

Stewart, Francis. "Beyond Krishnacore: Straight Edge punk and Implicit Religion." *Implicit Religion* 15, no. 3 (2012): 259-288.

Stewart, Francis. *Punk Rock is My Religion: Straight Edge Punk and 'Religious' Identity*. London and New York: Routledge, 2017.

Stuff You Will Hate, "HXC HISTORY: Hardline and how moshcore kids turned into vegan muslim fundamentalists (srs)." 2014. https://sergeant220.rssing.com/chan-34949831/all_p1.html

Svitil, Greg. "Interview with Karl Buechner (Earth Crisis)." Veils of Teeth. 20 July 1996. https://veilsofteeth.com/karl-buechner/

Taliyah al- Mahdi homepage. August 2002. https://web.archive.org/web/20020806210733/http://www.taliyah.org/

Tiffany/Indianapolis Hardline. "Hardline Women." *Vanguard* double issue 1+2 (1993): 13.

Torkelson, Jason. "Life After (Straightedge) Subculture." *Qualitative Sociology* 33, no. 3 (2010): 257-274.

Tsitsos, William. "An International Comparison of the Politics of Straight Edge." In *Music Sociology: Examining the Role of Music in Social Life*. Edited by Sara Towe Horsfall, Jan-Martijn Meij, and Meghan Probstfield, 202–210. NY: Routledge, 2013.

UNAxVOCE. Interview with Vegan Reich (by Julien). *UNAxVOCE* 1 (1990).

Vaďura, Šimon. *Cesta kršnacoru: vliv spirituality hnutí Haré Kršna na hardcore a straight edge 80. let. The journey of krishnacore: the influence of Hare Krishna spirituality on hardcore and straightedge of the 80s*. University Thesis. Prague, 2018. [Czech]

Valdez, Al. "The Straight Edge Scene: Rated XXX." *Police Magazine*. 1 September. 2000. https://www.policemag.com/338761/the-straight-edge-scene-rated-xxx

Value of Strength. "Upstate Hardline interview with Dave Agranoff." *Value Of Strength* 5 (1999): 52-56.

Vanguard. "The Way It Is." *Vanguard* 1+2(double issue) (1993a): 14.

Vanguard. "Vanguard." *Vanguard* 1+2 (double issue), (1993b): 2

Vegan Final Solution. "Preamble." *Vegan Final Solution.* 2020. https://web.archive.org/web/20200729083857/http://veganfinalsolution.com/about/

Vegan Reich. *Hardline*. 7". Hardline Records. 1990.

Vegan Reich. *Wrath of God*. Cassette. Hardline Records. 1992.

Vegan Reich. *Vanguard/Wrath of God 10"*. Uprising Records. 1995.

Vegan Reich. *Jihad*. Uprising Records. 1999.

Vegan Reich reunion 2017 video. "Sorry" (cover of 4 Skins song). 2017a. https://www.facebook.com/veganreich/videos/1743351289040788

Vegan Reich. "Vegan Reich Communiqué." 2 August 2017b. https://www.facebook.com/veganreich/posts/1697709530271631/

VEO. Vegan Power ad for Vegan Earth Order ad. *Maximum Rocknroll* 126 (November 1993): 114.

Wagner-Pacifici, Robin. *Discourse and Destruction: The City of Philadelphia versus MOVE.* Chicago: University of Chicago Press, 1994.

Wikipedia "Hardline," and "Hardline (Talk)." 2020. https://en.wikipedia.org/wiki/Hardline_(subculture) https://en.wikipedia.org/wiki/Talk:Hardline_(subculture)

Williams, Dina. "Review: Vegan Reich *Hardline* EP." *Factsheet Five* 44 (1991): 120.

Williams, James Patrick. *The Straightedge Subculture on the Internet: A Case Study*. PhD Dissertation. Knoxville, TN: University of Tennessee, 2003.

Wood, Robert. *Straightedge Youth: Complexity and Contradictions of a Subculture.* Syracuse: Syracuse University Press, 2006.

xCatalystx board. "Earth Crisis and Hardline Record rumors." *Catalyst Records homepage* 2009. http://www.xcatalystx.com/board/viewtopic.php?f=2&t=31339&sid=2ee5cac141c07317be5c2d2440a376a0

xCHIPxSEM. "Hardline Interview with David Agranoff." *Stuck in the Past*. 2010. http://xstuckinthepastx.blogspot.com/2010/06/hardline-interview-with-david-agranoff.html

xYosefx. "Original Interview with Steve Lovett from RAID (taken from a xCatalystx forum)." *Remain Upright*. 2010. http://remainupright.blogspot.com/2010/12/original-interview-with-steve-lovett.html

Young, Peter. *Liberate: Stories & Lessons on Animal Liberation Above the Law*. USA: Warcry Communications, 2019.

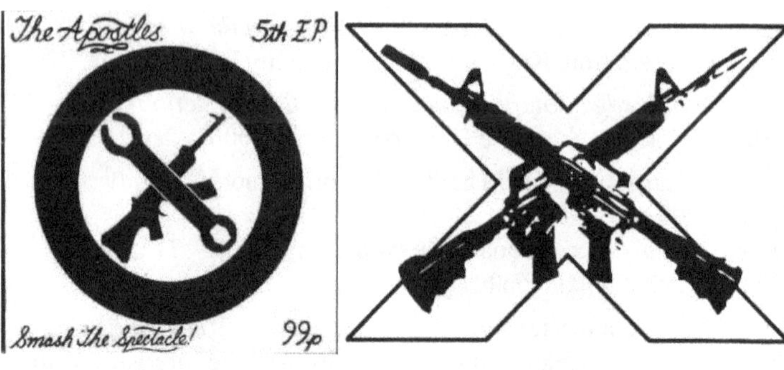

VEGANISMUS / UMWELT / TIERBEFREIUNG / ABTREIBUNG / DROGEN / SEXISMUS / RASSISMUS / GEWALT

VEGANISM / ECOLOGY / ANIMAL LIBERATION / ABORTION / DRUGS / SEXISM / RACISM / VIOLENCE

INFORMATION + FORWORD TO EDEN (A HARDLINE GUIDE) FOR 2 $ FROM
HARDLINE GERMANY (EUROPE DISTRIBUTION) P. O. BOX 157 4019 BASEL SWITZERLAND EUROPE

CRISIS OF FAITH

NO TOLERANCE FOR HARDLINE

STATEMENT
PREPARE FOR BATTLE
AHL-i ALLAH
ANIMAL RIGHTS
HUMAN RIGHTS
ONE STRUGGLE
ONE FIGHT!
VANGUARD
DECLARATION
CARING EDGE
Animal Rites
YOU CAN DECIDE TO BE
APATHETIC AND COMPLACENT,
AND HOPE FOR IT
ALL TO COLLAPSE,
OR
YOU CAN DECIDE TO
TAKE RESPONSIBILITY,
AND FIGHT TO DESTROY
THIS DEATH-MACHINE
...EITHER WAY YOU WILL
HAVE BLOOD ON YOUR HANDS.
IT'S JUST A MATTER OF WHOSE.
ANARCHIST
YOUTH
FEDERATION
HARDLINE
Three face jail, fines in anti-fur vandalism
Less Suffering
Hardline
direct action
More Living

FURTHER READING

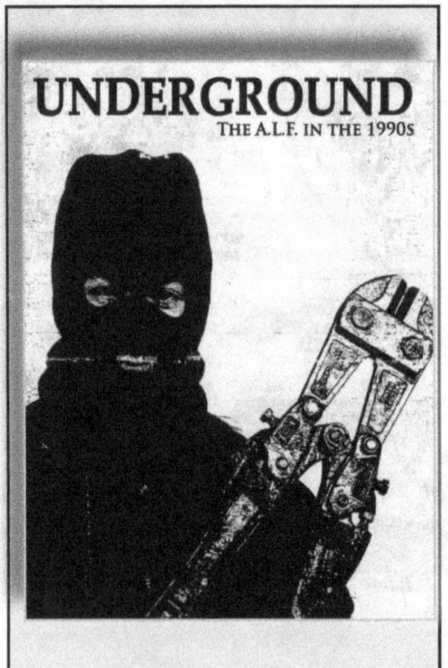

FURTHER READING

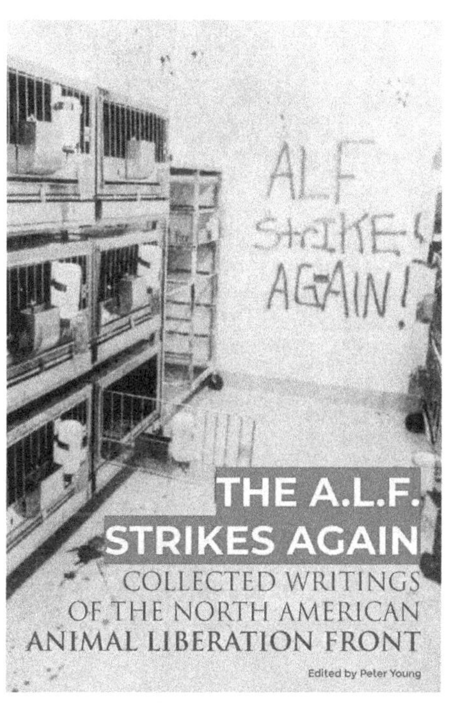

ALF
STRIKES
AGAIN!
THE A.L.F.
STRIKES AGAIN
COLLECTED WRITINGS
OF THE NORTH AMERICAN
ANIMAL LIBERATION FRONT
Edited by Peter Young

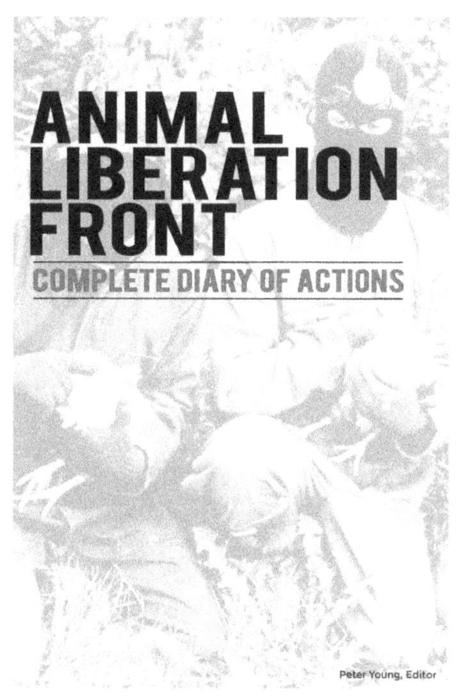

ANIMAL
LIBERATION
FRONT
COMPLETE DIARY OF ACTIONS
Peter Young, Editor

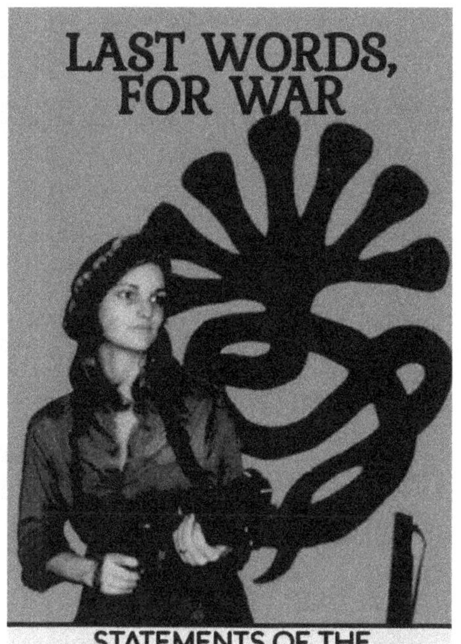

LAST WORDS,
FOR WAR
STATEMENTS OF THE
SYMBIONESE LIBERATION ARMY

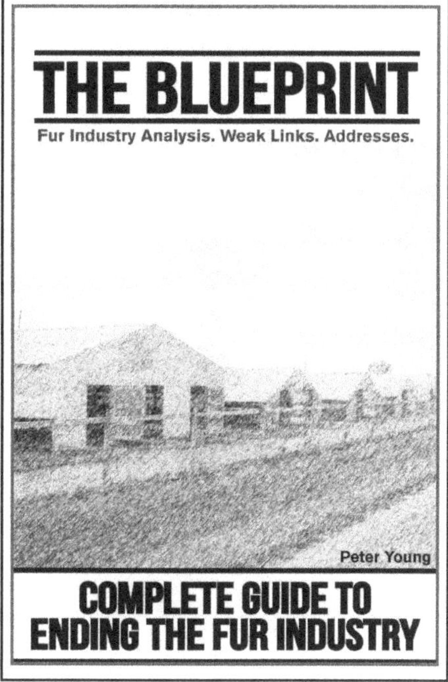

THE BLUEPRINT
Fur Industry Analysis. Weak Links. Addresses.
Peter Young
COMPLETE GUIDE TO
ENDING THE FUR INDUSTRY

CPSIA information can be obtained
at www.ICGtesting.com
Printed in the USA
LVHW102131070922
727846LV00020B/407